THE CAMBRIDGE ILLUSTRATED HISTORY OF THE
British Empire

F   G   H   I   J

India

Burma

Hong Kong

Aden

Ceylon

Penang

Labuan

Malacca

Singapore

Sarawak

Seychelles

Mauritius

Natal

British Kaffraria

New South Wales

Western Australia

Queensland

South Australia

New South Wales

Victoria

Tasmania

New Zealand

Territory under British rule

THE CAMBRIDGE ILLUSTRATED HISTORY OF THE

British Empire

edited by P.J. MARSHALL

CAMBRIDGE
UNIVERSITY PRESS

Published by the Press Syndicate of the University of Cambridge
The Pitt Building, Trumpington Street, Cambridge CB2 1RP
40 West 20th Street, New York, NY 10011-4211, USA
10 Stamford Road, Oakleigh, Melbourne 3166, Australia

First published 1996

Project editor: Sally Carpenter
Picture research: Callie Kendall
Layout: David Seabourne
Cartography by European Map Graphics Ltd, Finchampstead
Origination by HiLo Offset, Colchester

Printed in Great Britain at the University Press, Cambridge

A catalogue record for this book is available from the British Library

Library of Congress cataloguing in publication data

Marshall, P. J. (Peter James)
The Cambridge illustrated history of the British Empire / P. J. Marshall
p.   cm.
Includes bibliographical references and index.
ISBN 0-521-43211-1
1. Great Britain–Colonies–History.
2. Imperialism–Great Britain–Colonies–History.
3. Commonwealth countries–History.
I. Title.
DA16.M29 1995   941.08–dc20
95-14535   CIP

ISBN 0 521 43211 1 hardback

Page 1: The *Empire Windrush*
with Jamaican immigrants 1948.
Pages 2–3: *A patrol under the
Command of Captain Fisher
Charged by Macoma's Kafirs in
Van Beulen's Hoek* by Thomas
Baines.

Contents

Preface   6

INTRODUCTION: THE WORLD SHAPED BY EMPIRE   7
   P.J. Marshall

PART I THE HISTORY OF THE EMPIRE

 1 *The British Empire at the End of the Eighteenth Century*   16
   P.J. Marshall

 2 *1783–1870: An Expanding Empire*   24
   P.J. Marshall

 3 *1870–1918: The Empire under Threat*   52
   P.J. Marshall

 4 *1918 to the 1960s: Keeping Afloat*   80
   P.J. Marshall

PART II THE LIFE OF THE EMPIRE

 5 *For Richer, for Poorer?*   108
   David Fieldhouse

 6 *Power, Authority, and Freedom*   147
   A.J. Stockwell

 7 *Empires in the Mind*   185
   Andrew Porter

 8 *Imperial Towns and Cities*   224
   Thomas R. Metcalf

 9 *British Emigration and New Identities*   254
   Ged Martin and Benjamin E. Kline

10 *The Diaspora of the Africans and the Asians*   280
   P.J. Marshall

11 *Art and the Empire*   296
   John M. MacKenzie

PART III THE IMPERIAL EXPERIENCE

12 *Imperial Britain*   318
   P.J. Marshall

13 *Australia*   338
   K.S. Inglis

14 Africa   347
Toyin Falola

15 British Rule in India: An Assessment   357
Tapan Raychaudhuri

CONCLUSION: EMPIRE IN RETROSPECT   370
P.J. Marshall

REFERENCE GUIDE

British Imperial Territories from 1783   384
Further Reading   389
Contributors   391
Acknowledgements   392
Index   394

Preface

It is the editor's pleasant duty to acknowledge the debts he owes to many people who have made invaluable contributions to this book. Such acknowledgements must begin with the editor's warmest thanks to the authors of the individual chapters. The book was the brain-child of Dr Peter Richards. Sally Carpenter has not only been an indefatigable and meticulous project editor, but she has also been a most resourceful and creative one. The book owes a great deal to David Seabourne for his skill in designing it, and to Callie Kendall's ingenuity in tracking down illustrations. Richard Newnham compiled the index. The sources for the illustrations are fully acknowledged elsewhere, but special thanks are due to Terry Barringer for her help which enabled us to select items from the magnificent photographic collection of the Royal Commonwealth Society, now in Cambridge University Library. June Walker did much valuable work in preparing the text. Sections of the book have benefited from the critical eye and astute comments of Dr Gad Heuman, Mr Donald Simpson, and Professor Glyndwr Williams.

PJM

The World Shaped by Empire

INTRODUCTION

P. J. Marshall

For most of the nineteenth and twentieth centuries the British ruled over a colossal territorial empire, extending over a large part of North America, much of the Caribbean region, great tracts of Africa south of the Sahara, the whole of the Indian subcontinent and Australasia, territories in South East Asia and the Pacific, and even for a time much of the Middle East.

The British empire has profoundly shaped the modern world. Most present-day countries outside Europe owe their existence to empires, especially to the British empire. The British fixed boundaries by conquest and partition treaties. Huge movements of people took place within the empire, determining the ethnic composition of many countries. It was British people under British rule who were responsible for ensuring that, once indigenous peoples had been displaced, North American and Australasian societies would be overwhelmingly European in character. The British were also the major carriers of the estimated eleven million Africans shifted to the Americas as slaves. Most of those carried by the British went to Britain's own colonies in the Caribbean, whose present population are for the most part the consequence of that forced migration. From the middle of the nineteenth century large numbers of Indian and Chinese people went to labour in colonies ruled by Britain. Their descendants make up a large part of the population of many countries from Guyana and Trinidad to Fiji, Mauritius, Malaysia, and Singapore.

Street scene in Port Louis, Mauritius, 1881. The people and culture of the Indian Ocean island of Mauritius are a legacy of empires and their need for labour. The French, who ruled Mauritius until 1810, brought in African slaves to grow sugar and left their language behind them. The British brought in Indian immigrants to work the plantations and also left their language. Here people of African and Indian origin in various forms of European dress mingle in the streets of the island's capital.

Through their empire the British disseminated their institutions, culture, and language. No country in the present-day world can of course be regarded as anything approaching a carbon copy of what Britain was or is: national identities evolve by very complex processes of interaction between a society's own traditions and external influences. Occupation by an imperial power is, nevertheless, likely to have been a very potent external influence, especially when the imperial power was as self-confident in its values and institutions as Britain has been for most of its history. In varying degrees British influences can be detected in systems of government, religious adherence, patterns of education, the layout of towns and cities, cultural tastes, sports, and pastimes throughout the world. The claim of English to be a virtually universal language in the contemporary world is no doubt partly a reflection of the power of the United States. But the United States is of course an English-speaking society as a consequence of the British empire; so are very many other countries.

The British empire changed not only people but the land in which they lived. New patterns of farming, mining, or manufacturing all meant that the land and its resources were used in new ways. Sometimes environmental change was rapid and spectacular, as prairies were ploughed up or previously forested islands were turned into sugar plantations; the full effects of other changes that began in the colonial period have only become apparent in modern times with an increase in pressure to use the land and its resources to the full.

The contemporary world is sharply divided between rich and poor. The legacy of empire has played a part in bringing about this divide, although it is not a part that is easy to interpret. Some ex-imperial countries are rich; some are very poor. Does this simply indicate that, regardless of what the British did or did not do, some countries have favourable endowments of land, people, and resources, which have made economic growth possible, while others lack such endowments? Or does it mean that the experience of imperial rule by Britain was very different – enabling, for instance, white immigrant communities in Australia and Canada to improve their lot, while impoverishing Asians or Africans? Answers to such questions are rarely simple: economic change, like the evolution of cultures, involves a process of interaction. Colonial economies were shaped by the enterprise of the colonial people, as well as by the intervention of the British.

The history of the empire as a whole is indeed the study of interactions between the British and other people rather than of the British 'impact' on them. Interaction supposes that the peoples over whom the British ruled were not merely hapless 'natives' to whom the British brought blessings or misfortune. Before colonial rule, the peoples of Asia, Africa, the Americas, and the Pacific of course made their own history. Under British rule they continued to do so, as well as having it made for them by British power. The history of slavery, for instance, is the history of how the slaves developed their own culture and resisted their masters, as well as being the history of their oppression.

Ireland and the British empire

Whether Ireland – a separate kingdom with its own Parliament until 1801 and thereafter until 1922 an integral part of the United Kingdom, sending Members of Parliament to Westminster – should be treated as a British colony or as a partner in empire with the rest of Britain is a much debated issue.

Until the creation of the Irish Free State in 1922, a majority of Irish people probably regarded themselves as being held in subordination by the rest of the United Kingdom. In the eighteenth century this resentment was mainly expressed by Irish Protestants, who objected to London's domination of the Irish government. The Union of 1801 became an object of hatred for great sections of Irish Catholic opinion, who hoped to see it modified substantially to permit an effective Irish autonomy, if not repealed altogether to create an independent Ireland. For their part, many English people seem to have seen the Irish not as equal fellow citizens but as inferior beings to whom many derogatory stereotypes were applied. Whatever they might feel about the Irish, British opinion in general did not regard Ireland as in any sense a colony; for them it was an integral part of the United Kingdom. In important respects, however, Ireland was not governed like the rest of the United Kingdom: it had its own separate administration dominated by London.

Questions about Ireland also became imperial questions, especially in the later nineteenth century. Those who hoped to sustain and strengthen the British empire as a counterpoise to Britain's European rivals saw concessions to Irish nationalism as the first stage in imperial dissolution. Irish nationalists seem, however, rarely to have urged the dismantling of the British empire as a matter of principle. They were generally rather selective in their choice of colonial peoples with whom they were willing to identify as fellow victims. What they detested was an empire that frustrated the ambitions of a European nation like theirs. The ambiguous situation of Ireland is thus a major theme in British imperial history. Irish people of all kinds were actors in the story of empire – as emigrants, businessmen, administrators, and above all as soldiers, missionaries, and teachers – but many Irish saw themselves as the first victims of British expansion.

This *Punch* cartoon of 1846 is directed at the threat of a rebellion by the radical nationalist movement called Young Ireland. The simian countenance of the armed figure embodied certain British stereotypes about the Irish. *Punch* wrote of 'A creature manifestly between the Gorilla and the Negro', which 'belongs to a tribe of Irish savages'.

THE EMPIRE AND THE BRITISH

While the British changed others through their empire, empire changed the British. It shaped British people's view of their national identity as a people at the centre of a world-wide empire. Emigration took British people overseas to form new communities within the empire and it has brought new elements into Britain's own population from what was once the empire. Did Britain gain in wealth and power from the possession of an empire or was its development distorted by the pursuit of ambitions it ultimately could not fulfil? Are imperial assumptions still built into British culture? These are important questions for an understanding of contemporary Britain.

Who were the British who created the British empire? The Scots were as fully involved as the English, but were the Irish partners in the imperial enterprise or were they its first victims? Any answer to that very complex and contentious question depends in part on what sort of Irish person you happened to be. The Irish people as a whole were both imperial partners and a subordinated population, whose history has much in common with the history of other subordinated people within the empire. The history of the British empire is central to the history of Anglo-Irish relations and, although this book is concerned with British rule outside the British Isles, it is impossible to understand the history of the British empire without some awareness of Ireland.

THE LIFE-SPAN OF EMPIRE

There is little disagreement about when a history of the British empire should end: the colonial empire subsided with the last major round of decolonization in the 1960s, even if it left unfinished business in Rhodesia (Zimbabwe), Hong Kong, and the Falkland Islands. But when should a history of the British empire begin? An English empire overseas might be traced back to John Cabot's claiming of 'the New Found Land' for Henry VII in 1497 or, more plausibly, from the first permanent settlement in America, that on the James River in Virginia from 1607. This book starts in the late eighteenth century, specifically in 1783, the year in which Britain formally recognized the loss of most of its colonies in North America. Though there were many continuities before and after 1783 and the immediate impact of this disaster seems to have been surprisingly limited, in the long run the character of the British empire was to change profoundly with the loss of America. It ceased to be an empire overwhelmingly of colonies of white settlement. New communities of British origin were to be created in Canada and Australasia and southern Africa, but the empire became for the most part a system of rule over non-European peoples. Its centre of gravity would be in the Indian Ocean rather than in the Atlantic.

The first part of this book, THE HISTORY OF THE EMPIRE, consists of a narrative history of the development of the British empire from 1783 to the 1960s. This is followed by THE LIFE OF THE EMPIRE, in which the chapters are devoted to specific themes – economic relations within the empire, the political life of the empire, the emergence of identities and new nationalities that followed the movement of peoples within the empire, the diffusion of British culture and ideas, the cities of the empire, and its art. These themes have been chosen because they embody issues that illuminate the essential workings of the British empire and are at the heart of all attempts to assess its legacy to the present-day world.

THE EXTENT OF EMPIRE

Defining the extent of the British empire at any time may seem to be a simple matter. Territory ruled by the British outside their own islands was a part of the British empire. The legal basis of British rule varied greatly, as did the forms it took, but the outlines are clear enough. Ultimate authority emanated from the Crown and Parliament in Britain. Governors were appointed to exercise that authority, even if they shared it with local representatives in many cases, and recognizably British legal and administrative systems were in operation under the protection of the forces of the Crown. As everyone knows, British territory – whether it was technically a colony, a self-governing Dominion, a protectorate, or a mandate – was conventionally coloured red on the map. But there were also areas that Britain had no legal claim to rule and that were never coloured red on maps, but which are sometimes included in what is called Britain's 'informal empire'. Those who use the concept of an informal British empire argue that British influence extended far beyond the bounds of the empire ruled by Britain. They point, in the first place, to the world-wide deployment of British naval and military power and the way that this enabled Britain to intimidate and coerce weaker governments outside Europe,

A cricket match at Shanghai in the 1880s. A Chinese artist has captured the way in which British dominance could extend to commercial centres beyond the bounds of empire. In 1842 the Chinese government had been forced to permit foreign trade in certain ports. Parts of the city of Shanghai came to be designated as international settlements where the British built their churches and laid out their playing fields, while the Chinese inhabitants effectively lived under foreign rule.

especially in the nineteenth century. Secondly, they argue that the settlement of British communities overseas and the spread of British trade and investment, ideas, language, and culture enabled the British to exercise a dominant influence over certain countries. Examples of governments, like those of China or Iran, that were forced to make very great concessions to British power can certainly be found. A large proportion of the trade of other countries, such as Argentina or Chile at the end of the nineteenth century, was financed by British capital and passed through British hands. In cities like Shanghai and Buenos Aires British communities enjoyed the status of a privileged elite with their own institutions and way of life. In short, for much of the period covered by this book, Britain exercised influence to a powerful degree over certain parts of the world where British rule was not formally established. Nevertheless, there is a real difference between influence and rule. However strong the influence exerted by Britain, in most respects foreign governments still maintained their freedom of action. Within the empire British control might be weakly exerted, but in the last resort the system of government and the ultimate authority were in British hands. This book is primarily about the empire of rule.

A book such as this cannot comprehensively cover all of the countries within the empire of rule. The British did not give equal attention to every colony in their vast empire. India, with its immense population, its huge army, and its great importance to the British economy, always featured very prominently in their calculations. At the beginning of the period covered by this book the West Indies was still the jewel in Britain's imperial crown. At least from the middle of the nineteenth century, the hopes of those in Britain who took a serious interest in empire were overwhelmingly invested in what were called the 'colonies of settlement' – first in trying to build a 'Greater Britain' out of the white communities of Australia, Canada, New Zealand, and South Africa and later in the ideal of Commonwealth. The fact that such hopes have sunk out of the consciousness of most people in contemporary Britain is no reason for not giving them full coverage here. The emphasis in this book generally follows the concerns of the British in the past. The major themes of British imperial history are best exemplified in areas where the British were most deeply involved. Nevertheless, if little is said about some territories, this does not mean that the authors do not recognize that the imperial experience was an important one, very much worth studying, for, say, colonies in tropical Africa, or the Pacific, Malta, or Cyprus.

CONTROVERSIES ABOUT EMPIRE

The history of the British empire has always been a contentious subject. The way in which domination was being exercised over other people raised great moral issues about which the British themselves and those whom they ruled argued with passion throughout the period covered by this book. Although empire has been dissolved, the issues still arouse passion.

Both the British and the nations that emerged out of the British empire have defined themselves through their attitudes to empire. Since the American Declaration of Independence in 1776, with its ringing denunciation of 'a long train of abuses and usurpations' which made it both the right and the duty of the Americans 'to throw off such government', colonial nationalism has challenged the record of British rule in establishing its own legitimacy. New nations have nearly all felt the need to break with the imperial past, and condemnation of that past can still have a role in nation-building. Interpretations of what can be seen as British betrayals at Gallipoli in 1915 or at Singapore in 1942, for example, reinforce aspirations for a republican Australia (see page 344).

For many British people over a very long period possession of an empire has been an essential part of their sense of Britishness. Pride in a territorial British empire dates at least from the mid-eighteenth century and it continued until well after the Second World War. If few British people before the 1950s rejected the imperial connection altogether, there was much debate as to the values that the empire should embody. These were ultimately debates about Britain's own values. From the eighteenth century onwards, critics of the conduct of imperial administration argued that it betrayed British ideals of freedom. On the other hand, for many others the empire embodied the highest qualities of Britishness. These were often supposed to be manliness, courage, and discipline, but they also included self-sacrifice and disinterested service to others.

The imperial past still recurs in debate about the British present. For some British people, what they take to be an insufficiently critical view of the oppression of colonial rule is fostering contemporary racism and hindering the development of a truly multicultural society. For others, criticism of Britain's imperial record strikes a raw nerve: this record, they maintain, sets the British apart from other imperial powers, commonly supposed to have been far less disinterested. Margaret Thatcher, British Prime Minister during the 1980s, is reputed to have asked her fellow Commonwealth prime ministers to reflect on how lucky they were to have been ruled by the British.

Professional historians, like the authors of this book, recognize an obligation to keep the preoccupations of the present from distorting their interpretation of the past. But they cannot claim to approach the imperial past with complete detachment or to draw up a totally objective balance sheet of the British empire. Such a project is hardly conceivable. The history of the empire is subject to lively debates. Each of the authors approaches the subject with his own point of view and has his own interpretations to offer. The editor and the authors of the second section, apart from two Americans, are, however, all British, and it is appropriate that other voices should be heard as well. An Australian, an Indian, and a Nigerian have therefore been asked to give their verdicts on the British empire in the last section of the book, THE IMPERIAL EXPERIENCE.

Removing a statue of Lord Curzon, Viceroy of India 1899–1905, from Calcutta after Indian independence. As the capital of British India from the eighteenth century to 1911, Calcutta bore many visible marks of colonial rule, such as buildings in European styles or street names and statues commemorating British notables. The citizens of Calcutta, as of many other ex-colonial cities, sought to erase some of the marks of the imperial past.

The History of the Empire

PART I

CHAPTER 1

P. J. Marshall

The British Empire at the End of the Eighteenth Century

This book begins at one of the British empire's darkest hours. By 1782 a war for empire was about to be lost. Attempts to crush the rebellion of the thirteen colonies of British North America had failed and in the following year Britain was forced to recognize the independence of the new United States of America. King George III believed that Britain could never recover from such a defeat but would fall 'into a very low class among the European states'. He even considered abdication. But British expansion overseas was far too deep-rooted for its momentum to be seriously disrupted, even by so crushing a defeat. Britain was set on the course that would make it the pre-eminent European imperial power for the next 150 years.

The rest of the empire not only remained intact but continued to grow. The British colonies in the West Indies and those from which modern Canada was later to emerge did not defect. Twenty to thirty million Indian people were already living under British rule, most of them in the very rich province of Bengal. Britain was by far the largest naval power in Europe: for an emergency in a period of peace over ninety ships could be mobilized and Britain maintained naval bases at Halifax in Nova Scotia, at Jamaica and Antigua in the West Indies, and at Bombay. The loss of America did little damage to Britain's overseas trade. Britain was still the major distribution point through which the products of the non-European world, such as tobacco, tea, sugar, silk, or cotton cloth, passed to Europe and elsewhere. Within a few years after 1783 the value of British exports to the new United States of America would comfortably exceed the highest totals for the colonial period there. Britain also remained the biggest carrier of slaves from Africa to the Americas.

THE VIEW FROM BRITAIN

Some parts of the British Isles were more heavily involved in this great overseas network than others. In 1783 London was playing the major role, as it continued to do throughout Britain's imperial history. Westminster was the seat of imperial government, transacted in Parliament on occasions and by certain government departments in a somewhat haphazard and unco-ordinated way. The City of London was the home of the great overseas trading companies, of which the East India Company and the Hudson's Bay Company were the most important, and of numerous banking and business houses which financed the activities of planters and overseas traders and marketed their produce. London was a vast port from which the great East India ships sailed, as well as a host of smaller merchant ships bound for world-wide destinations.

The Atlantic trades – to West Africa, the Caribbean, and North America – were the special concern of a string of west coast ports. Bristol was heavily involved in

Opposite: London's West India docks, 1810. As the great array of ships indicates, the West Indies was still the biggest source of British imports: sugar and cotton worth over £10 million in contemporary values were shipped to Britain from the Caribbean in 1810. As well as being a major port for colonial trade, London was the centre from which most of this trade was financed.

sugar. Liverpool was the home of the bulk of slaving ships and also handled increasing imports of raw cotton for the growing Lancashire textile industry. Before the disruptions of the American Revolution, Glasgow had been the main outlet for the world's biggest tobacco exporters, the colonies of Virginia and Maryland. The tobacco trade declined after the war, but Glasgow remained heavily involved with the West Indies.

People from all parts of Britain were seeking new opportunities in the empire. In the fifteen years before the outbreak of the revolution, some 55,000 Protestant Irish, 40,000 Scots, and 30,000 English people had emigrated to settle in North America. Many Scots held senior civil service posts in India or became planters in the West Indies.

THE EMPIRE OVERSEAS

At the end of the eighteenth century British interests overseas fell into two main geographical areas: the Atlantic and Asia. Conditions in these two areas were fundamentally different.

The Atlantic world

Across the Atlantic the English were at first intruders in a world shaped by the Spanish and partially by the Portuguese. The Spanish had destroyed the great native American empires of South and Central America and introduced new economic systems based on mining, European farming, and new crops specially suited to tropical conditions. In the early seventeenth century the English began to infiltrate uncertainly on the fringes of Spanish or Portuguese claims. Confident enough to challenge Spain only on the margins of its empire, they settled in the outer islands of the Caribbean and on the uncontested coasts of North America, in the New England and Chesapeake areas.

In North America a native American population, already seriously thinned by disease, was largely displaced by the English settlers, some 200,000 of whom emigrated to the new colonies during the seventeenth century, mostly as servants to work the land. By the end of the century this white American population was reproducing itself very rapidly, probably at an average rate of about 3 per cent a year, as well as being reinforced throughout the following century by fresh waves of immigration, including some 175,000 slaves from Africa. Eighteenth-century British North America was subdivided into thirteen separate colonies. To the early seventeenth-century nuclei – the New England settlements of Puritan inspiration dominated by Massachusetts and the Chesapeake colonies of Virginia and Maryland – later foundations had been added. The most successful of these were Pennsylvania, which rapidly outgrew its Quaker origins, attracting a very cosmopolitan group of immigrants, including many Germans and Ulster people, and South Carolina, the destination of large numbers of imported Africans. All the colonies became increasingly autonomous during the eighteenth century, as elected assemblies of the local population wrested power from the governors appointed in Britain. The great prosperity of the eighteenth-century American colonies was mainly based on exploiting an abundance of land. From the Chesapeake southwards, tobacco, rice, and indigo were grown for export through Britain. To the north, surpluses of meat and grain, together with fish and timber, were shipped to the West Indies or to southern Europe. With what they earned from selling the produce of their lands Americans bought very large quantities of British manufactured goods.

In 1755 a new round of wars began in North America between the British colonies and the French settlements strung out to the north and west of them. By the time peace was signed in 1763 the lack of effective British authority over the colonies had become glaringly apparent. In a hard-fought war the colonies seemed to be unwilling to co-operate with one another let alone with the British army. Successive British ministers after 1763 tried to enforce trade regulations and to provide for the defence of what had become very valuable assets for the British empire. Americans would accept neither the measures themselves nor the right of the British Parliament to impose them. Protest and riot gradually grew into armed resistance, which the British tried to crush with troops. Fighting broke out in 1775. The war in America became a world war when France and other European enemies of Britain joined in on the side of the Americans after 1778. Although the British deployed over 50,000 men in America, they could never dominate enough territory to establish an effective 'loyalist' alternative to the Congress that had thrown off British rule. Isolated British armies were defeated and the British public eventually refused to continue to pay the costs of a war that had obviously become unwinnable. The war was formally abandoned in 1783.

But Britain's interests in the Atlantic survived defeat. Britain's dominance over the trade of the independent United States of America was quickly reasserted. Moreover, not all the colonies in North America were lost to British rule. In 1760 British armies had forced the surrender of the old French settlements along the St Lawrence river in Canada and had created the new British colony of Quebec. This colony, together with Nova Scotia, an older British foundation, were successfully defended from the Americans and remained in the empire.

The British West Indian colonies also remained in the empire. From the mid-seventeenth century, islands settled by the British began to specialize in the cultivation of sugar cane. Sugar spread from Barbados to the Leeward Islands and then to Jamaica. Other islands and territories were later incorporated into the

The surrender of the British army at Yorktown, 19 October 1781. A British army of 7,000 men under Lord Cornwallis had been blockaded at Yorktown on the coast of Virginia by French and rebel American forces. Although the main British army still held New York, the Yorktown defeat meant that no further offensive operations would be undertaken and that negotiations ending in American independence would follow. The centrepiece of the old empire had gone forever.

British empire: the Windward Islands after 1763 and Trinidad and what has become Guyana in the early nineteenth century. Most of the new acquisitions also became sugar producers.

The labour force for cultivating sugar consisted almost entirely of black slaves. These were usually people taken by African rulers in war or raids, condemned for some offence or otherwise considered disposable. British traders then bought them from African merchants or from the agents of African rulers on the west coast of Africa in a great belt from Senegal in the north to Angola in the south. By the end of the eighteenth century, the biggest number of slaves came from what is now Nigeria. In the late eighteenth century slaves were exported in huge quantities: current estimates are that in the decade of the 1780s about 350,000 were shipped out of Africa by the British and 420,000 in the 1790s. Whatever their status in Africa, once purchased by British merchants slaves became objects of property whose ownership could be transferred (see pages 281–83).

The West Indian sugar economy remained buoyant at the end of the eighteenth century. The American Revolution had caused serious dislocation, but after 1783 there was a new phase of growth, which was to be sustained well into the nineteenth century. More and more slaves were imported to produce ever more sugar and also cotton and coffee. In 1783 the West Indies was still regarded as a most valuable imperial asset and it continued to be so for many years to come.

The Asian world

The impact of early European expansion on the Asian world was much less dramatic than in the Atlantic. There were no great conquests or decimations of populations by epidemics of European diseases. No new economic systems were created. During the sixteenth and seventeenth centuries the strength of the great Asian land-based empires of the Ottoman Turks, the Safavids in Iran, Mughal India, and the Chinese emperors was growing. Europeans lodged themselves on islands or in coastal enclaves on the margins of the Asian empires from which they could draw off some part of Asia's existing trade and direct it round the Cape of Good Hope at the tip of southern Africa.

The British began trading in Asia early in the seventeenth century. By the middle of the eighteenth century the East India Company, which enjoyed a monopoly of British trade to and from Asia, was conducting a highly successful business importing Indian cotton cloth and silk and Chinese tea from trading settlements at Bombay, Madras, Calcutta, and Canton.

Very significant new developments were, however, beginning to occur in India at that time. The British and French began to manipulate Indian rivalries in the south, their contest culminating in the great British victory at Wandiwash in 1760. In Bengal the British provoked the provincial ruler into attacking their settlement in 1756. Calcutta was recovered by an expedition by Robert Clive who succeeded in bringing down the ruler of Bengal after the battle of Plassey in 1757. As a result

Ch'ien-lung, Emperor of China. At the end of the eighteenth century Europe, for all its technological and military prowess, was still kept at arm's length by the great empires of Asia. Britain's contact with China was confined to a very restricted trade at the port of Canton. In an attempt to get better access, a British embassy under Lord Macartney was sent to Peking in 1793. There he was permitted to do homage to the Emperor in the splendour of his court but was granted no concessions. This portrait of Ch'ien-lung was drawn by one of the embassy's artists, William Alexander, who had not been present at the audience, working from the sketches of those who had seen the Emperor.

of these events, by 1783 the British exercised a decisive political influence along the south east coast and had become the actual rulers of Bengal.

It is not easy to explain why this great transformation took place. Was it because a rapidly industrializing Britain could now deploy resources, powers of organization, and advanced military technology on a scale that no Asian state could withstand and thus it was simply India's misfortune to be picked on first? Or was it the case that eighteenth-century India, torn by political disintegration, was a society in terminal decline which had lost all capacity to resist any outside threat? There are serious flaws in both these views. Britain did not have superior firepower or manpower: the cannons and muskets used by the British in India were also used by the Indians themselves and the British employed very large numbers of Indian soldiers. Nor was eighteenth-century India an especially soft target for European aggression. With the fall of the Mughal empire, political fragmentation had certainly taken place, but new regional states were emerging, some of which, such as those of the Sikhs of the Punjab or of the Marathas of western and central India, were to prove effective opponents of the British. Sweeping explanations that stress either the power of the British or Indian degeneration are not very convincing. The success of the British seems to have been based on their ability to infiltrate and to take over some of the new Indian states rather than to destroy them by naked military power.

Early British rule was very Indian in character. Once the British had succeeded in taking over an Indian state, they had neither the capacity nor the inclination to introduce radical changes in the way that it was run. The famous British Governor of Bengal, Warren Hastings, ruled from 1772 to 1785 much as his Indian predecessors, the nawabs of Bengal, had done. To the dismay of many contemporaries, the British became 'oriental despots'. In North America and the West Indies the white population essentially ruled itself, through elected assemblies under the governors, and enjoyed most of the privileges of English common law. But in Bengal Hastings ruled through Indian intermediaries or through British officials, who enforced the collection of taxes, for which the consent of the population was not required, and who tried to administer Indian law. Although this form of authoritarian colonial government appeared to go against the British tradition of liberty, it would be used again in the future as British rule spread through Asia and Africa, bringing under its control people judged by the British to be quite unfit for self-government. But few such ventures were potentially as lucrative as the early government of Bengal, which generated a revenue from

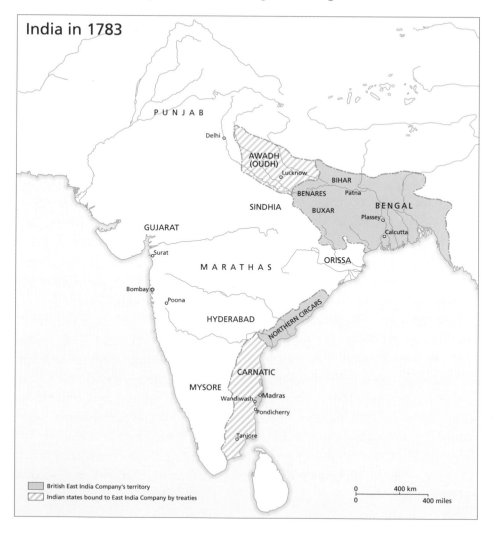

taxation of about £3 million in eighteenth-century values. Much of what was collected went on maintaining an army of some 70,000 Indian sepoys, as well as up to 15,000 British soldiers. The British Indian army of the future had come into being.

Once the British had assumed political power with its great financial rewards in Bengal and the south, other Indian states were threatened with infiltration and takeovers. Although it was official policy in London to limit Britain's territorial stake in India, processes of expansion had been set off and these would not be halted.

THE IMPULSES BEHIND EXPANSION

Territorial expansion in India was part of a wider movement of British expansion well under way at the end of the eighteenth century. It took many forms. In India more states were being taken over. The volume of trade with China was increasing greatly. More sugar was being grown in the West Indies. More slaves were being shipped out of Africa. The Pacific had been quartered by the great voyages of James Cook between 1768 and 1779. The British army and navy, which had been largely on the defensive during the American Revolution, were now ready to be turned loose on the overseas empires of France, Spain, and the Netherlands. British Christians were forming themselves into societies to convert the heathen all over the world.

To look for designs behind these multifarious processes of expansion is not very rewarding. For the most part, they were not directed or planned by ministers. They cannot be neatly demarcated into first and second empires. They do not have any very close relationship with the needs of the industrial revolution whose effects on British society as a whole were still limited. Expansion rather reflects the willingness of many sections of British society to seek opportunities for trade, plunder, land, office, knowledge – in short, advantages of all kinds from a world they and their governments were increasingly confident that Britain could dominate. Driven by different impulses at different times and taking different forms, expansion was to continue for most of the period covered by this book and an ever larger empire was to grow with it.

Expansion and the determination to maintain what had been acquired gave British imperial history a continuity that lasted from the eighteenth century at least until the Second World War. The three chapters that follow begin at what are conventionally seen as turning points in the history of empire: the rise of a 'second' empire out of the American defeat in 1783; the emergence of a 'new' imperialism from about 1870; and the beginning of a long decline with the ending of the First World War. The significance of what seem to be turning points or new phases must, however, be kept in proportion. Until the very end, the British commitment to empire was steadily and consistently sustained. All three chapters tell a story that is essentially the same.

Warren Hastings. Warren Hastings, British Governor of Bengal 1772–85, was much admired by some contemporaries as the man who brought stability to the government of the new British conquests in India, while holding off attacks on them by the French and by Indian opponents. To others he seemed to be ruthless and tyrannical. He was in fact put on trial for what were held to be crimes committed in the course of his government, but acquitted. This portrait by an unknown Indian artist reflects his close relations with the Indian aristocracy of his time and his interest in Indian art and culture.

1783–1870: An Expanding Empire

In 1870 Earl Russell (the former Lord John Russell and ex-Prime Minister) looked back on the growth of empire during the period covered by this chapter and concluded:

> There was a time when we might have acted alone as the United Kingdom of England, Scotland and Ireland. That time has passed. We conquered and peopled Canada, we took possession of the whole of Australia, Van Diemen's Land and New Zealand. We have annexed India to the Crown. There is no going back.

The conquest and settlement of new territory had in fact been only part of a much wider pattern of expansion. British trade had spread across the world. The planting of Christianity in non-Christian areas had largely been the result of efforts by British missionaries. British institutions and ways of doing things – from team games to representative government – were imitated far beyond the empire of rule. The eventual adoption of the Greenwich meridian as the universal meridian of longitude and of a universal system of time zones based on the Greenwich meridian were symbols of the ascendancy of Britain's influence. The naval officer, the Indian sepoy soldier, the emigrant, the merchant, the missionary, and the traveller: all had acted as agents in what had been very diverse processes of expansion.

THE VIEW FROM BRITAIN

The British government itself did not pursue a very active or interventionist role during this period. Its unwillingness to do so arose in part from the physical difficulties of communicating – for most of the period by sailing ship – with a far-flung empire, partly from a lack of a strong bureaucracy capable of imposing its will overseas, and partly from a lack of commitment to government intervention generally. Authority in Britain over imperial matters was divided between different bodies. Effectively from about 1812, a Colonial Office in Whitehall was responsible for the colonies. This was headed by a minister who became the Colonial Secretary. Although it attracted some very able officials, for most of the nineteenth century the Colonial Office was neither very well equipped to play an active role nor, except on a few great issues such as slavery, was it very assertive in using its authority. For the most part it saw its function as responding to developments overseas rather than initiating new policies. India was always a separate concern. Until 1858 the British government did not exercise direct authority over it. Detailed administration was left to the old East India Company, subject to the supervision of a government department on major issues of policy. The administration both of India and of the colonies was responsible to Parliament. Members of Parliament with any detailed knowledge of colonial affairs were always a small minority and Parliament did not generally engage in systematic supervision of colonial matters. On certain issues, such as slavery, it was, however, willing to assert its authority very vigorously indeed.

The lack of strong centralized control over the empire does not, however, necessarily indicate that British politicians or the wider public lacked interest in it. By the end of the eighteenth century it was generally accepted that Britain was at the centre of a great territorial 'British empire'. In spite of the American catastrophe and whatever difficulties Britain might later experience in governing and defending its colonies, a retreat from empire was never regarded as a serious proposition. Only a few isolated individuals ever advocated relinquishing it. Most people considered that the loss of empire would have dire consequences. These were rarely spelled out very explicitly, but the assumption was that they would entail a great reduction in the wealth and power at Britain's disposal as well as – less tangible but still keenly felt – the loss of a role in the world and of national prestige and identity.

The economic imperative

In the eighteenth century the British empire had been a closely integrated trading block: colonies had to send much of their produce to Britain and to buy British manufactured goods. During the first half of the nineteenth century, in accordance with strongly held beliefs in the virtues of free trade, this system of regulations was dismantled. Yet colonies continued to do most of their trade with Britain. Canadian wheat and timber, Australian wool, Indian cotton, jute, and tea, and West Indian sugar were mostly all produced for the British market. From Britain's point of view India was becoming a major market for British manufactured goods. In the years from 1850 to 1870 the empire provided around 20 per cent of Britain's imports and was the market for up to a third of its exports.

Trade with the empire was, however, only a part of the huge volume of trade that Britain was increasingly transacting with the world outside Europe. Britain had retained and indeed greatly expanded its stake in the economy of the United States and was successfully seeking opportunities in the former colonies of Spain and Portugal in Latin America, in the Ottoman empire in the Middle East, and in China. It seemed to make no significant difference whether a country outside Europe was in the empire or not: it still traded with Britain. If that was the case, was there any serious economic argument in favour of retaining the British empire? Why should Britain bear the expense of governing and defending colonies, which presumably would still trade with Britain if they became independent nations?

Contemporaries were well aware of these arguments, but few accepted that they could be applied in a real world. The economic case for empire rested on two principal grounds. In the mid-nineteenth century some independent countries, like the United States, gave Britain relatively free access to their markets; but they could restrict this at any time, as the Americans began to do from 1861. The assumption, albeit a mistaken one, was that so long as Britain kept a minimum of imperial control over the Australian or Canadian colonies, they would not be free to restrict British commercial access. Thus their markets would always remain open. As far as India was concerned, the economic value of imperial control seemed to be even clearer. The British had gone to great lengths to 'open up' India to free trade. This meant abolishing duties (which Indian rulers, left to themselves, might have imposed) and investing heavily in communications – in steamboats to ply the rivers and above all in railways. All this was greatly facilitating the flow of British trade by 1870. Would it have been possible without colonial rule? The example of Chinese and Japanese intransigence to British commercial penetration, even after they had been subjected to attack by warships, left little doubt in the minds of contemporaries. The value of British trade with China bore no comparison with the value of trade with India. Even in an era of free trade, empire retained an economic rationale.

The military imperative

To the eighteenth-century politician, the connection between the wealth that Britain derived from empire and its status as a great military and naval power was crystal clear: hence the insistence on trade regulations to ensure that Britain benefited to the maximum from the possession of empire. Government revenue from taxation – especially the government's capacity to borrow in the City of London at reasonable rates of interest, on which maintaining the armed forces depended – rested to a large degree on the riches of the colonial trades. By the nineteenth century the situation seemed to be rather different. A greatly expanded domestic British economy provided a much bigger base for taxation and borrowing. Moreover, after the defeat of Napoleon it seemed unlikely for several generations that Britain would have to mobilize its resources to the full to fight an all-out war for national survival. On the other hand, the defence of its colonies was a drain on Britain's resources. Only India was a conspicuous exception. An almost unlimited number of troops could be raised in India (by the 1820s over 200,000 Indian soldiers were under arms) and some 40,000 British troops were kept there, primarily at the expense of Indian not British taxpayers. The British Indian army was available for imperial purposes from the Red Sea to China. The colonies of settlement, however, could not contribute much to their own defence in any serious emergency. They had to be protected. British garrisons, for which little if any financial return was received, were strung out across the world from Quebec to Sydney. In 1848 nearly 40,000 British troops, out of total army of 130,000, were in colonial garrisons outside India.

In a permanently peaceful world empire might be regarded as a disposable military liability with much the same logic as it could be seen as a disposable economic liability in a world permanently committed to free trade. Very few contemporaries believed, however, that the intentions of the other powers were

'Officers and Privates of the 2nd and 11th Companies Gun Lascar Corps', Madras army. From the middle of the eighteenth century the East India Company recruited Indian soldiers, or sepoys, into its three separate armies – those of Bengal, Bombay, and Madras. With a total strength at the end of the century of some 200,000 men, the British Indian army was a much larger force than the British peacetime army. These are artillerymen, depicted in 1796 in the characteristic turbans of the Madras army.

Troops bound for Canada, December 1861. Until late in the nineteenth century Britain maintained garrisons in its North American colonies as a precaution against any attack from the United States. In a serious crisis reinforcements had to be sent across the Atlantic. These troops are boarding the fast steamship *The Great Eastern* as part of a build-up in response to the seizure by the forces of the Union during the American Civil War of delegates from the southern states travelling to Britain on a British ship.

permanently peaceful towards Britain. If Britain ceased to concern itself with the defence of its colonies, they might eventually fall into the hands of other powers with consequences that could not be risked. The empire must be defended.

European powers did not pose a serious threat to Britain's imperial possessions for much of the nineteenth century. Although the British often viewed French intentions with some apprehension, no European country possessed a navy sufficiently powerful to challenge the British empire by sea. But the territory of two major powers was growing at a rate that was carrying them overland into close proximity to British possessions. The first was the United States. By the middle of the nineteenth century Britain had to take very serious account of the capacity of the United States to dominate the western hemisphere, including of course Canada. Until late in the century Britain was fully committed to defending Canada should it ever be attacked from the south. In the event this was not necessary. When disputes arose they were settled by diplomatic means (for example, the agreements fixing the boundary between Canada and the United States along the 49th parallel), and Britain concentrated on building Canada into a viable state that could deal directly with the United States. Solutions to the other overland threat to the empire were much more difficult to find. At least from 1828 the expansion of Russia into Central

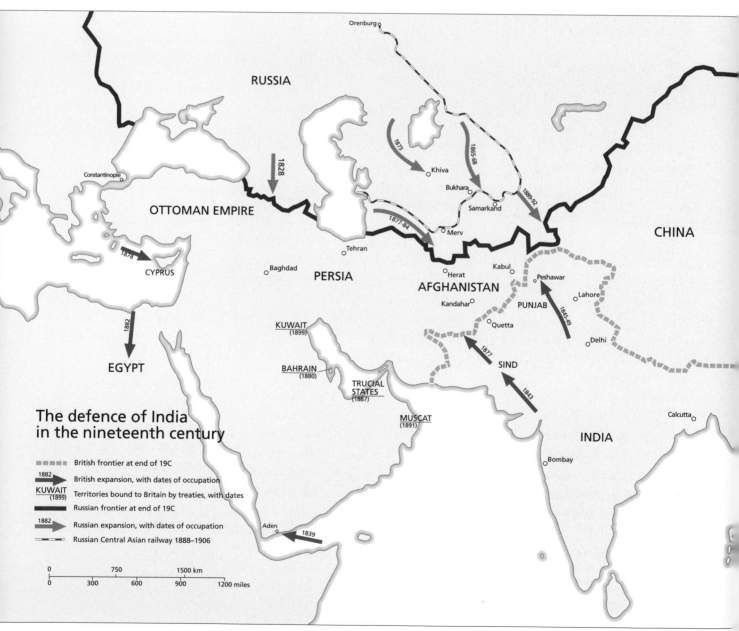

The defence of India in the nineteenth century

- British frontier at end of 19C
- **1882 →** British expansion, with dates of occupation
- **KUWAIT (1899)** Territories bound to Britain by treaties, with dates
- Russian frontier at end of 19C
- **1882 →** Russian expansion, with dates of occupation
- Russian Central Asian railway 1888–1906

0   750   1500 km
0   300   600   900   1200 miles

Asia and the Caucasus was seen as posing a direct threat to Britain's position in India. The fear was that as Russia established control over the khanates of Central Asia, Iran, and possibly Afghanistan and even the Ottoman empire, its influence would extend to the frontiers of India. The Russians could then foment revolt in India and Britain's supremacy would crumble. To counter such a threat Britain tried to establish a secure frontier in north-western India and to build up its own influence in the Middle East, on the Persian Gulf, and in Afghanistan to act as a protective screen for India. At times this involved the dispatch of armed forces beyond India's frontiers, as with the disastrous intervention to try to establish a favourable regime in Afghanistan between 1838 and 1842. What was later to be called the 'Great Game' of Anglo-Russian rivalry in Asia had begun. For the British, the defence of India was the stake in a game that was to last well into the twentieth century.

The moral imperative

To concentrate solely on the material and military incentive for expansion – territory conquered, people settled, or statistics of trade – would be to miss an important dimension of the British imperial experience. Empire was a vehicle by which a self-confident people exported their values and culture throughout the world. This process will be examined in detail in chapter 7 (see pages 185–223), but it should be noted here that confidence in Britain's ability to influence the world for the better was probably at its height in the early nineteenth century, even if imperial propaganda might be more strident in later periods. British emigrants took their values with them and adhered tenaciously to them. When they tried to rule other people British administrators in this period were not unmindful of the need to adapt to indigenous ways of doing things, but the assumption that British ways were the norm was usually inescapable. There were as yet relatively few competitors to set an alternative pattern of a successful society – open to change, yet apparently stable. British models were definitely for export, outside the empire as well as within it.

In the opinion of most of its citizens, if Britain lost its empire it would lose much of its status as a great power: it would be materially impoverished and militarily weakened. But the British people would also have lost much of their capacity to leave their mark on the world and would be diminished in their own eyes. Colonies of British immigrants were seen as distinctively British communities. They should remain British. Thus the thought that Canada, for example, should lose its British identity and be submerged by American republicanism was not a welcome prospect. Earl Grey, a major politician who involved himself deeply in colonial matters, wrote in 1853:

> I consider, then, that the British Colonial Empire ought to be maintained, principally because I do not consider that the Nation would be justified in throwing off the responsibility it has incurred by the acquisition of this dominion,

Map opposite: During the nineteenth century Britain and Russia extended their power over large parts of Asia. They were prompted by mutual fear: the Russians wished to prevent British penetration in Central Asia, while the British were trying to keep the Russians as far away from their Indian possessions as possible. British tactics were to extend the frontier of India up to the great mountain ranges of the north-west and to try to maintain Afghanistan, Iran, and the Ottoman empire as buffers against further Russian expansion. Concern for stable buffer states and for rapid communications for reinforcements to India drew the British into the Persian Gulf and into Cyprus and Egypt.

Queen Victoria. In 1858, when India was placed under the direct rule of the Crown, Queen Victoria committed herself and Britain: 'To stimulate the peaceful industry of India, to promote works of public utility and improvement, and to administer its government for the benefit of all our subjects resident therein. In their prosperity will be our strength; in their contentment our security; and in their gratitude our best reward.'

and because I believe that much of the power and influence of this Country depends upon its having large Colonial possessions in different parts of the world.

The possession of a number of steady and faithful allies in various quarters of the globe, will surely be admitted to add greatly to the strength of any nation; while no alliance between independent states can be so close and intimate as the connection which unites the Colonies of the United Kingdom as parts of the Great British Empire. Nor ought it to be forgotten, that the power of a nation does not depend merely on the amount of physical force it can command, but rests in no small degree, upon opinion and moral influence: in this respect British power would be diminished by the loss of our Colonies, to a degree which it would be difficult to estimate.

Where Britain ruled over non-European peoples, Grey believed that: 'The authority of the British Crown is at this moment the most powerful instrument under Providence, of maintaining peace and order in many extensive regions of the earth, and thereby assists in diffusing amongst millions of the human race, the blessings of Christianity and civilisation.' To most contemporaries, Britain's providential role for good in the world was most splendidly demonstrated in the way in which it had taken the lead in abolishing its own slave trade and slave system and was exerting its power to harry the slave trade of others. India offered another great field on which Britain's imperial role would be a beacon to the world. When the East India Company was replaced by direct Crown rule in 1858, a great new future, both for India and for Britain, was confidently anticipated.

THE EXPANSION OF EMPIRE

The British liked to assume that their role in the world was an essentially peaceful one: Britain protected its existing empire, while its trade and its culture prevailed on their intrinsic merits alone wherever free competition was allowed by others. Britain, its citizens believed, only resorted to force in self-defence. The reality was, however, a record of almost continuous conquest or violence overseas between 1783 and 1870.

There were some curbs on the use of force in this period, but they could usually be overcome without much difficulty. Concern about cost was the most effective restraint. Costs incurred in wars of conquest and in the creation of new administrations were unpopular with the British Treasury and with the House of Commons, if they were likely to fall on the British taxpayer. Early nineteenth-century wars on the frontier of the Cape in South Africa, for instance, attracted particularly vehement criticism. British sensitivity to the rights of subjugated peoples and to the loss of lives involved in wars of conquest or in other naval and military operations was usually somewhat selective, especially if the lives in question were those of non-European people. There were, however, groups who would complain on humanitarian and Christian grounds against aggression and the taking of life in an apparently unjust war and voices of protest, such as those of Edmund Burke, Thomas Fowell Buxton, or Richard Cobden, were heard in the House of Commons. Governments could usually survive such criticism without too much difficulty, but an overseas war that seemed to be unjustifiable, as well as being costly and not immediately successful, was the sort of embarrassment governments wished to avoid.

During the French Revolutionary and Napoleonic Wars from 1793 to 1815, the British were very heavily involved in conquest overseas. They took from their enemies places of strategic importance – the Cape of Good Hope, Mauritius, and Ceylon (Sri Lanka) – and kept them at the peace settlements. Huge British forces

'Captain Fisher charged by Macoma's Kafirs in Van Beulen's Hoek, Kat River' by Thomas Baines (see page 307). The Kaffir War of 1850–52 on the eastern frontier of the Cape Colony in South Africa was one of many local wars that pushed forward the frontiers of the mid-Victorian empire. The Xhosa people resisted extensions of British authority and white settlement: it took ten battalions to subjugate them.

A British naval officer in Japan, 1861. The masterful figure depicted by a Japanese artist symbolized an unmistakable threat to the old order in Japan. The exclusion of foreigners from Japan had been brought to an end in 1854, when the first treaties had been signed with western countries under the threat of American naval power. The warships of other countries, including Britain, also appeared in Japanese waters. Attempts by some Japanese lords to resist concessions were met by naval bombardments in 1863. British merchant communities were then established in Japanese ports.

were sent to the West Indies in attempts to conquer the French islands and, unavailingly, to subjugate the ex-slaves who had rebelled against the French and taken control of what was soon to be called Haiti. Trinidad was, however, taken from the Spanish and Guyana from the Dutch. The price of these wars was staggering. Between 1793 and 1801 some 89,000 British troops were sent to the West Indies, more than half of whom died there.

After the wars were over, the British empire continued to expand. For the most part growth was the result of local initiatives: settler communities moved into new lands, local garrisons chastized what they took to be refractory tribes on colonial frontiers, and governors-general of India used their military resources to annex independent states that seemed to threaten the security of British India. The lack of much direct involvement by the British government gives some plausibility to the famous aphorism that the British empire was acquired in a fit of absence of mind. Such an impression is, however, misleading. The British government may have had real difficulty in restraining unauthorized conquests, but it was usually inclined to accept what had been done without its authority. Except on occasions in South Africa, conquests were not renounced and colonial governors or Indian governors-general who waged wars on their own initiative were rarely reprimanded or recalled. Whatever may have been the official rhetoric, most British politicians seem tacitly to have accepted that the empire could not remain in a steady state: preserving it almost inevitably meant allowing it to grow. Claims that Britain was solely concerned with standing on the defensive outside Europe and with protecting its long-established interests against other predators are hard to reconcile with great additions of territory to the empire.

THE EXPANSION OF INFLUENCE

British dominance was not confined to the acquisition of territory. In the mid-nineteenth century Britain had opportunities, which it had never enjoyed before and was never to enjoy again, for extending its influence throughout the world. As the world's biggest market for tropical produce and the world's main supplier of manufactured goods, Britain could forge links with less developed economies on its own terms. Moreover, since the Royal Navy had only limited competition from the fleets of France and the United States, there was little to restrain Britain from using force against those who declined to trade as it wished. Economic dominance could be sustained by the limited application of force.

Most British politicians were very strongly committed to the ideal of free trade. Lord Palmerston, who directed British policy for long periods between 1830 and 1865, called free trade one of 'the great standing laws of nature'. He had a vision of 'commerce ... leading civilisation with one hand, peace with the other, to render mankind happier, wiser, better ... This is the dispensation of Providence ...' Since Britain was likely to be the main beneficiary of free trade agreements, this may look somewhat cynical. Palmerston and his contemporaries did not, however, see anything cynical about equating the interests of Britain with those of humanity and with the will of the Almighty. Palmerston had no doubt that Britain was a force for good in the world and that on occasions the use of violence to bring about improvement could be justified. Agreements about free trade were assiduously sought with other European countries, with the United States, with the Latin American republics, throughout Asia, and, where possible, in Africa.

In some cases agreements for freer trade with Britain were readily conceded by countries who considered it to be to their advantage to do so. In other cases reluctance was overcome by diplomatic pressure or even by force. Resort to force was most blatant on the China coast, where Opium Wars were fought between 1839 and 1842 and again from 1856 to 1860. Each war ended in a treaty in which the Chinese were compelled to grant increased access for western trade. In 1863 naval bombardment of the Japanese port of Kagoshima helped to subdue opposition to trade concessions to the west. The British navy was also extremely active off the coast of West Africa in trying to suppress slave trading and in forcing African rulers to sign treaties banning slaving and facilitating alternative forms of trade.

Efforts to secure agreements for freer trade, backed by the implied threat and sometimes the overt use of coercion, have been called 'the imperialism of free trade'. Forceful imperialist tactics were on occasions used to establish free trade. But whether Britain's success in pursuing such policies ever amounted to the creation of an informal empire, as is sometimes claimed, is another matter. The issue has already been briefly discussed in the Introduction. There are good grounds for being cautious about the extent of any informal empire for the period down to 1870. Informal empire assumes effective domination. Economic domination is a somewhat nebulous concept, but whether Britain in this period was able effectively to dominate the economy of any region of Latin America, Africa, or Asia (except where colonial rule had been established in India) seems very doubtful. The volume of trade passing to and from Britain was not likely ever to have been great enough for that. The market for British goods was too limited and so was the capacity of most non-European countries to produce commodities for export. Above all, major developments in transport were required. A 'shipping revolution', enabling bulk cargoes to be moved cheaply and rapidly by large steamships, was not complete until the 1870s. The full development of railways outside Europe was also not achieved until the later nineteenth century (see pages 116–20). British merchants might seek new opportunities, but trade on any scale outside Europe could only be carried on in this period in limited coastal areas or in countries with relatively developed economies, like the United States, where any form of coercion was impossible.

The practical effects of Britain's naval supremacy were limited. Britain had neither the means nor the will to practise 'gunboat diplomacy' all over the world or to impose a system of peace and order throughout the world, which contemporaries liked to call the 'Pax Britannica'. Concern for American susceptibilities, for instance, put some limits on what Britain would attempt in the western hemisphere. British merchants could not expect the automatic support of British warships whenever they encountered commercial difficulties. The Victorian Royal Navy was, however, very widely dispersed. There was a powerful British presence in the Mediterranean. Further afield, bases such as Aden, Singapore, and Hong Kong were acquired. Squadrons operated in the Indian Ocean, the West Indies, the south Atlantic, and the Pacific. In the Persian Gulf, the China seas, and off the coast of Africa British sea power was at its most uninhibited. Here Britain could exercise informal authority, based on force or the threat of force. Even so, British naval authority did not extend far inland beyond Zanzibar, the Gulf coast, the ports and great rivers of China, or the Niger delta.

THE EMPIRE OVERSEAS

In the period from 1783 to 1870 there can be no doubt of Britain's ambitions, or, to be more exact, of many British people's ambitions. Britain was a restless society. British people were leaving the British Isles, seeking commercial advantages and propagating their values throughout the world. A considerable part of this restless energy spilt over beyond the bounds of the British empire, but its most lasting memorial was an expanding empire of rule. If always essentially British in fundamentals, this empire took very different forms in different parts of the world.

Colonies of settlement

When Britain conceded American independence in 1783, Quebec and Nova Scotia formed the nucleus of the colonies that constituted Britain's remaining stake on the North American continent – British North America. The population of these colonies was swelled by the arrival of about 50,000 'loyalists' – people who for various reasons had chosen to leave the rebellious colonies and continue to live under British authority. Those loyalists who moved to Quebec introduced a major non-French element to the province for the first time. In 1791 the English-speaking districts of Quebec were turned into a separate province of Upper Canada from which modern Ontario has grown. Over the fifty years after the ending of the European wars in 1815, more than a million British immigrants entered the provinces, although more than half of those eventually moved down to the United States. Of those who remained in British North America, the majority settled in Upper Canada. The old Quebec, later Lower Canada, was dominated by French-speakers. Even if they received no new immigrants, their natural rate of population increase was still spectacular. The French Canadians remained a strongly cohesive community, preserving their language, their Roman Catholicism, and parts of their own legal system. But although the French continued to dominate Quebec, continuous immigration from Britain meant that the French Canadians were no more than a powerful minority in British North America as a whole by the mid-nineteenth century.

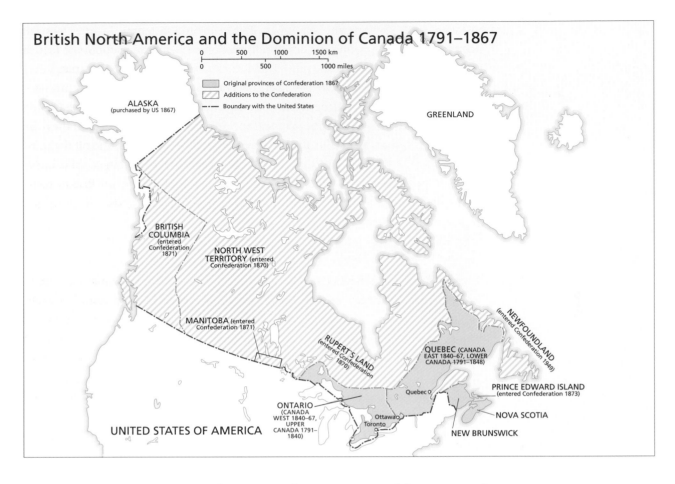

British North America and the Dominion of Canada 1791–1867

The British North American colonies were the proving ground for systems of government considered appropriate for sizeable white communities anywhere within the British empire. British policy was generally to ensure an adequate degree of imperial authority – exercised by a Governor appointed in London – over what were regarded as essential matters, while letting the colonists run their own affairs in all other respects through their own assemblies or local parliaments with as little interference as possible. Close supervision over colonies of white settlement was never desired. In the Canadian colonies by the middle of the nineteenth century and later in other colonies dominated by whites, most of the Governor's powers came to be exercised by local ministers who could command a majority in the Assembly. This was the system eventually known as 'responsible government', under which British colonies became for all intents and purposes internally self-governing, while remaining within the empire and accepting British control over their relations with foreign countries. In retrospect, responsible government was a device of which the British came to be very proud. It seemed to combine freedom for the inhabitants of British colonies to run their own affairs with guarantees that imperial links would survive and therefore that a British identity would be preserved.

The scattered British colonies left in north-eastern America by the revolt of the thirteen colonies began to come together with the union of the two Canadas in 1840 and the forming of a Confederation in 1867. This new Dominion of Canada was able to incorporate the lands to the west and spread itself across the continent from the Atlantic to the Pacific.

Responsible government was first achieved in British North America but not without difficulty. So long as there was a French majority in Canada, the British were wary of handing over real power to a local leadership that might not ultimately prove to be loyal to Britain. (A part of the French population had even taken up arms in revolt in 1837.) The British strategy was first of all to try to bring the provinces of British North America together in a larger block. The larger the unit, the smaller would be the French component in it and the greater would be its chances of resisting the seduction of being absorbed into the great republic to the south. A prosperous, stable, united Canada could stand on its own and make its own terms with the United States. In 1840 English-speaking Upper Canada and Quebec (or Lower Canada), with its French-speaking majority, were joined together. It was becoming clear that a new French leadership was willing to co-operate with English-speaking Canadian politicians, on the implied condition that Quebec would keep its religion, language, and identity within a union. This union was enlarged by the act creating the Canadian Confederation of 1867, patiently engineered by Canadian politicians with encouragement from London, which united the Canadas and the two main maritime provinces. The act made specific provision for the new Canada to incorporate all the lands claimed to the west by Britain, including the territory of British Columbia on the Pacific in 1871.

In 1788 a British colony was established in a part of the world totally remote from any European colonizing enterprise in the past. After a prodigious journey round the Cape of Good Hope and across the Indian Ocean, a fleet of eleven vessels containing 736 convicted criminals, a Governor and some officials, and an escort of marines founded a British colony on the eastern coast of Australia in what later became New South Wales. This was to be the first European settlement of any kind in Australasia, an area about which very little was known in Europe. The site for which the first fleet was aiming had been visited in 1770 by Captain James Cook as he sailed up the coast of Australia on the first of his great voyages of exploration into the Pacific. The briefest of calls into what was named Botany Bay suggested that it might be a habitable location for Europeans. Seventeen years later a British government chose to act on that suggestion and dispatch the fleet.

This was a stroke of extraordinary boldness, not to say foolhardiness. Although New South Wales in fact turned out to be an environment in which European settlers would eventually flourish, the British government had no sure knowledge as to what conditions there would be like, and the new colony only survived its initial problems with a great deal of good fortune. Why then did British ministers run such risks? One widely held view is that they were playing for high imperial stakes – that they considered it important for British interests to establish a base somewhere in the Pacific and that the convicts were the best means of getting a new colony off the ground. While it seems to be beyond doubt that British ministers were to some degree interested in the possibilities of the Pacific, no conclusive evidence has yet been found to support theories that settlement in Australia in 1788 was sought primarily for commercial or strategic ends. The traditional explanation that New South Wales was colonized to provide a convict settlement is more plausible. Transportation was an important part of the British penal system. Convicts had been transported in the past to colonial America but after the revolution America was no longer available. No alternative destination could be found, in spite of determined efforts to do so, and very large numbers of convicts awaiting transportation were accumulating in Britain. They had to go somewhere – New South Wales was where they went. That is not the whole explanation for the founding of white Australia, but it seems still to be the major factor.

Once the new colony was established, the British government continued to pour out convicts, some 160,000 of them, without significant interruption until 1852. Who the convicts were, how they were treated, and what sort of society emerged among them are all subjects of lively debate. What is beyond question is that they were the basis on which the first two Australian colonies, New South Wales and Van Diemen's Land (Tasmania), were built.

From the landing of the first fleet, non-convict 'free' settlers also went to Australia. Their numbers gradually increased as the opportunities for making a new life in Australia began to become apparent. Australia offered the resources of the Pacific Ocean, particularly seals and whales, convict labour, and an abundance of land from which a thinly-spread Aborigine population – probably around 750,000 on the eve of the first white settlement – could be displaced. (This settlement was accompanied by more violence from whites and more resistance by Aborigines than was once assumed.) The land was used in particular for raising sheep, wool being

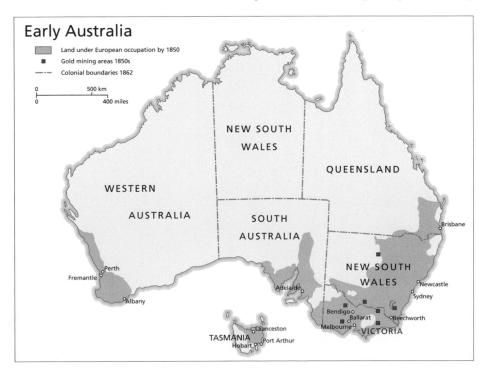

Early Australia

- Land under European occupation by 1850
- Gold mining areas 1850s
- Colonial boundaries 1862

0   500 km
0   400 miles

WESTERN AUSTRALIA

NEW SOUTH WALES

QUEENSLAND

SOUTH AUSTRALIA

Brisbane

NEW SOUTH WALES

Perth
Fremantle
Albany

Adelaide

Newcastle
Sydney

Bendigo
Ballarat
Melbourne
Beechworth
VICTORIA

TASMANIA
Launceston
Hobart Port Arthur

a cargo whose value in relation to its bulk was sufficient to defray the costs of the immense voyage. By the 1830s Australia was becoming a major supplier of wool to the British textile industry.

The cost of the long haul out to Australia, by comparison with the relatively short trip across the Atlantic, always limited 'free' emigration from Britain. But enough people were encouraged to move, often by schemes of assisted passages in which there was some degree of government involvement, to enable new colonies to be

Convict Australia

View of Sydney, *c.*1821. This section of a panorama shows something of the progress made in just over thirty years of European settlement on the coast of New South Wales. Sydney had become a thriving port with the beginnings of some industry, such as flour and timber mills, brewing, or making pottery, leather, woollen cloth, and bricks. The labour of convicts, shown on the left of the picture, was crucial to these developments.

The convicts and the system to which they were subjected have been interpreted in many different ways throughout Australia's history. For some later Australians, convict origins were a source of shame. Others have been proud to claim descent from people who, they liked to believe, were either the innocent victims of an inhuman system or, if they were guilty at all, were only guilty of acts of justifiable defiance. Some accounts stress the barbarous severity with which convicts were treated in Australia, creating – in the words of Richard Hughes's *The Fatal Shore* – a 'not so-small, not so-primitive ancestor of the Gulag' of Joseph Stalin; other historians insist that most convicts had a real measure of control over their lives and

that 'the making of a free society' had been going on in New South Wales 'almost since the day it began'.

Studies of convicts suggest that they should not be unduly romanticized. They were the victims of a system of British criminal law that no doubt now seems to be intolerably severe, but most of them seem to have been persistent offenders who were not lightly or frivolously sentenced according to the standards of that law. Most of those transported were thieves, usually from urban backgrounds. There were some 'political' offenders, including some Irish ones, but not very many.

Those who stress that convict society was more or less 'normal' and those who

established without convicts. In 1826 settlement began in Western Australia. The new colony of South Australia was sanctioned by act of Parliament in 1834. In the same year settlers from Van Diemen's Land moved across the straits to take up land in what is now Victoria. The success of that settlement was revolutionized by the great gold discoveries of the 1850s, which brought waves of new immigrants to the workings in Victoria and New South Wales. The white population of the Australian colonies jumped from 437,665 in 1851 to over a million in 1861.

stress its brutality are both right in different ways. For the majority, especially in New South Wales, life was not necessarily intolerable. Part of most sentences was remitted, and much of the work done by those under sentence was done for material reward. Convicts could tacitly bargain for their labour. Marriage was encouraged and a new population of 'country-born' children grew up healthy and well nourished. However, for a small minority in New South Wales and a much larger proportion in Van Diemen's Land (Tasmania), authority could be extremely violent and vindictive. Those who were judged to have offended again in Australia were likely to be flogged relentlessly and sentenced to places of very ill repute indeed, such as Port Arthur in Van Diemen's Land or Norfolk Island. Horrendous punishments are well documented, but it must be stressed that the ordinary convict was too valuable a commodity to be an object of sadism. The new colonies were built on their labour. A new society emerged from the endurance and ingenuity of cargoes of urban thieves.

The flogging of the convict, Charles Maher. The convict system was at its most brutal in penal settlements like Norfolk Island in the Tasman Sea. In 1800 the settlement was under a sadistic officer called Major Joseph Foveaux, who was said to 'believe in the lash more than the Bible'. The sketch shows a man receiving 250 lashes, which left his back 'quite bare of skin and flesh'.

Some whites from New South Wales crossed over into New Zealand to use it as a base for voyages into the Pacific and to trade with the Maoris. By the 1830s the lands of New Zealand were coming to be of interest to groups in Britain who wanted to ship out emigrants. In 1840 the British government intervened to try to impose a new order in New Zealand. It was annexed for Britain and white settlement under regulation was officially sanctioned, while under the Treaty of Waitangi guarantees were given to Maori representatives. The new order had eventually to be imposed by force. Maoris resisted the loss of land and of their capacity to rule themselves and proved to be very formidable fighters. In a series of Maori Wars and other skirmishes from 1845 to 1872 British regiments were fully extended and often badly mauled. The outcome of the wars and of the continuing flow of new British immigrants into New Zealand, stimulated by gold rushes in South Island, was to reduce the Maoris to a minority of the total population. By 1870 there were 250,000 whites to some 50,000 Maoris.

As in Quebec, when the British annexed the Cape of Good Hope in 1806 they acquired new European subjects who were not of British origin – in this case the Afrikaners, a population of about 30,000, who, outside the considerable port of Cape Town, were for the most part thinly scattered as farmers (hence 'boers') across a wide area. In addition to the Afrikaners, the Cape was also inhabited by its indigenous people, the Khoikhoi, by slaves brought in by the Dutch, and by communities of people of mixed race. On the frontiers of the area claimed by the Dutch, there were formidable African peoples, especially the Xhosa on the eastern Cape frontier, who disputed the further expansion of European settlement.

Until the great discoveries of minerals in the later nineteenth century, South Africa was not regarded as a major economic asset and it attracted relatively few British immigrants. British interests in this highly complex society were at first mainly limited to maintaining a stable order around the strategically vital harbour of Cape Town, the half-way house to India. Stability was not, however, easy to ensure. At any time rural Afrikaners were inclined to migrate in search of fresh grazing land. Under the British they felt that they had added incentives to move. Some found British rule alien and heavy-handed, a threat to the distinctiveness of their culture and institutions and especially to their labour supply: the British eventually abolished slavery throughout the empire, while imposing regulations on other forms of labour. Instead of rebelling, as some French Canadians had done in 1837, a part of the Afrikaner population took itself away from British jurisdiction by trekking out of the Cape into apparently vacant land to the north. Between 1836 and 1846 about 14,000 Afrikaners embarked on the Great Trek. Their migration created fresh problems for the British. The lands of the north were not of course vacant. They were claimed by African peoples with whom the Afrikaners came into violent conflict. War in the interior, which threatened to spread south into British territory, was added to the more or less endemic war with the Xhosa on the eastern frontier. After a brief attempt to bring under control the new Afrikaner republics of

A romanticized engraving of an ox wagon crossing the Cradock pass in the eastern Cape in 1840. The Great Trek took Afrikaners away from British rule in the Cape Colony to new lands to the north where they founded their own states.

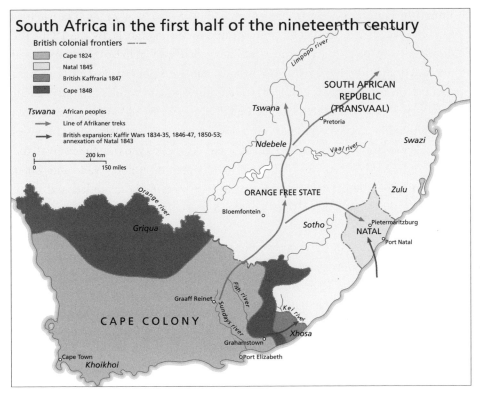

South Africa in the first half of the nineteenth century

British colonial frontiers —-—

- Cape 1824
- Natal 1845
- British Kaffraria 1847
- Cape 1848

Tswana African peoples

→ Line of Afrikaner treks

→ British expansion: Kaffir Wars 1834-35, 1846-47, 1850-53; annexation of Natal 1843

0   200 km
0   150 miles

the Orange Free State and the South African Republic (Transvaal), the British for the time being more or less washed their hands of the interior, leaving the trekkers alone. Nearer the coast, however, British involvement continued to be expensive and unrewarding, as a series of Kaffir Wars were fought against the Xhosa and Natal was annexed.

At the Cape, in the Australian colonies, and in New Zealand the British established constitutional arrangements on the same principles as they had done in British North America. Essential imperial control was to be maintained, but otherwise the white communities were to rule themselves as far as possible. Initially elected assemblies were established and eventually the government of the colonies was made 'responsible' to these assemblies as in Canada. Most Australian colonies got responsible government in 1855, New Zealand in 1856, and the Cape in 1872. As with British North America, the British were also concerned to see individual colonies merge into larger and, it was hoped, more stable units, capable of undertaking their own defence. The Australian colonies were not, however, to come together until 1901. The intractable problems of uniting the old British colonies of the Cape and Natal with the Afrikaner republics of the Orange Free State and the Transvaal were not to be overcome until after South Africa had been convulsed by war at the end of the century.

By 1870 British politicians could take some satisfaction from the growth and development of colonies in Canada, South Africa, Australia, and New Zealand. They had stayed within the imperial fold, while developing their own local autonomies. Even the French Canadians and the majority of Afrikaners who remained at the Cape had been kept within the empire. A part at least of the civilizing mission that the Victorians had set themselves had been fulfilled: British values had been preserved in 'British' communities overseas. In terms of wealth and power, Britain stood to gain too. The growth of the white population in Australia, Canada, and New Zealand was to make them by the late nineteenth century 'steady and faithful allies' (as Grey had put it in 1853) of real value to Britain as sources of high-quality military manpower in future wars. As their economies grew, and that of South Africa was transformed by gold and diamonds, their value as trading partners with Britain and as homes for British investment was to grow enormously.

There was, however, a blot on the record of success. The protection of vulnerable non-European peoples was another part of the Victorian civilizing mission. By and large Britain had abandoned this part of its mission in what were emerging as 'white' colonies. British opinion had taken very little notice of the problems of the native American population of Canada or of Australian Aborigines. The Maoris of New Zealand and the Khoikhoi and the Africans of South Africa had, however, featured prominently in the concerns of British humanitarians. The attitudes of British governments had reflected some of this concern, but in the end Britain was not willing to go very far in interposing its authority on their behalf against the wishes of the dominant white communities, and indeed had provided the military power through which these wishes had been enforced. The Xhosa of the eastern Cape in South Africa and the Maoris of New Zealand, for example, had lost their lands as a

Tasmanian Aborigines in the 1860s. There were probably 4,000–6,000 Aborigines in Tasmania at the beginning of European settlement. Within a few years most of the population had been destroyed by European diseases or by violent encounters with the whites. The remnants were removed to small islands off the coast, where they too perished. The last member of this group, photographed at Oyster Cove near Hobart, died in 1876.

result of defeat by British forces. Those who wished to take pride in Britain's role as protector of the weak found it more edifying to reflect on what had happened in the West Indies.

The West Indies and West Africa

At the end of the eighteenth century, Britain was the biggest exporter of slaves from West Africa and operated the biggest and most successful slave-worked plantation system in the world. With the destruction by slave revolts of St Domingue (Haiti), the immensely successful French West Indian enterprise, and with the Royal Navy able to eliminate the slave and sugar trade of Britain's enemies after the outbreak of war in 1793, the British West Indies had few competitors as sugar, coffee, and cotton producers. Trinidad and what is now called Guyana, territories with a very high potential for plantation agriculture, were added to the British empire by conquest. Yet by the middle of the nineteenth century the West Indian colonies were for the most part in decline and other producers were capturing most of the world market.

The years in which the British West Indies shifted from riches to decline were marked by two major decisions of the British Parliament. In 1807 Britain abolished its trade in slaves before all its major competitors did the same and in 1833 it decreed the abolition of slavery throughout the British empire, again before others did so. The relationship between these two decisions and the decline of the British West Indies is the subject of intense historical debate. The case is often made that the decline of the British West Indies was inevitable, owing to the exhaustion of the older plantations and the lack of abundant new lands. Since the British West Indies could no longer compete effectively with new producers like Cuba, it cost the British relatively little to indulge their humanitarian emotions by getting rid of their slave systems, knowing that their population would be supplied more cheaply with plantation produce from foreign sources. The abolition of Britain's slave trade and of slavery in the empire was not therefore the great triumph of virtue that contemporaries and so many later historians have generally believed. It was a piece of relatively enlightened self-interest. This view is particularly associated with the late Eric Williams, who was Prime Minister of Trinidad, as well as being a distinguished scholar and author of *Capitalism and Slavery*.

Other historians maintain that the decline of the British West Indies was the direct result of the ending of the slave trade and of British slavery. They suggest that had Britain been able to maintain the supply of labour from Africa and to impose the control over it that slavery permitted, the British West Indian islands would have remained competitive with Cuba or with Brazil, both of which continued to import and use slaves until much later. The British humanitarians who were responsible for the ending of slavery therefore destroyed an entirely viable system. Thus, far from being in the economic interests of Britain, the abolition of slavery was a triumph of altruism or an act of foolishness, according to one's point of view.

Anti-slavery medallion. Josiah Wedgwood, the great manufacturer of pottery and himself an enthusiastic campaigner against the slave trade, began to distribute copies of this medallion made of jasper in 1787 to coincide with the first parliamentary investigation of the trade. The medallion proved to be extremely popular. 'Am I not a man and a brother?' was one of the great slogans of anti-slavery.

William Wilberforce. Wilberforce, here depicted in old age, led the campaign against the slave trade in Parliament from 1787 until its abolition in 1807. As a deeply committed Christian, he was also active in many other causes, such as the propagation of Christianity in India.

Those who argue that slavery was abolished because of the pressure of the humanitarians can point to the fact that the mobilization of British opinion against the slave trade and slavery was very successful indeed. The humanitarians had massive popular support and vast numbers of people signed petitions. A petition from Manchester at the beginning of the campaign in 1787 attracted 11,000 signatures, about 20 per cent of the town's population. One and a half million people petitioned in the last campaign in 1833. The leadership of the movement consisted of highly religious men and women, such as William Wilberforce and Thomas Clarkson, whose sense of Christian justice was outraged by slavery. Committed Christians were clearly a major part of the movement's support, but opinion of all sorts rallied to a cause that appealed both to radicals, who wished to destroy the privileges of the West Indian planter oligarchy and vindicate the rights of man, and to conservatives, who were concerned with Britain's honour.

Powerful as the public pressure undoubtedly was, sheer numbers could not be translated into votes in the House of Commons, given the nature of the representative system before the 1832 Reform Act and indeed after it. The British political elite had to be convinced that no irreparable damage would be done to Britain's national interests by abolition. It is not easy to see why they were so convinced in 1807, when the trade was abolished. At that time some 60 per cent of the world's sugar supplies was coming from the British colonies. It seems, however, that Members of Parliament were willing to believe that Britain could continue to produce sugar successfully using existing slave labour and indeed that Britain's lead could be preserved far into the future if slave trading by all countries was cut off and if Britain could then permanently enforce a total ban. This is not what happened. With the ending of the great wars against France in 1815, many countries apart from Britain resumed slave trading and their colonies became very serious competitors with the British West Indies. The British colonies began to get into difficulties. World sugar prices fell rapidly in the 1820s, while costs increased. At the same time the slaves themselves took a hand. Slave resistance became increasingly vigorous, culminating in a major revolt in Jamaica in 1831. Low prices and slave revolts were the setting in which a massive final petitioning movement throughout Britain brought down slavery in the British empire in 1833.

The humanitarians and the politicians who abolished slavery thought that life in the British West Indies would continue much as before – slaves would still work on the plantations, but as free men for wages. In smaller islands this is what generally happened. In larger territories ex-slaves showed less inclination to stay on the plantations. Where land was available, they moved off to become small cultivators on their own. In Trinidad and Guyana planters eventually had to meet their labour needs by another form of imperial immigration: from the 1840s large numbers of Indians were induced to sign indentures and travel round the world to become labourers in the Caribbean (see pages 284–85).

The Krio: black Englishmen in Sierra Leone?

In 1807 Britain turned against the slave trade, and the Royal Navy polished its peacetime efficiency by chasing slave ships and freeing their cargoes. In the next half century, 84,000 'liberated Africans' were released in Sierra Leone, gradually fusing with the original settlers – Jamaican 'Maroons', shipped via Nova Scotia, and the 'Black Poor' who had been rounded up in London and settled at Freetown in 1787. The abolitionists who had founded the colony – serious-minded evangelicals from Britain – hoped to create a new type of 'black Englishman' who would become the cultural intermediary to 'civilize' West Africa. Like the West Indian slaves, the 'Krio' of Sierra Leone hid an African reality under their black English veneer. Even their name – the badge of identity – was a source of misunderstanding, with Europeans interpreting a word probably of Yoruba origin as 'Creole' (from Spanish).

Freetown became an important commercial centre with several Christian churches. Missionaries established Fourah Bay College – one of Africa's oldest universities – in 1827 and went on to endow the colony with schools. A Krio, James Africanus Horton, was almost certainly the first black African to take a degree at a British university, in medicine from Edinburgh.

Yet in reality, influences from Britain contributed very little to Krio culture compared with the amalgam of influences from many parts of Africa. In the late nineteenth century the boundaries of Sierra Leone were expanded by the annexation of the indigenous hill tribes to form a protectorate of some 27,000 square miles. At the same time the number of white officials increased: advances in tropical medicine (especially the availability of quinine) meant that West Africa was no longer 'the white man's grave'. These white civil servants pushed the Krio aside. In 1892 the Krio held eighteen of the forty-seven government posts; by 1912 they had only fifteen out of ninety-two posts, and five of those were soon to retire. Education was no longer encouraged: in 1902 the British decided that white doctors were automatically senior to Krio practitioners, irrespective of qualifications. The British comforted themselves with the belief that the newly annexed hill tribes did not like the Krio: it was therefore necessary for the whites to become the intermediaries themselves. For their part, the Krio could not or would not merge with the indigenous Africans and they became increasingly isolated. In a classic exercise of 'divide and rule' the small Sierra Leone colony – the Krio area around Freetown – was administered separately from the inland protectorate until the eve of independence in 1961. By this time, accepted neither by the Europeans in spite of their partly Europeanized ways nor by the Africans, these descendants of the ex-slaves were not so much 'black Englishmen' as condemned to the political role of being white settlers with black skins.   [BEK]

Charlotte School in the 1880s. Charlotte was one of the villages established in Sierra Leone for the 'liberated Africans' rescued from the slaving ships. Founded in 1830, this school was one of the earliest attempts to provide western education for African girls. Christian missionaries believed that girls should be educated to become suitable companions for their husbands who had been to Sierra Leone's schools or colleges.

Proud as British people might be of the abolition of slavery, the state of the British Caribbean was not a generally happy one by the middle of the nineteenth century. Many plantations were struggling but little was being done to produce an alternative to them. The communities of smallholders were often impoverished. Full civil and political rights were not conceded to ex-slaves. Resentment in Jamaica exploded in the rebellion at Morant Bay in 1865, which was repressed with extreme violence.

For British humanitarians the question of West Indian slavery was closely linked with the question of West Africa. Once it became apparent that international slave trading had not stopped with British abolition, Britain sent naval patrols to the African coast to intercept slave ships and to back diplomatic efforts to persuade African rulers into giving up the trade. British interest in West Africa, however, went further. The humanitarians believed that one of the great crimes involved in the slave trade was that it spread war and devastation in Africa. They thought that abolition of the trade would begin what some British people liked to think of as the regeneration of Africa. Enthusiasts believed that Britain could have a more positive role in bringing about this regeneration. The spread of trade was again seen as the panacea and various projects were devised to teach Africans new skills and thus draw them into new trades. The settlement of Sierra Leone was the most enduring of these projects. From 1787 a series of attempts had been made to establish communities of black people from Britain or America on the West African coast at Sierra Leone. The settlers were to grow new crops and to encourage trade among neighbouring African peoples. Most of the hopes invested in Sierra Leone proved groundless, but a permanent British colony did take root. Freetown in Sierra Leone came to house a remarkable community of ex-slaves of various kinds, who established churches, schools, and commercial businesses. Hopes that such a community might have a transforming influence throughout West Africa were, however, naive.

Dhian Singh. The Sikh state of the Punjab was a formidable obstacle to British expansion. Ranjit Singh, its ruler from 1799 to 1837, built up a modern army, supported by an efficient administrative system under the direction of Dhian Singh, who was effectively chief minister of the state from 1818 until after Ranjit Singh's death.

India

Once British conquests began in the middle of the eighteenth century, the scale of the involvement in India dwarfed every other British imperial enterprise. The acquisition of Bengal brought the British at least twenty million new subjects and a public revenue of £3 million in contemporary values, with which they could start to create a huge new army and construct an elaborate civil administration. Waves of expansion by conquest or the annexation of Indian states produced many millions more subjects, vast increases in resources, and even greater expenditure on defence and administration. When the first census of India was taken in 1871 it indicated that a population of at least 236 million lived either directly under British rule or in Indian states protected by treaties with Britain. The public revenue of the British government of India was then approaching that of Britain itself and its army was much bigger.

The boundaries of India under British rule were effectively established in the first half of the nineteenth century. This was the consequence of several phases of wars and annexations, with the East India Company's frontiers moving forward more rapidly at some times than at others but with few prolonged intervals of peace. These wars were rarely planned or sanctioned in Britain. Until the effective operation of the telegraph in the 1860s, communications with India took up to a month (six months round the Cape in the early nineteenth century). Wars therefore began on the initiative of men in India itself, above all of those who held the office of Governor-General. Some governors-general made little secret of their willingness to extend British rule on almost any pretext. This was true of the Marquess Wellesley between 1798 and 1805, of the Marquess of Hastings between 1813 and 1823, and of Lord Dalhousie from 1848 to 1856. Others professed their abhorrence of war, above all because of its effect on the finances of the government of India. Yet few avoided war altogether. For all its immense military power, British India was constantly apprehensive about its security. Stable relations with states on the British frontiers or within them must be maintained at all costs. Any Indian state that appeared to offer a challenge to the British or to be lapsing into disorder as the British interpreted it must be brought under control before it spread its contagion into British India. Official explanations for British policy constantly portray the British as reluctantly intervening to stabilize their frontiers or remove unsatisfactory rulers. What such accounts do not explain is that the instability that

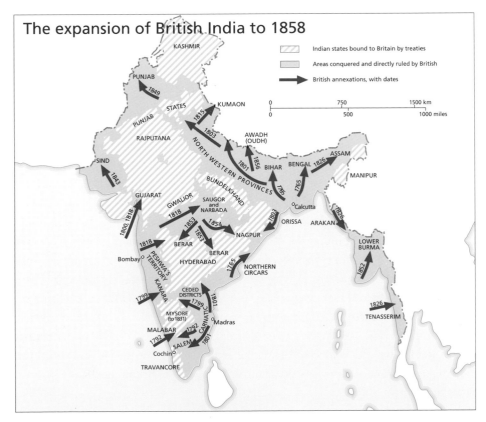

The expansion of British India to 1858

the British deplored and feared was often produced by British pressures for military alliances, for financial contributions, or for commercial access. Nominally independent states were required to make financial contributions to the British, provide for British troops, or accept British guidance to the point where the authority of the rulers was undermined and co-operation with the British broke down. The most costly of all the wars of conquest, the two wars against the Sikhs of the Punjab in 1845–46 and in 1848–49, were a direct consequence of the breakdown under British pressure of the state built up by its ruler Ranjit Singh .

With many local variations, a pattern of administration that had developed for the first conquered provinces was extended all over India in the wake of each new annexation. The central preoccupation of early British India was financial – the raising of taxes. It was the existence of indigenous systems of taxation immediately available to the British that made India so valuable by comparison with colonies where tax resources were very small or where they depended on votes by representative assemblies of Europeans. In India the main tax contribution was extracted from those who cultivated the land. The principal local British administrator, appropriately called the Collector, was responsible for assessing the level of taxation and seeing that it was paid. Concern for taxation gave the British a concern for maintaining an orderly society and for stable property relations with clearly defined rights to land, on which they believed rural prosperity to depend. Much British administration was therefore concerned with law and justice. British jurists tried to codify Indian law and British judges tried to administer it.

Collecting taxes, maintaining law and order, and presiding over courts remained the basic functions of the Raj – as the British government in India was known throughout its history. Other more elaborate ones were added. The government

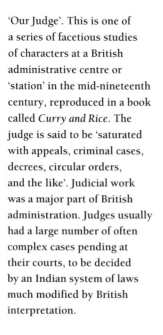

'Our Judge'. This is one of a series of facetious studies of characters at a British administrative centre or 'station' in the mid-nineteenth century, reproduced in a book called *Curry and Rice*. The judge is said to be 'saturated with appeals, criminal cases, decrees, circular orders, and the like'. Judicial work was a major part of British administration. Judges usually had a large number of often complex cases pending at their courts, to be decided by an Indian system of laws much modified by British interpretation.

took some responsibility for promoting education and for the development of public works such as irrigation and improved communications – above all for a great programme of railway building from mid-century. By contemporary standards the government of British India was an ambitious one, at least in its intentions. Its ambitions were those of an authoritarian regime invested with a great deal of power and disposing of a large public revenue. Many of the most innovative minds in early nineteenth-century Britain applied themselves to questions as to how Britain should use its power to govern India. Radical programmes of reform were proposed. Some pressed for the Christianizing of India; others urged secular panaceas, such as reforming Indian law according to the principle of the greatest happiness of the greatest number. Running through these debates was a genuine concern for improvement for its own sake, as expressed in Queen Victoria's proclamation of 1858 (see page 30), together with a keen sense of British interests. British officials in early nineteenth-century India liked to think of themselves as the proprietors of a great landed estate. The prosperity of their tenants, the people of India, was directly linked to the prosperity of the landlord, Britain. Any improvement in the material welfare of the people of India would be reflected in higher tax yields for Britain and a greater capacity to buy British goods and to supply the British market.

The government of India was served by a professional bureaucracy of British officials unique in the empire. What was known as the Indian civil service was well paid and attracted some people of outstanding ability, although its critics regarded it as a privileged body, mostly concerned with maintaining its own status. From 1853 the Indian civil service was filled by open competition through examinations in what were considered to be appropriate academic subjects. In spite of claims that official posts were open to candidates of all races, senior civil servants were virtually all white until well into the twentieth century. Very large staffs of subordinate Indian officials were, however, the essential intermediaries between this small foreign elite and the great mass of the Indian population.

It is always easier to describe what any government claimed to do than to assess its impact on the people it governed. For most of the nineteenth century, Britain did not make significant changes in India. Reform programmes generally remained on paper. For Indians, the most important effects of imperial rule were probably those related to the basic functions performed by the British administration. The level of assessment of taxes and how they are paid are vital questions for any society. It is likely that under early British rule Indians faced quite steep tax demands. Beyond that, the new regime had very little direct contact with its subjects. Except in a few instances, like the banning of widow burning (suttee), the British were reluctant to use the law to enforce social change on Indians and it is doubtful whether they had much capacity to do so. New educational initiatives as yet affected only limited groups in towns. Public works programmes did not develop on any large scale until late in the nineteenth century.

What seems to have been the relatively limited impact on Indian society of early British rule must be borne in mind in any attempt to explain the great upheaval of 1857, the huge revolt against British rule conventionally called the Indian Mutiny. By and large Indians were not trying to overthrow a government that had ruthlessly interfered in their lives and tried to impose 'modernization' on them. That was not the kind of government to which they were subjected. But Indian soldiers and the rural population over a large part of northern India showed their mistrust of their rulers and their alienation from them. British India's concern for its security had good grounds. For all their talk of improvement, the new rulers were as yet able to offer very little in the way of positive inducements for Indians to acquiesce in their rule.

The Indian Rebellion of 1857

In 1857 British authority disintegrated over a large and densely populated tract of northern India and it took much desperate fighting for it to be restored. Yet most generalized explanations of this great uprising are unsatisfactory. Many Indians took up arms against the British, if for very diverse reasons. On the other hand, a very large number actually fought for the British, while the majority remained apparently acquiescent. Explanations have therefore to concentrate on the motives of those who actually rebelled.

At the centre of the rebellion were the soldiers of the Bengal army. Recruited overwhelmingly from certain areas of northern India, these were peasant soldiers, in that they had an agrarian background, but they prided themselves on their status, which was well above that of an agricultural labourer. Service in the Bengal army was largely hereditary and over the years it had become a highly respected and privileged occupation. By 1857 many soldiers felt that their privileges and their status were under threat, as the British imposed new conditions of service. The issue of cartridges, apparently coated with ritually impure animal fat, provoked resistance and this spread very rapidly throughout the Bengal army.

In 1857 the sepoys seized control in most of the cities of northern India. The soldiers were joined by parts of the urban population and, of much greater consequence, sections of the rural population as well. The rural rebellion was in general limited to the areas of the military revolt, but even here it was not universal and motives were varied. In some places discontented landlords and former rulers, who had lost their eminence under British rule, took the lead and brought out their followers. (Nana Sahib, held by the British to be responsible for massacring British prisoners, including women, at Cawnpore (Kanpur), was a person in such a situation.) In the province of Awadh (Oudh), only just annexed by Britain in the previous year, the new British administration had aroused widespread fear and dislike and was widely opposed, particularly by peasants who often had family connections with the soldiers. In older areas of British rule some peasant communities also resorted to violence even though they were not necessarily among the very poorest. They evidently felt that they had been badly treated by British taxation or resented the gains made by rival peasant communities, such as new opportunities for selling their crops or irrigating their lands.

The rebellion was clearly not a 'modern' or a 'nationalist' one. But it is also misleading to see it as a 'traditional' reaction to modernizing British rule, even if the rebels had no alternative but to call on old sources of authority to replace the British, especially that of the Mughal Emperor. There was nothing as yet very modern about British rule by 1857, especially in the areas that actually rebelled. The British had created an army and then lost its confidence. They had also intervened in Indian rural society, altering the balance of wealth and power within it. The soldiers gave those who felt themselves aggrieved the chance to strike back.

The cost of the rebellion in terms of human suffering was immense. Two great cities, Delhi and Lucknow, were devastated by fighting and by the plundering of the victorious British. Where the countryside resisted the British, as in parts of Awadh, villages were burnt. Mutineers and their supposed supporters were often killed out of hand. British civilians, including women and children, were murdered as well as the British officers of the sepoy regiments.

The gap between the aspirations behind British rule in India and its actual achievements is characteristic of the empire as a whole in the period from 1783 to 1870. The British of this time were a confident and often an idealistic people, but their capacity to change the world was limited. Slaves could be liberated, but a prosperous Caribbean or a 'regenerated' West Africa (whatever that might have been) did not come into existence. European settlers could be shipped off to New Zealand but hopes that they would live peacefully side by side with Maoris, who would be uplifted by their example, ended in war. High ideals on one hand and violence and dispossession on the other were equally characteristic of the Victorian empire.

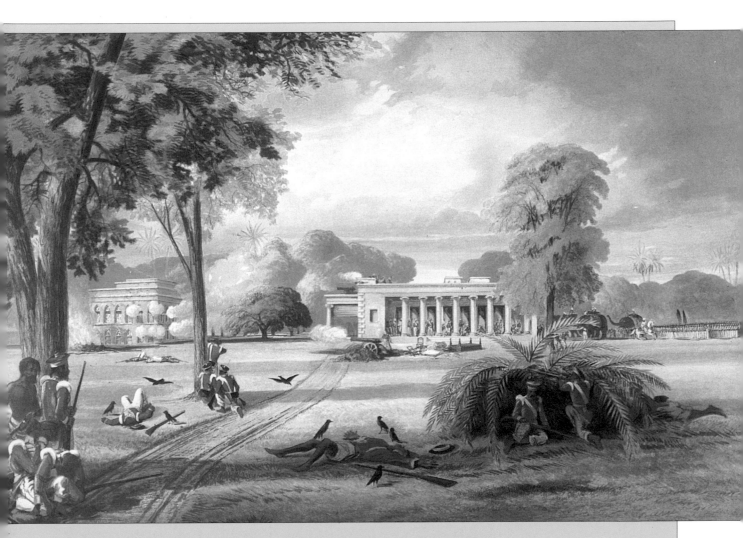

The siege of Arrah House. Arrah House, the headquarters of the administration of a district in Bihar in eastern India, was held for eight days by sixty-nine British and Indian defenders against a large force of rebellious sepoys and the supporters of a disaffected nobleman.

<table>
<tr><td>CHAPTER 3
P.J.Marshall</td><td></td></tr>
</table>

CHAPTER 3
P.J.Marshall

1870–1918: The Empire under Threat

Queen Victoria celebrated her Diamond Jubilee in 1897 and the British people as a whole indulged themselves in celebrating their imperial power at its fullest extent. A great parade in London was the climax of the jubilee. James (now Jan) Morris has memorably described the imperial elements in it.

> There were cavalrymen from New South Wales – gigantic soldiers, the papers reported, with an average height of five feet ten and a half inches and an average chest of thirty-eight inches. There were hussars from Canada and Carabiniers from Natal, camel troops from Bikaner and Dyak head-hunters from North Borneo, wearing bright red pillbox hats and commanded by Captain W. Raffles Flint. The seventeen officers of the Indian Imperial Service troops were all princes and the Hong Kong Chinese police wore conical coolie hats. There were Malays, and Sinhalese and Hausas from the Niger and the Gold Coast, Jamaicans in white gaiters and ornately embroidered jackets, British Guiana police in caps like French gendarmes, Cypriot Zaptiehs whose fezzes struck so jarring a chord that some of the crowd hissed them, supposing them to be Turks, and a jangling squadron of Indian lancers led by a British officer in a white spiked helmet.

These festivities were spectacular evidence of the very high degree of enthusiasm for empire in Britain at the end of the nineteenth century, a period often described as the age of a 'new imperialism'. At home, there was a vocal minority in British public life who had a new vision of what empire could and should mean to Britain. The mass of the British public was being made aware of empire to a much greater extent than ever before through spectacles like the jubilee parade, coverage in the new popular press, the music hall, and adventure stories. Overseas, Britain was encountering competition from other powers on a scale that it had not faced since the eighteenth century and was being drawn into deep involvement in areas previously only of marginal importance – Africa, South East Asia, and the islands of the Pacific.

Yet the novelty of the new imperialism, at least in essentials as opposed to displays, needs to be kept in proportion. While some new departures can be dated from the late nineteenth century, the history of empire in this period in general followed courses set firmly in the past. With one or two important exceptions, those who directed British policy at home were not motivated by visions of a transformed empire. Like their predecessors of the earlier nineteenth century, they believed that the empire must be fully maintained and accepted that growth might be the inevitable consequence of this. The British public as a whole celebrated the relief of Mafeking in 1900 with much the same fervour as their ancestors had greeted the fall of Quebec in 1759 and in the same spirit – as a great national deliverance after much adversity. British national pride was strongly focused upon empire, but there is little to suggest that, even when they understood them, the public as a whole endorsed new ideas about Britain's imperial destiny.

The growth of Britain's territorial empire and of its world-wide interests beyond the empire was very marked in the later nineteenth century; but for the most part growth was along lines established in earlier periods. The volume of British trade with countries outside Europe or the United States increased greatly and there was a spectacular growth in the investment of British funds overseas. By far the largest part of trade with the empire and investment in it was, however, directed to old established imperial domains, not to new acquisitions. Major developments took place in nearly all parts of the existing empire: the colonies of white settlement continued to evolve as distinct entities in their own right, and their population and economies grew very rapidly; in India the British hold strengthened and deepened, and social and economic change affected the people to a much greater degree than in the past.

Mafeking Night in London. News of the raising of the siege of Mafeking, defended by a British garrison under Robert Baden-Powell, reached London on 18 May 1900 and set off demonstrations of enthusiasm throughout the country – reflecting a sense of relief after so many national humiliations in the early years of the South African War. In London 'staid citizens ... were to be seen parading the streets, shouting patriotic songs with the full force of their lungs, dancing, jumping, screaming in a delirium of unrestrained joy'.

THE VIEW FROM BRITAIN

What was strikingly new about the later nineteenth century was the intensity of public debate about empire. Central to this debate was concern about how Britain now stood in relation to other European powers.

The challenge overseas

It was becoming obvious that in many parts of the world Britain would no longer enjoy the free hand that it had been able to take for granted for so long. Anxieties about American dominance of the western hemisphere abated, but old fears about Russian territorial expansion in Asia became much more acute in the 1870s. In 1873 the Russians established their control over Khiva, the last of the major independent khanates of Central Asia. By 1884 they were firmly established on the borders of Afghanistan and a railway network was being constructed, which, the British feared, could sustain a powerful Russian army within easy striking distance of India.

By the 1880s assumptions that, because of Britain's absolute naval supremacy, the only serious threats to the empire would be from powers able to attack British colonies overland no longer seemed to be valid. The naval building of France and Russia caused anxiety in the 1880s. By the end of the century Germany was embarking on the first of its programmes of naval expansion and Japan, Italy, and the United States were also all acquiring fleets of modern warships. In 1897, in spite of a great expansion of the British fleet, the battleships of the other powers outnumbered the Royal Navy by ninety-six to sixty-two. Britain had lost its naval monopoly.

Thus from the 1880s other powers were acquiring the means to support probes into areas where Britain had not faced serious competition before, especially in the Far East and in Africa. In South East Asia the foothold established by the French in the 1860s in Indochina (Vietnam) was pushed outwards towards southern China

'Wake up there! If you mean to continue to rule the waves'. This cartoon illustrates widespread concern about Britain's naval capacity. A Navy League was founded in December 1894 to campaign for higher spending to build more and better warships and 'to spread information as to the vital importance to the British Empire of Naval Supremacy, upon which depend its trade, food supply and national existence'. The League had 100,000 members by 1914. The *Pall Mall Gazette* was its favoured newspaper.

and Siam (Thailand). The French were joined by the Germans in seeking commercial concessions and grants of coastal enclaves from the Chinese. Germany also claimed territory in the Pacific, occupying part of New Guinea. Russia joined Germany and France in disputing what had effectively been British commercial and diplomatic dominance of China's relations with the outside world. In 1891 the Russians started to build a great railway across Siberia. They claimed Manchuria as their special sphere and, like the French and Germans, they took over a coastal enclave.

In Africa south of the Sahara more assertive French policies became evident in 1879. Expansion from old coastal trading settlements gathered momentum in the 1880s and 1890s, culminating by the end of the century in a vast French territorial empire in tropical Africa. In 1884–85 the Germans were also challenging Britain in Africa: their initial annexations became the colonies of South West Africa (Namibia), Tanganyika (Tanzania), and Togo and Cameroon in West Africa.

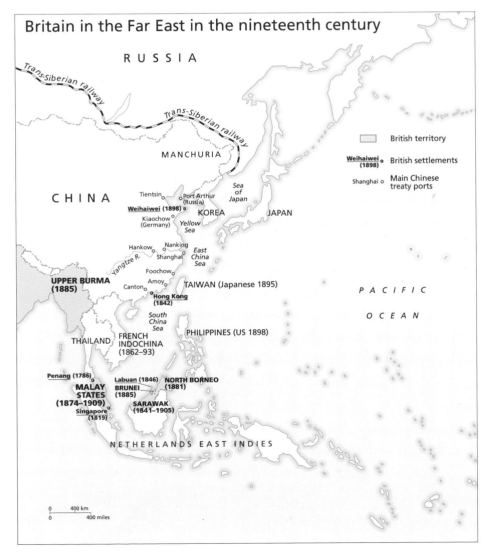

Britain in the Far East in the nineteenth century

Until the last quarter of the nineteenth century, Britain enjoyed a position of dominance in the Far East. Through the treaty ports that China had been forced to open to foreigners or through enclaves under British rule – such as Hong Kong and Singapore, most of the region's international trade was controlled by the British. From the 1880s, however, Britain had to contend with European competition: what seemed to be a policy of Russian territorial expansion to the north of China, a new French empire in Indochina, and increasing German interest. Britain's response to the French was to annex territory in Burma and Malaya, leaving Thailand as a buffer. To sustain their interests in China, the British, like other powers, tried to extract further concessions from China in the 1890s.

The challenge in Europe

To many British people, the more active roles being played by the French, Germans, and Russians outside Europe were symptoms of much deeper changes on the continent itself. The appearance of increasing numbers of German merchants selling German goods and supported on occasions by German cruisers throughout the world was just one manifestation of the great transformation of Germany. By far the most spectacular and threatening evidence of this transformation was the overwhelming of France in war in 1871 and the completion of German unity in the same year. The new Germany had clearly harnessed great industrial power and a highly efficient state machinery to waging war with an altogether new intensity. In eighteen days, over a million German soldiers had been mobilized and 462,000 of them had moved into France. France was defeated, but it reformed its armed forces and tried to recover its position in Europe and the world. Tsarist Russia was engaged in a transformation much more uneven and much less total than Germany's, but still impressive. A great European war in which the survival of Britain or of its fundamental interests would be at stake had seemed a remote possibility after the defeat of Napoleon. Now it no longer seemed so remote. Were such a war to break out would Britain be capable of holding its own with the new leviathans?

The imperial contribution

This question was debated in many ways and many solutions were suggested. Underlying nearly all of them was the recognition that size was fundamental, but that size alone was not enough. Modern wars were won by manpower but also by high-quality armaments. Britain might have to raise troops on a scale to compete with modern continental armies. It would also need the financial resources and the industrial base to arm and equip these men to the highest levels and to expand its fleets to try to outbuild any likely combination of enemies. Concern about what seemed to be questions of survival in a dangerous world led to debate about many aspects of British life: the efficiency of British industry, the health of the people, their standard of education. Anxieties about the future also prompted a searching examination of the state of the British empire. If proper use was made of it, the empire might provide the manpower for war and the economic resources that would enable Britain to maintain its status as a first-class power and to avoid the decline to mediocrity assumed to have been the fate of other imperial powers – Spain, Portugal, and the Netherlands.

India was the most obvious source of additional manpower. Indian troops had long been used for imperial purposes outside India in other parts of Asia and in East Africa. In 1878 a symbolic movement of Indian troops was made to Malta during a crisis with Russia over the Balkans. This was intended to signal that India's manpower could have a role in Europe. British military planners also began to take note of Canada, Australia, and New Zealand as sources of manpower. As late as the

1860s, when British garrisons started to be withdrawn, the colonies of settlement had been seen as something of a military liability, requiring the posting of troops from Britain to keep them secure. By 1897, however, the Colonial Secretary Joseph Chamberlain was anticipating a doubling of their populations 'in the lifetime of our descendants' and the emergence of 'great nations' tied to Britain by a 'principle of mutual support and of a truly Imperial patriotism'. 55,000 'colonial' troops served in the South African War from 1899 to 1902. The colonies of settlement were also urged to make financial contributions to the Royal Navy.

Even if cold winds had not been blowing out of Europe, the empire's economic contribution to Britain would have been re-examined in the later nineteenth century. However, the belief that military power now depended on industrial strength gave this re-examination a much keener edge. A number of developments were strengthening Britain's economic links with the world outside Europe. More and more of Britain's food and of the raw materials for its industry came from such sources, though not necessarily from the empire. Half of the food that British people ate was imported by 1914. By the end of the nineteenth century Britain needed to import most of the wheat it consumed. Here the empire was a major supplier: by 1913 nearly half the wheat imported into Britain came from the empire. The proportion of British exports going to countries created by European colonization overseas (Latin America as well as the British colonies of settlement) increased from 21.2 per cent in 1871–75 to 28.5 per cent in 1909–13 and the proportion going to African and Asian markets rose from 31.6 per cent to 36.2 per cent. By contrast, Europe's share declined slightly and that of the United States fell markedly.

Increasing British trade with countries outside Europe was made possible by a number of developments in the later nineteenth century. The steamship and the railway brought down the costs of moving commodities around the world. Cheap communications enabled the farmers of the colonies of settlement to exploit their advantages – above all, their access to an abundance of cheap land – over the farmers in Europe. Many of the improvements in communications across the world, such as the great railway networks of North and South America or Australasia, were to a large extent financed by Britain. Between 1870 and 1914 British savings were invested overseas on a massive and totally unprecedented scale. Little of this investment, probably only some 13 per cent, went to Europe. Over half of it went to North and South America and 16 per cent to Australasia. Only small amounts went to Africa outside South Africa or indeed to any other tropical area. In short, the British invested overwhelmingly in countries of recent white settlement, whether they were British colonies or not. Although only 40 per cent of total investment went to the empire, the heavy concentration of this imperial investment on colonies of settlement (Australia, Canada, New Zealand, and South Africa) still did much to stimulate their rapid development. Even more rapid development in the future would, it was hoped, be brought about by appropriate British policies.

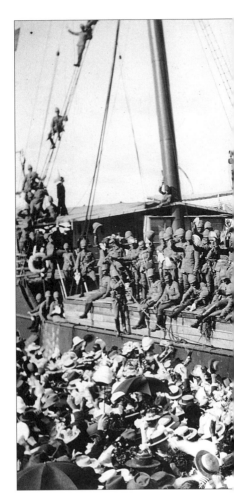

Australian volunteers for the South African War. 16,000 Australian troops served in South Africa, part of a colonial contribution of 55,000 men. Although some sections of Australian opinion opposed the war, volunteers came forward in large numbers, especially after the early British defeats. The contribution made by the colonies of settlement was much praised in Britain.

William Ewart Gladstone.
As the leader of the Liberal party for most of the period from 1866 to 1893, Gladstone played an important part in the late nineteenth-century debate on empire. He insisted on 'the equal rights of all nations' and denounced imperial wars and conquests, but his governments sanctioned some major extensions of British rule, such as the occupation of Egypt in 1882.

THE EMPIRE AND BRITISH POLITICS

Debates about the implications of empire began in the 1870s, when party politicians took to defining positions on empire in a way that was largely new. In the past there had been a consensus that empire was fundamental to British interests and to its standing in the world, and that it must be sustained. In the 1870s Benjamin Disraeli, as leader of the Conservative party, began to assert that the Conservatives were uniquely the party of empire and that their Liberal opponents were unsound on imperial questions, pursuing policies that would lead to the weakening and might even end in the dismemberment of the empire. In a speech at the Crystal Palace in 1872, Disraeli asked his fellow citizens whether 'you will be content to be a comfortable England, modelled and moulded upon Continental principles and meeting in due course an inevitable fate, or whether you will be a great country, an Imperial country ...?' Disraeli was doing no more than articulate conventional platitudes, generally acceptable to people of all parties. His concerns were not to produce new policies for either consolidating or expanding the empire, but to win political support at home. The Conservatives were bidding to be the party that was particularly identified with British nationalism. Disraeli believed that enthusiasm for empire could be an effective part of a nationalist programme: appeals to nationalism were part of a strategy for winning votes from an electorate that had been considerably expanded by the parliamentary Reform Act of 1867.

From Disraeli's time onwards, the Conservatives remained the party of empire, even if other parties were also committed to empire. Disraeli's successor as leader of the party, Lord Salisbury (Prime Minister 1886–92 and 1895–1902) was very much an upholder of the British empire. But with Salisbury, as with Disraeli and the main body of the Conservative party, it is necessary to make a clear distinction between what they believed and what those who called themselves 'imperialists' came to believe. Salisbury remained sceptical about any policy of unlimited acquisitions or restructuring the empire on radically new lines to produce some kind of union of the white 'British'. The imperial enthusiasts never captured the Conservative party, let alone British public opinion as a whole. They remained a very vocal pressure group.

Attitudes to empire became an issue of intense party rivalry from the 1870s. Yet the issues of substance dividing the parties were not very great. When Disraeli made his bid to annex the imperial issue in British politics to the Conservative party, Gladstone did not try to disassociate the Liberals from empire. In his view, 'The sentiment of empire may be called innate in every Briton.' He responded to Disraeli with an alternative version of Britain's imperial role. In the process, the Liberals coined two words that were to have a long life in polemic: Disraeli was accused of 'imperialism' and of 'jingoism'. Both accusations assumed that the Conservatives had departed from the traditional imperial policy of the past, in favour of a demagogic nationalism and vainglorious boasting about Britain's power. Britain's true imperial policy, according to Gladstone, was to avoid new acquisitions and foster the development of the existing colonies towards self-government within the empire.

The imperialists' programme

By the 1890s programmes for the radical overhaul of the empire were being formulated by self-styled 'imperialists' who wanted to see positive action taken to direct British foreign trade into specifically imperial channels. They argued that Britain was being pushed out of some of its older markets by protective tariffs in the United States and by the tendency towards protection in many European countries. The free trade world of the mid-nineteenth century was, they believed, coming to an end. The major nations of the world were pursuing self-sufficiency. Britain must do the same. It should pursue that goal not on its own but with its empire. The empire would provide the food and the raw materials that Britain needed. In return, Britain must supply the empire with capital, immigrants, and manufactured goods. If appropriate policies were pursued, the British empire could become an economic superpower, at least the equal of the United States or Germany. Since in the modern world economic power was the basis of military power, the British empire would be a military superpower, invulnerable to any enemy. This or a variation on it became the programme of those who were proud to call themselves 'imperialists' by the end of the nineteenth century. Lord Milner was certainly one of those. In a speech of 1906 he pointed out that:

> Physical limitations alone forbid that these islands by themselves should retain the same relative importance among the vast empires of the modern world which they held in the days of smaller states – before the growth of Russia and the United States, before united Germany made those giant strides in prosperity and commerce which have been the direct result of the development of her military and naval strength. These islands by themselves cannot always remain a Power of the very first rank. But Greater Britain may remain such a Power, humanly speaking, for ever, and by so remaining, will ensure the safety and prosperity of all the states composing it, which, again humanly speaking, nothing else can equally ensure.

For Milner 'Greater Britain' meant that 'every white man of British birth' should 'be at home in every state of the empire'. Such an aspiration was representative of much imperialist thought. The competition that made the modern world such a dangerous place was not just a competition of states; it was a competition of 'races'. According to the vulgarized theories of evolution that were currently fashionable, races evolved through struggle. The British race was locked in conflict with 'Teutons', Slavs, and others. The colonies of white settlement had dispersed the British race throughout the world: its elements must be reunited. Britain had much to gain from such a reunion with what Rudyard Kipling called 'the Younger Nations

Alfred Milner. Milner was an imperial enthusiast who did all he could to foster the cause of a stronger, more closely united empire. As High Commissioner in South Africa from 1897 to 1905, he did much to provoke war with the Afrikaner republics and attempted to create a new order after the war. He was a member of the War Cabinet from 1916 and was Colonial Secretary from 1918 to 1921.

... the men who could shoot and ride'. Empire was indeed a way to regenerate British society and make it fitter for the great struggles ahead. Life in the Australian outback or on the Canadian prairies produced a people fitter in all senses than those who spent their lives in the cities of Britain.

For nearly all imperialists, the British race was an exclusively white one. The non-white peoples of the empire were its subjects. They were citizens of the empire in the sense that they had rights, but they were not regarded as full citizens, capable of controlling their own destinies. For the imperial statesman and novelist John Buchan, the British empire should be a 'closer organic connection under one crown of a number of autonomous nations of the same blood, who can spare something of their vitality for the administration of vast tracts inhabited by lower races – a racial aristocracy considered in their relation to subject peoples, a democracy in their relation to each other'.

The closest that 'high' imperialists came to determining policy was in the Conservative governments of 1895 to 1905. Then a very prominent politician, Joseph Chamberlain, chose to be Colonial Secretary. Chamberlain had a strong sense of a national crisis. He believed that Britain was losing in the industrial and military competition with other powers and that it had serious social problems at home. The effective development of the empire was, in his view, the solution to all Britain's difficulties. A reorganized empire would be the basis of a great industrial recovery for Britain. Not only would much new employment be created, but the wealth generated by the empire would fund ambitious programmes of social reform, such as the provision of state pensions. Thus the loyalty of the working class to the British state would be ensured. But Chamberlain's concerns, like those of other imperialists, were not simply material. Empire was a cause through which the moral fibre of the British people would be greatly improved. He wished the public to be fully educated about empire, so that it could rise to its great responsibilities as an imperial people.

Central to Chamberlain's programme were policies to create a union between Britain and the colonies of settlement. At his most ambitious he contemplated full unions for defence or trade in which Britain and the colonies would pool sovereignty and create joint councils or even an imperial parliament to run the affairs of the empire. Well aware that opinion either in Britain or in the colonies was most unlikely to follow him to such lengths, Chamberlain eventually committed himself to what he thought was a politically practical set of proposals. This was the programme called Tariff Reform, which he launched in 1903. Britain would give up its commitment to free trade with the whole world in favour of tariffs on foreign imports. These duties would be waived for imports from the colonies. Thus, for instance, Canadian wheat would win an even bigger share of the British market, since American wheat would be burdened with a tariff. In return, the colonies would reduce the tariffs they put on British imports. This, Chamberlain believed, was a programme by which the economic development of the colonies and of

Britain would go forward together. But it was more than that. For Chamberlain, it was the first step towards imperial unity.

Unusually for a major British politician, Chamberlain's interests extended beyond the colonies of settlement and India. He also wished to make the best of colonial territories in the tropics, especially in West Africa and the West Indies, and he began to formulate ideas about 'colonial development', a concept that was to have a very long life in British imperial history. Tropical territories were poor, in Chamberlain's view, because they lacked investment. They would not attract normal investment on commercial principles because the prospect of any profitable return was low by comparison with the colonies of settlement. There was therefore a role for the government – either to provide capital or to offer extra inducements for private investment in such projects as African railways and harbours or shipping lines to the West Indies.

Joseph Chamberlain. Chamberlain was a successful Birmingham manufacturer who was a radical Liberal for the first part of his political career. He broke with the Liberals in 1886 over concessions to Ireland and allied himself with the Conservatives, becoming Colonial Secretary in their governments from 1895 to 1903. By 1895 he had come to believe that 'England had not yet realised what the British empire really stood for or what a part it might play in the world or of what developments it was capable and he meant to try and make England understand'.

Harnessing public opinion

It was an essential part of Chamberlain's imperialism that the British public must be won over to the cause of empire. He saw himself as an educator about empire and did his best to put the issues, as he saw them, before the electorate in his speeches. Others also took a hand in the business of propagating imperial values. British culture at many levels in this period was permeated by imperial themes, images, and motifs. Music, the theatre, music hall entertainment, novels, poetry, literature of all sorts for young people, exhibitions, and advertisements all spread awareness of empire.

For the most part, this relentless exposure of the British public to material about empire was not an orchestrated propaganda campaign, and it was certainly not directed by some sort of imperialist high command. Writers and publishers presumably took their own commercial decisions when they gave their popular songs or children's stories an imperial setting. Advertisers were concerned with selling their goods, not with propagating imperialist ideology. Expectations that the public would buy articles to which imperial connotations had been attached is, however, important evidence that the British people in general were presumed to be well disposed to empire and likely to respond enthusiastically to allusions to it.

However, some deliberate attempts were made to turn this public enthusiasm into commitment to policies to create a union of the white citizens of the empire or the regeneration of Britain through imperial service. Rudyard Kipling, for example, although a supreme artist rather than a crude propagandist, had a highly personal and deeply committed imperial vision and he intended that his readers should be aware of that (see pages 218–19). Those who founded youth movements such as the Boys Brigade or the Boy Scouts had values they wished to propagate and commitment to the empire usually had a prominent place in those values. Many schoolmasters in the public schools were very much committed to imperialism. In state schools, attempts were made to include what was regarded as 'sound' imperial material in the curriculum and to institute what were intended to be popular festivals of empire, such as Empire Day.

Plates from *ABC for Baby Patriots*, 1899, by Mary Frances Ames. As this example shows, children's books that aimed to instil imperial and patriotic values started with very young readers.

British youth and empire

The readers of a book for girls published in 1912 were told that:

> While boys and girls are learning
> To be their empire's fence
> We needn't really be afraid
> Of national decadence.

For a quarter of a century before 1912 intensive efforts had been made to teach children 'to be their empire's fence' through formal education, through what children read, and by trying to induce them to join clubs and associations, such as the Boys Brigade (1883), the Boy Scouts (1908), and the Girl Guides (1912).

Public school headmasters, like J.E. Wellden of Harrow in 1899, were fond of reflecting that their pupils 'are destined to be citizens of the greatest empire under heaven'. They must be inspired with 'faith in the divinely ordered mission of their country and their race'. History and geography books used in state elementary schools tended to depict the acquisition of empire in glowing terms and to extol its value to Britain. Schools were encouraged to celebrate Empire Day on 24 May, Queen Victoria's birthday. *The Boy's Own Paper*, eventually claiming a readership of over a million, was launched in 1879. A strongly imperial tone appeared in its output from the 1890s. The title of the short-lived *Boys of Our Empire* speaks for itself. G.A. Henty, author of a string of books with titles like *With Wolfe to Canada, With Kitchener to the Soudan,* or *With Roberts to Pretoria,* is probably the most famous of many writers of fiction for children with imperial settings. Young people who joined military cadet forces were told that they were being trained to be defenders of empire. The Boy Scouts was founded by one of the heroes of the South African War, Robert Baden-Powell.

While there can be no denying the very high level of imperial content in what was being offered to the young, its impact is very difficult to assess. The resistance of children to unacceptable uplift was memorably evoked in Kipling's *Stalky and Co,* where an effusively patriotic Member of Parliament is dismissed as 'a Jelly-bellied Flag-flapper'. Moreover, those who sought to interest the young in empire did not speak with one voice or have one view of the values that they believed the British empire to embody. A scout was to learn how 'to shoot and to drill and to take his share in the defence of the empire'. But Baden-Powell was a particularly complex imperialist. He disliked conventional military training. In later editions, *Scouting for Boys* became increasingly internationalist in tone. 'Remember that a scout is not just a friend to the people round him, but "a friend to all the world". Friends don't fight each other. If we make friends with our neighbours across the sea in foreign countries, and if they keep friends with us, we shan't want to fight.' Scouting has spread very easily through every part of a multiracial Commonwealth.

Children, except for the very deprived, would have encountered much material about the empire, but this material was very diverse and they were unlikely to have formed a single view of it.

Robert Baden-Powell with scouts from all over the empire at the Imperial Jamboree, London, 1924.

The activists who campaigned for greater imperial awareness were usually members of societies like the Royal Colonial Institute. Certain individuals, like Lord Meath, a man of wealth but of no real political consequence, were involved in nearly all of them. Such people did not, however, constitute the contemporary 'establishment'. Imperial enthusiasts were mostly, but not exclusively, Conservatives, but they tended to be the radical right and, with the exception of Chamberlain, outside the main councils of the party.

Crisis of empire

For all their fervour, debates about the future of the empire in Britain were for the most part abstract discussions of what might be or ought to be. What people said or wrote in Britain and what actually happened overseas were not closely related. Nevertheless, at the very end of the century there was an imperial crisis of gigantic proportions. This was in a very real sense the consequence of views adopted by men then in power in Britain and in its turn it had very important effects on British opinion about empire. The crisis was the South African War of 1899–1902.

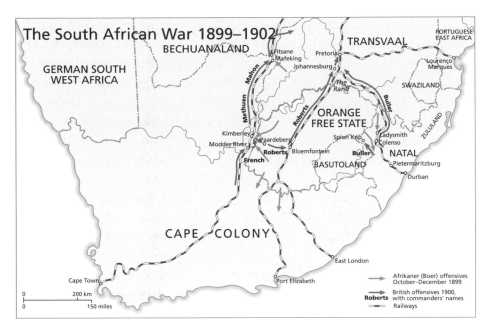

The South African War 1899–1902

GERMAN SOUTH
WEST AFRICA

BECHUANALAND

TRANSVAAL

PORTUGUESE
EAST AFRICA

Pitsane
Mafeking
Johannesburg
Pretoria
Lourenço
Marques

The
Rand

SWAZILAND

ORANGE
FREE
STATE

ZULULAND

Kimberley
Modder River
Paardeberg
Roberts
Bloemfontein

Spion Kop
Ladysmith
Colenso
Buller

NATAL
Pietermaritzburg

French

BASUTOLAND

Durban

CAPE   COLONY

East London

Cape Town

200 km

150 miles

Port Elizabeth

Afrikaner (Boer) offensives
October–December 1899

British offensives 1900,
with commanders' names

Railways

The South African War
began in 1899 with Afrikaner
advances into British territory
and a series of severe British
defeats. In 1900 large British
armies under the direction of
Lord Roberts overwhelmed
the Afrikaners and captured
their towns. This was not,
however, the end of the war.
Small groups of Afrikaner
commandos maintained an
extremely effective guerrilla
resistance. This kept the
British army at full stretch
until 1902.

After the exodus of Afrikaners from the Cape on their treks a rough *de facto*
division had been established between the British colonies of the Cape and Natal
and the Afrikaner republics of the Orange Free State and the Transvaal in the
interior. In the second half of the nineteenth century this division began to break
down. The British were no longer inclined to leave the Afrikaner republics alone.
The establishment of a German presence on the coast of South West Africa in 1884
raised fears that the Afrikaners might form an alliance with Germany. By then the
discovery of diamonds at Kimberley in 1867 had already begun to create instability
in the interior, and this was greatly exacerbated by awareness after 1886 of the
extent of the gold deposits on the Rand of the Transvaal (see page 135). The gold of
the Rand was exploited by companies from outside the Transvaal, such as the
Consolidated Gold Fields of Cecil Rhodes. The mines brought a mass of non-
Afrikaner Europeans (the *uitlanders*) into the republics, set off a scramble for
African labour, and gave the Transvaal government access to greatly increased
resources. These developments caused anxiety to the British. If the Transvaal could
not be tied soon into the British empire, it might become strong enough to escape
altogether and eventually to take the Afrikaners of the Cape with it. British
governments therefore tried to isolate the Transvaal from contact with other
European powers and put pressure on it to come to terms with the empire, and
especially to give votes to the *uitlanders* who, it was hoped, would vote in a pro-
British government. In 1895 Chamberlain even gave covert support to Dr Jameson's
project for attempting to overthrow the republican regime of President Kruger of
the Transvaal by an armed coup. The failure of the Jameson Raid exacerbated the
Afrikaners' suspicions of British intentions and stiffened their determination to
resist. British ministers, including Chamberlain, hoped that pressure short of war

Opposite: Cecil Rhodes at
Kimberley during the siege,
October 1899 to February
1900. Rhodes played a
prominent part in the affairs of
southern Africa at the end of
the nineteenth century. He
made a great fortune out of the
diamonds of Kimberley (where
he went to protect his interests
on the outbreak of war) and
the gold of the Transvaal. He
became Prime Minister of the
Cape from 1890 to 1896, tried
to overthrow the government
of the Transvaal through the
Jameson Raid in December
1895, and founded a new
colony of Rhodesia through his
British South Africa Company,
which was given a charter in
1889. In retrospect, at least,
Rhodes came to see his
'profession' as 'that of making
additions to Her Majesty's
empire'.

might be enough to force Afrikaner compliance, but they were not prepared to compromise. For them the issue was now one of Britain's credibility. If Britain could not be seen to have got its way in southern Africa, an area of vital interest to Britain, its position as a great power would be seriously compromised. Although Chamberlain wished to avoid war if at all possible, he had consistently presented relations with the Transvaal as a test of Britain's will to hold its own in the world. He and his Cabinet colleagues had thus left themselves with little room for manoeuvre. Negotiations broke down and the Afrikaners launched a pre-emptive strike before the British army could be reinforced. The war lasted from 1899 to 1902. The Afrikaners won striking initial successes and even after 1900, when British forces had gained mastery, Afrikaner resistance was extremely hard to suppress. The war eventually involved nearly 400,000 imperial troops at a cost of £250 million. It is not surprising that British public opinion began to turn against the war in its later stages.

Was the war a squalid capitalists' war to protect the investments in the gold of the Transvaal by great mine owners like Cecil Rhodes? Rhodes certainly wanted to overthrow the Transvaal government, but it is impossible to prove that he and those who thought like him had any real influence on forcing the British government to war. Gold, by enormously strengthening Kruger, created the threat of instability in southern Africa, which alarmed British ministers. Their own heavy-handedness was then largely responsible for a crisis, out of which they felt that they could not escape with anything less than total victory – by peaceful means if possible, by war if need be. If there had been no gold in the Transvaal, it is most unlikely that there would have been a war; but that is not the same thing as saying that the war was about control of the gold.

In its early years the South African War was given strong popular support and British successes were greeted with great displays of public enthusiasm. In the general election of 1900 the Conservative government won an impressive victory. Sir Henry Campbell-Bannerman, the leader of the Liberal opposition, criticized the policies that had led to the war, but insisted: 'I have never uttered a pro-Boer word: I have been anti-Joe [Chamberlain] but never pro-Kruger.' Only a small minority were openly sympathetic to the cause of the Afrikaners. In the later stages of the war, however, nearly all Liberals became critical of the way in which it was being conducted and of the harsh treatment, including incarceration in 'concentration camps', to which Afrikaner civilians were subjected in operations to crush guerrilla resistance. When Chamberlain launched his Tariff Reform proposals in 1903, Liberals attacked them with vehemence as a violation of the principles of free trade and a threat to the living standards of the poor. Disillusionment with the war and the unpopularity of any proposal for tariffs on imported food probably played a significant part in the sweeping Liberal victory at the general election of 1906.

Liberal governments were to hold power up to the outbreak of war in 1914. But although the Liberals abandoned policies associated with Chamberlain and tried to

Burning a Boer farm house during the South African War. In 1900 British forces succeeded in defeating the main armies of the Afrikaner republics and occupying their towns. The war was not, however, over. Vigorous guerrilla resistance was waged by the Afrikaner mounted commandos. To deprive them of support in the countryside, the British destroyed farms and took the women and children into what were called concentration camps. 116,000 Afrikaners were eventually placed in badly prepared camps where they were very vulnerable to disease. 28,000 people died, most of them children. The concentration camp policy was strongly criticized and helped to turn public opinion in Britain against the war.

avoid confrontations with Afrikaners or other potentially disaffected colonial subjects, their approach to the empire was, in essentials, very similar to that of previous governments. Differences over the empire between the majority of Conservatives, apart from imperial enthusiasts like Chamberlain, and the bulk of the Liberal party were still not very significant. The Liberal governments were fully committed to preserving the British empire.

There were, however, some on the left of the Liberal party who were not willing to support the general consensus about empire. A minority of Liberals had openly opposed the South African War, becoming 'Pro-Boers' in the eyes of their opponents. During the war dissenting Liberals and some supporters of the new Labour movement began to formulate an explanation for the war and other acts of imperial expansion which involved a fundamental critique of what they called British 'imperialism'. *Imperialism* was in fact the title of the very influential book of 1902 by J.A. Hobson in which this critique was expounded. Hobson was struck by the huge volume of British investment going overseas. He argued that this was symptomatic of the injustices underlying British society: a few rich people accumulated great wealth, while the mass remained poor. These rich 'capitalists' sought profitable outlets for their investments in new colonies. Their political power was so extensive that they could dictate the course of British colonial policy. The South African War was their war, since it was a war fought to secure the gold resources of South Africa for a few capitalists. In general, British imperial expansion was a capitalist plot. This identification of 'imperialism' with 'capitalism' was to have a very long life. It was to be taken up by European writers in the Marxist tradition, most famously by Lenin in 1916. Similar arguments were also used by the British left, but their use did not necessarily signal a total rejection of empire. Most supporters of the emerging Labour party, for example, seem to have believed that, while capitalist excesses should be prevented, empire should be preserved until its various peoples were 'ready' for its dissolution.

The most intense phase in the debate about empire began in the 1890s and came to an end in 1906. By then it was clear that the imperialists' programme for restructuring the empire and for reforming Britain through such a restructuring had failed, at least for the time being. The creation of a closer union between Britain and the self-governing colonies of settlement was the crucial issue in all the imperialists' projects. Opinion in the colonies was not necessarily hostile to ideas of closer union, but whether any terms that Britain was prepared to offer would have been acceptable to their governments and peoples is another matter. It was a question that was not, however, to be put to the test, since the Liberal victory in 1906 ensured that no such offers were to be made. But if the empire was not going to be reformed, it was not going to be dismantled either. An unreformed empire demonstrated its vitality and cohesion in the years of war after 1914.

THE EMPIRE OVERSEAS

Great additions were made to the British empire in this period but, by every criterion of importance, the colonies of settlement and India continued to be the vital components of the empire.

Colonies of settlement

In the white societies of Canada, Australia, and New Zealand there was spectacular growth in the period from 1870 to 1918. Their populations grew rapidly with new waves of immigration: from 1890 to 1900 only 28 per cent of those leaving Britain had gone to imperial destinations; from 1901 to 1912 63 per cent went to the empire. Canada, especially western Canada, which was also drawing in a large volume of immigration to the prairies from continental Europe, attracted the greatest number, but in 1912 for the first time more British people went to Australia than to the United States. There were many new British immigrants among those who volunteered so readily for war in Australia, Canada, and New Zealand in 1914. White dominance was reinforced by the exclusion of Asian immigration: this was the period in which a 'white Australia' policy was enforced and Asian immigration into British Columbia was severely restricted.

Cities such as Montreal, Toronto, Sydney, or Melbourne grew to maturity as Victorian cities, comparable to those of Britain itself. 'Marvellous Melbourne' had a rateable value in 1891 only exceeded within the empire by London and Glasgow. Settlement spread. In Canada the transcontinental railways were completed and new provinces across the prairies began to prosper as wheat exporters. British investment played a major role in financing the development of cities and communications, while the British market provided the stimulus for expanding agriculture and mining. In 1901 the Australian colonies followed the example of

Canada in forming a union. By 1914 the population of Australia, Canada, and New Zealand amounted to one third of that of Great Britain and their national wealth (gross national product) amounted to some 40 per cent of Britain's. Their potential as partners was clear for all to see.

Once Britain had conquered the Afrikaner republics, South Africa followed a path beaten by the other colonies of white settlement. In South Africa's case whites were of course a minority in a very large African population. African peoples had, however, been systematically subordinated as the white population moved outwards from the Cape from the 1830s. The most formidable of all the African military powers, the Zulu, were crushed by the British army in 1879. Except to a limited extent in the Cape (where there was a qualified non-racial franchise), non-whites were allowed no part in the creation of the new political order in South Africa.

This new order began to take shape when Britain returned authority in the conquered Transvaal and Orange Free State to Afrikaner political leaders after the South African War. The decision to do this was taken by the Liberal government after their 1906 election victory. It was represented at the time as a brave and imaginative gesture, but no British government was in fact prepared to keep a white population within the empire under direct British rule for very long, and attempts to make the Transvaal British rather than Afrikaner by mass immigration after the war had clearly failed. There was no real alternative to coming to terms with the Afrikaners. The new Afrikaner leaders, Louis Botha and Jan Christiaan Smuts, were evidently willing to accept that South Africa should remain within Britain's sphere, thus ending the old anxieties about Britain's strategic interest at the Cape, but they wished to be masters of a new united South Africa. Britain did not stand in the way of such a union and it came about in 1910, when the Transvaal and the Orange Free State joined with the Cape and Natal to become the Union of South Africa. With the Union, self-government within the empire was granted to the whites of South Africa. This meant that, in spite of lobbying by, among others, those who were to form the African National Congress, Britain renounced nearly all powers to protect African rights in southern Africa, powers that it had long since ceased to exercise effectively anyway.

The new South Africa acquired the same status in 1910 as that already enjoyed by Canada, Australia, and New Zealand. By then hopes that these communities would enter into some kind of formal union with Britain had failed to get off the ground. Nevertheless, the colonies co-operated in an effective alliance with Britain. Britain was economically extremely important to them and the expansion across the world of French, Russian, and German power worried them as it worried Britain. Common interests led to close consultation, if not to anything like formal union. From 1887 the prime ministers of the colonies of settlement met regularly in London to discuss common interests. The outbreak of war in 1914 was a test of the alliance, demonstrating that it was a reality.

Jan Christiaan Smuts. Smuts held office in Kruger's Transvaal and fought through the South African War against the British. After the war he saw his task as ensuring the survival of Afrikaner dominance in South Africa through accommodation with the British empire. In this he was largely successful, although he earned the mistrust of Afrikaner nationalists, who saw him as much too accommodating and finally drove him from office in 1948. To the British he was a great imperial statesman to whom many honours were given: he became a member of the British War Cabinet in 1917 and, greatly admired by Winston Churchill, was made a Field Marshal in 1941.

India

On no very convincing evidence, it was commonly assumed by British opinion that the Indian Rebellion of 1857 had been the response of a deeply conservative society provoked by ill-considered and intrusive programmes of reform. Because of this belief, the later nineteenth century was ostensibly marked by caution. Indian society was to be left undisturbed. Elaborate rituals were devised to give Indian princes and other 'traditional' notables a place in a hierarchy of authority. The reality was rather different. British rule had a much deeper impact on India in the late nineteenth century than before 1857. Indian society changed very significantly, obliging the British to take account of the views of some other Indians, as well as the princes and landowners.

The completion of a great railway network, cheaper shipping, and the opening of the Suez canal linked India to an ever-increasing extent to world trade. Like farmers in Canada, Australia, and New Zealand, many Indian peasants grew crops, such as sugar cane, cotton, wheat, groundnuts, or jute, for overseas markets, while the railways greatly increased the internal markets for basic foodstuffs. Peasant farmers in the tropics were usually much more vulnerable under market conditions than more substantial farmers in the colonies of settlement. But world prices for Indian commodities were quite buoyant in the later nineteenth century and some peasants did well. They could acquire extra land and in some cases benefit from improved irrigation introduced by the government. Parts of provinces like the Punjab enjoyed a genuine prosperity. The mass of the poor in the countryside evidently did less well. When harvests failed in droughts at the end of the century, they died in huge numbers in the great famines (see pages 132–34).

India remained overwhelmingly rural until far into the twentieth century, but towns grew and there was a patchy development of modern industry. Iron and coal deposits were exploited and cotton mills were established in western India in the teeth of competition from Lancashire's exports to what was still its most important market.

Early in the nineteenth century new schools and colleges were opened in the Indian cities where there was a strong colonial presence. Education provision expanded very rapidly in the later nineteenth century. The British administration prompted and tried to direct, but the initiative for opening new schools and colleges came mostly from Indians themselves. The results of this expansion were very uneven, no doubt inevitably so in a highly stratified society. A small number of people were educated to a very high level: the first Indian universities were sanctioned in 1854. On the other hand, it proved impossible to secure anything remotely like universal primary education in the villages. Lord Curzon, the British Viceroy of India at the beginning of the twentieth century, thought that only one quarter of Indian villages had schools in them and that only one fifth of the boys of primary school age were actually getting any schooling. The figure for girls getting educated would have been minuscule. Nevertheless, even a small proportion of the

Maharani's School, Mysore, India. This pioneering venture in female education was opened in the princely state of Mysore in 1881. At first confined to 'high caste girls', its aim under lady superintendents recruited from Cambridge was said to be to find 'an acceptable compromise between western methods and eastern views as to the appropriate subjects of female education'. In 1906 two of the school's students became the first female Bachelors of Arts in India. This remarkable institution needs, however, to be seen in the context of an almost total lack of educational opportunity for Indian girls: in Mysore state in 1891 just over 3 per cent of girls of school age were believed actually to be attending a school.

Indian population is a huge total. Millions of people were now fully literate in Indian languages and a good number of those had a working knowledge of English as well. In 1882 there were 150,000 pupils in English-medium secondary schools.

New opportunities for acquiring wealth and education brought a significant number of Indian people into closer relations with the government. Some of those served it in official positions, although still generally positions that were subordinate to Europeans; others came into contact with it through their businesses or through professions like the law or teaching. The British depended on the services of a literate intelligentsia to carry on the administration of India, but such people also formed a public opinion that began to pass judgement on that administration in newspapers and in meetings of clubs and associations.

The most obvious evidence of increasing political consciousness was the formation in 1885 of the Indian National Congress. This was at first little more than an annual meeting to discuss public affairs. It certainly did not constitute a revolutionary challenge to British rule. It did, however, begin to formulate criticisms and to ask for a greater role in the government for Indians. British administrators professed to despise Congress and its criticisms, but they were increasingly aware that India was developing a political leadership that could give direction to deeper popular discontents with British rule. There were clear signs of this in a formidable agitation with strikes and boycotts of British-made goods in 1905 against a ruling that the province of Bengal should be divided into two separate provinces. To many Bengalis, this amounted to vivisection of their homeland. In an effort to bring educated Indian opinion back into co-operation with British rule, the Liberal government elected in Britain in 1906 authorized a very limited programme of reforms. These reforms of 1909 allowed for Indian representatives – chosen by the British in some cases, elected on a very narrow franchise in others – to become members of the councils that advised the Viceroy or assisted in the making of laws. The general acceptance by the Indian public of the full commitment of India to the British war effort after 1914 seemed to vindicate this policy. The war, however, raised expectations and created problems for the British administration, which made it inevitable that there should be a major reconsideration of the way in which India was governed once the war was over.

The partitions of Africa and South East Asia

Until late in the nineteenth century, Britain's interests anywhere in Africa north of the Limpopo or throughout South East Asia were confined to West African coastal enclaves, such as Sierra Leone, The Gambia, or a string of forts on the Gold Coast (Ghana), and to Singapore, Malacca, and Penang on the Malay coast. Trading networks, such as those on the Niger river, penetrated further inland, but the British presence was still a strictly limited one. Yet by 1900 Britain had acquired huge territorial possessions in both areas. A string of British colonies had been established in East and Central Africa as well as in West Africa. The British had also occupied Egypt and the Sudan. In South East Asia the British had extended their authority over the whole Malay peninsula and had conquered the kingdom of Burma.

Traditionally, Britain's spectacular territorial gains in the last quarter of the nineteenth century have been explained in one of two ways. One view is that Britain acted to secure the resources and markets of the tropics for its increasingly hard-pressed industries; the other view is that Britain's aim was to protect vital strategic interests. Neither explanation on its own survives close examination. By most standards the stakes in these spectacular partitions were not very high. Quite valuable trades were already being carried on in some areas, such as the palm oil trade of the Niger or the tin trade of the Malay states. Should these trades be seriously threatened, they were certainly worth protecting from Britain's point of view, but they hardly justified massive annexations. Egypt, which had a large population and a sophisticated economy and where large sums had already been invested by western concerns, including British ones, was the only major economic asset at stake. The strategic importance of the control of Egypt was also obvious and it had been enhanced by the construction of the Suez canal. But it required some ingenuity to invest most of the rest of the territory about to be partitioned with much strategic significance.

Rather than attempt any overall explanation of the partitions, it is important to recognize that conditions varied markedly between the 1880s and the 1890s. The story of the partitions is one of gathering momentum: in the 1880s annexations were still limited; they became unrestrained in the 1890s.

In the 1880s, the British appeared to be reacting to the initiatives of other powers. As France and Germany made new claims, Britain felt compelled to match

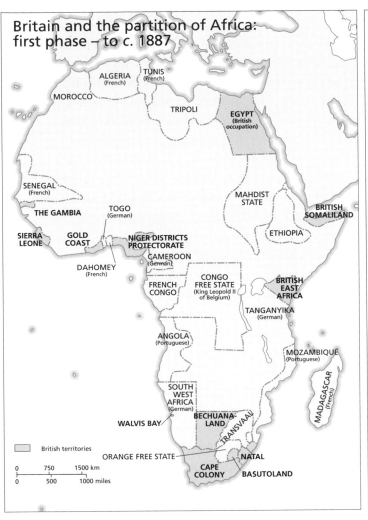

Britain and the partition of Africa: first phase – to c. 1887

Britain and the partition of Africa: completed – 1914

them by defining its own claims to areas where British traders had usually been operating for many years. Most interpretations date the partition of Africa as starting with French actions between 1879 and 1882 – an expedition from Senegal towards the upper Niger and the ratification of a treaty with an African ruler on the Congo. German interventions followed in 1884. British responses in the 1880s were generally limited and hesitant. Counter claims were put forward and Britain participated in the Berlin conference of 1885 which tried to limit expansion and define claims. When Britain claimed territory, there was a strong preference for using private bodies – companies to which the British government awarded charters, entitling them to occupy and administer territory. The Royal Niger Company was chartered in 1886 to implement British claims on the Niger. In 1888 the Imperial British East African Company took over territory allocated to Britain in East Africa by the agreement with Germany of 1886. Cecil Rhodes's British South Africa Company was chartered in 1889 to occupy the future Rhodesia (Zimbabwe) and exclude Afrikaners or other Europeans from the area. A company was chartered for the administration of British claims to North Borneo in 1881. In Malaya British authority was also established by indirect means as a series of treaties were signed from 1874 to take rulers under British protection.

In Egypt British intervention was direct and involved the dispatch of considerable forces of the Crown to bombard Alexandria and to invade Egypt in 1882. Even here the British claimed to be acting on the defensive, arguing that law and order had broken down under a new Egyptian regime. The Egyptian army was defeated at the battle of Tell el-Kebir. Egypt never formally became a British colony as such: it was 'occupied' by Britain and what purported to be its own administration was placed under close British supervision. Through this fiction what was in reality a formidable and ambitious structure of colonial rule was constructed, second only to the government of India in its scope, its resources, and the quality of its personnel. The Khedive's ministers were 'guided' by a British Consul-General, an office held for a long period by the redoubtable Evelyn Baring (later Lord Cromer) and a staff of advisers: the Egyptian financial system was directed by British financial advisers; Egyptian irrigation schemes were managed by British engineers; judicial advisers devised reforms of the legal system; Egyptian schools were inspected by British inspectors; the Egyptian army was commanded by a British Sirdar. In short, the British presence became increasingly intrusive: there were 170 British officials in Egypt in 1883 and 662 in 1906.

The occupation of Egypt was a spectacular act of imperial expansion. It was sanctioned, very much contrary to its declared principles, by the Liberal government of Gladstone. The British government's explanation for the invasion was that it was engaged in an operation to restore order and then to create a stable government and that it would have done this with French co-operation, had that been forthcoming. Much was said, after the invasion had actually been launched, about protecting the Suez canal. Critics, however, pointed to the large sums of money lent to the Egyptian government and detected the kind of capitalist plot that they were later to see in South Africa. There is no evidence that Gladstone intervened specifically to protect the bondholders who had lent money to the Egyptians. On the other hand, just as there would have been no South African War without gold, so there would have been no invasion of Egypt if so much western money, and with it much western interference, had not been poured into Egypt, creating resentment among Egyptians and the instability that the British feared so greatly. In a situation of world-wide European rivalry, the British were not prepared to leave Egypt alone. Doubts about its stability were resolved by the use of force.

The other major act of British aggression in the 1880s was a war against Burma. The kingdom of Burma had already lost territory to Britain, but in 1885 the Viceroy of India used his army in the way that his predecessors had done so often to subdue what he regarded as a recalcitrant neighbour, in whom the French showed some interest.

Opposite: Auctioning loot from the palace at Mandalay, 1885. In wars ending in 1826 and 1852 the British conquered and annexed the coastal regions of Burma but the kings of Burma continued to rule over Upper Burma until a third war began in 1885. King Thibaw was accused of allying with France and obstructing British trade: his kingdom was invaded, his capital was occupied, and he was deported. His palace contained European jewellery as well as Burmese ceremonial objects and figures of the Buddha. Choice gifts were selected for the British royal family and the rest were auctioned.

Egypt and Burma apart, British acquisitions of territory during the 1880s were generally conducted in a low-key manner: limited gains were made, usually avoiding major confrontations with other powers. In the 1890s British policy was more assertive. The outlines of the future colonies of the Gold Coast and Nigeria began to be filled in by forceful actions against African peoples. On the Niger French claims were brusquely rebuffed in a sharp crisis. In 1885 the British had pulled back from the Sudan, even though General Gordon had perished in the withdrawal, an episode that attracted intense public concern and much resentment against a government that was accused of allowing him to die a Christian martyr's death (see page 301). In 1896 the government of Lord Salisbury decided that the Sudan must now be conquered. A powerful expeditionary force under General Kitchener drove south from Egypt and destroyed the forces of the Islamic Mahdist regime in the Sudan in 1898 at Omdurman. As in West Africa, there was now to be no compromise with French claims. The French tried to establish their right to the

Upper Nile by sending a small expeditionary force overland from West Africa to a village called Fashoda in 1898. The British insisted that the French withdraw. War was the alternative if they did not. The French accepted the situation and withdrew.

Britain's role in the partition of Africa is often depicted as the 'new' British imperialism in action overseas. For the 1880s at least, this is misleading. Throughout the decade, outside Egypt, the British edged forward cautiously, making piecemeal gains. Only the death of Gordon seems to have aroused deep public concern. For the 1890s, however, there is a much closer connection between imperial attitudes at home and what happened in Africa. Serious imperialists were primarily concerned with reuniting the dispersed British race, not with conquering African territory. Nevertheless, the Conservative government elected in 1895 was committed to maintaining Britain's position in every part of the world, almost regardless of cost. Challenges must be faced, by force if necessary. The French yielded to the threat of force on the Niger and the Nile. The Afrikaners did not. The ensuing South African War with its cost and eventual unpopularity was a great setback for imperial idealism.

Wars and threats of war over Africa in the 1890s, together with ambitious programmes to reconstruct the empire and thus to regenerate Britain itself, are striking new developments in the history of the British empire. But by 1914 the British empire had not been reconstructed and in the newly acquired territories, apart from Egypt, very little had been done to create effective administrations or to realize such economic potential as they might possess. The continuities between the period 1870 to 1914 and the earlier nineteenth century are in fact more striking than the changes. Too much should not be read into the great parade for Queen Victoria's Jubilee in 1897.

THE TEST OF WAR

Even if plans to integrate the empire had come to nothing, the war of 1914–18 was unmistakable proof of its vitality and power. Although Britain devoted by far the largest part of its men and resources to the trench warfare of France, the war still had very important imperial dimensions. The empire made significant contributions to Britain's capacity to wage a war on the continent of Europe on a scale and of a duration that virtually no one had foreseen. In 1914 Britain could declare war on behalf of the whole empire but it could not commit the troops of its self-governing colonies or Dominions, as they were now coming to be called. While Indian and African troops were at Britain's disposal, Dominion troops fought in the war, first of all because men volunteered, at least until conscription was introduced later in the war, and secondly because their governments were willing to dispatch troops overseas. Neither the men nor the governments flinched. Troops from the Dominions and from India took often prominent places in the British line of battle in France and fought with great distinction. The empire also supplied important raw materials for the British war effort and was a major supplier of food. German food supplies ultimately failed; British food supplies, in part at least due to the empire, did not.

In the war outside Europe the imperial contribution was even greater. There the British empire was generally on the offensive, attacking Germany's colonial territories and eventually dismembering the Middle Eastern empire of Turkey, Germany's ally. A very large force of Australians and New Zealanders was committed both to the disastrously unsuccessful attempt to knock Turkey out of the war by landing troops at Gallipoli in 1915 and to the offensive from Egypt which drove the Turks out of Palestine and Syria in 1917–18. Great numbers of Indians were also involved in that campaign, and the attack on the Turks in Iraq began as an operation exclusively by the British Indian army.

During the war some steps were taken towards implementing parts of the programme of the prewar imperialists. When the Liberal government gave way to a Conservative-dominated coalition in 1916, strong prewar imperialists, such as Milner and Curzon, returned to office, while David Lloyd George, the new Prime Minister, became something of a convert to imperial causes. Empire suppliers were given preferences in British markets. Schemes for future imperial self-sufficiency were discussed. There was even a perceptible move towards joint decision-taking, which enthusiasts might interpret as a first step to institutionalized imperial unity.

'My Boys'. This cartoon of 1914 reflects enthusiasm in Britain at the empire's response to the outbreak of the First World War. Australia immediately offered a force of 20,000 men, while Canada offered a division. These numbers were to grow enormously during the course of the war.

To meet pressure from colonial leaders, who wanted some say in the way in which the British command used the troops which they contributed, the prime ministers of the Dominions together with nominated Indian representatives were invited to join the British War Cabinet in London in 1917. This so-called Imperial War Cabinet met for two sessions but it was never an effective cabinet of the empire. The governments of the Dominions were not prepared to surrender their powers to what was essentially the British War Cabinet with additions from the Dominions. Nevertheless, it seemed to be an appropriate symbol of the reality that the war of 1914–18 had been a war fought by the British empire as a single great power.

The empire and the First World War

King George V declared war in 1914 against Britain's enemies for the whole empire. South Africa's participation in the war was disliked by many Afrikaners and there was some armed resistance. Elsewhere, in the early years of the war, men volunteered in great numbers, the main problems in putting imperial troops into the field being the limited capacity to train and equip them, rather than any shortage of recruits. From 1916, however, conscription was instituted in the Dominions as well as in Britain. This proved divisive. Conscription was opposed by some sections of opinion in Australia and very bitterly contested by many French Canadians.

A high proportion of the adult male population of Australia, Canada, and New Zealand took part in the war, nearly 20 per cent in the case of New Zealand. They fought in some of the most ferocious engagements in France and at Gallipoli, and gained much esteem for doing so. The record of the Indian army was more patchy. Initial defeats in Mesopotamia (Iraq) revealed serious deficiencies in logistics. The Indian corps in France suffered heavy losses and, with fears that its morale was deteriorating, it was withdrawn after a year.

The empire contributed not only front-line troops, who in many cases took very heavy casualties in battle, but also large numbers of people who worked as labourers and carriers behind the lines or supplying the fighting men. 90,000 Chinese were recruited as labourers for France in the British settlement of Weiheiwei. Black and coloured South Africans did not bear arms, but they too were recruited to work in France. The biggest number of human porters were required for the long-drawn-out process of conquering the German colony of Tanganyika (Tanzania) in East Africa. Up to one million men were enlisted in British East Africa, often by compulsion. The labour forces may have been spared death by machine gun, but they were not immune from disease. Some 100,000 porters probably died in East Africa.

Non-combatants suffered very severely from the indirect consequences of war. World wars may not be the actual cause of epidemics, but the war of 1914–18, in which millions of people were moved around the world, provided the conditions in which the influenza epidemic of 1918–19 could spread on a catastrophic scale. The most authoritative estimate is that seventeen million people died of influenza in India, and perhaps 2 per cent of the total population of Africa may have perished.

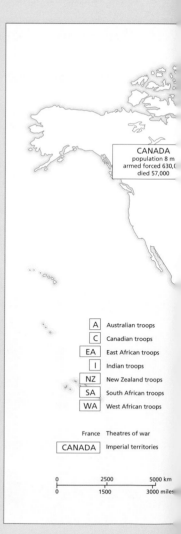

CANADA
population 8 m
armed forced 630,0
died 57,000

A	Australian troops
C	Canadian troops
EA	East African troops
I	Indian troops
NZ	New Zealand troops
SA	South African troops
WA	West African troops

France   Theatres of war

| CANADA | Imperial territories |

0   2500   5000 km
0   1500   3000 miles

Indian soldiers at the Somme, July 1916. Although the main Indian army corps that had been dispatched to France in October 1914 was moved to the Middle East in 1915, two divisions remained on the western front.

The imperial contribution to the First World War

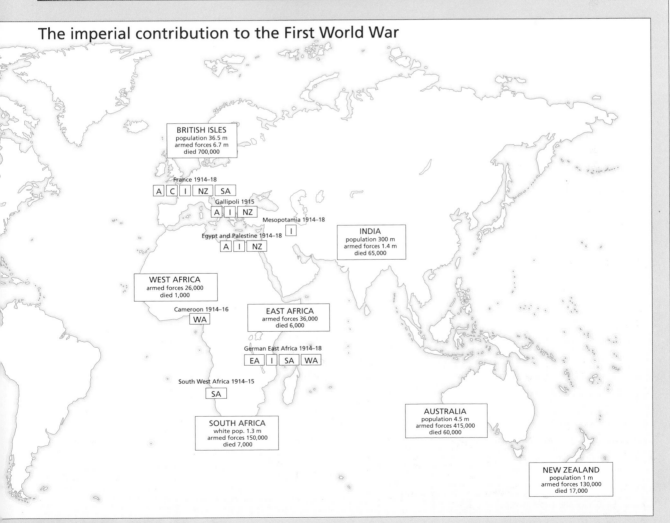

BRITISH ISLES
population 36.5 m
armed forces 6.7 m
died 700,000

France 1914–18
A   C   I   NZ   SA

Gallipoli 1915
A   I   NZ

Mesopotamia 1914–18
I

Egypt and Palestine 1914–18
A   I   NZ

INDIA
population 300 m
armed forces 1.4 m
died 65,000

WEST AFRICA
armed forces 26,000
died 1,000

Cameroon 1914–16
WA

EAST AFRICA
armed forces 36,000
died 6,000

German East Africa 1914–18
EA   I   SA   WA

South West Africa 1914–15
SA

SOUTH AFRICA
white pop. 1.3 m
armed forces 150,000
died 7,000

AUSTRALIA
population 4.5 m
armed forces 415,000
died 60,000

NEW ZEALAND
population 1 m
armed forces 130,000
died 17,000

CHAPTER 4

P. J. Marshall

1918 to the 1960s: Keeping Afloat

Gurkhas at the victory parade in London, 19 July 1919. Imperial troops took a prominent place on the parade, symbolizing the empire's support for Britain throughout the First World War. Gurkhas from Nepal had been recruited into the British Indian army since 1815 and were highly esteemed as fighting men. 55,589 Gurkhas served during the First World War.

This chapter, like the last one, will begin with an evocation of a parade. Last time the parade was that to mark Queen Victoria's Diamond Jubilee in 1897 and the interpreter was Jan Morris; this time it is the victory parade of 1919 to mark the end of the First World War and the interpreter is Correlli Barnett. As in 1897, there was a strong imperial element in the parade of 1919. Barnett writes of '... slouch-hatted Australians and New Zealanders; Canadians and Newfoundlanders; Indians dark under their turbans; contingents to represent all parts of the empire that had rallied to Britain's side in her time of peril'.

The evocation is sparser than Jan Morris's and the message is very different. Her book was entitled *Pax Britannica: Climax of an Empire*; his is called *The Collapse of British Power*. She commented that: 'There was a great deal of brag to the Britain of

the nineties, but then there really was a good deal to brag about.' He is only too aware of 'fundamental anomalies and weaknesses in British power'. For him the empire was one of the greatest of these anomalies and weaknesses. By 1939 and the outbreak of the Second World War it had become 'a colossal burden'. In short, Morris offers an interpretation of the late nineteenth century as apogee; Barnett sees decline and fall by the mid-twentieth century.

Those who see the writing on the wall for the British empire from the First World War have good reasons for doing so. What the imperialists of a previous generation had feared was coming about. Industrial and military power were being effectively harnessed by countries with a much greater capacity than Britain. The United States had emerged as a potential world power of the first magnitude, while the eclipse of Germany by military defeat and of Russia by revolution would be at best temporary. Currents of nationalism were strong in the Dominions and in India and Egypt. It was not likely that nationalism and an effective British empire could be reconciled. Political and social change in Britain might well make it very difficult for a consistent commitment to empire to be maintained by British governments.

Yet the British empire sustained no major loss of territory until the Second World War and that war was to be conducted as a joint imperial effort, comparable to that made by the empire between 1914 and 1918. To depict the period from 1918 to the 1960s as one of unrelieved decline is therefore to misrepresent it. The potential weaknesses are undeniable, but potential weaknesses only became actual ones under certain specific conditions. When the British people, or at least their political leaders, lost their will to retain an empire, when Britain was shown to be unable to protect its empire by armed force or diplomacy from the assaults of other powers, and when it could no longer enforce its rule against its subjects or – what was usually of much greater consequence – when it could no longer retain the consent or loyalty of enough of them by means other than coercion: then the empire would disintegrate.

Until well into the 1940s, such conditions did not exist. Britain's political leaders of both the main parties were still committed to empire. The price of sustaining an empire was evidently not as yet one that the British people refused to pay. The vulnerability of the empire was not openly exposed until the Japanese launched their assault on it in 1942. The extent of the support given to Britain in the Second World War suggested that the aspirations of most of the peoples of the empire could still be met within an imperial framework. Both gloom about the parade of 1919 and euphoria about that of 1897 should be tempered. On both occasions the empire continued to do business much as usual.

THE WILL TO EMPIRE

Contemporaries who watched the imperial contingents parade through London in 1919 are most unlikely to have felt many forebodings of gloom about Britain's future as an imperial power. There could be no doubt about the British people's continuing commitment to empire. The war that had just ended seemed to have demonstrated conclusively that the empire made a crucial contribution to Britain's standing as a great power.

The imperialist revival

During the war politicians with a very strong commitment to empire were again in office in Britain and they were to have an important influence during the first years of peace. The Imperial War Cabinet of 1917 seemed to symbolize the union of the British empire in war. At the peace conference of 1919 the empire again acted as a unit. The British delegation was called the British empire delegation: Dominion

---

The Palestine mandate

Palestine had long been a part of the Ottoman province of Syria. In the closing stages of the First World War the Turks were driven out of it by British forces. On 31 October 1917, while the war was still far from over, the British entered into a momentous commitment about the future of Palestine. In a declaration issued under the name of the British Foreign Secretary, A.J. Balfour, the British government stated that it viewed 'with favour the establishment in Palestine of a national home for the Jewish people ... it being clearly understood that nothing shall be done which may prejudice the civil and religious rights of existing non-Jewish communities in Palestine'. Thus began one of the most troubled and inglorious episodes in Britain's colonial history.

In 1922 Britain was formally awarded the mandate of Palestine in a document that endorsed the commitment of the Balfour Declaration to a Jewish national home, although only 11 per cent, some 67,000 people, in the territory entrusted to Britain were actually Jewish. The vast majority – around 600,000 – were Arabs, most of whom were Muslims.

From the outset, the British politicians who made policy for Palestine in London and those who tried to administer the mandate in Palestine itself faced uncertainties and contradictions. What did a 'national home' mean? Was a Jewish state to be created or something less than that? Was any form of national home for Jews consistent with maintaining the 'civil and religious rights' of the Arabs? It quickly became clear that the contradictions could not be resolved. Zionists, whose ideals were fixed on Palestine, wanted massive Jewish immigration and the eventual creation of a Jewish state. Arabs wanted no more Jewish immigration and no Jewish state. Neither side would co-operate with the British in trying to create a united Palestine.

The British were left to administer Palestine as best they could. In the 1920s, with a low rate of Jewish immigration,

tension could be more or less contained. But violent Arab–Jewish conflict occurred in 1929. In the 1930s Arab opinion throughout the Middle East was increasingly mobilized to defend the rights of the Palestine Arabs, as Jewish immigration built up with persecution in Europe. By this time the Jews had become nearly 30 per cent of the population with their own institutions, including their own armed force, the *Haganah*. In 1936 a major Arab revolt began.

The Second World War made the situation even more fraught. The British government believed that it could not risk in wartime the hostility of Arabs and other Muslims from Egypt to India. In 1939 it committed itself strictly to limiting future Jewish immigration. As the scale of the Nazi holocaust became increasingly apparent, there was a mounting Jewish sense of outrage against British policy, especially in the United States.

The Palestine problem inherited by the Labour government in 1945 was utterly intractable. A united Palestine was inconceivable. Yet a partitioned Palestine, which would create a Jewish state, would have to be forced on Arabs. Jews were insisting that refugees from Europe must be let in. They began to use terrorism against the British, who were for a time still determined to maintain a position in Palestine as a future base in the Middle East. In their efforts to find a settlement the British sought to involve the United States but Ernest Bevin, the British Foreign Secretary, became convinced that the Americans would only act as partisans of the Zionists. By February 1947 he saw no solution but to abandon Britain's commitment and return Palestine to the United Nations. A United Nations commission produced a plan for a partitioned Palestine, which the British refused to enforce. All British troops were to be withdrawn from Palestine by May 1948, leaving it to the inevitable Jewish–Arab war. The state of Israel emerged from Jewish victory in war.

prime ministers served on it as full members with British Cabinet ministers. Lloyd George, the British Prime Minister, hoped that the involvement of the Dominions in joint policy-making with Britain would continue into the future. 'There was a time', he said in 1921, 'when Downing Street controlled the Empire; today the Empire is in charge of Downing Street.'

The war seemed to have revived Britain's appetite for territorial acquisitions. The redistribution of German colonies and Turkish provinces gave abundant opportunities for indulging this appetite. British forces had been mainly responsible for expelling the Turks from Palestine, Syria, Iraq, and the Arabian peninsula by 1918. In any future settlement, Britain was determined that its interests in the Middle East – still primarily the traditional one of maintaining the defence of India – must be safeguarded as securely as possible. The Turks must certainly be replaced, but it was less clear who was to replace them. On the one hand, Britain – most flamboyantly through the legendary T.E. Lawrence 'of Arabia' – had encouraged the peoples under Turkish rule to rebel, implying that they would obtain their independence after the war. Promises for future Arab states were made. On the other hand, Britain had entered into commitments for the partition of Ottoman territory with its allies, France and Russia. Britain also had its own ambitions for direct control over the area. Yet further complications were introduced by the Balfour Declaration of 1917 which promised, among other things, 'a national home for the Jewish people' in Palestine – a bid for the support of Jewry throughout the world to the allied war effort.

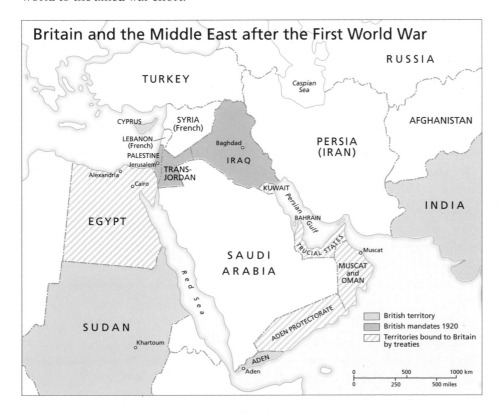

Britain and the Middle East after the First World War

T.E. Lawrence. 'Lawrence of Arabia', as he came to be known, was recruited by British military intelligence in Egypt during the First World War. He spent two years from 1916 in the field with the Arabs who had rebelled against Turkish rule, dressing and living as an Arab. Lawrence became a heroic cult figure in postwar Britain, although he felt deeply disillusioned with what he regarded as the betrayal of the Arabs. The Arabs 'did not risk their lives in battle to change masters, to become British subjects or French citizens, but to win a show of their own', he wrote.

In the event, the French could not be kept out of the Middle East and they obtained control of Syria. Britain acquired large gains for itself: Palestine (and with it a commitment to implement the pledge to the Jewish national home), Transjordan (Jordan), and Iraq became British 'mandates'. Britain also aimed to secure a strong position in Iran by obtaining a treaty recognizing its dominant influence. With the Middle East largely under British control, the defence of India was at last assured. Lord Curzon was the Foreign Secretary who presided over this immense extension of British power and influence in the Middle East. This was a fitting reward for a man who, as Viceroy of India at the very end of the nineteenth century, had struggled to curb the influence of Tsarist Russia over the region. Far from beginning a long decline, the British empire seemed to be much more secure in 1920 than it had been in 1900.

The term 'mandate' indicated a change of language and sentiment, if not necessarily a change in practice, in the way in which Europeans ruled other people. German colonies as well as Turkish provinces were given new masters after the war. Ex-German territories went to Britain and also to some of the Dominions: Australia and New Zealand were allocated areas in the Pacific, while South Africa was entrusted with South West Africa (Namibia). What were transferred were technically mandates, not colonies. Those who held mandates did so formally as the trustees of the League of Nations and were bound to 'promote to the utmost the material and moral well-being and social progress' of the indigenous peoples. The distinction between mandates and colonies did not, however, seem very real to many contemporaries. Britain had made sizeable territorial gains.

Imperialism in moderation

The Indian summer of old-style British imperialism did not last long. The careers in office of Lloyd George, Curzon, and Milner all effectively ended in the early 1920s. They were replaced by men who were totally convinced of the need to maintain Britain's standing as an imperial power, but were wary of over-extending Britain's commitments and of ambitious schemes for imperial co-operation over foreign policy or for an imperial trading block fenced off by tariffs from the rest of the world.

From the 1920s a rough consensus about imperial policy began to emerge in British politics and this was to endure until the winding up of the dependent empire after the Second World War. The main body both of Conservatives and of the Labour party (which replaced the Liberals in 1918 as the alternative party of government) accepted that empire must be maintained, but that overt coercion should be kept to the minimum and that dreams of formal structures for imperial unity had little relevance in the conditions of the mid-twentieth century.

The strength of the consensus was most strikingly demonstrated in the final stages of the British empire. The dependent empire came to an end in two great phases of decolonization: from 1947 to 1948 British rule ended in the Indian subcontinent and the Palestine mandate was surrendered; from 1957 to the mid-1960s independence was granted to colonies in Africa and the Caribbean and to Malaya. The first phase was presided over by a Labour government; the second by Conservative governments.

Neither party had been committed in advance to ending the British empire. Labour had a tradition of scepticism about 'imperialism' and suspicion about its capitalist links. It was a party that prided itself on standing for justice for colonial peoples and its activist wing would take up issues of apparent injustice with some of the enthusiasm of Wilberforce, Buxton, or Cobden in the past. Most radical critics of colonial administration tended, however, to stress the need for more vigorous British protection of indigenous people against 'exploitation', rather than to call for the removal of Britain's protecting hand. In the 1920s the development of colonial self-government was stated by Labour to be a desirable objective, but in 1943 Labour still felt that most colonial peoples would not 'be ready for self-government ... for a considerable time to come'. On India, a group within the Labour party, which included Clement Attlee, was genuinely enthusiastic about constitutional progress. But recognition of the need to concede immediate Indian independence only came under the pressure of events in the Second World War. Labour governments after 1945 were committed to constitutional reform for African colonies with self-government as an ultimate objective, but that objective was still distant for many of them.

If Labour was not the party of decolonization, Conservatives were not committed to resisting all change. Winston Churchill, a maverick Conservative in the interwar period who was to come into his own as the great Prime Minister of the Second World War, was an exception to this. Churchill was not a 'high imperialist' in the Chamberlain sense: he was a free trader and had no interest in equal partnership with the Dominions, whom he frankly did not regard as equals. But he had a total aversion to concessions that might weaken the empire and therefore reduce Britain's standing in the world. He was deeply moved by 'the humiliation of being kicked out of India by the beastliest people in the world next to the Germans', by which he meant the Indians. The main body of the Conservative party did not accept these views. They were responsible for the two great Indian reform acts of the interwar period, which took India towards internal self-government. Although these reforms carefully safeguarded what were considered to be vital British interests, the 1919 and the 1935 Government of India Acts were regarded as major concessions at the time and the 1935 act drew bitter opposition from Churchill for undermining the empire. Conservative ministers accepted even in the 1920s that the aim for British colonies was self-government at some unspecified point in the future. They did not generally oppose the policies of the post-1945 Labour governments in India or the colonies and when the Conservatives returned to power in 1951, they tended to follow precedents set by Labour.

THE CASE FOR EMPIRE

Although the will to empire remained essentially intact among all shades of opinion in the mainstream of British politics, it was not an unconditional will to empire at all costs. The empire should be preserved only so long as the advantages seemed to be real and the costs did not appear to be excessive.

The military case

Did the empire remain an essential prop for Britain's status as a great military power or did it draw Britain into commitments so over-extending that Britain could not respond effectively to real threats to its vital interests? For some years after 1918 such questions did not pose themselves with any urgency. In the 1920s there was little sense of impending danger. Of Britain's potential rivals, Germany had been crippled by defeat and the Russian Communist regime had turned inwards to consolidate its grip on its own society. France was formally Britain's ally. There seemed to be no need to keep the imperial alliance in a state of readiness for a future European conflagration. Lloyd George may have sincerely welcomed the prospect of the empire running Downing Street, but as international tension eased this seemed a less attractive prospect to others. The British Foreign Office was not

The Japanese incite Indians to throw off British rule. By 1942 the Japanese had driven the British out of Malaya and Burma and had reached the eastern frontier of India. Leaflets such as this one were smuggled into India. Its message reads: 'All British colonies are awake. Why must Indians stay slaves? Seize this chance, rise'. Churchill's Indian servants are shown Burmese nationalists belabouring the British. The Japanese victories represented a severe shock to British rule in India. Nevertheless, the British were able to hold their position in India, which made a huge contribution to the war effort.

The empire and the Second World War

The two World Wars were very different in character and so was the imperial contribution to victory. The weapons used in the Second World War were much more technically sophisticated. This meant that, even though the mobilization of men and women was to be on an even greater scale than between 1914 and 1918, the number of actual combatants would be much smaller. A huge premium was placed on industrial capacity and on those who worked in industry, while many of those in the armed forces were in fact concerned with servicing equipment or with supply.

Although high-quality fighting men were needed as much as ever, and the colonies and Commonwealth again provided these in abundance, the transformation of war by technology to some extent limited the value of the imperial contribution. With the exception of Canada, colonial and Commonwealth countries lacked an industrial base capable of making a significant contribution to the production of munitions. Nearly 70 per cent of the munitions used throughout the whole Commonwealth were in fact produced in Britain itself, and a further 20 per cent came from the United States. As the

map shows, what the Commonwealth and the colonies supplied above all was people. This contribution went beyond their own forces. For instance, nearly 40 per cent of the air crews of the British Royal Air Force were provided by the Dominions or colonies.

With fewer combatants, casualties in battle were lower than those of 1914–18, but non-combatant civilians again suffered the indirect effects of war on a vast scale. In 1943 some three million people died in Bengal in a famine caused by the loss of rice-surplus areas in South East Asia to Japanese conquest, the unwillingness of the allies to divert shipping from obvious military purposes to transporting food to India, and artificial scarcities produced by inept attempts at price regulation.

The war was particularly traumatic for Australia. Many Australians, both at the time and since, have felt that, while requiring Australia to send troops to the Middle East, Britain did far too little to safeguard South East Asia against a Japanese attack. After the great Japanese victories, Australia turned to the United States for its defence (see page 345).

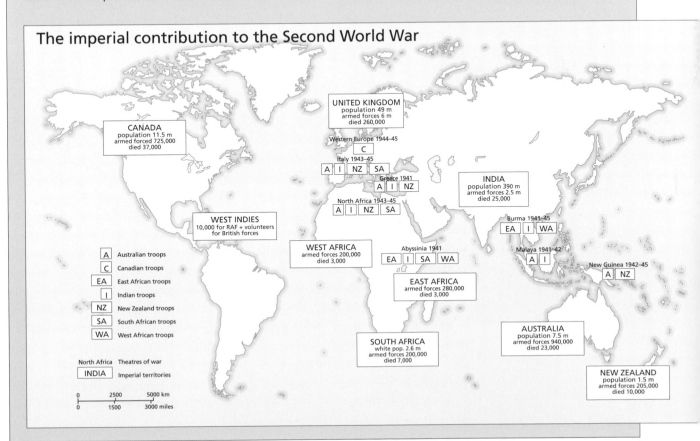

The imperial contribution to the Second World War

enthusiastic about having to make policy with the agreement of the Dominions. Once the wartime armed forces of the Dominions had been demobilized, their capacity to render active assistance to Britain in any emergency was minimal, as was their willingness to accept any formal obligations to do so. Consultation with them, in the eyes of British policy makers, merely gave them an opportunity to delay and object. Britain should be free to make its own foreign policy and if the price of that freedom was allowing the Dominions to do the same, that was not considered an excessive price, at least until the international situation got very much worse in the 1930s.

For most of the period between the two World Wars, British defence policy was primarily focused on the needs of the empire. The British army resumed its nineteenth-century role of providing imperial garrisons. Troops were deployed not so much to deter foreign aggression as to maintain British rule against internal disaffection. In the immediate aftermath of the First World War the empire faced turbulence in Ireland, Egypt, the new mandates of Iraq and Palestine, and in India. This required a deployment of British troops on a scale that seriously strained available resources and forced British planners to reduce some commitments, especially in the Middle East. Even so, in 1938 there were more British infantry battalions stationed in India, the Middle East, and the Far East than there were in Britain itself.

Britain's Indian army was still regarded as an imperial asset of great importance, even though the uses to which it could be put were being restricted. In 1923 the British conceded that the Indian army could not be deployed outside India without the consent of the government of India and that in such a case the cost would have to be borne by Britain. In 1938 the British government agreed to pay the costs of the modernization of a reduced Indian army which would be·available for service overseas. Full use was to be made of the Indian army in the Second World War, whatever the financial cost to Britain.

In the 1930s, as the international situation again became threatening, British political leaders once more looked to the empire for support. Each crisis in relations with Germany, Italy, or Japan led to exchanges of views with the Dominions. Any immediate military contribution by the Dominions at the start of a war would inevitably be on a small scale and not much notice was taken of the advice they offered, but ministers still did not wish to see Britain go to war without their assured support. The effect on British opinion of a divided empire was clearly thought to be an important consideration. When war came in 1939, all the Dominions, with the exception of Eire (later the Republic of Ireland and a Dominion since 1921), declared war on Britain's enemies. India and the colonies were, as in 1914, automatically committed to war by Britain.

As in the First World War, imperial manpower eventually made a massive contribution to the British war effort between 1939 and 1945. Large contingents of troops from the colonies and the Dominions again fought on the European fronts:

a Canadian army corps took part in the liberation of France in 1944 and Indians
and New Zealanders fought their way through Italy in 1944–45.

For most of the war of 1914–18 the British empire had been on the offensive
outside Europe; between 1939 and 1945 the empire had to fight desperate defensive
actions before it could begin to push back its enemies. Egypt was under periodical
attack from Italians and Germans operating out of Libya before the eighth army,
with large contributions from Australia, India, New Zealand, and South Africa,
cleared the enemy out of North Africa. In 1941 Japan entered a war in which Britain
was already very hard pressed. In a brilliant campaign, the Japanese overran
Malaya, sank the main units of the British fleet in the Far East, and forced the
surrender of some 130,000 imperial troops at Singapore. The Japanese were
eventually held on the border between Burma and India and in New Guinea.
British, Indian, and Australian forces were slowly regaining lost territory when
American naval victories, followed by the use of the atomic bomb, brought the war
to an end in 1945.

The global scale of the Second World War meant that the empire ceased to be just
an asset to be drawn upon for resources for the European war, as it had been in
1914–18; it also made claims on British resources in its own hours of need. Faced
with hard choices, British planners attached a very high importance to the defence
of Egypt and the Middle East, but otherwise they consistently gave priority to home
defence and to Europe. The theory was that Germany would be beaten first and that
then Britain would turn its full attention on Japan. But in the desperate crisis caused
by Japan's initial offensive, reinforcements, however inadequate, had to be rushed
to Singapore, and thereafter British forces had to be committed to the defence of
India and the Indian Ocean, if not to the defence of Australia. Churchill liked to
think that 'the peoples of Hindustan' had been 'protected from the horrors and
perils of the World War ... on the shoulders of our small Island'. He paid tribute to
the 'glorious heroism and martial qualities of the Indian troops', but he was also
indignant at the thought of the huge bill India was charging Britain for the use of
its resources. Few historians would agree with Churchill's version of the
British–Indian relationship, but it shows how the experience of the Second World
War made even Churchill begin to see that in military terms the British empire
could be a burden as well as an asset.

After 1945 few British strategists believed that empire could contribute
significantly to Britain's military strength. Britain was immediately locked into a
permanent defence commitment on the continent of Europe in the NATO alliance,
in which the United States was the senior and indispensable partner. Until the
collapse of Communism in 1989, the defence of Europe was the overwhelming
British priority. Interests outside Europe were by no means abandoned, but in any
conflict over resources Europe would always prevail. Any possibility that imperial
contributions could still be levied for commitments outside Europe was greatly
reduced after 1947, when a partitioned Indian army was no longer available for the

Suez, 1956: a British soldier gives water to a wounded Egyptian. In 1954 the Egyptian leader Gamal Abdul Nasser began to pursue anti-colonialist policies which seemed to threaten Britain's position in the Middle East. A crisis came to a head in 1956 when Nasser nationalized the Suez canal. Anthony Eden, the British Prime Minister, saw this as a challenge that must be met by force. Britain enlisted the support of France and Israel. Israel attacked Egypt and Britain joined in, landing troops at Port Said on 5 November. Under widespread international condemnation and intense American pressure, the operation was called off.

British, even if they paid the bills. Commonwealth forces were to fight together in Korea and in Malaysia in the 1950s, and Gurkhas have remained a part of the British army, but it became inescapable that, if Britain wished to see its world-wide interests supported by a military presence, it would have to provide that presence itself.

In 1956 the British made a desperate attempt to shore up their position in the Middle East by invading Egypt. Their allies in this Suez adventure were not, as would have been the case in the past, the forces of the empire, but those of France and Israel. Only Australia and New Zealand viewed the venture with any sort of sympathy. The attempt to recover lost ground outside Europe by a major military operation at Suez was very much against the consistent trend of British policy after 1945. Britain still saw itself as a world power, but with the inescapable commitment to Europe and in the economic conditions prevailing in postwar Britain, it could not afford to sustain imperial responsibilities for long. The Egyptian base had been abandoned in 1954. In 1967 a major decision was taken to run down all commitments 'east of Suez'.

The economic case

The value of the imperial contribution to Britain's potential as a great military power was not seriously questioned until the Second World War. Thereafter, there could be no real doubt that empire, simply in military terms, had become a burden to Britain. The contribution that empire might be expected to make to the British economy was not questioned until even later: it was only in the late 1950s that scepticism about the relevance of empire to Britain's economic future gained wide currency.

Hopes that Britain might be transformed economically by ambitious programmes of imperial development and integration, of the kind advocated by Joseph Chamberlain, won little support after 1918. Such programmes had been based on assumptions that Britain and the empire, especially the Dominions, had essentially complementary interests: Britain would manufacture and the empire would supply food and primary products. However, the growing industrialization in Canada, India, and Australia meant that this was no longer true.

Nevertheless, in the difficult economic conditions of the 1930s and during the Second World War and its aftermath the volume of trade between Britain and the empire increased considerably. In 1909–13 the British empire took 35 per cent of Britain's exports and provided 26.9 per cent of its imports; in 1934–38 the proportion of exports going to the empire had risen to 41.3 per cent and imports from it to 41.2 per cent. India's share was declining as its own industries developed, given some protection by the British government of India, but the share of the Dominions grew markedly. Trade within the empire was boosted by the ending of Britain's long commitment to world-wide free trade. In 1931 Britain introduced tariffs to counter a severe balance of payments crisis. Negotiations were then opened at Ottawa for the Dominions and Britain to decide what tariff reductions they would offer one another to stimulate imperial trade. What emerged was something far short of free trade within the empire. A mass of piecemeal concessions were negotiated, which tended to favour imports of the Dominions' produce by Britain rather than British exports of manufactures to them. Economic activity within the empire was further co-ordinated by the establishment of the sterling area: most of the empire and some other countries agreed to fix their currencies in relation to sterling and to hold their reserves in a sterling pool to be managed by Britain.

War again increased the economic importance of the empire to Britain. Soon after the outbreak of the Second World War trade with Europe ceased as did access to the Far East. Canada and colonies in Africa therefore played a major role as suppliers to Britain. Sales of colonial produce to the United States enabled Britain to pay for essential American food, raw materials, and munitions. During and after the war, Britain intervened in the economic life of the colonies in a largely new way, fixing prices and trying to increase output by government investment. Another of Chamberlain's ideas, the use of action by the state to 'develop' colonies, seemed to have been revived. In fact schemes for colonial development had been proposed again in the 1920s. The first major Colonial Development Act was passed in 1929. This was mainly intended to ease British unemployment by giving colonies funds with which to buy British goods. More generous acts followed in 1940 and 1945, allocating much larger sums of British taxpayers' money to colonial projects. Developing the colonies was a serious interest of the Labour government after 1945. The motives were somewhat mixed: British investment would in the long run provide the flourishing economy on which eventual self-government could be built; in the short run it would enable the colonies to produce more commodities for sale to the United States, earning dollars which, under the sterling area arrangements, would be at Britain's disposal for purchases in America.

The imperial economy launched in the 1930s was wound down in the 1950s. World trade began to recover and Britain shifted back towards international free trade. From taking more than half British exports up to 1950, colonial and Commonwealth markets sank back to taking about one third in the mid-1960s. Preferences and the sterling area were abandoned. The schemes to force on African development by large state-financed projects had brought no significant return for a very large outlay. Developing impoverished colonies in the tropics could only become an open-ended burden on the British taxpayer, from which few realistic returns could be expected. Trade with rapidly growing markets in Europe was a much more inviting prospect.

In terms of national wealth and power, the colonial empire and the Commonwealth clearly could not provide Britain with the security and the opportunities it required in the world that was emerging after the Second World War. Britain was bound to seek closer relationships with the United States and with a reviving western Europe. Yet throughout the 1920s and 1930s Britain's defence policies had been designed to protect imperial interests, whose economic contribution to Britain's welfare was on an upward curve. In retrospect, the Second World War showed that the contribution of the United States had been much greater than that of the empire in providing the economic and military support that had enabled Britain to avoid defeat; it also showed that Britain was no longer capable of defending a world-wide empire. At the time, however, the contribution to the defeat of Germany and Japan of an empire that had rallied yet again to the aid of Britain could hardly be doubted. Calculations of an adverse balance sheet in military and economic terms were not to undermine the British will to empire until after the elation of victory had evaporated in a new postwar world.

The moral case

The will to empire in Britain had never been based solely on calculations of benefits in terms of wealth and power. It was also sustained by pride in empire as an essential part of Britain's national identity and as defining Britain's role in the world. Pride in an imperial role was largely moribund by the 1960s, but it is important yet again not to apply too much hindsight. Large numbers of British people retained an emotional commitment to empire far into the twentieth century. The fervour of those who in the late nineteenth century had tried to depict the destiny of the British race as an imperial one, by which all its disparate elements would be reunited and fulfilled in rule over other peoples, found few takers after 1918. Instead there was something of a reversion to what had been mid-nineteenth-century imperial idealism. The British people liked to believe that, through their empire, they spread freedom and improvement across the world.

What came to be called the Commonwealth seemed, to the British, to embody that freedom. The term 'Commonwealth' was consistently used from 1917. In that year General Smuts, the South African leader, spoke about a 'community of nations, which I prefer to call the British Commonwealth of Nations'. That community consisted of the Dominions together with Britain. Its institutions were the meetings of prime ministers which had begun in 1887, had become regular occurrences before 1914, and were to continue during and after the war. It was usually easier to define the Commonwealth by what it was not rather than by what it was. It was certainly not a federal union of the sort hoped for by Chamberlain and others before 1914. The prime ministers took no binding decisions – they made suggestions that individual members might or might not wish to adopt. The most ambitious attempt to define what the Commonwealth was appeared in the Balfour Declaration of 1926 which described it as 'a group of self-governing communities ... autonomous ... within the British Empire, equal in status, in no way subordinate one to another in any aspect of their domestic or external affairs, though united by a common allegiance to the Crown, and freely associated as members of the British Commonwealth of Nations'. Many British people came to see the Commonwealth as an expression of particularly British virtues. It rested on loyalty to the Crown and

British values, but on an unforced loyalty freely given. This symbol of the like-mindedness of the old colonies of settlement was surely proof of the success of the Victorian mission to spread British values through the migration of British people. Optimists believed that Afrikaners and French Canadians had also freely accepted these values and that in time other peoples of the empire would be included in this great brotherhood of the Commonwealth.

In 1947 India and Pakistan achieved independence as Dominions and members of the Commonwealth. Virtually every other ex-colonial territory was also admitted into the Commonwealth in due course. Idealistic British people liked to believe that the old vision of a white British race had been replaced by a new one of people of every sort of ethnic background united by their loyalty to the Crown and a commitment to the British values of freedom and democracy through the Commonwealth. Such idealism did not on the whole wear well. Assumptions that the Commonwealth would develop into a vehicle to propagate British institutions and values throughout the world were no doubt naive. The reality was somewhat different. The British monarchy retained a symbolic role in the Commonwealth, but since 1949 more and more of its members have become republics. Periods of military rule or the creation of one-party states in some Commonwealth countries were regarded by jaundiced British observers as distinctly un-British.

Full membership of the Commonwealth as independent states came to be accepted in the 1950s as the destination towards which nearly all peoples under British colonial rule were now heading. Up to and beyond the Second World War, however, Britain's imperial mission was seen less as preparing its subjects for eventual freedom than as exercising an almost indefinite 'trusteeship' over them. This language of trusteeship was similar to that used to describe the mandates of the League of Nations. Twentieth-century sensibilities required that rule over other peoples should be clearly stated to be rule in the interests of the ruled. In Africa, especially, the British prided themselves on having developed a deeper understanding of what really constituted the interests of the ruled. Their knowledge was embodied in theories such as that of indirect rule developed by Lord Lugard in northern Nigeria. 'Native' peoples were to be protected within the British interpretation of what were their own indigenous institutions, while they adjusted at their own pace to the pressures of the modern world. The British meanwhile acted as their benevolent guides and protectors. Doctrines of trusteeship gave British rule, at least in the eyes of the British, a strong ethical purpose and one that they considered to be unique to them. Opinion both on the left and the right of the political spectrum strongly endorsed doctrines of trusteeship. During the Second World War well-intentioned Americans were inclined to suggest that the British should place their colonies under international administration after the war. Such proposals were indignantly rejected by British opinion of all political shades. Britain could not give up the task of administering its own colonies in its own way.

Lord Lugard and Nigerian emirs. Frederick Lugard is flanked by the Sultan of Sokoto on his right and the Emir of Kano on his left. They were visiting Britain in 1934 to be presented to King George V. Sokoto and Kano were northern Nigerian states which Lugard had compelled to submit to him by force in 1903. He had then incorporated them into what he regarded as the benevolent system of trusteeship called indirect rule, by which the institutions and forms of the rulers' government were preserved, while they were placed under the supervision of a British Resident. Lugard took his guests to see the London Zoo.

Nevertheless, the task of administering other peoples was soon to be abandoned, as colonial nationalists rejected the trusteeship of others and claimed the right to rule themselves, and as no very significant British interest seemed to be served in contesting those claims. For many British people, however, the doctrine of trusteeship had invested the will to empire with an ethical purpose which helped to sustain it beyond the Second World War. For a generation not yet disillusioned with the Commonwealth, it was comforting to suppose that enlightened trusteeship was giving way to membership of a Commonwealth supposedly based on British ideals. Such beliefs helped to cushion the shock of the eventual loss of empire for many British people and enabled them to see the granting of independence as the fulfilment of mission, not as the collapse of British power.

EXTERNAL PRESSURES ON THE EMPIRE

The British were remarkably successful in defending their colonies against their rivals. Only the Japanese during the Second World War succeeded in taking territory out of the British empire by force. These losses were, however, restored in 1945. Nevertheless, the Second World War still had important consequences for the empire.

In the Middle East the strains of war made it impossible to maintain the Palestine mandate. The tight control that Britain had imposed on Egypt during the war aroused intense opposition to the continuation of British dominance after the war. In the Far East Britain was never again to be a dominant power after the loss of Singapore. It was the United States that had defeated Japan and in future the Australians would rely for their defence on the Americans and not the British. Japanese victories had shown Asian peoples how the British could be defeated. Not surprisingly, large sections of the ex-colonial populations identified with the victors, especially in Burma where effective British rule was never to be restored.

In India the British had to cope with a serious revolt in 1942. This was put down and India continued to make a major contribution to the allied cause. But commitment had its price. A great expansion of the Indian army and of India's war production required a major increase in the employment of Indians in the higher levels of government and in the armed forces. In 1939 there had been 697 Indian officers in the army; in 1945 there were 13,947, some of whom had attained very senior commands. The army was now an Indian army – no longer a force of mercenaries who would do any imperial bidding. Promises had again been made for the future. In an attempt to persuade Indian politicians to support the war, Sir Stafford Cripps, an emissary of the British government, had given a pledge that after the war the people of India would be free to choose whatever future they wished, including complete independence.

The pressures of war obliged the British to conciliate their allies as well as their imperial subjects. American opinion was not enthusiastic about including the preservation and restoration of colonial empires on the agenda of aims for a war

A British planter and his escort during the Communist insurgency in Malaya. In 1948 Communists among the Chinese population began a campaign of terrorism. European planters were the main target; it is estimated that one in ten of them was murdered. The colonial government replied by declaring an emergency and deploying 40,000 troops and 70,000 police against at the most 8,000 guerrillas. By the mid-1950s terrorism had subsided.

that was ostensibly about liberating peoples from foreign oppression. President Roosevelt shared these views. The British government always resisted giving precise undertakings about granting independence or placing its colonies under international supervision. However, it seemed politic even to Churchill to issue general statements about 'the progressive evolution of self-governing institutions' in the colonies. Desire to disarm American critics meant that a great deal was done to try to present British colonial rule in an amiable light. This desire gave an extra impetus, for instance, to programmes of economic development.

The American alliance persisted after the war. As the British empire crumbled after 1945, it was common to assume that the Americans had played an important part in bringing about its demise in order to increase their own world power and to encourage the British to concentrate their energies on Europe. On occasions, such as the ending of the Palestine mandate in 1948 or in their reactions to the Suez

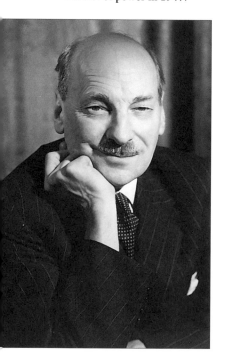

Clement Attlee. Attlee led the British Labour party from 1935 until 1951 and was Prime Minister from 1945 to 1951. He wished to sustain Britain's role as a world-wide power, but believed that outright rule should, where possible, be replaced by influence. He was therefore enthusiastic about the Commonwealth. He had no plans to dismantle the colonial empire, but was very much committed to the independence of India and played a crucial role in the transfer of power in 1947.

adventure of 1956, the Americans did apply direct pressure, but in general there is little evidence of it. With the outbreak of a cold war with the Soviet Union, Americans saw their interests as best served by stability rather than unpredictable change. The British empire offered some stability. American acquiescence in the continuation of the British empire could not, however, be presumed to be completely open-ended. Awareness of American concern probably reinforced the inclination of the British to avoid conflict with their subjects or an unacceptable degree of repression.

Russia was the British empire's ostensible enemy after 1945, as it had been in the later nineteenth century. Britain considered that the danger now lay not so much in military invasion of any part of the empire as in subversion by local Communist parties in the colonies. These could be curbed by police action, but it was the belief of the Labour government in particular that Communism must also be contained by removing grievances through reforms. Fear of potential Communist infiltration of the Gold Coast (Ghana) was a reason for working with Dr Nkrumah whom the British otherwise considered to be a very intransigent nationalist. Outside pressure again reinforced trends already present in British colonial policy.

The twentieth-century empire had been buffeted by two great wars, but in the short run it had shown remarkable powers of recovery. The enemy without had either been kept at bay or, in the case of the Japanese, driven back, but the price of keeping external enemies at bay had been to strengthen pressures for change within the empire.

INTERNAL PRESSURES ON THE EMPIRE

The British empire was eventually to break up into a series of independent nation states, as the British lost the will and the capacity to contain the claims to separate nationhood of their subjects. Was the loss of the will to empire on the part of the British more important in bringing the empire to an end than the strength of internal opposition to it? Put more crudely, were the British pushed out of empire by their former subjects or did they jump out of it voluntarily? It is difficult to offer any simple answer to such questions. Individual cases varied widely. In some instances the British commitment to maintaining their rule was weak, and their subjects had little difficulty in persuading them to leave. In other cases the British stood their ground and faced determined nationalist opposition. One overall trend is, however, clear: after 1945 the British will to preserve empire was rarely strong enough to induce them to fight a very prolonged military rearguard action. A weakening of the will to empire gave nationalists their opportunity, but they still had to show skill and resolution in taking it.

The Dominions
The process by which the British relinquished control over Canada, Australia, New Zealand, and South Africa was already far advanced by 1918. Grants of

responsible government at various times meant that all four had become internally self-governing. Certain powers were retained by the Crown, advised by British ministers and by the British Parliament, but these powers were virtually never used. What was a major limitation on their status was their lack of any international standing. Dominions in 1914 did not have foreign relations of their own. For international purposes they were subordinate to Britain, which negotiated treaties on their behalf and committed them to war or peace.

By 1918 these territories with their mixed populations, including Afrikaners and French Canadians, had developed a sense of national identity. The experience of war, in which Canadians and Australians, for instance, had taken the predominant part in certain famous engagements, as at Gallipoli or Vimy Ridge, had been a powerful stimulus to national integration and national sentiment. This sentiment was not necessarily anti-British. As a Canadian historian put it in 1915: 'It never occurred to the average Canadian, even when his country reached national stature, that he could not remain both a Canadian and a Briton.' Nor was Dominion nationalism necessarily anti-imperial. Membership of the empire or of the Commonwealth gave individual Dominions a role in the world which they could not hope to play on their own. But they still insisted on clear recognition by Britain of their autonomy within an imperial or a Commonwealth framework.

Britain had little difficulty in conceding this recognition. In a series of changes, of which the most important were the Balfour Declaration of 1926 and the Statute of Westminster of 1931, Britain's formal powers over the internal affairs of the Dominions were eliminated and the Dominions gained what amounted to full

The winding up of the British colonial empire began shortly after the Second World War and continued into the 1980s. Both the major British political parties, Labour and Conservative, were fully involved in it. Labour were in power in the first wave of decolonization – which included India, Pakistan, Palestine, and Burma – in the late 1940s. The next wave in the late 1950s and early 1960s – involving, among others, Ghana, Nigeria, Kenya, and Zambia in Africa, as well as Malaya, Jamaica, and Trinidad – was the work of Conservative governments.

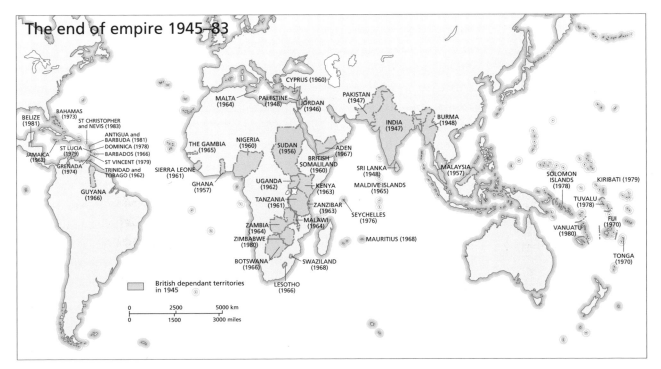

The end of empire 1945–83

CYPRUS (1960)
MALTA (1964)
PALESTINE (1948)
JORDAN (1946)
PAKISTAN (1947)
BELIZE (1981)
BAHAMAS (1973)
ST CHRISTOPHER and NEVIS (1983)
ANTIGUA and BARBUDA (1981)
DOMINICA (1978)
BARBADOS (1966)
ST VINCENT (1979)
ST LUCIA (1979)
JAMAICA (1962)
GRENADA (1974)
TRINIDAD and TOBAGO (1962)
THE GAMBIA (1965)
NIGERIA (1960)
SUDAN (1956)
ADEN (1967)
BRITISH SOMALILAND (1960)
INDIA (1947)
BURMA (1948)
SRI LANKA (1948)
MALAYSIA (1957)
SIERRA LEONE (1961)
GHANA (1957)
UGANDA (1962)
KENYA (1963)
MALDIVE ISLANDS (1965)
SOLOMON ISLANDS (1978)
KIRIBATI (1979)
TANZANIA (1961)
ZANZIBAR (1963)
SEYCHELLES (1976)
TUVALU (1978)
ZAMBIA (1964)
MALAWI (1964)
FIJI (1970)
VANUATU (1980)
ZIMBABWE (1980)
MAURITIUS (1968)
BOTSWANA (1966)
SWAZILAND (1968)
TONGA (1970)
LESOTHO (1966)
GUYANA (1966)

British dependant territories in 1945

0   2500   5000 km
0   1500   3000 miles

recognition as states in their own right. In 1939 they declared war on their own authority. The story of Dominion relations with Britain is, however, more complex than questions of status in legal terms. The Commonwealth was not just an alliance of free and equal members. It reflected the Dominions' need for close association with Britain, particularly in the difficult economic conditions of the great recession of the 1920s and 1930s, which had a devastating effect on the economies of Australia, Canada, and New Zealand, and in the deteriorating international climate of the years before 1939. The dominance of Germany and Japan that would follow the defeat of Britain was seen as a dire threat to all the Dominions. There was little alternative to supporting Britain in war.

The war and its aftermath revealed the limitations of what Britain could do for what it was now becoming anachronistic to call the Dominions. Britain had not purported to be able to defend Canada for a long time and it showed in 1942 that it could not defend Australia either. Canada never joined the sterling area and the rest disengaged from it. Britain remained central to the economic welfare of New Zealand, but others coped with the dislocations of Britain's eventual entry into the European Economic Community with less difficulty. While the alliance of interests was being whittled away, the ethnic composition of populations was becoming less British from the 1970s, as Australia and Canada in particular drew on new sources of immigrants from all over Europe and from Asia. Nationalist sentiment, even for Afrikaners, might still not be markedly anti-British, but links with Britain now had a diminished relevance. There was a progressive weakening on both sides of the will to maintain at any high level what had originated as an imperial connection.

India

Relations between Britain and the old Dominions underwent a long period of gradual adjustment, as both sides came to appreciate that they neither needed nor desired a very close association. The issues in British–Indian relations were much starker. Britain's will to empire in India remained very strong until the Second World War but in 1918 it was already under intense pressure from an extremely vigorous nationalist movement, which was to grow even stronger in the years ahead.

Even before the outbreak of the First World War, Indian nationalism had ceased to be a movement with a limited following and limited aims. The Indian National Congress was committed to self-government for India from 1906. It supported the war in 1914, but during the war restated its insistence on home rule as soon as possible. To secure maximum public support for the war, the British government wanted to avoid open confrontation with India. Ambiguous promises of future constitutional progress were therefore made.

Congress was also moving towards becoming a mass movement. The creation of a unified political movement in a society as diverse as India was an extremely difficult task, but Congress was becoming the focus through which different

Amritsar, 1919. The first of Gandhi's great campaigns to redress grievances by non-violent means took place in 1919. Violence, however, broke out in the city of Amritsar in the Punjab, involving the killing of some Europeans and the beating up of a female doctor called Marcia Sherwood. Counter measures of a most ruthless kind were taken by the British commander, General Dyer. An illegal meeting was broken up by indiscriminate shooting, which led to many deaths, and an order was issued that any Indian using the lane where Dr Sherwood had been attacked must, as this picture shows, crawl along it.

communities could articulate their specific grievances against the British. With the ending of the war a new leader emerged, one who was capable both of extending Indian nationalism's popular following and of fusing diverse demands and programmes into some kind of unity.

The new leader was Gandhi (see page 180). Even if there had been no Gandhi, the British government of India would have faced a wave of turbulence in postwar India; what he did was to give discontent a degree of central direction. In response to Gandhi's demands that specifically named grievances be remedied, people all over India were asked to take non-violent action – through strikes, protest marches, and refusing co-operation with the government. The government did not make concessions and violence took place, especially in the Punjab where General Dyer, the local military commander, ordered shooting in Amritsar, leading to 380 deaths. The mobilization of masses of Indians to support Gandhi's first wave of campaigns, lasting from 1919 to 1922, had been extremely impressive. There could be no doubt that Indian nationalism had become a popular force.

The British strategy for containing nationalism was devised before Gandhi launched his challenge. Indian opinion was to be encouraged to work with the British regime rather than to oppose it. This would involve transferring certain functions of government to elected Indians. Indians should be permitted to take responsibility for many domestic matters. Whatever may have been said later, transferring authority in certain areas to Indians was not regarded at the time as an education for independence. That was not on any agenda for the foreseeable future. What was intended was a kind of partnership: the British would maintain control over the issues of crucial importance to them, especially foreign policy, the army, and security, while many other matters would be transferred to representatives of Indian opinion, who, it was hoped, would work 'responsibly' for the good of India, as the British interpreted it. The first instalment of this policy was launched in an act of 1919. Under further nationalist pressure, in 1929 the British made a more explicit declaration of their intentions. India would attain 'Dominion status' at some time in the future – that is, it would acquire the status already enjoyed by Canada and Australia. The other major Indian reform act, that of 1935, offered India something still short of that status. The provinces were to become almost completely self-governing and areas of responsibility began to be demarcated for Indian ministers at the centre. Essential British interests, however, still remained under the direct authority of the Viceroy. After much debate, Congress leaders agreed to work within the framework of the act and Congress formed the government within a majority of provinces. The 1935 act was as far as Britain intended to go for a long time to come. On the eve of war in 1939, most British policy makers assumed that a fully effective British presence in India would last for another twenty or thirty years.

War shattered such expectations. The British committed India to war without formal Indian consent and the Congress ministries refused to stay in office under

Muhammad Ali Jinnah, 1946. Although Jinnah was the founder of Pakistan, for much of his life he campaigned for an independent India rather than for a separate Islamic state of Pakistan. Jinnah only accepted the partition of India in 1947, after many attempts to win from the British and the Indian National Congress guarantees of what he regarded as proper rights for Muslims in a united India.

those terms. In 1942 the Cripps mission offered participation by Indian politicians in the central direction of the war together with the prospect of independence after the war. Believing that the Japanese would win the war anyway, Congress rejected the terms and went into open opposition, including a major rebellion in northern India. For the rest of the war Congress, and with it the main body of Indian nationalism, was successfully repressed by British authority. The Raj was still intact. India made a very large contribution to the allied war effort.

Members of Congress were not, however, the only nationalists in the field. The Muslim League, headed by Muhammad Ali Jinnah, claimed to speak for the quarter of the population who were Muslim. Until the outbreak of war the League's programme was similar to that of Congress, but with safeguards for Muslim rights and interests. In 1940 the Muslim League put forward a rather imprecise claim for a separate Muslim state in any independent India. During the war the League was able to strengthen its hold on Muslim opinion. It seemed clear to the British that any postwar settlement must now have the acceptance of the League as well as Congress.

Such a settlement had to be pursued with urgency as soon as the war ended. The British had been able to survive the 1942 rebellion, but with an army, police, and administration that was now Indianized to a high level, there seemed to be no chance of their surviving another rebellion. Even if there were not to be a revolt, the conflicting claims of the Muslim League and Congress about the future were leading to communal violence in which Hindus and Muslims were killing one another. There was every prospect that this violence would spread widely. India was becoming ungovernable and there was no vital British interest left in continuing to try to govern it.

British viceroys and the British government therefore initiated round after round of negotiations with the Indian politicians. While Jinnah dominated the League and demanded partition, Jawaharlal Nehru led the Congress attempts to preserve a united India. The British hoped to be able to satisfy Muslims short of an actual partition and to retain some link with a future India, if possible involving a continuing connection with the Indian army. Such terms could not be obtained. The Labour government under Attlee insisted that a settlement must be reached within a time limit. It appointed as the last Viceroy, Lord Louis Mountbatten, a kinsman of the royal family and distinguished wartime commander. Mountbatten was permitted to make the best terms he could: India was partitioned, but both the new states that came into existence in August 1947, as India and Pakistan, remained within the Commonwealth.

Until well into the Second World War Britain had assumed that India would remain linked to Britain, at least for foreign policy and defence. To preserve that link, it had made concessions. Those concessions had of course been forced out of it by nationalist pressure, but, down to 1939, nationalism had been more or less contained. War created the conditions under which nationalism could not be

Black and white in Central Africa 1953–80

At the end of the nineteenth century, mainly through the personal ambitions of Cecil Rhodes, Britain had acquired a large territorial domain in Central Africa. This territory was divided into three separate colonies: Northern and Southern Rhodesia and Nyasaland. European settlers had moved into Southern Rhodesia in considerable numbers, dispossessing Africans of land and engaging in farming and mining. Fewer whites were permanently settled in Northern Rhodesia, but the colony had become one of the world's main copper producers. Nyasaland had a large and generally poor African population. In Southern Rhodesia the white population had been able to take political power and to win what was effectively internal self-government for themselves in 1923. Northern Rhodesia and Nyasaland were under the authority of the Colonial Office and were administered by British officials.

In planning for the future after the Second World War, a union of the three territories had considerable attractions for British policy makers. There were fears that the whites of Northern and Southern Rhodesia might throw in their lot with South Africa, where an Afrikaner-dominated Nationalist government had been elected in 1948. A stable political regime was needed for the copper mines. It was also hoped that the wealth of Southern Rhodesia could be used to develop Northern Rhodesia and especially Nyasaland. Behind proposals for a federation was an underlying idealism that whites and blacks would be able to work together in 'partnership', a very fashionable concept for Africa in the 1950s.

A Central African Federation was created in 1953 in the face of opposition by Africans in Northern Rhodesia and Nyasaland, who feared that partnership would mean white domination. In the years after 1953 the extent of opposition became unmistakable, as a powerful African leadership emerged under Kenneth Kaunda in Northern Rhodesia and Hastings Banda in Nyasaland. In 1959 there was a crisis in Nyasaland. Rising African protests were crushed and Banda was put into detention. If the federation could only be maintained by repression, the government of Harold Macmillan began to doubt whether it should be maintained at all. It was decided to let the Africans of Nyasaland and Northern Rhodesia go their own way. They inevitably chose independence, which was granted to them in 1964, as Malawi and Zambia respectively.

This left the future of Southern Rhodesia to be decided. Its white population asked for independence as well. The British government replied that independence would only be granted after the existing constitution had been amended to give Africans greater representation in the Rhodesian Parliament. This was unacceptable to the white politicians of the Rhodesian Front, who decided to take independence for themselves through their Unilateral Declaration of Independence in 1965. The British Labour government of Harold Wilson declined to meet the white rebellion with force. Sanctions were imposed against the new Rhodesia; meanwhile periodic negotiations took place between the British and the Rhodesian Prime Minister, Ian Smith. White Rhodesia was eventually brought down not so much by international sanctions as by the guerrilla war launched in the 1970s by black Rhodesians operating out of neighbouring African countries. The Smith regime finally conceded the principle of majority rule and power passed to an African government, which established the new republic of Zimbabwe in 1980.

The end of the Central African Federation. Africans in Blantyre, Nyasaland (soon to be Malawi), celebrate the end of the Federation on 1 January 1964 with a mock-funeral at which the oration was to be delivered by Hastings Banda, Malawi's first Prime Minister.

contained any longer. Indian independence took the centrepiece out of the British empire. But it by no means followed that independence would automatically be granted to other colonies. Political change in Africa, in particular, followed its own momentum.

Africa

British contact with the West African coast went back to slave-trading days. At some points of prolonged contact, such as Freetown in Sierra Leone or Lagos and Accra, sophisticated African commercial communities grew up, whose members were usually Christians and fully literate, often in English. By the end of the nineteenth century such people were being entrusted by the British with some responsibility for the government of small coastal enclaves. But when the British suddenly extended their rule inland over huge territories as part of the European partition of Africa, authority in the new order tended to be delegated to what were regarded as traditional African leaders – chiefs or other dignitaries. In parts of East and Central Africa European settlement was encouraged and the settlers inevitably claimed political rights for themselves.

Thus by 1918 two rough models of African colonies had emerged: colonies under 'traditional' local rulers, often described as being colonies under indirect rule, and colonies of white settlement with some European representation on councils as well as a structure of administration by British officials. Emirs or chiefs wielded authority over most of West Africa, as did their equivalents in Uganda, Tanganyika (Tanzania), Nyasaland (Malawi), and parts of Northern Rhodesia (Zambia). European settlers were gaining control of Southern Rhodesia (Zimbabwe) and were trying to do the same in Kenya. In neither type of colony was there much scope for anything that could be called African nationalism.

From the 1920s, however, opinion in the coastal regions of West Africa began to protest against the lack of political rights for the mass of the people. In Kenya the power of settlers was at first contested by Indian immigrants rather than by Africans. Significant political changes in colonial Africa did not, however, occur until the end of the Second World War. By then indirect rule and the authority of chiefs were beginning to look somewhat outmoded. The war had created many new opportunities for Africans to gain experience overseas (both West African and East African divisions had fought in Burma) or to acquire new jobs at home. Some had been enriched, while others felt cheated by government price-fixing on crops such as cocoa, which prevented them from getting the benefit of high wartime prices.

After the war the British government at first proposed to move slowly by providing opportunities for a wider range of Africans to get involved in local affairs. A mixture of the idealism of some Labour politicians and what appeared to be pressing problems in individual colonies pushed forward change at rather greater speed. What seemed to be a serious challenge to the colonial regime emerged in riots in Accra in the Gold Coast in 1948. Concerned to head off further disorder,

Hong Kong - Britain`s Chinese city-state

Hong Kong came to Britain as part of the spoils of the Opium War, which began in 1839 when the Chinese seized opium at the port of Canton. Britain took advantage of the war greatly to improve its commercial access to China. Certain Chinese ports, later called treaty ports, were to be opened to international trade and a thinly inhabited island, called Hong Kong, was ceded to Britain. In 1860, after another bout of war with China, Britain took territory opposite the island. In 1898 a much large area of the mainland, called the New Territories, was granted to Britain until 1997 under a ninety-nine-year lease. This brought the land under British control to approximately 400 square miles.

Trade dominated the life of Hong Kong until the mid-twentieth century. In the colony`s early years, opium was the major item of its trade. Hong Kong also became an important staging post for exports from Britain to China. The most famous of all British companies trading to China, Jardine Matheson, operated from Hong Kong from the very beginnings of British rule and the great Hong Kong and Shanghai Bank was founded in 1864. Chinese merchants did business both on their own as as compradors - agents or brokers - for the European businesses. The commercial success of Hong Kong attracted increasing numbers of immigrants from China as labourers, artisans, shopkeepers, and clerks and its population grew from 15,000 in 1841 to 1.7 million in 1941.

In 1941 Hong Kong was seized by the Japanese and subjected to a rigorous occupation until 1945. After the war, however, Hong Kong recovered remarkably quickly and was transformed by waves of new immigrants fleeing from the new Communist regime in China. Its economic progress was spectacular: it became a great exporter of manufactured goods and developed into a major financial centre.

Throughout the colony`s history its government remained under tight British control, with British officials retaining ultimate authority although they consulted the leaders of the Chinese community. In 1984 the British agreed to transfer authority in 1997, at the end of the lease on the New Territories, not to the elected representatives of the six million people of the colony - as in virtually every other case of decolonization - but to the government of the People`s Republic of China.

Hong Kong, 1848. When the British annexed it in 1842, the island of Hong Kong had a largely rural population of some 5,000 people. Within a few years, as this picture shows, it had become a flourishing port with government buildings and the houses of the British merchants. Large numbers of Chinese people had also begun to move in from the mainland.

the British government accepted that constitutional change should be rapid. The beneficiary of this was Kwame Nkrumah, leader of a powerful nationalist party that was capable of winning elections over most of the country. With active encouragement from the British, Nkrumah took the Gold Coast to independence as Ghana in 1957. Other West African colonies followed with little difficulty. They met most of what were thought to be the conditions for sustaining independence: their economies were quite well developed, education was widely diffused, and there were no significant European minorities to be considered.

The colonies of East and Central Africa posed difficult problems. Europeans were entrenched in Southern Rhodesia and Kenya and many of the other colonies were extremely poor. Yet stirrings of African nationalism were evident in both areas. In Central Africa the British government brought Northern Rhodesia and Nyasaland into a federation with Southern Rhodesia in 1953. This Central African Federation was intended to block any tendency by South Africa to absorb the white populations of the Rhodesias and to divert some of the wealth of Southern Rhodesia into the development of the other two much poorer colonies. Within a few years African opinion was rejecting what it saw as the dominance of the Southern Rhodesian whites and calling for an end to the federation. In Kenya the Mau Mau insurrection of the early 1950s showed the vulnerability of a regime based on settler privilege and administration by officials. Since the interests of white populations were involved, any decision to yield to African pressure would be politically a difficult one. Yet such decisions were taken in the early 1960s by the Conservative government headed by Harold Macmillan. The Central African Federation was

The Mau Mau rebellion in Kenya: a woman accompanied by a female British police officer searches among suspects for her husband's murderer. The Mau Mau movement in Kenya was largely confined to the Kikuyu people, who suffered from an acute shortage of land and from unemployment and poor conditions in the towns. The government declared an emergency in 1952. From then until 1956, when the revolt fizzled out, 11,000 rebels were killed and 81,000 people were detained. As with the episode depicted here, most of the victims of Mau Mau violence were other Kikuyu.

broken up and Northern Rhodesia became the new African state of Zambia, while Nyasaland became Malawi. Kenya was given independence under the rule of an African government.

Some colonial problems still remained outstanding. Southern Rhodesia was the most obvious one and African rule was not established there until 1980. Problems of the Falkland Islands and of Hong Kong remained after that. Yet the wave of independent states created during the Macmillan government marked the effective end of the British colonial empire. Macmillan's motives have been the subject of much debate. Had the will to empire died completely in him and been replaced by hard calculations that colonial territories would only cost money and trouble and that the decks must in any case be cleared for Britain's entry into Europe? Current assessments are generally that there was no master plan to liquidate the last of the African empire. Each case was looked at on its merits, but in the climate of the 1960s each case had very little merit. Britain was no longer interested in sustaining settlers or ruling very poor African communities. The will to empire had evaporated on the British side, but the African nationalists had played their part. They could not defeat the British, but they could make trouble and almost any trouble was too much for the British empire of the 1960s.

END OF EMPIRE

The British empire came to an effective end in the 1960s. Historian's hindsight reveals a pattern of decline stretching far back in time, to the First World War or earlier. In retrospect, Britain's military and economic capacity were less and less capable of sustaining a vast world-wide empire, nor was it in Britain's own best interest to try to do so. Instead of over-extending its resources in a commitment to an empire that could not solve its problems anyway, Britain had no real alternative to coming to terms with its diminished status and seeking closer connections with the United States or Europe. Even if Britain did not heed the promptings of its own interests, nationalist pressure within the empire would eventually force it to do so. What happened after the Second World War was only the last act in a drama whose outcome had been clear for a long time.

That is not, however, a version of events that British people at the time would have recognized. They continued to believe in empire. It was what gave Britain a unique role in the world, and in return Britain had drawn strength from its empire to enable it to survive two great wars that had wrecked so many of its competitors. Imperial management in the twentieth century was fraught with many potential difficulties and dangers, but there was nothing new about that. British statecraft could weather the storms by skilful adjustment and compromise, as it had done in the nineteenth century. Only when the cards were impossibly stacked against it after the Second World War did Britain seek to make its exit, as gracefully as possible, from its imperial commitments. Such a version of events is not entirely based on hubris. The British empire had remarkable qualities of endurance.

The Life of the Empire

PART II

F. Dadd

CHAPTER 5

David Fieldhouse

For Richer, for Poorer?

There are two conflicting interpretations of empire – as a mutual self-help association or as an engine to enable capitalism to maximize the exploitation of colonies. These lie at the heart of the modern debate about the economic legacy of the empire: did it create 'development' or 'underdevelopment'? Imperialists argue that empire helped the development of colonies in whatever form best suited their own needs. Anti-imperialists claim that empire 'underdeveloped' colonies – that alien capitalism not only prevented development, but actually cauterized the innate capacity of third-world countries to develop at all, leaving them in a worse condition than they had been before western powers incorporated them into the evolving world economy. The following quotations encapsulate the debate.

> All the countries named as 'underdeveloped' in the world are exploited by others; and the underdevelopment with which the world is now pre-occupied is a product of capitalist, imperialist and colonialist exploitation. African and Asian societies were developing independently until they were taken over directly or indirectly by the capitalist powers. When that happened exploitation increased and the export of surplus ensued, depriving the societies of the benefit of their natural resources.

> In fact, colonial empire in Africa was one of the most efficacious engines of cultural diffusion in world history. Imperial rule involved a vast transfer of human and physical capital to Africa. Much of Africa benefited not merely from enormous private and public investments in brick and mortar, but also from a great transfer of human abilities to Africa. The efforts made by privately subsidized mission societies and similar organizations alone form an outstanding chapter in the history of civilization … The Western powers brought a host of new economic, medical, social, and administrative techniques to Africa; these in turn have played a decisive role in the history of the continent.

Which of these two contrasting views is borne out by the facts of the British empire?

HOW THE EMPIRE WORKED

The British imperial system worked in very different ways during the period covered by this book. The economic management of the empire can, however, be divided into three main phases.

The end of mercantilism (1800–1850)

At the end of the eighteenth century the British imperial economy was still run much as it had been since the Navigation Acts were passed in the seventeenth century. All trade between Britain and the colonies had to be carried in ships owned

Ships loading timber at a Canadian port. The timber industry of British North America was a conspicuous example of one that flourished under mercantilist policies of imperial self-sufficiency. Russia and other countries round the Baltic were Britain's traditional suppliers of imported timber. But after Napoleon had tried to blockade the Baltic in 1807, Britain encouraged colonial supplies by putting a heavy duty on all other imported timber. In spite of having to be floated down rivers for up to 600 miles before being loaded at the ports for the long Atlantic voyage, British North American timber won a large share of the British market until the duties on foreign timber were drastically reduced in 1846.

and manned by Britain or the colonies. No foreign vessel might enter a colonial harbour. All colonial imports and exports (with a few specified exemptions) had to come from or go to a British port in the first instance, even if they came from or were destined for a European country. In addition, lower duties were paid on British goods than on foreign goods on entry to a colony, and some colonial exports had a similar tariff preference on entry to Britain.

This system was based on two widely held assumptions. The first assumption was that no European country held any significant technical advantages over another and thus the only way to achieve technical and therefore political superiority was through the possession of exclusive colonial markets and sources of raw materials. The second assumption was that the total of the world's trade and wealth was finite: if one country became richer, it must be at the expense of a rival.

By the early nineteenth century both these assumptions were weakening. The beginning of the industrial revolution in Britain showed that people's productive powers were greater than had been supposed and that one country could gain an advantage by superior industrial or even agricultural efficiency. Meanwhile Adam Smith, in his influential book *The Wealth of Nations*, had argued that in most circumstances wealth was indefinitely expandable.

In response to this new thinking, British policy changed from the early 1820s. The British now wanted a world market for their exports and were prepared to open their own and colonial markets to foreign countries in return. They did this at first on a reciprocal basis, later without conditions. Moreover, after 1846 they ended preferential duties in Britain and the colonies.

The era of free trade (1850–1932)

By the 1850s Britain had a free-trading empire, though already self-governing colonies such as Canada were beginning to protect some of their new industries against all imports, including those from an outraged Britain. This sense of outrage, accentuated by the refusal of Canada to take what the British regarded as a fair share in the costs of its own defence, was characteristically expressed by *The Times* in June 1862.

> Opinion in England is perfectly decided that in the connexion between the Mother Country and the Colony the advantage is infinitely more on the side of the child than of the parent ... We cannot even obtain ... reasonably fair treatment for our manufactures, which are taxed 25 per cent on their value to increase a revenue which the colonies will not apply to our or even to their defence. There is little reciprocity in such a relation.

Up to 1932 (apart from the First World War) Britain and its dependent empire remained rigorously free-trading. Theoretically it made no economic difference to a colony that it was part of an empire. Enthusiasts for free trade argued that under this system there could be no exploitation. Increased specialization in export crops was to the advantage of the peasant as well as to the British consumer.

Nevertheless it is significant that, even under free trade, Britain retained a disproportionately large share of the trade and investment in its own colonies. This

Australian wool drays, *c*.1900. Because of its quality, relative cheapness, and the huge quantities produced, Australian wool was able to flourish in an age of free trade. It did not need special protection to become Britain's main supplier and, by the time when these wagons were taking their wool to the railhead, to win markets all over the world.

Money – an imperial tool?

Until the early 1900s there were almost as many local currencies as there were territories within the British empire: Britain and the non-American self-governing colonies used sterling, based on gold; India, Ceylon (Sri Lanka), British East Africa, and other Indian Ocean territories used silver rupees; Malaya had silver dollars; African territories had a mixture of traditional exchange devices, such as bronze manillas and cowrie shells. Such variety proved inconvenient for imperial trade, especially since the sterling/gold value of silver coins varied with the price of silver. This meant that businessmen in British colonies could never predict precisely what return they might receive for exports or how much they would have to pay for imports. Starting with West Africa from 1912, East Africa in 1920, and ending with India in 1927, the British therefore established the sterling exchange standard. All colonial currencies were tied to the current value of sterling at fixed rates, though by different means. African colonies had local currencies in British denominations, exchangeable at face value. The rupee and dollar colonies retained their coinage but

their value was now fixed in relation to the pound. This system survived until independence. It certainly facilitated commerce, but some colonial interests thought it worked to their disadvantage. In West Africa there were complaints that the Currency Board insistence on 100 per cent cover for colonial currencies (in gold or securities) in London had a deflationary effect; Indian businessmen maintained that the rate at which the rupee was tied to sterling was too high for Indian exports to be competitive internationally, especially with Japan. At independence all British ex-colonies adopted their own currencies, by contrast with most ex-French colonies, which continued to tie their local francs to the French franc.

'Schroffs' or money-changers testing silver dollars, Canton, 1873. Trade with nineteenth-century China was hampered by a complex currency system that used both copper and silver.

was due largely to the way trade was organized. Colonial governments automatically bought official imports (including the very expensive railway equipment) from Britain because it was simpler to do so and because they felt it to be their duty. Trading firms dealt mainly with Britain. Furthermore, the use of a common language and a common or tied imperial currency greatly strengthened this two-way trading connection.

A return to protectionism (1932–1960s)

With the Ottawa conference of 1932 the emphasis swung firmly back to protectionism. Under pressure from the Dominions, as they were now called, to provide them with preferential markets for their temperate food exports in return for preference on British exports and in response also to demands from hard-pressed British manufacturers and farmers, Britain at last dropped free trade. A general tariff was adopted in Britain, potentially (though in fact food and raw materials were exempt) covering all imports. Imports from the empire were given preference (reduced rates of duty) or quotas (a guaranteed share of British markets for certain of their products). The Dominions agreed willingly – they were able to increase their sales in British markets. The dependencies, which had no choice, were compelled to give British imports preference over foreign goods: only the Gold Coast (Ghana) and Nigeria, which were covered by international treaties, did not do so. This was one-sided: apart from sugar, tobacco, and one or two other commodities, colonial exports to Britain gained no advantage, since there were no duties on imports of such things to Britain. From 1934, moreover, Britain imposed limits on the import by the colonies of certain goods (notably cotton textiles) from foreign countries. This was primarily aimed against Japan, whose devaluation of the yen made its goods much cheaper than those of embattled British manufacturers. Inevitably, colonial consumers, forced to buy the more expensive British goods, paid more for their purchases, but there was a significant increase in the proportion of trade carried on within the empire. Between 1930 and 1950 British imports from the empire rose from 26 per cent to 44 per cent and British exports to the empire rose from 40 per cent to 52 per cent.

These changes undoubtedly shifted the balance of advantage against many (though not all) of the non-self-governing colonies, and worse was to follow from 1939. During the Second World War the British Ministry of Food imposed bulk-buying contracts on most commodities exported by the colonies. This meant that a colony had to sell its entire crop to Britain for a fixed price and prices were set deliberately low to minimize the cost to Britain. Moreover, the colonies' earning from this trade were partly frozen in credit accounts in London because Britain could not provide the goods that the colonies wanted to buy with this money. This system continued into the early 1950s, until Britain at last honoured its obligations and slowly unfroze the accounts. In these ways the British imperial economy became more exploitative of the colonies during the two decades after 1932 than at any previous time; and the effects of rationing imports by the colonies – which generated shortages, particularly of consumer goods such as textiles, and therefore inflation – became a potent political factor, particularly in West Africa, between 1945 and the early 1950s.

The imperial economy in this form was wound down in the early 1950s and disappeared with colonial independence. Imperial preferences had gradually lost their force after 1948, since the British commitment under the General Agreement on Trade and Tariffs (GATT) was to run down existing preferences and controls and not to introduce new ones. The newly independent countries of the Commonwealth showed no enthusiasm for retaining special economic relationships with Britain and all that was left of the mechanisms of the old imperial economy were those resulting from established contacts, language, and business organizations. Britain was left on its own with no special partners. This led naturally to Britain's first attempts in the 1960s, and its eventually successful application in 1973, to join the European Economic Community.

THE INFRASTRUCTURE OF EMPIRE

In order to perform their allotted imperial functions as providers of raw material and buyers of British exports, the colonies needed an adequate infrastructure. Initially this was lacking. Except possibly for India, the colonies did not possess fleets of ocean-going ships to carry long-distance trades. They lacked deep-water harbours and port facilities to handle the increasingly large cargo ships of the steam era. Their internal communications were generally very poor. Except where there were navigable rivers (in northern India, The Gambia, the lower Niger region, and the St Lawrence) inland transport was by human porter, pack animal, or bullock cart. Given the huge distances usually involved, a large-scale import/export trade could only develop in places with no useful river by building railways and, once lorries were available, all-weather roads.

To create such communication systems was beyond the scope of small, struggling, and fragmented pre-colonial states, and also of early white settler communities. The great indigenous rulers of India and Ceylon (Sri Lanka) had once built and maintained road, river, and canal systems, but these were decayed by the time the British took over these countries. Thus imperial rule, by unifying large regions politically, made it possible to construct modern communications to link the interior with the coastal ports. Britain, moreover, could provide both the capital and the technology these systems required.

Ships and shipping

The British empire was a maritime one – communications were its life-blood. Until the early nineteenth century distance was an enemy both of trade and control. In that era of relatively primitive sailing ships it took even the large East India Company ships perhaps six months to sail to Calcutta and, given monsoon

Passengers being lowered into surf boats at Sekondi, Gold Coast (Ghana), 1916. This photograph illustrates the difficulties encountered in developing trade on a large scale on coasts where port facilities were lacking. Along the Gold Coast people and goods had to negotiate a raging surf until a new harbour was built at Takoradi after the First World War.

conditions, some two years for a round voyage. The time factor, coupled with the limited cargo capacity of ships of this type, seriously affected British links with Asia, though less so with the Americas. Commercially it was not possible or profitable to carry large amounts of bulk commodities. Another problem in India was that the main artery into northern India was the Ganges: however, it was virtually impossible to sail against the current into the interior, so inland trade was extremely slow.

India presented the problem of distance in an acute form, but the same things inhibited British trade and communications with the Americas and West Africa. The British solved them during the mid-nineteenth century by developing both the steamship and the telegraph. By the end of that century no part of the empire was more than about six weeks' sail from Britain, and all colonies could be contacted by telegraph within seconds.

Between 1837 and 1843 the British built and operated the first true iron-hull, ocean-going ships, and in 1843 Isambard Brunel launched his *Great Britain*, then the largest ship ever built, which had a steel hull and a screw in place of the less efficient paddle wheels. But its steam engines were still relatively inefficient – in their early days, steamships consumed so much coal that they could carry very little other cargo. The development in Britain of the compound steam engine during the 1850s more than doubled the efficiency of the marine steam engine, enabling steamships to trade economically with the Far East. The opening of the Suez canal in 1869 and the development of the triple expansion steam engine in the 1870s completed the shipping revolution. At the same time sailing ships reached their highest state of efficiency, still able to compete for bulk cargoes such as grain when there was no time constraint. There was no part of the empire or the world whose bulkiest trades were uneconomic: it was now cost-effective to bring even the guano of the Pacific islands to help British farmers to compete with the North American prairie farmers.

The steamship was also critical for effective British development of inland regions. In India paddle steamers were operating on the Ganges by the early 1830s and remained important for Calcutta's trade until the railways took over in the 1850s. Steam was even more important for the penetration of West Africa. For centuries after Europeans had first investigated the coastlines of West Africa in the later fifteenth century, further activities had been impeded by disease and poor communications. The obvious way into the interior of West and Central Africa was via the Niger or the Congo. The Congo, however, was barred by the falls near its mouth, between the modern Kinshasa and Matadi – it was not until 1898 that a railway bypassing them made the Congo commercially viable. The Niger, apart from shifting bars, presented no such problems for steamships: Macgregor Laird successfully steamed up the Niger to its confluence with the Benue in 1833–34. But the death toll from malaria was so serious that it was not until the use of quinine as a prophylactic had been established in the early 1850s that the Niger could be used

The Suez canal

The advantage of a canal through the isthmus of Suez was obvious. Trade between Asia and Europe had two alternative routes: overland, via the Red Sea or the Persian Gulf; and the sea route via the Cape of Good Hope. The overland routes were expensive and involved splitting up bulk cargoes for carriage by, for example, pack animals such as camels. The Cape route was long and slow: London to Bombay was 10,667 sea miles via the Cape but would be only 6,274 sea miles via a canal. Once the Suez canal was opened, the sailing time was cut by a half.

The French were enthusiastic about building a canal – technically quite easy because no locks would be needed – from at least the end of the eighteenth century when Napoleon saw a canal as a means of taking the French fleet into the Indian Ocean and thus challenging British predominance there. The British were for long opposed for that very reason. The Egyptian khedives also were unenthusiastic until 1854 when the new ruler, Muhammad Said, gave a concession to the French engineer and Consul, Ferdinand de Lesseps. De Lesseps actively cultivated British interests, notably the shipping companies and those who traded with India, and the British government weakened. In 1859 de Lesseps founded the Compagnie Universelle du Canal Maritime de Suez, mostly subscribed to in France, though the Khedive was given 40 per cent of the shares in return for providing the human labour. The canal was eventually opened in 1869. In 1870 486 ships, whose total capacity was 436,609 tons, 66.25 per cent of it British, passed through the canal. By 1910 total tonnage had risen to 16,581,898, of which 62.86 per cent was British. Meanwhile, in 1875, the British Prime Minister, Benjamin Disraeli, had bought the bankrupt Khedive's shares in the company for £3.9 million as a flamboyant gesture to demonstrate his country's huge interest in the canal. In 1882 the British occupation of Egypt provided military insurance against hostile control of the canal, and its protection remained a major plank in British foreign policy until the Suez war of 1956.

French warships pass through the newly opened Suez canal.

as a serious trade artery. By the 1870s several British companies were sending steam trading vessels up the Niger; and the formation in 1879 of the United African Company by George Goldie Taubman (later known as Sir George Goldie) from four of these companies led to the foundation of the chartered Royal Niger Company in 1886, and so to effective British control of what became northern Nigeria.

Steam had thus conquered distance both across the oceans and up continental rivers: it was to do the same up the Irrawaddy in Burma and, beyond the limits of the formal British empire, into the interior of China and up the Mekong into South East Asia. The great age of steam (later the steam turbine and the diesel engine) as an imperial phenomenon lasted until more efficient alternatives replaced it.

Across the oceans steamships remained the main bulk carriers to the end of the twentieth century, though as a passenger carrier they were gradually ousted by the aeroplane, whose final victory came after 1950. Britain, in common with other European countries, quickly saw the importance of aviation for its empire. In 1924 Imperial Airways was set up (see page 119), with government subsidy, to provide links with the overseas empire. By 1937 its routes extended to Hong Kong and a route was planned to the Cape of Good Hope in South Africa.

Railways

Railways were the main agent of economic development in most parts of the British empire. Like the steamship, the steam railway was a British invention of the early nineteenth century. It also became one of the great British exports, carried round the world by railway entrepreneurs such as the great Thomas Brassey. After building lines in Britain and Europe, Brassey turned overseas. The Grand Trunk railway in Canada, 1,100 miles long, was partly his work. In the 1860s he had work in hand in Europe, India, Australia, and South America. Publicly owned railways were paid

Temporary bridge on the Haputale railway, Ceylon (Sri Lanka), 1893. Ceylon became a major exporter of tea in the late nineteenth century. The opening of new plantations depended on adequate communications to get the tea to the ports. That meant railways. This line ran to Uva, one of the prime tea areas.

for by governments, who commonly raised the money by selling bonds in London. Private lines were financed by companies, again usually London-based, who relied on an efficient railway for their profits. A hybrid combination of the two varieties was the privately built and run railway whose profits were guaranteed by the colonial government as a minimum percentage of their capital cost.

Railways were essential because they conquered distance and made it possible to develop bulk-commodity trades in the colonies. Without them it would have been uneconomic to open up the Canadian prairies, whose grain began to flood British markets from the 1890s. Railways made it possible to expand the Indian cotton- and jute-growing industries, linking the hinterland with the mills of Bombay and Calcutta, and carried rice and wheat to the ports for overseas markets. They were vital to the opening up of Australia, greatly reducing the cost of carrying wool and wheat. They were equally important in New Zealand; and in South Africa they were the key to expansion from the Cape into the interior.

Railways also had important political aspects. Some historians have even talked of 'railway imperialism', implying that the ability to finance and build railways gave the imperial power considerable control over even a self-governing colony such as Canada. In the colonies of settlement such as Canada, Australia, New Zealand, and South Africa, railways were the largest single investment of the age. They were also the greatest source of political patronage available to poverty-stricken colonial politicians. Borrowing in Britain for the construction of a railway, whether state or privately owned, caused money to flow into an economy, enabling politicians to provide employment and enrich their supporters with contracts or sub-contracts. Railways also increased the value of land that had previously been worthless because it was inaccessible. In short, railways were the key in these colonies of settlement to both economic and political success in the second half of the nineteenth century.

But, because both the technology and the capital for railways had to come from Britain, the colonies had to pay a price. This meant demonstrating both their loyalty and their economic stability. It might also mean accepting dictation from the imperial government. The classic case of this was Canada. Completing the Intercolonial railway and starting the Canadian Pacific railway – essential if Canada was to link east with west and keep out the United States – required British government guarantees on the capital. London in turn tried to use its ability to refuse such guarantees to induce the Canadian government to adopt desirable policies, notably on defence and, in the mid-1860s, to encourage the federation of the colonies into the Dominion of Canada. Although such imperial levers had limited effect, they certainly helped to tie Canada to Britain.

But it was in non-self-governing colonies such as India that railways played the most obviously 'imperial' role and proved most controversial. The difference stemmed from the fact that in the colonies of settlement railways were built because the self-governing colonists wanted them and were prepared to pay for them. In other colonies the inhabitants also paid, but had no choice: the imperial authorities determined what sort of railway system should be built and what purposes it should fulfil.

Construction of railways in India began in 1850 and was the result of combined pressure on a reluctant East India Company by a number of vested interests: railway entrepreneurs and engineers; the Lancashire cotton industry, which wanted an alternative source to the United States and required a finer quality of raw cotton than resulted from carriage of Indian cotton to the ports in bullock carts; the Pacific and Orient shipping line, which would benefit from additional cargoes; British idealists, who wanted to open up the heart of India to western ideas and religion; and bankers, who saw favourable profit opportunities.

India's railway system had a huge impact on the Indian economy. It generated an engineering industry that was to provide the basis for much of India's economic development and created for the first time something approaching an integrated economy. It also had a considerable influence on Indian society, making possible large-scale movement of people. Railways ironically also made possible an effective nationalist movement by enabling its leaders to move freely.

But the railways had a further major purpose and result: running as they did from the main ports through northern India, they made it possible, with a relatively small but now increasingly mobile army, to control half a continent. The first railways contributed to the suppression of the Indian Rebellion of 1857 by facilitating troop movements: thereafter the government pressed on much faster with their

Incline on the Uganda railway, *c*.1900. The purpose of this line was essentially political: to maintain a British presence in Uganda by linking it to the sea at Mombasa. This scene illustrates the complicated engineering skills so often required for colonial railways – in this case making an incline down the steep sides of the Kenya Rift Valley – as well as the huge deployment of labour needed. The work-force for this railway consisted of 32,000 labourers brought from India.

construction, partly at least for strategic reasons. Why otherwise build a narrow-gauge railway right up to the Khyber pass when there was almost no trade to Afghanistan?

India was not the only British colony in which railways were built at least partly for strategic reasons. The Mombasa–Uganda railway, started in the 1890s, was intended mainly to enable the British to forestall projected French attempts to claim the eastern Sudan. In order to make it pay, the British government eventually encouraged British settlement in what became known as the White Highlands of Kenya (the areas near Nairobi that were reserved for European settlers). The railway from the Cape through Bechuanaland (Botswana) was intended primarily to enable Cecil Rhodes, representing the British interest, to outflank the Afrikaner republic of the Transvaal and possibly the Germans in the rush into Central Africa: Rhodes intended his railway to continue along the spine of the mountain system, hoping that it would eventually reach the Nile, and so ensure British domination of all East–Central Africa. But the Cape to Cairo dream was blocked by German

Imperial Airways

The First World War had demonstrated the potential of powered flight in maintaining imperial communications, especially through the speedy delivery of mail. An Imperial Airways company was set up in 1924 with a government subsidy. The first regular service between London and India was established in 1929 with a weekly service to Cape Town in 1931 and a mail service to Australia from 1935.

Imperial Airways in Africa.

occupation of Tanganyika (Tanzania) and was never completed. The main lines in West Africa, built inland at right angles to the main ports, mostly had a double function: they linked the interior areas of commodity production with the sea but also made it possible to move troops rapidly to problem areas.

Roads were never a major imperial concern, mainly because steam preceded internal combustion; and colonial governments, with a large financial stake in the railways, stood to lose if goods moved from rail to road. It was only from the 1920s that colonial governments began to take road building seriously; and by the mid-twentieth century most British colonies in tropical Africa still had very limited all-weather road systems.

Rivers and canals

The British could claim to have been among the great improvers of rivers and builders of canals. Their first major overseas achievement was the improvement of the St Lawrence/Great Lakes seaway system in Canada. Work began in the later eighteenth century to give access to Lake Ontario. The canals were deepened after the union of the two Canadas in 1840 and again after the establishment of the federation in 1867. Simultaneously the Welland canal was built to overcome the height difference between Lakes Erie and Ontario. These were colonial responsibilities, but much of the finance was provided by Britain, along with technical expertise.

India was the greatest example of British canal building. The British were not, of course, pioneers. Earlier rulers had built many canals and water tanks; but by the later eighteenth century many of these had fallen into disrepair as political conditions became insecure. As the inheritors of Mughal power, the British had a moral obligation at least to repair existing works. Beyond that their main incentive was to avoid political problems by increasing food production and offsetting the effects of monsoon failure.

Serious work on canal reconstruction and building began soon after 1800, as the British Raj was consolidated, and continued throughout the British period. In the early years the East India Company repaired old canals; but from the later 1830s they, and the imperial government that replaced the company after 1858, began to develop new canals on a huge scale. Their greatest achievements were in the Punjab and northern India – using the seasonal flood waters of the Indus, Ganges, and their tributaries to irrigate vast areas of desert and land with insufficient or uncertain rainfall. By 1942 India's irrigated area had risen to fifty-seven million acres – of which thirty-two million was from government works, the rest from a large number of privately built wells, tanks, and channels.

This was a huge achievement; yet it was later criticized by the successor Indian and Pakistan governments as totally inadequate. Why was more not done? There were in fact three main constraints during the British period which did not apply in the post-colonial period.

The first was money. Apart from a short period in the 1850s and 1860s when private companies, rather than the state, undertook new canal building with very little success, the government always had great difficulty in financing construction. Since the British government of India was not allowed to raise loans for canals in London, costs had to be met from the limited budget of the Public Works Department. This restricted the amount of work; it also meant that canals has to pay their way from fees paid by the Indian cultivators who used the water they provided. Unless profit could be expected, a canal was unlikely to be built. It was only after independence that the Indian and Pakistan governments, free from such restrictions, were able to devote large sums to irrigation whose reward would be measured in increased food production rather than in fees received.

Building the Aswan dam, 1902–06. After their occupation of Egypt in 1882 the British applied many of the lessons learnt in Indian irrigation to the problems of the Nile. The Aswan dam created a resevoir in which summer flood water was stored and then released to enable peasant farmers to grow two or three crops a year.

The British empire not only changed people's lives; it changed the face of the land in which they lived. Until recently, most British people have believed that such changes were generally beneficial. Through them, it could be argued, the potential wealth of the tropics or of the temperate grasslands of North America and Australasia was realized for the first time. In the tropics, British people, British technology, and British capital made fruitful what had once been wilderness or lands that at best had been misused by African or Asian peasants. As a result, indigenous people were able to lead lives that were more healthy as well as being far more productive.

Many people now dispute this optimistic version. Before the coming of the British, it is claimed, non-European peoples lived in harmony with their environment. British intrusion destroyed this harmony, degrading both the lives of the people and the land off which they lived. Mass poverty, epidemics, and high death rates are seen as much more characteristic of the colonial period than new opportunities and longer life.

Simple versions of environmental change under British rule can be discounted. To suppose that people lived in happy harmony with nature before the coming of the Europeans may gratify the yearnings of contemporary western society, but probably has little historical foundation. Environmental changes produced by human agency and epidemics have occurred in all periods. Nevertheless, certain kinds of change certainly can be attributed to European dominance in general and to British colonial rule in particular. More land was brought under cultivation and lands previously cultivated were generally used more intensively. New crops were raised and new animals introduced. Methods of tilling the land changed greatly. The principles governing access to land also changed. To suggest that non-European peoples had no sense of private property until the British foisted it on them would be much too crude; but the British had little sympathy with concepts of collective ownership of land or of rights to the use of land that did not involve outright ownership. They believed that only secure property would be effectively developed and improved. Early British governors of New Zealand, for instance, encouraged Maoris to claim personal ownership of blocks of tribal lands which they could either sell to Europeans or cultivate intensively themselves. The general tendency in British colonial law was to establish unequivocal rights to property in land, vested in an individual owner.

The cumulative effect of such changes was to turn what were regarded as unproductive woodland, grazing land, or hunting land into clearly demarcated holdings, be they great estates, sizeable farms, or peasant plots. Thus the land might indeed be used more productively, able to support a much larger

Salination caused by canal irrigation in northern India. For all their beneficial effects in improving the supply of water, canals can also take land out of cultivation, as this photograph illustrates. The white patches show land made infertile by salts rising to the surface as a result of waterlogging caused by impeded drainage around the canal built in the 1930s.

population, as with newly irrigated lands in the Punjab, or to feed the urban masses in distant countries, as with the Canadian prairies. But there were obvious dangers of environmental deterioration being brought about by deforestation, overcropping of the land, or overstocking it with too many animals.

British colonial authorities were aware of these dangers. Concern began with the West Indies, where intensive sugar cultivation totally changed the face of islands like Barbados. By the middle of the nineteenth century the British government in India was taking steps to preserve forests that were rapidly disappearing in the face of the needs of cultivation and the demand for fuel and sleepers for the railways. In the 1930s anxiety began to be expressed about what were thought to be 'dustbowl' conditions in East and Central Africa. Measures such as terracing were later enforced to try to conserve the top soil. But however well-intentioned, regulations by colonial authorities to keep people out of forests or to try to compel them to farm differently were often very much resented and even resisted.   [PJM]

Above: Cutting railway sleepers in the Kashmir forests, 1907. The Indian railways' need for timber took a huge toll of India's forests.

Below: Deforestation in South Island, New Zealand. Serious soil erosion has been caused by sheep grazing and sluicing for mining.

The second main problem faced by the British was ignorance. In modern times no one in any part of the world had undertaken such vast irrigating operations, and there was no available body of technology. The British had therefore to gain experience by using rule of thumb. Most of those who surveyed and planned the canals, dams, and bridges were army officers with little or no specialist training, though some travelled extensively to learn how Italians and others tackled specific problems. But, although many expensive mistakes were made, it has been said that 'The fundamentals of hydraulic science and the practices of irrigation engineering came out of the great irrigation works of India itself.'

But the third and perhaps most surprising constraint on canal construction in India was that, in an age of steam power, it was done almost entirely by human and animal muscle. Slow though this made construction, there were good reasons for it. The basic technique of building dams and other works went back many centuries and had always relied on human effort. Since Indian labour was cheap – or free in cash terms if convict labour was used – most of the excavation was done by labourers using mattocks and the earth was carried in baskets by donkey or ox carts. After the conquest of the Punjab in 1849, work on the Upper Bari Doab canal was done mostly by former Sikh soldiers, who were rewarded with plots of irrigated land. It was not until the late 1920s that modern western building and transport methods were adopted, with the use of bulldozers, dump trucks, graders, and reinforced concrete. Thus the Indian canal system could technically have been built at almost any period of known history. What the British added was above all the power of a unified and authoritarian state, which acted because it saw the danger of drought and famine to its rule. Limited though it might be, irrigation in India was one of the greatest achievements of the British empire.

Infrastructure – rewards and costs

The British achievement was substantial but it invites two questions. Who were seen as the chief potential beneficiaries of these technological inputs – the imperial power and its citizens or the colonial subjects? And who paid the financial costs?

The first question has been much debated. Empire builders and rulers always maintained that facilities were provided mainly for the benefit of the peoples of the colonial territories. Conversely, nationalists usually alleged that they were built mainly for the benefit of the British as soldiers (needing strategic communications), exporters (wanting good access to inland markets), manufacturers (wanting cheap transport of raw materials to the ports), and expatriate owners of mines, plantations, and so on.

Such questions are extremely complex and can probably never be resolved. But on the second question – who paid for such amenities – there can be no possible doubt. At least until the Colonial Development Acts of 1929, 1940, and thereafter, which made limited loans and grants for development purposes, all investments in the colonial infrastructure were financed either by private investment – mostly by

British companies or individuals – or by public investment by the colonial government. If the former, profits were expected; and in the case of railways it was common for the colonial government to encourage the contractors by giving a guaranteed minimum rate of profit on their investment. In the case of public activities, the capital was usually raised by selling government bonds in the London money market; and the interest plus capital repayment had to be paid from colonial taxes. Either way, a colony only got the infrastructure it could afford to pay for, through charges for use of services such as water or railways or through taxation. Thus poor colonies got very few public services, while rich colonies (notably the colonies of settlement) did very much better.

But if it is impossible to determine who benefited most from the provision of infrastructure, of the achievement itself there can be no doubt. By the twentieth century all British colonies had at least the infrastructural facilities needed to link their economies with the empire and the wider world.

AGRICULTURE

Since Britain became a predominately industrial society during the nineteenth century, it expected its colonies to provide markets for its manufactures and to supply both food for a population that was then outgrowing the capacity of domestic agriculture and the raw materials its industries needed.

The relationship was not, however, as artificial as this statement suggests. In practice, at least initially, most colonial economies were naturally agricultural rather than industrial: the only significant exception was India, whose industries were nevertheless pre-capitalist and for long unable to compete with modern industrial products from Britain. Moreover, the main need of a primarily agricultural community was an assured overseas market. During the nineteenth and the first half of the twentieth century Britain was virtually the only country in the world that provided such a market, particularly for temperate foodstuffs and some industrial raw materials. Thus the imperial–colonial relationship was potentially productive for both parties, provided that there were no artificial constraints on either side.

There was, however, a fundamental difference between the types of agriculture found in the temperate colonies of settlement and the tropical dependencies, and within each there were major contrasts in methods of production.

Farming in the colonies of settlement

The British emigrants who went to the colonies of settlement aimed to construct as nearly the same lifestyle as they had, or would have liked to have, at home. The most important initial difference was that ample land was available at relatively very low prices. This meant that, provided other factors such as soil and rainfall were favourable, settlers could run large farms with little or no rent or mortgage to pay. Their two main problems in the early nineteenth century were to find products for which there was a profitable overseas sale and lack of internal communications. The second was solved gradually by the building of railways, the key to profitable farming, and improved land values. Markets were found by trial and error with different crops at different times.

In Canada exports depended for long on fish, timber, and beaver skins. It was only after the 1870s, when the Canadian Pacific railway was pushed westwards into the prairies, that wheat became the chief staple, along with beef from the far west and a variety of fruit products from the east. From then until the beginning of the world wheat boom in the 1950s, the British market was critical for the Canadian economy. Canada was the first colony to press for protection in Britain for colonial foodstuffs, summoning the Ottawa conference of 1894 and offering preferential import duties on British goods in return. The British refused then, and again in the early 1900s, to concede this; and it was not until the Ottawa conference of 1932 that they gave way. Canadian wheat and other farming products were then given a guaranteed import quota.

The typical farming unit of eastern and prairie Canada was the family farm, though to the west there were large cattle ranches. These farms were large by European standards. In the mid-twentieth century the average size of farms in the three main prairie provinces – Manitoba, Saskatchewan, and Alberta – was 420, 686, and 645 acres respectively. The combination of large acreages, a short growing season, and shortage of labour resulted in a high degree of mechanization. Indeed agricultural machinery was one of the earliest important Canadian industries to develop, mainly in Ontario.

Harvesting wheat in southern Alberta, *c.*1900. The Canadian prairies were brought under cultivation primarily to grow wheat for export, especially to Britain. The boom in the demand for wheat lasted from the late 1890s into the First World War. In 1901 six million acres of prairie land were under cultivation; in 1916 the total was thirty-four million acres.

In Australia distance from possible markets and the cost of sea transport was a major consideration until the development of larger steam and sailing vessels later in the nineteenth century. In its very early days New South Wales had great difficulty in finding any staple other than whale oil with which to pay for its imports. Wool proved the salvation of the Australian economy and largely conditioned land use. Allegedly introduced by John Macarthur early in the nineteenth century, the merino flocks throve on the arid pastures of the outback. Wool had three special virtues: it did not deteriorate during storage; its bulk, and therefore transport cost, were low in relation to its value; and the British and European woollen industry was growing very fast in this period, rapidly outstripping the supply from Spain and from Saxony in Germany. It is not too much to say that the Australian economy grew on the back of the sheep.

But sheep and limited rainfall combined to impose severe constraints on the type of settlement possible. Sheep required very large runs. Yet it was official policy in Australia from the early 1830s not to make large land grants and to charge a 'sufficient' price for all freehold land – the aim being to produce intensive rather

'Shearing the rams' by Tom Roberts. Shearing teams moved from farm to farm. A skilled man could shear 70 to 80 sheep a day; with the introduction of mechanical shears in the 1890s, he could expect to shear 120.

than dispersed settlement. Australian wool farmers got round this by the ingenious combination of 'squatting' and 'spotting' – getting short leases for large runs and buying the critical parts of their runs that provided water. Since it was then impossible for would-be small settlers to use the legislation passed in the 1850s to enable them to select freeholds, the large sheep-run, often bought outright when the profits from wool allowed, became the symbol of Australian pastoralism. By the second half of the century most squatters had bought their runs, fenced them, and built irrigation systems to reduce dependence on unpredictable rain. By 1891 wool exports were worth £117 million, over half the value of all exports, and by 1893 there were reckoned to be 106 million sheep in Australia.

Wool was not the only major Australian farming product. Wheat became an important export crop in the more fertile regions of New South Wales, Victoria, and South Australia and a wine industry was developed in South Australia. On the margins of grazing country there were huge cattle stations. Until the 1880s their products, apart from local consumption of beef, were chiefly tallow and hides. But with the development of refrigerated ships, frozen beef, mutton, and lamb became major exports, almost entirely to Britain. Another important crop, though it was grown mainly for domestic consumption, was sugar, produced in Queensland on the well-watered Pacific coastal strip.

New Zealand initially followed the Australian example. From the 1850s wool became the export staple, produced mostly in the South Island and the Hawkes Bay area of the North Island. But the development of refrigerated ships during the 1880s opened up new possibilities in those parts of the North Island that had a sub-tropical climate and ample rainfall: they could grow grass for eleven months in the year. This led to a rapid development of dairy farming, producing huge quantities of butter and cheese far more cheaply than was possible in Britain, whose farmers had to rely on hay or concentrates for half the year. Dairy produce along with lamb became the mainstay of the New Zealand export economy, earning it the reputation of being the farmland of Britain. This also meant, however, that when Britain joined the European Economic Community in 1973, New Zealand faced a very serious problem of finding markets for its produce and consequently it turned to Japan.

Agriculture in these three self-governing colonies had at least two things in common. Firstly, with the early exception of Queensland sugar (which depended on semi-servile Polynesian labour from the South Pacific islands until this was banned after 1900), all farming was done by the labour of Europeans. This meant farms were run by the whole family, with some itinerant labour particularly for sheep-shearing. Secondly, it was mainly the profits of farming (to which the relatively short gold booms merely added impetus) that paid for the huge investment in infrastructure – railways, roads, urban amenities, and housing. Each colony borrowed extensively in the London market, where interest rates were substantially below those available in the colonies, but none ever did so beyond its capacity to service the debt (though Australia and New Zealand each came near the edge in periods of low agricultural prices or natural disasters). In this sense these colonies showed that specialization in export crops can provide a route to affluence, despite their apparent dependence on Britain.

South Africa, the other area of temperate agriculture, was different. There were many white settler farmers; but from the beginning of Dutch settlement in the mid-seventeenth century, farmers had relied on black Africans for their labour force. Indeed, particularly in the Transvaal, many white landowners did not so much farm as let out their land to African farmers on a share-cropping basis: Africans provided the seed, the draft animals, the equipment, and the human labour, and received perhaps half the product. These were 'squatters' in a different sense from those in Australia; and it was not until the evolution of mechanical aids to farming, perhaps from the 1930s, that white landowners generally took over cultivation of their own land. Even then they still relied on a black labour force, now as labourers rather than farming partners.

From early days South Africa was a large-scale exporter of wine (produced mainly near Cape Town) and wool: indeed the original Australian sheep came from South Africa. There was also a substantial sugar industry in Natal, though there the labour force was provided by Indian indentured immigrants. Maize was the main grain crop, an important export, as was citrus fruit. But the second main difference between South Africa and the other colonies of settlement was that agriculture never played the dominant role in paying for infrastructural investment and economic development. That function was provided by diamonds and gold. As early as 1901–05 gold provided 50.5 per cent and diamonds 24 per cent of the value of South African exports; whereas food and drink (mainly wine, maize, and sugar) contributed only 0.2 per cent and wool, which had been 69 per cent of exports in the early 1870s, only 18 per cent. It was diamonds and gold that financed the economic development of South Africa: and gold, like agriculture, depended largely on cheap black labour.

Peasant farms in the tropics

Temperate colonies grew or produced crops that were already available in Britain or Europe, but did so more cheaply or efficiently owing to advantages of soil, space, or climate. Tropical countries, by contrast, mainly produced things that could not efficiently be grown in Britain because they required greater heat or rainfall. Since most tropical producers were peasants who grew cash crops as a sideline to their subsistence agriculture, they usually accepted the price they were offered by middlemen or exporters – producing more, not less, if prices dropped, and so sending prices still lower. What they got was determined by the international commodity markets, which were governed solely by supply and demand. If such commodities – typically sugar, cocoa, coffee, groundnuts, copra, oil palm products – were in over-supply, prices might be forced very low. Moreover, since world consumption of these things was virtually static over the short to medium term, a very small over- or under-supply had dramatic effects on the price; and this in turn would greatly affect the return to the producer.

Typically, a peasant farm consisted of a piece of land that one family could cultivate with very little mechanical equipment, though perhaps helped by non-family labour at peak times of the year. Provided they owned or had secure tenancy of their land, peasant farmers had the option of producing for the market if it was profitable to do so, or withdrawing from the market and producing subsistence crops if it was not. But with restricted land and no mechanical aids – in most of tropical Africa not even animals, wheels, or ploughs – peasant farming could not provide any substantial surplus for the peasant himself or his society as a whole.

Until early in the twentieth century British officials made no attempt to protect African or Asian peasants from compulsory land purchase by white farmers, as in southern Africa, or plantations, as in South and South East Asia. Thus, by about 1900 much of the best land in South Africa had been acquired by Europeans, even if they still often relied on African farmers to till it for them. Equally in Kenya, once it became clear that only large-scale European-type farming in the White Highlands could make the railway pay its costs, London had no hesitation in encouraging white settlers, even though this involved extensive eviction of the Masai and other groups. Until the first years of the century, also, land was made available for plantations in parts of the newly British territories in West Africa.

But then came a change of policy, particularly in West Africa. Partly because peasants there proved willing and able to produce the export crops needed by the traders, partly because the traders feared the effects of large-scale plantation companies on their trade (since such companies would export their own crops and

Empire Marketing Board poster, 1927. The Empire Marketing Board was established in 1926 in an effort to make the British public more aware of the economic benefits of empire. In spite of its old-fashioned stereotypes of Africans, this poster makes extremely optimistic claims about the potential of tropical Africa with its largely peasant agriculture as a market and a source of raw materials.

import goods to sell to their workers), but partly also because they feared political repercussions, the British authorities began to disallow sales of land by Africans to Europeans. By the 1920s it was generally accepted by the Colonial Office that West Africa was a land of peasant agriculture. Thereafter virtually no land was taken for European agriculture and British West Africa remained a society of peasant producers.

This had important consequences. On the one hand it preserved the structure of rural society and prevented the sort of social division between whites and blacks that resulted from large-scale European agriculture in South, Central, and East Africa. On the other hand it also made it impossible for West Africa to compete successfully in the production of commodities such as palm oil with Sumatra and Malaya, where plantations, aided by more favourable soil and climatic conditions, provided much higher yields and lower costs. This did not affect all crops: for example, cocoa produced in the Gold Coast and Nigeria was able to compete successfully with rival producers, partly because the unit of production was often much larger than the normal peasant holding. Nor was groundnut production badly affected.

What in the end proved the most serious handicap to the peasant producers of West Africa was the introduction of the marketing boards during and after the Second World War. These boards imposed state purchase of export crops, paying the peasant producers a fixed price below the market price. Surpluses, intended to subsidize payments if the market slumped, were accumulated. By the 1960s producers generally were getting half or less of the value of their crops and this had a seriously deterrent effect on their will to produce. The worst effect was in Ghana, which lost its position as the world's leading cocoa exporter, but there were similar results in all ex-British colonies using the marketing board system.

Plantation farming

The alternative to peasant production was the plantation. If properly organized, a plantation was in theory a much more efficient method of production than peasant agriculture. But it had two major limitations. Firstly, it needed a large labour force and, given the nature of plantation work and the deep prejudice against a system once based on slavery, this could be difficult to recruit and retain. Secondly, a plantation involved substantial investment: when the market was depressed a plantation (unlike the peasant) had to continue producing what it was designed to produce or it would rapidly deteriorate. Given the instability of commodity markets this was a serious consideration.

From the seventeenth century, plantations – particularly for sugar, tobacco, and cotton – were developed in the British colonies of North America and the West Indies. Up to 1807 the British imported slaves to work them but in that year the slave trade was abolished and in 1833 slavery was made illegal throughout the British empire. To solve the labour problem the British planters revived the system of indentured labour whereby men and women agreed to work for a period of years in return for the cost of their passage. From the 1830s until 1917, when the Indian government banned such recruiting, over 400,000 Indian 'coolies' were brought to the British West Indies – mostly to British Guiana, Trinidad, and Jamaica – bound to work for a period, usually fixed at five years. They were also taken in large numbers to Mauritius, Fiji, and Natal in South Africa.

Indentured labour, mostly Indian but sometimes from China or the Pacific islands, became the basis of plantations in many other parts of the British empire where local labour was unwilling or unable to provide the necessary work-force. In British colonies plantations were set up for sisal in Kenya and Tanganyika; for coffee and tea in Ceylon and Kenya; for tea in India; for sugar in Mauritius and Natal; for rubber and palm oil in Malaya and North Borneo; for coconuts (producing copra) in the Solomons; for sugar in Fiji; and for sugar in Queensland, Australia.

Plantations were, in varying degrees, critical for the economic development of all these territories. On the other hand the brutalities of the system of forced labour under indentures (see page 284), and the fact that the workers were generally paid very low wages for hard and often unpleasant work, always gave the plantation a bad image.

Drought and famine

In the later nineteenth century there was a series of disastrous crop failures in India, leading not only to starvation but to epidemics. Most were regional, but the death toll could be huge. Thus, to take only some of the worst famines for which the death rate is known, some 800,000 died in the North West Provinces, Punjab, and Rajasthan in 1837–38; perhaps 2 million in the same region in 1860–61; nearly a million in different areas in 1866–67; 4.3 million in widely spread areas in 1876–78, an additional 1.2 million in the North West Provinces and Kashmir in 1877–78; and, worst of all, over 5 million in a famine that affected a large proportion of India in 1896–97. In 1899–1900 more than a million were thought to have died, conditions being worse because of the shortage of food following the famines only two years earlier. Thereafter the only major loss of life through famine was in 1943, under exceptional wartime conditions.

In pre-colonial societies scarcity and famine often caused large losses of life, though peasant groups were usually extremely efficient at weathering such disasters by mutual help. But empire, by unifying large regions and linking territories under a single rule, and helped by technical innovations such as railways and telegraphic communications, made it possible to alleviate the effects both of drought and other disasters (such as that scourge of Africa, the locust). Natural disaster would only result in famine if the colonial state failed to recognize and shoulder its responsibilities.

It was in India that famine relief was most necessary and where the British eventually accepted that it was the duty of the state to organize relief. Until the end

Famine in India. At the end of the nineteenth century repeated years of drought destroyed crops, forcing up the price of what food was available and leaving the poor to starve in huge numbers.

of the East India Company period in 1858 there was no co-ordinated policy to counter the effects of drought, apart from some relief works and distribution of charity. But after the British Crown took over from the company, serious investigations took place after each of the later famines. The Famine Commission of 1867 laid down general principles: public works were seen as both a form of short-term relief, enabling the Indians who were employed on them to buy food during famine, when high prices rather than availability of food was the main cause of starvation; and also as a means of improving transport, so that food could be moved quickly to affected areas. Irrigation must be expanded to minimize the effects of shortage of rain. The Famine Commission of 1878–80, following the terrible famines of the previous two years, recommended the establishment of definite rules of procedure – famine codes – by the provincial governments. In 1881 a famine insurance fund for relief in future emergencies was set up into which about £1 million a year was paid.

By the early 1900s these various strategies began to have effect. In the province of Bombay Presidency, for example, employment on 'relief works' was available to those in the countryside who were unable to earn because of failure of rains so that they could buy grain, 'gratuitous relief' was administered by the village officers to those unable to find work, loans were made to farmers and other private employers to enable them to provide work, and loans were also made to farmers to enable them to restock after a famine.

The result of such relief measures, together with improved food production, the ability to move foodgrains quickly on the railways, and government alertness to the onset of famine, was that after the great famine of 1899–1900 it seemed that the problem had been solved. Thus the great famine of 1943 in the north east of India, particularly in Bengal, was a great shock. Wartime problems of communication, the huge inflow of refugees into Bengal from Burma, and the presence of large numbers of troops were all obvious reasons. But Indians blamed the British authorities for not reacting adequately.

In the twentieth century the British accepted the obligation to take precautions against famine in other parts of their empire. In East Africa, for example, a combination of drought and locusts in 1919 caused widespread famine; but in the early 1930s successive years of low rainfall caused no serious mortality because by then famine relief measures had been properly organized. In 1914 failure of rain and inadequate flooding by the Nile in the Sudan would have caused widespread famine had the government not arranged for large imports of grain from India.

Even if precautionary and relief measures became increasingly effective, critics of British rule, especially in India, still argued that colonial rule had actually caused the conditions that produced famine. The mass of the population were said to be so impoverished that they were at the mercy of fluctuations in the supply of food, fluctuations that were accentuated by the encouragement given to the growth of cash crops for export rather than food grains. If, as is probably the case, Indian society as a whole was not made poorer as the result of British rule, the British had still not been able significantly to improve the lot of the mass of the population. Until such improvements could be brought about, many Indians would live on a knife edge and would be in danger whenever there was a failure of the monsoons and therefore of the harvest.

MINING

From the very start of European expansion the great hope of most colonists was to discover precious metals and 'get rich quick'. For a new economy, gold, in particular, could provide the means of paying for essential needs such as railways, ports, and roads. A gold strike always led to a dramatic increase in immigration and often resulted in a long-term settlement. A few colonies were lucky, most were not. Apart from tin in Nigeria, gold in the Gold Coast, and diamonds in Sierra Leone, few viable minerals were found in British West Africa. East Africa was also deficient in desirable minerals except for some gold in Tanganyika and Kenya – expensive to extract and thus profitable only when the price of gold was relatively very high (as

Gold mining in South Africa

Probably the most momentous mineral discovery of the nineteenth century was the Witwatersrand gold reef in 1886, when a prospector, George Harrison, stumbled on a gold-bearing outcrop of rock near Johannesburg. Though there were deposits near the surface, which led to the normal rush of small prospectors, and, later, to surface mining, the main wealth of the reef lay deep down. The ore had to quarried, brought to the surface, crushed, and the minute particles of gold, after filtration, separated out by the then new process using cyanide. The cost of such enterprises was enormous. Initially, considerable amounts of local capital were available from the profits generated by the Kimberley diamond mines, developed since 1869, which had resulted in the formation of a monopoly organization, the Diamond Syndicate. This syndicate, dominated by Cecil Rhodes and Wernher Beit, was itself a fusion of Rhodes's De Beers Consolidated Mines and Beit's company. Since these companies had bought out other mine owners, men such as J.B. Robinson and Barney Barnato also had ample funds to start mining on the Rand, as this area soon came to be called. They were soon joined by others, including Rhodes and Beit; and all those with claims began to sell shares on the British and continental stock markets. The result was the unprecedented 'Kaffir' share boom of the early 1890s, when thousands of small investors in Europe bought shares as a gamble, often an unprofitable one. The Rand soon contained the largest collective capital investment in Africa and one of the largest in the world, possibly £60 million by 1900 and over £100 million by 1910. By 1902 there were 120 companies involved, arranged in nine groups, most of them co-operating closely through the Chamber of Mines. Labour was provided by some 12,500 white workers, many of them from Kimberley or earlier mining booms elsewhere, and around 100,000 black Africans. The latter were normally recruited on contract from rural areas, often far distant. They were closely controlled, lived in compounds, and made to return home at the end of their period of contract in order to avoid having what was seen as a potentially dangerous unemployed population if production was cut back. Friction between the mine owners and white workers on the one hand and the Afrikaner government of the Transvaal on the other was a contributory cause of the South African War of 1899–1902, though the idea that Britain started the war primarily to ensure that this gold production remained within the British empire is probably wrong.

'Kaffir boys' at a Johannesburg gold mine, 1896. The mines required a huge force of labourers, recruited throughout southern Africa.

'Zealous gold diggers', Bendigo, Victoria, 1852. During the Australian gold rushes of the 1850s very small areas were allocated to individuals: a typical claim has been described as 'no larger than the floor of a moderate suburban bedroom or dining room'. The prospector worked his claim to a depth of between two and six feet with pick and shovel before moving on to another claim. Mining was a lottery in which individuals had more or less the same chance of success.

in the 1930s). The main mineral discoveries in British Africa were in Central and South Africa: copper in Northern Rhodesia (Zambia), coal and gold in Southern Rhodesia (Zimbabwe), and diamonds and gold in South Africa.

The discovery of gold on the Witwatersrand in South Africa in 1886 was only one of the major gold strikes in the British empire during the nineteenth century but it was the most important and the only one that has remained a major producer to the present day.

The first gold strike was in Australia, where a miner who had left the Californian gold fields – opened in 1849 – discovered gold near Bathurst in New South Wales in 1851. That discovery produced the first gold rush; but the same year far more promising deposits were found at Ballarat and Bendigo, some sixty miles from Melbourne, capital of the recently established colony of Victoria. During the next fifteen years Victoria produced gold worth £124 million – one third of the then total world production – and New South Wales a further £25 million.

This first Australian gold rush was unusual in that the ore was relatively accessible and did not require deep mining or large capital investment. It was the classic example of mining by individual diggers who came from many parts of the world, notably Cornwall, whose tin mines were entering their final declining phase. The mines introduced many thousands of immigrants to Australia, many of whom stayed on after the Victorian mines began to run dry in the 1860s. They, and the wealth the gold produced, made a major contribution to the early phase of manufacturing which had developed in Victoria by the 1860s.

There was a later wave of gold discoveries in the 1880s, when deposits were discovered in Queensland (though this proved unimportant) and at Kalgoorlie, in the previously depressed Western Australia. Kalgoorlie gold required comparatively deep mining and companies were formed drawing on capital from Britain. By that time British capital had also been attracted to other Australian mining ventures – such as the Broken Hill Proprietory Company Ltd (BHP) in New South Wales, initially to mine silver, but later a wide range of other minerals and even to undertake ship building. BHP became one of the largest concentrations of capital in the southern hemisphere.

After Australia, New Zealand. There gold was discovered on the west coast of the South Island in the 1860s, and a stream of diggers duly arrived from California and Australia. The same pattern followed: small claims were amalgamated into large companies and surface washing was replaced by mining, with capital coming from Britain. The gold era in New Zealand did not last long; but it came at a critical period for the economy, at the end of the debilitating Maori Wars, and provided the confidence needed for the government to float large loans in London to finance the construction of railways.

The last of the famous gold strikes in the empire was on the Yukon, in the extreme north west of Canada. It was also the shortest. Gold was discovered round the Klondike river in 1897 and some 100,000 men and women, the majority of them Americans, arrived to make their fortune. Very few did so. Those that did were mostly veterans from the Californian gold rush of 1849; most of those who failed to get as far as Dawson City, the archetypical gold-rush town, were novices who could not face the appalling trek up the Chilkoot pass with the year's supplies on which the Canadian Mounted Police insisted. The rush lasted only two years; and then Dawson City became a ghost town, along with most of the other mining towns of other gold rushes.

Probably more important in the long run for economic development than most of these gold mining episodes, except that in South Africa, was the development of coal mining in India. The British had known about the huge Raniganj coal field, north of Calcutta, since the later eighteenth century, but it was only when the building of the East Indian railway in 1855 connected the coal field with Calcutta that mining there became profitable. In 1867 geologists discovered the Gondwana system, one of the world's largest coal reserves. Indian coal was of relatively low quality. But it was easily accessible and mining labour was very cheap. Operated by Calcutta-based companies under the direction of British managing agents, mostly using capital raised in Britain, Raniganj coal became the basis for the early stages of Indian industrialization: it fuelled the jute factories of Calcutta and the cotton mills of Bombay and it powered the railways. From 1911 coal from the better-suited Jharia coal fields, along with new finds of iron ore, made possible the start of India's first large-scale modern iron and steel complex at Jamshedpur.

INDUSTRY

Before independence there was only limited industrialization in the British colonies. It was a consistent complaint among colonial nationalists from the 1890s onwards that the British did not encourage the development of manufacturing outside Britain itself. Indians went further, claiming that the British had 'de-industrialized' their economy, once far more advanced in manufacturing than that of Britain itself, by imposing free trade and then making it impossible for Indians to protect their infant modern industries against British goods. It has even been suggested that in the later nineteenth century there was an informal conspiracy between British manufacturers and capitalists to prevent British investment in certain industries in India, notably iron and steel, which might compete with those of Britain. Colonial nationalists considered modern industry to be essential to economic development and they believed that the British empire prevented development by its refusal to allow colonies to protect their industries until they were able to stand on their own feet.

It is true that from the mid-nineteenth century to at least the 1920s it was established British policy to insist on an open door and no protection in all those colonies over which they had effective control. This did not include the self-governing colonies, later Dominions. Once these colonies had responsible government – in most cases from the 1850s – they had the legislative freedom to protect growing industries if they wished to do so. In 1859 the Canadian government imposed a number of import duties on manufactures, most of which came from Britain. Since the goods chosen were mainly those that were also being made in Canada, and since the British were at the time supplying large numbers of troops, at British expense, to protect Canada against a possible American attack, this caused an outcry in Britain. It had no effect: the Canadians denied that the new duties were overtly protectionist, claiming that they were now responsible for their own budgeting and must therefore be free to raise revenue as they saw fit. The British never again tried to fight that battle.

The result of Canada's victory was that most of the self-governing colonies adopted protectionist tariffs whenever it seemed economically desirable to do so. This typically occurred in periods of economic recession when there were numbers of unemployed people in the towns for whom work needed to be found: for example, in Victoria in the 1860s and in New Zealand in the early 1890s. Manufacturers would then appeal to the government for protection and were usually given it for a specific product. The predictable consequence was a number of relatively high-cost and economically inefficient industries which absorbed the unemployed and provided profits for industrialists. Such industries also constituted a tax on the farmers whose export prices were set by international market conditions but who had to pay above international prices for many of their inputs. It was partly for this reason that New South Wales held out against protection until it joined protectionist Victoria in the federation of 1901.

Britain could do little to keep these colonies of settlement in what it regarded as the only true road to economic development. But it did have the power to prevent other dependencies from going against free trade. Those British manufacturers for whom the colonies were an important market fought tenaciously against protection or any other artificial stimulus to colonial industrial development. The classic case was the Lancashire cotton complex of mill owners and traders. In some colonies British officials also opposed local manufacturing, but for very different motives. Particularly in British West Africa, the colonial officials were generally hostile to modern industry because it was inconsistent with their model of a society based on an autonomous rural peasantry.

Even in dependent colonies, the British could not, however, insist on total free trade. All colonies were responsible for balancing their own budgets. If they could show that this was impossible without greatly increased import duties, they were in a position to use the same lever as the Canadians had used in 1859. This is what the British government of India did between 1917 and 1921. Hitherto the home government had insisted that if duties were imposed on goods imported to India, a similar tax must be placed on the same goods when manufactured in India. In practice this had only affected cotton textile piecegoods, to the fury of the Indian mill owners and their nationalist supporters. But in 1917 Britain insisted on India taking responsibility for servicing £100 million of British war debts. In return India was allowed to raise the import duty on cottons without taxing

A dye jigger at work in the government of India's textile printing factory. By the beginning of the twentieth century British India had developed a small industrial sector: about 500,000 people out of a total population of over 285 million were engaged in manufacturing. The direct role of the government was limited to pioneer factories, such as this one, intended to encourage the use of new technology.

Indian-manufactured cottons. In 1921 a 'fiscal autonomy convention' was established which left India free to protect any industry it wished, provided that a Tariff Board, set up in 1923, was convinced that the industry concerned had natural advantages, could eventually do without protection, and would not need government support. Thereafter India, while still not self-governing, rapidly became a highly protectionist economy, particularly from 1932, though it was forced to provide tariff preferences for Britain. Predictably, protection stimulated a wave of new consumer industries, especially sugar refining, detergents, matches, rubber tyres, cement, paper, and light engineering goods. By 1939 India was virtually self-sufficient in textiles and iron and steel products, though still weak on a wide range of engineering goods.

The Indian example has often been used as evidence that it was only imperial policy that held back industrial development in other British dependencies. Indeed before the 1950s there was very little modern manufacturing in any African colony apart from Southern Rhodesia, whose comparatively large manufacturing sector – 16 per cent of the gross domestic product in 1960 – was the highest in the continent, apart from South Africa and the Mediterranean countries. In Nigeria the proportion was then 4.5 per cent and in the Gold Coast 6.3 per cent. Was it, then, the selfish imperial stranglehold that blocked modern industrial development in these places?

A country will only develop large-scale industries when there is an adequate market – at home or overseas – to justify even the minimal scale of production that modern industry needs if it is to be economically efficient, sufficient capital to provide the machines and cover working costs, a grasp of the technology involved, and a trained labour force. The absence of the last three does not constitute an absolute bar to industrialization: capital can be borrowed, technology hired and learned, a labour force trained. The really serious obstacle is the absence of an adequate market. The essence of modern manufacturing lies in economies of scale: often there is a minimum size for a machine below which production becomes uneconomic. The main obstacle to industrialization in most parts of tropical Africa and the smaller countries of South East Asia and the Pacific was simply that the population and their disposable incomes were both too small to justify establishing local modern manufactures. This meant that the average cost of production for so limited a market would be above, and often far above, international prices. Moreover, unless it embodied new technology, a new colonial venture could not compete with an established company elsewhere because to the latter the colonial market was marginal to its main production and could price exports accordingly.

In a free market, therefore, as in free-trading British colonies, it would have been suicidal for a private enterprise to set up a modern industry in most fields. Although the raw materials might be grown locally, as cotton for example was in northern Nigeria, and the local wage rate might be far below that paid in Lancashire, the unit cost of production was likely to be higher than that of imported goods. Even in

India, which not only produced cotton but had a relatively very large market for cottons, local mills could not compete on price or quality with imported British textiles: until the coming of effective protection after 1917, therefore, the Indian cotton industry relied mostly on making and exporting cotton thread and weaving cloth that did not attempt to compete with Lancashire products. Equally, when the Tata family eventually succeeded in building India's first modern iron and steel plant in 1911 it relied on government orders and survived only because of military demand during the First World War and protective tariffs thereafter.

It is clear that the only large-scale industries likely to develop in the tropical colonies under free-trade conditions were certain bulk products whose transport from Europe constituted a substantial proportion of their value and which might therefore profitably be made locally, provided there was a substantial local demand. Beer and soft drinks, consisting mainly of water, were early examples in most colonies. Cement was another, where there were suitable local raw materials and the building industry was active. These and a few other industries, such as soap, were established under free-trade regimes by the 1940s in a number of British colonies.

Traders' warehouse in Nigeria, *c.*1912. The river system of southern Nigeria enabled British goods to circulate far inland and, as this photograph shows, to give local customers a choice of textiles and other imported manufactured goods. Local textiles had difficulty in competing with British ones.

Western medical skills were made available to much of the world through the British empire. The achievement of the men and women involved in colonial medical services was a remarkable one. On the other hand, the British empire also spread disease and high death rates. The balance between the empire as agent of death or preserver of life only came down decisively in favour of the preservation of life in the years after the First World War.

The first contact of non-European peoples with the diseases brought by Europeans produced catastrophic results. British penetration into previously isolated parts of the world was followed by a dramatic decline in indigenous populations, most notably in the nineteenth century in New Zealand and Australia. In India and Africa, by contrast, colonial rule seems to have been accompanied by an increased severity in the incidence of diseases already established there. Colonial rule greatly increased the mobility of people and therefore of infection. It also produced environmental deterioration, concentrating people into urban slums or densely populated rural areas, where they were vulnerable to disease. One of the unintended consequences of some irrigation schemes was to create a favourable environment for the anopheles mosquito, the spreader of malaria. India was ravaged by cholera (twenty-three million people may have died in epidemics between 1865 and 1949), by the plague (an estimated twelve million victims died in the great pandemic that started in 1896), and by malaria, influenza, and tuberculosis. The European conquest of much of Africa at the end of the nineteenth century was accompanied by great epidemics. Sleeping sickness spread, as did malaria. Rinderpest decimated cattle. Africa too was badly affected by the great influenza outbreak following the First World War. Death rates only started to fall in India in the 1920s and did so even later in Africa.

Most of the early attempts to improve health in colonial territories were aimed at keeping Europeans alive in the tropics. Cholera epidemics in Calcutta in the 1830s and 1840s eventually led to schemes for sewage disposal and to piped, filtered water, which mainly serviced European parts of the city. The slums and shanty towns of the poor in African or Indian cities remained outside any effective health provision. The use of quinine was by far the most important advance in tropical medicine in the nineteenth century. Although the causes of malaria were not understood until much later, it was discovered by the 1820s that

an extract of the alkaloid of quinine from the cinchona bark (which then came only from the Andes) could provide protection from malaria. By the mid-1840s some Europeans in West Africa were beginning to take quinine regularly. By the end of the century supplies of cinchona bark were available from India and Indonesia, and West Africa was no longer necessarily 'a white man's grave'.

By the end of the nineteenth century the British schools of tropical medicine, set up in London and Liverpool in 1899, and the government and missionary hospitals in the colonies had acquired a formidable body of expertise for countering the diseases of Africa and Asia. Resources were, however, only slowly made available to enable this expertise to be applied on a scale that would have any real effect on the life expectation of the mass of the population. Insecticides such as DDT were, for instance, only widely used against insect-borne diseases, such as malaria, during and immediately after the Second World War. It was medical missionaries rather than public servants who provided most of the hospitals and dispensaries to which Africans and Indians could go. Only after independence did the British ex-colonies begin to devote substantial resources to preventative medicine   [DKF/PJM]

Above: The Medical Officer of Northern Nigeria on his rounds, 1912. In an area where medical provision was tightly stretched to meet the needs of a large population, the doctor is using a railway trolley to get around.

Right: Colonial War Memorial Hospital, Suva, Fiji, in the 1950s. As was so often the case elsewhere, early colonial contacts brought heavy mortality to Fiji: about one quarter of the population died of measles in an epidemic of 1875. By the end of British rule, however, Fiji had become one of the colonial medical service's notable successes with a death rate as low as that of New Zealand.

Opposite: Plague precautions in Bombay, 1896. The British authorities tried to counter a major plague epidemic in western India by a rigorous programme of disinfecting. Houses were broken into and, as this picture shows, the poorer inhabitants were often roughly treated, eventually provoking much popular resentment.

It is not necessary to look for hostile imperial policies or British capitalist conspiracies to explain the limited industrialization in the British dependent empire. The main reason was that the very restricted market in virtually all territories other than India offered no attraction to either foreign or local capitalists. Only state encouragement – by protection, official orders for products, and restriction on imports – could have generated extensive manufacture; and this was something that only the British government of India was able or willing to do during its last two decades.

THE BALANCE SHEET

Did the colonies, on balance, do better as British colonies – part of what was in theory a complementary commercial system – than they might have done had they not been colonies?

On the credit side, Britain in its economic heyday, before 1914, provided benefits which no other imperial power could match and to which the colonies would not have had the same access had they not been part of the empire. Britain was then the world's leading source of both technology and capital. It was also the most important trading and shipping centre. Britain could provide every economic service that colonies might need. Moreover, colonies could buy some of these services in Britain more cheaply than foreign states could do: borrowing, for example, was cheaper because British capital had faith in the economic and fiscal reliability of British possessions. Moreover the Colonial Stocks Act of 1900 enabled colonial governments to sell bonds on the London money market with the security of British gilt-edged securities, and so offer lower interest rates.

'The natives before and after working in the mines': Kimberley, South Africa, 1873. The listless 'savages' on the left of the picture have been turned into the prosperous wage earners on the right after a spell in the new diamond mines. In the early stages of South African mining many Africans accumulated some savings and did indeed often buy guns, as the picture shows. The great waves of later migrants were, however, generally driven by poverty and the pressure of taxes in the countryside to work in the mines for low wages.

The Shanghai staff of Butterfield and Swire, 1883. This group is characteristic of the hierarchy in a European company. Managerial posts are filled by British people; the Chinese serve as brokers or agents (usually called 'compradors' on the China coast), who dealt with 'native' customers and suppliers.

Britain was probably even more important as a market than as a lender. As late as 1939 it remained the best, and in some instances the only, market for many colonial foodstuffs and industrial raw materials. For a young colonial economy, whether a colony of settlement or a tropical dependency recently linked to the international trading world, Britain was the key to establishing profitable export staples, which in turn provided the resources that could be used to create an effective infrastructure.

Against these undeniable benefits there were disadvantages and limitations in being part of the British empire, particularly for a non-self-governing colony. Because Britain's interest lay in colonial economies being complementary to its own, it showed no interest in stimulating types of development, notably in industry, that might have resulted in colonial competition, though it never banned these. The services Britain provided, such as shipping, banking, and trading, were owned and run by British nationals: there was little scope for indigenous merchants to compete with the managing agencies of India or the big trading companies of West Africa. In a general sense, also, the empire was racist. Until well into the twentieth century senior posts in both colonial administration and commerce were held by Britons: the business world of Calcutta, for example, was almost exclusively British until the 1920s. These factors limited the ability of tropical colonies to benefit from the potential transfer of economic skills.

Above all, perhaps, the basic principle of British imperial rule until the 1930s, and in practice until the 1950s, was that colonies must pay their own way. There was a good reason for this: however rich, Britain could never have afforded to support the economic development of so large an empire from its own resources. If a colony wanted to build a railway or a port it had to borrow the money and service the debt. The result was that poor colonies stayed poor unless they struck lucky with gold, diamonds, or some other mineral bonanza. It was only after 1940, with the Colonial Development and Welfare Acts, that Britain seriously began to provide unrequited aid to its colonies; and even then it was not until the early 1950s that its own economy, weakened by the Second World War, was capable of putting much capital into the colonies. Meanwhile, between 1939 and about 1951, the empire was milked of its foreign earnings and exploited by bulk buying of its exports at below world prices; and once that phase was over British politicians began to consider decolonization as a possible way of escaping from the intolerable burden of financing colonial development.

None of this applied to the colonies of settlement, such as Australia or Canada. Once they had self-government and were free to determine their own economic strategy, empire was entirely beneficial – at least to the white settlers. This is shown clearly by a comparison between, say, Australia and Argentina, which otherwise had much in common and were both booming economies in the early twentieth century, heavily dependent on the British market for their exports. Before 1932 and imperial preference Australia's main advantage was its ability to borrow more cheaply from Britain than a foreign country could do. After 1932 quotas for empire imports helped Australia and harmed Argentina. But in the longer term perhaps the most significant difference between Australia and Argentina lay in Australia's greater political and social stability, partly at least a product of its adoption of British political institutions.

Clearly the economic effects of empire were not uniform. But in its context, and particularly before 1914, it was probably more beneficial than harmful. Decolonization removed most of the constraints of empire and enabled the ex-colonies to draw on loans and grants from a wider world. This, in conjunction with the international trade boom of the two decades after 1950, gave the impression that increasing third-world affluence was the direct consequence of the end of empire. But by the 1980s it had become clear that this was largely an illusion. By then world conditions had turned against less developed countries. International aid became less freely available. External debts grew as the enterprises and infrastructural facilities for which they had paid proved unable to service their liabilities. In retrospect, the age of empire, with its tight financial and economic disciplines, came to seem increasingly less unattractive: indeed, in many ex-colonies the orthodox economic regime once imposed by London and thrown off with independence, was reimposed by international agencies such as the World Bank and International Monetary Fund.

In a nutshell, then, empire as run by the British was economically conservative. It provided facilities that helped colonies to help themselves but did little for those that could not. On balance, most of the dependencies probably developed faster and more soundly than they might have done had they remained independent or had they belonged to any other European power. Beyond that it is impossible to be certain.

Power, Authority, and Freedom

For Harold Macmillan, the British Prime Minister who presided over the unscrambling of colonial Africa, power itself was illusory: 'when you achieve it, there is nothing there'. Many of his predecessors in the age of empire had probably felt much the same.

Although the gulf between British power – economically, technologically, and militarily – and the non-European world was overwhelming, the extent of British control over the empire was severely limited. The constraints on the effective use of power in maintaining an empire were very real. And just as modern nuclear powers have not been able to impose their will on Asian peoples in Vietnam or Afghanistan, so the British could not rule by power alone. They had to deploy managerial devices and rhetorical flourishes to disguise or compensate for the patchiness of their actual strength. Sometimes indeed British power (like Japanese power since 1970) was wielded most effectively when free of imperial burdens. And just as the power of the imperial authorities was limited, so too was the power of nationalists. These movements, whose identities were significantly shaped by British rule, were neither solely responsible for the end of empire nor singlemindedly intent on dismantling the imperial legacy.

Harold Macmillan in Basutoland, 1960. During his tour of southern Africa in 1960, Macmillan made his classic statement about the transitoriness of imperial power. He warned the white South African Parliament that: 'The wind of change is blowing through this continent, and whether we like it or not, this growth of national consciousness is a political fact.' However, he also visited places where the wind of change was thought to be blowing less fiercely, as in Basutoland (Lesotho), where he was photographed greeting a crowd.

BRITISH WORLD POWER

State power – the ability to initiate, sustain, or arrest action and to influence and control people – can be assessed in relation to economic strength, social cohesion, technological expertise, military might, and government organization. By such criteria Britain was the most powerful nation in the world between 1815 and 1914.

The growth in Europe's population after 1750 was accompanied by, and indeed contributed to, unprecedented increases in economic productivity. In the years 1760–1830 Britain was responsible for two-thirds of Europe's industrial output; in the same period its share of the world's manufacturing production rose from 1.9 per cent to 9.5 per cent, and this doubled over the next thirty years. By 1860 Britain was conducting 20 per cent of the world's commerce and 40 per cent of world trade in manufactured goods. Technological advances contributed not only to productivity but also to the integration of the United Kingdom which, far from collapsing under the strains of economic change, proved highly resilient, with the result that (Ireland apart) British society was more cohesive than that of, say, unified Italy or unified Germany.

Thus, in the nineteenth century at least, the British were well endowed with the 'tools of empire': their steamships and telegraph cables encircled the earth; their railways opened up 'dark' continents; advances in medical science dispersed the spell of the 'white man's grave'; military technology – and especially the Maxim gun which, in the words of Hilaire Belloc, 'we have got [but] they have not' – allowed

British warships off Weihaiwei in China. In 1898, to counter the Russian annexation of Port Arthur, the British China squadron – at that time the most powerful naval force in the Far East – was ordered to assemble off the Chinese coast to support Britain's demand for a lease of the port of Weihaiwei.

small numbers of British soldiers to subdue poorly equipped African and Asian armies. Underpinning British world power after 1815 was the Royal Navy. In 1900 its tonnage – at over one million – was double that of the combined might of any other two powers and was supported by a global chain of bases and by a massive merchant fleet. Despite a relative decline industrially after 1870, in 1900 Britain still boasted the highest per capita level of industrialization, the second largest share of the world's manufacturing output, and by far the largest fleet.

GOVERNING THE EMPIRE

All these attributes of Britain's material civilization fuelled the motor for expansion overseas and helped to create and sustain an empire under which at least a quarter of the world's population was living by the late nineteenth century.

A gangling bureaucracy

The mechanisms by which power was exercised radiated in a complicated network from the hub of London to district offices on the rim of empire. Central and supreme were the monarchy and Parliament. But Parliament remained remote from the actual management of empire: members debated imperial issues infrequently and divided over them even less often. Parliament was not in any case competent to administer the empire, a task that was shared amongst a large number of departments and agencies throughout the gangling bureaucracy of Whitehall. The machinery grew in fits and starts, generally in response to the acquisition and loss of territory, the ebb and flow of the economy, the conduct of war, and revelations of maladministration, corruption, and scandal. For much of the period – indeed, probably until 1940 – efforts by the British government to impose its will on the empire were usually a response to international challenges and to events in the empire itself.

It was in times of war rather than in peace that successive British governments tried to bring about imperial unity or attempted to exert a firmer grip on imperial organization. During the prolonged Anglo-French conflict between 1793 and 1815 the Colonial Office began to take shape and newly conquered colonies were put under direct administration from home. Similarly, the colonial wars and uprisings of the 1850s, such as the Indian Rebellion, the Maori Wars in New Zealand, and the Kaffir Wars on the Cape frontier in South Africa, more or less coinciding as they did with the Crimean War, led to a shake-up in Whitehall and a review of colonial security. The demands and reverses of the South African War of 1899–1902 likewise provoked a reappraisal of imperial defence, while national survival in the two World Wars necessitated the exploitation of imperial assets on a massive scale, which inevitably required closer supervision of the colonies from home.

When attempts at imperial consolidation were made during peacetime, they tended to reflect British weakness rather than strength. In the 1880s and 1890s, for example, as other powers overhauled Britain's economic lead, competed with its

British officers in the Egyptian service, *c.*1900. Officially, Egypt was never a British colony; it kept its own government under the British occupation of 1881. Within a few years, however, British control became increasingly intrusive. By 1900 500 British officials held key posts in what were still Egyptian ministries – hence the wearing of fezzes. 'English heads and Egyptian hands' was a common slogan.

navy, and disputed its pre-eminence in Asia and Africa, so Britain set about occupying what it had hitherto regarded as its own spheres of influence, formalizing control over client states in Malaya, Uganda, Zanzibar, and in Egypt which the British had occupied in 1882. There Britain began to give its position as temporary occupying power some formal legal status by appointing Sir Evelyn Baring to be Agent and Consul-General, an office that he interpreted as giving him the right to supervise and reform the government of Egypt. At the same time Britain also experimented with proposals for the constitutional integration of the empire. Late nineteenth-century schemes for imperial federation – most of them confined to the colonies of white settlement – did not follow a single model: some looked forward to colonial representation at Westminster; others envisaged an imperial parliament set apart from Westminster. Many proposals were floated but each was scuppered by ingrained Dominion mistrust of British centralization and by a corresponding reluctance amongst British politicians to tamper with the sovereignty of Britain itself. The one practical result of all these schemes – the organization of colonial (later imperial) conferences which later became the forum where compromises were hammered out between Britain and the Dominions on international crises, constitutional relations, and tariffs and trade – fell a long way short of the grandiose aspirations of the 'new imperialists'. Of these, the most energetic and constructive was undoubtedly Joseph Chamberlain, Colonial Secretary from 1895 to 1903. But, political giant though he was, Chamberlain did not bestride the whole empire: India, together with British interests in the Middle East, China, and Latin America fell outside his remit, while, even in his own sphere, his plans for imperial federation proved abortive and his recipes for colonial development were frustrated by lack of support from the Treasury and businessmen. Chamberlain's experience indicates the constraints on the easy operation of imperial power.

Imperial government never amounted to a monolithic structure. Instead, its administrative, commercial, and military functions were shared between a variety of Whitehall departments. Some of these (like the Colonial, India, and Dominions Offices) had exclusively imperial functions; others (like the Board of Trade or War Office) played leading roles on the non-imperial stage as well. Apart from the Cabinet, which tended to concern itself with specific problems rather than dictate an imperial strategy, there was no over-arching department in which imperial authority was vested. Diffusion of control was compensated for by liaison between departments at official and ministerial level, although it was not until the 1940s that inter-departmental co-ordination became systematized.

Yet although specific tasks relating to individual parts of the empire were divided between departments that were relatively junior in the hierarchy – when compared with the mighty Treasury, Foreign Office, and Home Office – it would be wrong to conclude that the overseas empire was ever low in the priorities of successive governments. The fact that imperial matters involved such a wide range of departments of state suggests, on the contrary, that imperial issues could not be separated easily from home and foreign policies and that imperial management – however haphazard – was woven into the fabric of British government as a whole.

Just as the government in Britain left much to private initiative, so the management of its empire was not restricted to institutions of state but involved a large measure of private enterprise. Indeed the reason why some felt that the empire had been acquired in 'a fit of absence of mind' was doubtless because it was the product of many different minds: of merchants and manufacturers; of settlers with family ties to Britain; of missionaries, explorers, and learned societies; of slavers, convicts, and drop-outs; of the City as well as Westminster and Whitehall; of Edinburgh and Glasgow, Manchester and Birmingham, as much as London; of Scots, Irish, Welsh, and Hanoverians in addition to the English; of, in short, very many different men and women. Links between the innumerable elements of British society and communities in countries overseas were generally forged without government intervention. So far as dependent territories were concerned, such bonds were usually established long before the government took over and continued to survive for some time after it had relinquished control to nationalist regimes (hence the resilience of British hopes for continuing influence through the Commonwealth). While the British government could not be said to be in the pocket of any of these groups, it was aware of their concerns, even though these concerns did not necessarily coincide with each other or with what was perceived to be the 'national interest'. On one matter, however, there was general agreement in Britain – the desirability of low taxation. For this reason the British government was generally loath to take on responsibilities overseas and, if and when it did so, it tried to shift the financial burden onto the shoulders of others, particularly subject peoples in dependent territories. The House of Commons was very reluctant to vote British taxes for colonial purposes.

British colonies were formally possessions of the Crown, acquired by settlement of areas not legitimately claimed by other European powers (the claims of the indigenous inhabitants might or might not have been given the recognition of a treaty) or by conquest. Authority over the first overseas colonies was usually delegated by the Crown to be exercised by certain individuals (Sir Walter Raleigh's Virginia grant is a famous early example) or by groups of people, such as the Massachusetts Bay Company. During the seventeenth century those who had received the Crown's grants shared some of their authority with representative bodies chosen by the white settlers in the North American or West Indian colonies. Usually known as a Colonial Assembly, this body voted taxes and made local laws for the colony with the Governor, who acted for the holder of the grant or increasingly for the Crown itself, as most of the grants were cancelled in the eighteenth century.

From the end of the eighteenth century different patterns of colonial government evolved. In the period covered by this book this **representative system** of royal Governor with a local Assembly survived in the older West Indian colonies and was established in newly acquired territories where European populations settled – in Canada, Australia, New Zealand, and South Africa. At various times from the mid-nineteenth century onwards, these colonies of settlement, with the exception of the West Indies, moved to **responsible government**. That meant that the business of government was carried on not by officials appointed by the Governor but by ministers 'responsible' to – that is, owing their position to votes in – the Assembly, which became the Parliament of the colony. A responsible government colony was, for all practical purposes, internally self-governing. In the early twentieth century it became customary to refer to such colonies as **Dominions**. Changes during the interwar period, especially in 1926 and 1931, removed all theoretical British authority over their internal affairs and gave them full recognition in international affairs. The term 'independence' was usually avoided before 1945, but thereafter 'Dominion' dropped out of use and in every respect the ex-Dominions were regarded as independent sovereign states, even though there were no formal declarations of independence.

Other colonies acquired by Britain from the end of the eighteenth century followed a rather different course. They were placed under the direct authority of the Crown without at first any delegation of authority to representative bodies. Rule was in the hands of the royal Governor. This came to be called **crown colony** government. It was first applied to colonies conquered from other powers in the great wars of 1793 to 1814, such as Ceylon (Sri Lanka) or Trinidad. Crown colonies were colonies where the population was overwhelmingly non-European and therefore considered unfit for representative government. It was the basic system of government in Africa and the Pacific. In time,

representative bodies were conceded, usually called Legislative Councils. After the Second World War responsible government was quickly telescoped into full independence in the great waves of decolonization, which began in 1948 with the ending of British rule over Ceylon.

In the later nineteenth century Britain acquired **protectorates**. In legal terms Britain did not possess sovereignty over protectorates; their own rulers kept sovereignty while placing themselves under the protection of the British Crown. Most of the protectorates after a time became crown colonies under full British rule. Some rulers, like Malay sultans, however, remained as the rulers of protected states and Egypt, which

Britain had 'occupied' in 1882 became a protectorate between 1914 and 1922.

After the First World War Britain was awarded **mandates** by the League of Nations. These mandates were former provinces of the Ottoman empire or colonies of Germany. In the Middle East, Transjordan (Jordan) and Iraq were treated as protectorates; Palestine and the ex-German African colonies were ruled as crown colonies.

India was always an exception. **Indian provinces** were at first ruled by the East India Company under grants of the Mughal Emperor. The sovereignty of the Crown over the conquered areas of India (hence 'British' India) was effectively recognized by 1813, although the East India Company remained the agent of the Crown for governing India until 1858. Large parts of India, known as **princely states** or **native states**, were never conquered but were bound to the British Crown by treaties – hence their rulers were also 'protected'. In 1858 the Crown assumed direct responsibility for British India and after 1876 British monarchs also had the title of Empress or Emperor of India. Representative government of a very limited kind was introduced into British India in 1861, only becoming significant in the twentieth century. The Indian princes retained their status as protected allies of Britain down to the granting of independence to India and Pakistan in 1947. [PJM]

The annexation of South East New Guinea, 1884. In response to German claims to parts of New Guinea, Britain also claimed territory. The annexation depicted here was formally proclaimed by the commander of a British warship on 6 November 1884. Fifty chiefs had been assembled to witness the ceremony. They were given gifts, such as butchers' knives, shirts, cloth, and tobacco, and were told that Queen Victoria now 'guards and watches over you, looks upon you as her children'.

James Brooke and the Sultan of Brunei, 1842. Sarawak was a most unusual type of colonial possession, even in an empire as diverse as the British one. From 1841 until 1946 three generations of the Brooke family ruled it as white rajahs. James Brooke, the founder of the dynasty, is here shown extracting confirmation of the grant from the Sultan of Brunei.

A hotch-potch of colonial governments

The diffusion of responsibility throughout Whitehall was matched by a devolution of power to the empire itself. Apart from a commitment to the defence of its colonies – and the demarcation between imperial and local defence was a perennially contentious matter – London came to expect local authorities to cope with local matters. From the late eighteenth century, when the East India Company embarked on the conquest of more and more territory primarily in order to collect more taxes to pay for its growing administrative responsibilities, it became accepted that subject peoples, not the taxpayers in Britain, should pay the cost of their own subjugation.

In practice, a wide variety of forms of colonial government developed. The oldest form was the representative system. This lasted in the West Indies until the 1860s when the plantocracies, starting with the Assembly in Jamaica, voluntarily surrendered ancient privileges in exchange for the protection afforded by crown colony rule against the possibility of black uprisings. Crown colony government, with its Governor, Executive Council, and Legislative Council, provided for the direct administration and military protection of territories acquired from the late eighteenth century onwards in the Caribbean (for example, Trinidad 1797), on the coast of Africa (for example, the Cape 1815), in the Far East (for example, the Straits Settlements 1867), and in Australasia (for example, New Zealand 1840). Responsible government developed in the white settlements of Canada, Australia, and New Zealand during the mid-nineteenth century and later in South Africa. With ministers answerable to locally elected legislatures, this system afforded a large measure of self-government, although London retained control over defence and foreign affairs at least until the 1920s. British India – those provinces (like the Punjab) that had been conquered and annexed – was directly administered by British officials, while the several hundred princely states (of which Hyderabad was the largest) concluded agreements whereby they surrendered to the Crown control over external affairs in return for a good deal of internal autonomy. In the late nineteenth century new chartered companies established British control over large tracts of Africa through the agency of freelance imperialists, such as George Goldie, William Mackinnon, and Cecil Rhodes, all of whom operated under the supervision of the Foreign Office. There were also protectorates whose indigenous rulers, like Malay sultans, remained theoretically sovereign. In condominiums, power was vested in two imperial partners – as in the Sudan where control was legally shared with Egypt, or the New Hebrides, which was jointly administered with France. After the First World War, Britain, Australia, New Zealand, and South Africa acquired mandated territories from Germany's lost colonies and the Arab lands of the old Ottoman empire, for whose administration they were answerable to the League of Nations. A diversity of type of colony produced a diversity of overseas services, segregated from one another – for example, the Indian, Sudan, and other civil services. (There was no unified colonial service until 1930.) Nevertheless, there was a significant amount of transfer from dependency to dependency of personnel, constitutional forms (such as the crown colony model), and administrative devices (such as federal schemes and methods of policing).

The hotch-potch of constitutional forms was largely determined by local circumstances, by topography, and by the nature of the societies in the empire. It also reflected something of the nature of the British themselves, who preferred rhetoric to theory, distrusted precise definitions as hostages to fortune, made a virtue of compromise, and revelled in ambiguity. However, the varied dependencies were commonly grouped, for the purposes of generalization if not administration, in one of several categories: the colonies of settlement, India, and the tropical colonies. As far as the first category was concerned, it was assumed that the destiny of white people was to rule themselves. Appropriate for the other two, on the other hand, was indefinite government by 'heaven-born' white males who agreed with Alexander Pope that 'what e'er is best administer'd is best', placed good government above self-government, authority above liberty, and the preservation of traditional

societies above the introduction of alien parliamentary institutions. This duality
stretched back to the late eighteenth century when American colonists defended
their rights as 'free-born Englishmen' and Edmund Burke, in his attacks on Warren
Hastings and the abuses of early British rule in India, enunciated the principle of
'trusteeship' to guide British rule over non-Europeans.

The government of India perhaps presented the starkest contrast to the limited
involvement of the state in liberal England. Until the 1930s the colonial
government in India, independently of the British Treasury and contrary to British
traditions, raised sufficient revenue to cover the cost of an enormous standing army.
As what Lord Salisbury saw as 'an English barrack in the Oriental Seas', it not only
kept law and order in India and secured the frontiers of the Raj, but was called upon
to quell disturbances in other parts of the empire as well. It was accepted, moreover,
that Britain's Indian experience and the models established there for administering
lands and assessing taxation were applicable, at least in general terms, to other non-
European dependencies. However, each colony had its own traditions and practices
of administration, and none ranked with India in economic and international
importance or in sheer prestige. In fact, before 1945 governments of tropical
colonies lacked the funds, manpower, and expertise to perform much more than
the basic functions of maintaining law and order and raising taxes.

The 'informal empire'

The various categories of imperial government considered so far were all formally
attached to Britain by constitutional or administrative links. But British influence

The Sultan of Zanzibar and his
British advisers, *c*.1902. Sultan
Seyyid Ali, who succeeded in
1902 aged eighteen, had been
educated at Harrow. Nominally
an independent ruler, he was
very much dominated by the
British Agent and a British
First Minister, who acted as
regent at the beginning of his
reign. Informal empire was
in this case turning into
outright rule.

was not limited to this formal empire. Much British trade, investment, emigration, and culture affected societies lying outside those parts of the world painted 'British red' on the map – notably China, Latin America, and the Middle East. Such regions, which retained nominal independence while succumbing to British influence, are often described as Britain's 'informal empire'. Here, with the help of local collaborators, Britain was able to enjoy power without the costs of responsibility. Sometimes British influence took the form of commercial agreements with ostensibly sovereign states, such as Argentina, China, and Siam (Thailand). In other cases Britain secured its interests in strategically vital territories through diplomatic pressure and the appointment of key advisers. This was the case with Zanzibar, for example. In 1832 Seyyid Said, the Arab ruler of Oman in the Persian Gulf, laid the foundations of Zanzibar's importance by transferring his capital there from Muscat. Soon Zanzibar became the principal city in East Africa: it commanded the African coast of the Indian Ocean and held the key to the interior. 'If you play on the flute at Zanzibar,' ran an Arab proverb, 'everybody as far as the lakes dances.' By treaties and gun-boat diplomacy, Britain played on the flute to good effect: in 1890 France and Germany recognized the supremacy of British interests in the sultanate; the following year a government was constituted with a British representative as the Sultan's First Minister; in 1896 British warships bombarded the palace in order to reinstate the Sultan who had been overthrown by a member of the royal family. By the First World War, the offices of the British Consul-General and the Sultan's First Minister had been merged in the newly-created post of British Resident.

Were such relationships really 'imperial' at all? Those who dispute this argue that local economies – of, say, West Africa, Latin America, and China – did not revolve exclusively round British business interests and they cite numerous occasions when the British government was either unwilling or unable to get its own way in areas of so-called 'informal empire'. What is clear, however, is that the divide between empire and influence was often indistinct. Even in the formal empire Britain's presence was neither established simply by force nor sustained solely by British personnel; rather it depended upon the tacit acquiescence of the majority and the active and widespread support of indigenous leaders. In the informal empire, on the other hand, the co-operation of local leaders was underpinned by their perceptions of British power and their assumption that a solitary Briton on the spot could, if he chose, call up superior forces which were believed to be lurking beyond the horizon.

Britain's changing relationship with Egypt illustrates the difficulties of drawing a clear line between empire and influence. Following the Khedive's bankruptcy in 1875, Britain joined France in the dual control of Egypt's finances: Britain did so partly to strengthen the khedivate and partly to prevent the French taking command of the route to India. The British government wished to avoid seizing Egypt for itself but an Egyptian revolt led to British military intervention in 1882 and the installation of a British Agent and Consul-General. Thereafter, Sir Evelyn Baring (later Lord Cromer), who was British Agent from 1883 to 1907, and succeeding British representatives in Cairo acted as the power behind the throne. In February 1942, during the Second World War, Sir Miles Lampson (later Lord Killearn) surrounded Abdin Palace with tanks and imposed upon the Egyptian King Farouk a Prime Minister who was reliably hostile to the Axis powers. All this suggests that, despite their lack of legal sovereignty, the British had drawn Egypt into their formal empire. Yet throughout their seventy-year occupation of the country, Britain's freedom of manoeuvre was circumscribed by the waywardness of Egypt's rulers, the truculence of Egypt's nationalists, and the presence in the country of competing international interests.

THE LIMITATIONS OF POWER

Although some element of force, whether overt or latent, was always present in the acquisition of territory, eradication of resistance, collection of taxes, and deployment of labour, coercion was of limited value in the running of an empire.

The use of force could backfire and damage a government's standing at home. Colonial wars and the ruthless suppression of revolts excited bitter controversy; liberal critics of empire condemned militarism and feared it presaged the growth of authoritarianism in Britain. For example, James Brooke's punitive expedition against the piratical sea Dyaks of Sarawak created a furore which was only resolved when a royal commission cleared his name in 1854. The infinitely more horrific atrocities and reprisals carried out by both sides during the Indian Rebellion of 1857 rocked Victorian self-confidence to its foundations. Governor Eyre's merciless handling of a black rising in Jamaica in 1865 – after which 439 people were hanged, a further 600 were flogged, and thousands of homes were destroyed – rekindled the fiery debate, with the philosopher and Liberal Member of Parliament, John Stuart Mill, raising the question 'whether the British dependencies, and eventually, perhaps, Great Britain itself, were to be under the government of law or of military licence'. The costs of war, together with vociferous parliamentary opposition to taxation, further inhibited the government's freedom of action.

Using force could also complicate Britain's relations with other powers. Although Britain won major concessions in China as the result of the Opium Wars of 1839–42 and 1856–60, a major reason why governments held back from territorial expansion there was the danger of provoking Russia, France, and the United States. Britain's occupation of Egypt in 1882 and subsequent expansion into the Sudan so alienated the French that the two European powers almost went to war over the Upper Nile in 1898 when Colonel Marchand confronted General Kitchener after the British victory at Omdurman.

In the colonies themselves, the resort to arms might result in all sorts of untoward developments. Since British troops were not invincible – indeed they suffered humiliating defeats at, for example, Isandlhwana by the Zulu (1879) and

Paul Bogle. Bogle, a Baptist deacon, was one of the leaders of the Morant Bay rising of black people in Jamaica in October 1865. On the suppression of the rebellion, he was tried under martial law and hanged. Such atrocities were much criticized in Britain and produced a vigorous altercation between those who held the Governor responsible and his defenders.

Majuba Hill by the Afrikaners (1881), the use of force risked calling Britain's bluff. Moreover, even when it was initially effective, the pronounced assertion of power could ultimately prove its very undoing, as happened when, having achieved supremacy in North America at the end of the Seven Years War (1756–63), the British government aroused colonial resistance by unprecedented interference in local affairs – above all by trying to impose British parliamentary taxes.

Conquest, direct rule, economic exploitation, social engineering – each in its different way provoked local resistance to the British connection more readily than did 'salutary neglect' or simply leaving people to their own devices. Not only might the naked use of power set in train ultimately triumphant opposition movements, so, too, could revelations of its ineffectiveness.

The defeat of Sir George Colley at Majuba Hill, 26 February 1881. The Afrikaner republic of the Transvaal had been annexed to the British empire in 1877. When a revolt broke out in 1881, British troops under Colley were sent to the Transvaal, but were driven off Majuba Hill with the loss of ninety-two killed (including Colley) by a force of Afrikaner 'Boers'.

Another consideration was the shortage of manpower, which often stretched to breaking-point the thin red, white, and blue lines of soldiers, administrators, and police. In India during the 1930s, for instance, a mere 4,000 British civil servants assisted by 60,000 white soldiers and 90,000 civilians (who for the most part were businessmen and planters) were attempting to control more than 338 million people. Reliance on locally recruited troops could undermine Britain's military presence, as happened in the Indian Rebellion of 1857 and again in 1947. Furthermore, in spite of awe-inspiring improvements in communications, the 'tyranny of distance' prevented the empire from shrinking to the proportions of a 'global village', with the result that outposts could be left militarily exposed, as was the fate of Gordon in Khartoum in 1884–85. Finally, the unfamiliar environments of jungle or desert could negate the effectiveness of military tactics and materials developed for other conditions, as the British discovered in fighting colonial wars and, later, wars of decolonization.

The Antigua cricket club with the Governor, 1913. Sport was one of the means by which British values were instilled into the peoples of the empire. Here in the Caribbean people from different ethnic groups have been inducted into the rituals of cricket under imperial patronage. But cricket could also threaten the imperial order. West Indians used it to express their own sense of identity, as when largely black teams defeated England in test matches. Even more subversive behaviour was reported from Ceylon where a British engineer was considered '"socially impossible" because he used to play cricket with his half-caste bastards'. The objection was 'not that they were bastards or half-castes or, altogether, that he played cricket with them, but that he did so on the ground adjoining the Lawn Tennis Club's court'.

Compensating for difficulties

Conscious of the tenuousness of their grip, the British often eased their task by limiting the objectives they set themselves: having intervened in the first place to secure a frontier or defend a trade route or discover an additional source of revenue, thereafter they generally restricted themselves to the maintenance of law and order and the collection of taxes. Additional interference might well result in trouble: the spectre of uprising hung over the Raj from the time of the 1857 rebellion to 1947, and civil services elsewhere recalled similar incidents, like the Perak War in Malaya in 1875, when excessive zeal had provoked resistance. Using India's Grand Trunk road as an allegory of the limitations of British rule, Kipling wrote:

> A stone's throw out on either hand
> From that well-ordered road we tread
> And all the world is wild and strange.

Keeping order was not just a matter of keeping out of trouble; it also required strict adherence to rules and regulations. A culture of orderliness contributed to colonial stability and to an extent compensated for the superficiality of the imperial presence. Orderliness was expressed in British perceptions of themselves and in their attitudes to subject peoples. British self-esteem and the integrity of their regime were buttressed by social hierarchies and codes of behaviour which were themselves underpinned by government gazettes, the rhythms of the imperial calendar, the white tribalism of the club, 'manliness', and the cult of games.

Collaboration

Even in the pursuit of limited objectives, colonial regimes had to make up for their lack both of expatriate manpower and of a capacity to coerce their subjects by involving some of them in the business of administration. This became another constraint upon the exercise of power, as the more astute imperial practitioners were well aware. Indigenous and creole communities were not passive recipients of British influence. Nor did they merely react to the British presence; they operated from their own power bases and pursued their own objectives. The fact that emerging colonial societies were rarely homogeneous compounded the problems of control: some were geographical expressions, many were peopled by immigrants, and most were riven by racial and ethnic feuds. Thus British authorities attempted to arbitrate in Canada between the French majority in Quebec and the British minority, who wished to be subject to English rather than French law, and in South Africa between English-speakers and Afrikaners about whose language or whose system of law was to apply where. In Asia and Africa indigenous rulers were frequently in positions to shape the course of imperial advance and the pattern of colonial occupation. Where colonial officials had few resources at their immediate disposal, Asians and Africans sometimes succeeded in retaining significant elements of traditional authority or in winning places in the new colonial state. Even where colonial states were solidly constructed, the imperial authorities were not immune from challenge: on the contrary, the more elaborate, sophisticated, and pervasive the administration became, the more it depended upon creole and indigenous collaborators interested in taking over the direction of the system. India, for example, could only be governed with the assistance of very large numbers of Indian officials, who were even recruited in increasing numbers into the ranks of the previously all-white Indian civil service after the First World War.

In general terms colonies were either administered 'directly', by British officials, or indirectly, through British supervision of 'native' authorities. In the exercise of direct rule, as in provincial India or coastal West Africa, officials required the services of western-educated clerks, whom they otherwise held in some contempt as 'denationalized natives'. But where European influence had had less of a disruptive impact, colonial officials patronized traditional indigenous leaders like Indian princes or Fulani emirs or Malay sultans. The scheme of indirect rule, which the colonial administrator Frederick Lugard developed in northern Nigeria, became the orthodox method of 'native administration' throughout tropical Africa during the interwar period. But it was little more than the rationalization of a pragmatic response to the problems of controlling huge tracts of land with meagre resources. Here political officers conducted local government through African chiefs. Ruling through chiefs triggered a quest for chiefs: in societies where there were no chiefs – for example in southern Nigeria or among the Kikuyu of East Africa – the British created them. In so doing, they encouraged the new science of anthropology and led administrators to advance some ethnic groups over others. In

Pledging allegiance to the Governor of the Gold Coast at Kumasi, 1946. Indirect rule through 'traditional' chiefs persisted over most of the Gold Coast even after the Second World War, although many Africans were by then were rejecting the authority of the chiefs and claiming the right to participate in democratic politics.

Indirect rule: British relations with Malay sultans

British Malaya consisted of nine Malay states together with the Straits Settlements. Control over the Malay states rested on agreements concluded with Malay sultans between 1874 and 1914, not on conquest or annexation, and the people remained the subjects of the sultans; in the Straits Settlements they became British citizens.

Resembling Britain's relationship with the Indian princely states, the residential or advisory system of Malaya confirmed the sultans as sovereign yet obliged them to accept their British advisers' guidance in all things other than religion and custom. Such a sharp distinction was in fact inappropriate to the conduct of Malay government and the first Resident of the Malay state of Perak, James Birch, overstepped the mark in 1875 when he attempted to take over the chiefs' customary rights to taxation and to abolish their customary right to make slaves of those who could not pay their debts. Birch was speared to death in a riverside bathhouse and Perak erupted in a short colonial war. Subsequent residents – such as Hugh Low (Resident of Perak, 1877–99) who recognized that the British 'must first create the government to be advised' – were more subtle in maintaining the fiction of Malay sovereignty while building up an administrative system geared to British needs. The British presence had contradictory effects on the position of the Malay sultans: it enhanced their authority but it reduced their power. As Malaya prospered, the wealth and status of the sultans increased but their governmental functions were taken over by the Malayan civil service.

A young British civil servant described the situation at Trengganu in eastern Malaya where he was posted in the 1930s. On his arrival he was introduced to 'His Highness the Sultan ... one of the most dignified men I have ever met', together with the Malay Chief Minister and State Secretary. Although he felt that the 'senior Malay officials in Trengganu still regarded the British presence as a scarcely tolerable intrusion', the real power was exercised by the British Adviser (he was called the Resident in other states) who directed the administration. Under him were a British Commissioner of Lands and Collectors of Land Revenue. British officials sat in the high court with judges appointed by the Sultan. Thus the British controlled the essential functions of government, the allocation of land, the raising of finance, and the administration of justice. British officials were also put in command of the state's police and its public works and medical departments.

India the British were accused of deliberately highlighting the differences between Hindu and Muslim the better to control them, and in Cairo the British Consul-General shored up the Turco-Egyptian khedivate against Egyptian nationalism. In Nigeria political officers favoured the Hausa against the 'coast African'; and the Malay was preferred to the migrant Chinese in Malaya. Collaboration with some was matched by discrimination against others; ethnic stereotypology was another instrument in the administrator's toolbox assisting him in 'divide and rule'. Subject peoples were identified as princes or peasants, as warriors or clerks, as nomads or labourers, as Hindus or Muslims, as 'denationalized' (that is, western-educated) or 'real' (that is, uncorrupted by European influences). They were corralled in various quarters by map makers and census takers, town planners and recruiting officers, ethnographers and medical practitioners. This contributed to the compartmentalization of colonial societies and the multiplication of communal identities.

Consolidation

Both the way in which the British saw their subjects and their administrative practices tended towards fragmentation. What were presumed to be different groups of people were treated differently. Yet very fragmented societies are almost

Opening of the first Parliament of the Union of South Africa at Cape Town, 4 November 1910. The Duke of Connaught, uncle of King George V, reads the royal message at the ceremony that marked the end of a long and often bitter quest for unity by the white population of South Africa.

impossible to govern. So the managers of empire at home and on the spot were constantly on the lookout for opportunities to draw together the components of a dependency and to consolidate control over a wider region. Schemes of closer association, union, or federation were devised to improve the administrative efficiency, economic development, and security of scattered dependencies, as well as to release Britain from the chores of routine local government. For example, Lord Durham, who was appointed High Commissioner to examine the government of Canada following the risings of 1837, recommended the union of Upper (English) and Lower (French) Canada. This was implemented by the Act of Union, 1840, and followed up in 1867 by the British North America Act, creating the Dominion of Canada as a federation of Quebec, Ontario, Nova Scotia, and New Brunswick.

Subsequently joined by other provinces, this federal state allowed Canadians to open up the west and keep United States expansionism at bay. Other federal plans took much longer to come to fruition. The disparate Australian colonies were jealous of their separate identities and did not take up federal suggestions when the Colonial Secretary put them forward in the late 1840s; however, international threats posed by French and German expansion in the 1880s and the economic depression of the next decade spurred their closer association, with the result that the Commonwealth of Australia (a federation whose central powers were weaker than those in Canada) came into being on 1 January 1901. Closer association of British colonies and Afrikaner republics in southern Africa, mooted as early as the 1850s, was rejected by the Afrikaners until, following their defeat in the South African War of 1899–1902, the recolonized republics of the Transvaal and Orange Free State (renamed the Orange River Colony) were granted responsible self-government in 1906–1907. They were then inspired to leap-frog cautious schemes of federation to embrace a union constitution (the Union of South Africa) in 1908–10. Vain attempts were made to federate the Leeward and Windward Islands in the Caribbean during 1870s and 1880s, but an initiative in Malaya did result in the inauguration of the Federated Malay States in 1896.

After 1945, as Britain prepared to withdraw from empire, its interest in the 'closer association' of adjacent territories turned into more active attempts at 'nation-building'. This task was made more difficult by Britain's incapacity both to reverse the legacy of its earlier policy of 'divide and rule' and to contain the force of nationalist movements. Civil servants and constitutional lawyers engineered elaborate federal plans in order to strike a series of balances between central and provincial powers, majority and minority rights, national independence and safeguards for British interests. But, despite their good intentions, these were frequently cumbersome, impractical, and shortlived, if not still-born. In India, for example, a convoluted federal scheme contained in the Government of India Act of 1935 never bore fruit largely on account of the mistrust of Indian princes for Indian politicians and of Indian politicians for each other – a mistrust to which British rule had significantly contributed in the past. Such was the intensity of communal politics by the end of the Second World War, that the Viceroy, Lord Mountbatten, achieved a negotiated settlement with the Indian National Congress and the Muslim League only by paying the price of partition. Similarly, as regards Africa in the 1950s and early 1960s, the British lamented that plans for regional integration were overwhelmed by the politics of component territories and that 'nation-building' was obstructed by what they chose to call 'tribalism', a phenomenon that prewar indirect rule had in some measure shaped. Thus inchoate plans for the union of Britain's three East African colonies were swept aside by nationalist movements in Kenya, Tanganyika (Tanzania), and Uganda, while the Central African Federation (1953–64) could not survive the antagonism between Africans and Europeans (see page 101). Another disappointment was the Federation of the

West Indies which, having been conceived in the closing months of the Second World War and inaugurated in 1958, disintegrated within a few years and before independence had been attained because Jamaica and Trinidad aspired to separate nationhood. On the other hand, the Nigerian federation survived bloody civil war in the late 1960s and the Malaysian federation outlived the secession of Singapore in 1965. Scattered 'fortress colonies' and 'city-states' – such as Gibraltar, Hong Kong, and the Falkland Islands – posed special problems in the era of decolonization. Their imperial function had been to watch over vital sea lanes, serve as coaling stations, act as listening posts, and provide links in a chain of world-wide communications. But their size and vulnerability ruled them out as candidates for 'nationhood'. Consequently, while their isolation prevented their amalgamation with similarly placed territories, it was considered irresponsible to offer them independence on their own.

THE PROJECTION OF POWER

Largely because it was diffuse and decentralized, Britain's seaborne empire posed huge managerial problems. Bombastic portrayals of a far-flung empire over palm and pine upon which the sun never set called attention to appearances of British might and imperial unity but disguised the real constraints upon British power both 'on the spot' in individual territories and in the administration of the empire from London. Sometimes imperial power seemed a burden; yet frequently it was something of an illusion. Contemporary apologists for the British empire, therefore, used ceremonial set-pieces and images of its institutions to justify its existence, soften its impact, or disguise its weakness, and to mollify its subjects, counter its critics, or discipline its practitioners. In short, they took pains to present the acceptable face of Britain's imperial power by projecting Britain's imperial authority.

Authority, or the right to exercise power, ultimately depends on a mental attitude – on the confidence of the rulers and the acceptance of subordination by the ruled. During the time of the British empire, much of this was shaped by the sheer display of power. In addition to regular but ephemeral military parades and naval reviews, more lasting and no less ostentatious pronouncements of imperial authority were made in brick and stone. Public buildings were a metaphor of power (see page 238). Sharp differences between the *laissez-faire* state of liberal England and the authoritarianism of colonial regimes are conveyed, for example, in the contrast between the unprepossessing residence of the British Prime Minister in Downing Street and the grandeur of almost any of the government houses decorating British dependencies from India to the West Indies.

The projection of empire began in the capital itself. The need to remind British citizens of their imperial duties and to impress visiting colonials with the grandeur of Britain were central to plans of architects and empire builders alike for redesigning London. One such visionary was Sir James Pennethorne, who became

adviser to the Office of Works in 1854. Pennethorne wanted to construct an imperial capital that would eclipse Paris, Rome, and Vienna: 'I looked upon the Metropolis as belonging to the Empire … [and] the Empire ought … to pay for beautifying the Metropolis … It is visited perhaps by a million out of the country and foreigners every year, and every man in the Empire is interested in [its] appearance … [its] open space and public buildings.' A century later Churchill similarly looked forward to the day when 'the whole of the area from the Central Hall to the Houses of Parliament, and from Great George Street to Westminster Abbey [might] be cleared of buildings [so that] a great square could be laid out as a truly noble setting for the heart of the British Empire'. By then both Churchill and his empire were in their dotage, and, had his scheme come to pass, it would have been something of a counter-reformatory gesture, like the rebuilding of New Delhi by Sir Edwin Lutyens and Sir Herbert Baker from 1912 (see pages 242–43). As it was, the institutions involved in the management of empire were scattered about Westminster and Whitehall, their loose architectural configuration being more or less indicative of the varying commitment and capacity of the British state to control the activities of the British overseas during two centuries of imperial expansion and contraction. Yet, although the capital boasted no Baron Haussmann, its landmarks are redolent of Britain's imperial experience, from Trafalgar Square to Waterloo Station, from commemorative statuary in London's squares to Matthew Wyatt's magnificent Durbar Court in the India Office. The British Museum, Natural History Museum, Science Museum, and Kew Gardens were imperial monuments of another kind. Treasuries of art and temples of science, they were also

Government House, Dar es Salaam. Tanganyika (Tanzania) was taken from the Germans during the First World War. The British built an imposing new Government House in 1922 in 'the Moorish style' on the site of the old German Governor's residence.

Crown, Parliament, and Law

Colonies before the eighteenth century were solely the concern of the English monarch. In as far as any control was exercised over them, it was done by the monarch's personal servants on his or her Privy Council. English settlers in new colonies took the common law of England with them. Conquered peoples were allowed to keep their own laws at the discretion of the Crown. Local laws were made by assemblies, subject to the approval of the Crown through the Privy Council.

In a rough way these principles were still applied in the later empire. There was, however, one major additional complication. Parliament became involved in colonial affairs as a part of the general assertion of its right to be concerned with the business of government from the eighteenth century onwards. The officials who supervised colonial government were still in name the servants of the Crown exercising its powers, but in reality the head of colonial administration, the Colonial Secretary, was a minister responsible to Parliament and great issues of colonial policy were decided by the British Cabinet. The Privy Council, however, still exercised the royal prerogatives to review local laws and to be a final court of appeal from colonial courts until the end of empire.

From the eighteenth century the British Parliament also made laws for the colonies and for a time tried to tax them. The taxing power was given up in 1778; the law-making power remained until colonies became independent or until 1931 in the case of the Dominions when Parliament renounced its powers in the Statute of Westminster. Great issues, such as those affecting the constitutional development of colonies, were the subject of British parliamentary legislation, but Parliament generally left the initiative for local law making to local legislatures.

In the colonies law tended to evolve roughly along the lines established in the remote past. British emigrants took the common law with them and adapted it to local conditions by their own law making. Elsewhere the legal traditions of people who had been conquered and incorporated into the empire were drawn upon: Roman-Dutch law in South Africa, Islamic law in India or Malaysia, Hindu law also in India, what were believed to be customary 'tribal' laws in parts of Africa. The evolution of local legal systems was extremely complex. British principles were applied to what was inevitably a selective use of other sources of law, whose actual workings

were not always well understood. What emerged was often a kind of hybrid between British and non-British traditions, as in the British–Indian legal codes which began with the work of the famous historian, Thomas Macaulay, in 1835, and have become the basis for the law of modern India. With each colony making law in its own way through legislation and the decision of its own courts, the British empire developed a huge variety of legal systems, which combined British statutory law, English common law, and the codification of local customary law. Visiting the Malay states in 1879 during the early days of the British advisory system, that intrepid Victorian traveller, Isabella Bird, observed that 'a most queerly muddled system of law prevails under our flag'. Here Islam and the belief that the Sultan was the fount of justice were complicating factors but, even though Malay custom and religion were left to traditional authorities, the sphere of *adat* (custom) and religious law were increasingly circumscribed and redefined by the colonial system.

British people liked to believe, however, that certain principles – such as equality before the law, the independence of the judiciary, and the rule of law – were present in all of them. Against that must be set an historian's verdict that in Africa new rulers learnt from the British that 'law consists of the directives of the state and is a prime means of securing its goals and exercising its powers. The colonial period provided no foundation for the use of law by citizens in defence of their rights.' [AJS/PJM]

Thomas Babington Macaulay. Macaulay, politician and man of letters, compiled the Indian criminal code during his Indian service from 1834 to 1838.

memorials to British expansion and acquisitiveness overseas. In displaying knowledge of the world, these permanent exhibitions also conveyed a confident capacity to control it.

The British constitution and the empire

In these and other ways power was displayed – perhaps the more vigorously when either its reality or its legitimacy was suspect. But Britain's imperial authority was also projected – both to a British public at home and to those whom Britain ruled overseas – through demonstrating the moral virtue of its rulers as well as the efficacy of its institutions. 'The power of Great Britain', wrote Sydney Smith Bell in 1859, 'is … founded entirely upon the moral, social, and political qualities of my countrymen, fostered and encouraged, as these are, by the free institutions which

Previous page: The 1903 Delhi
durbar. A durbar was a
ceremony at which subjects
paid homage to their ruler,
while the ruler or a
representative appeared
before them with a massive
display of military power. The
British held enormous durbars
for Indian princes – here
shown in procession on their
elephants, to salute their
sovereign. In the durbar of
1903, Edward VII, whose
accession to the throne was
being celebrated, was
represented by the Viceroy,
Lord Curzon. In 1911 George
V attended the last great
durbar in person.

they enjoy.' The British compared themselves favourably with foreigners and
contrasted their imperial rule with that of other Europeans or with the atrocities
and abuses perpetrated by non-Europeans on each other.

Such virtue could be sanctified by law and custom, and would be sustained by
the Crown, Parliament, and the courts, which supposedly provided subjects with
redress against injustice and arbitrary decisions through a chain of appeal leading
from the colonies to the judicial committee of the Privy Council. (This committee
took into account the different legal systems in the various territories of the empire.
As colonies advanced to self-government so they withdrew the right of appeal to the
judicial committee, though some retained it even after achieving independence.)

Right: Nigerian cloth
commemorating the silver
jubilee of George V, 1935. This
adire cloth, with stencilled
motifs, is an example of
the projection of monarchy
throughout the empire.
The heads of the King and
Queen Mary were added to
conventional Islamic designs.

The rule of law – that is, the principle that justice, fairness, and due process are applied automatically and indiscriminately to all by every organ of state – could underpin authority. With the law supreme, both tyranny and arbitrary government would, the British believed, be prevented.

The most powerful symbol of British authority was the monarch, to whom all in the empire and Commonwealth owed allegiance. The image of the monarch was manipulated by successive prime ministers from Disraeli to Churchill. Despite the retreat of the 'widow of Windsor' from the public eye, Victoria was portrayed in splendour as Empress of India or more simply as 'great white mother' to all her peoples. The cult of crown imperial linked to an immemorial past was part of the nineteenth-century rediscovery of tradition, gothic revivalism, and a return to Camelot. Stamps and banknotes, medals and coins all bore the monarch's portrait. New chivalric orders were created for the reward of loyal servants and in recognition of valued allies: the Most Distinguished Order of St Michael and St George (1818), the Most Exalted Order of the Star of India (1861), the Most Eminent Order of the Indian Empire (1868), the Royal Victorian Order (1896), and the Most Excellent Order of the British Empire (1917). The ritual and pageantry of the coronation service, investitures, and durbars, and the celebrations surrounding the monarch's birthday and anniversaries of accession (as in 1887, 1897, and 1935), joined in the twentieth century by the Christmas broadcast, royal tours, and Empire Day, all contributed to the invention of an imperial tradition.

The monarchy was the emblem of stability, unity, and order both at home and overseas, whereas Parliament, which stood as the guarantor against arbitrary rule, symbolized freedom within the empire. Although it was somewhat removed from the routine control of dependent territories, Parliament was of prime and constant importance to those who were preoccupied with upholding Britain's global position. It was equally important to those who were committed to the protection of imperial subjects. The monarch's loyal ministers, servants, and officers overseas were accountable to Parliament whose members accepted responsibility for the rights and interests of those subjects who were not represented there as well as those who were. Parliament could, for instance, call to account unruly colonial officials, as it did in the case of Robert Clive in the 1770s or the prison officers guilty of atrocities in Kenya's Hola Camp two centuries later. It was through parliamentary action that slavery was eventually outlawed in the British empire and it was upon the parliamentary model that first the white Dominions and later moderate political leaders elsewhere aspired to self-determination.

Those seeking redress of grievances in the colonies placed their trust in the British Parliament. Apart from the Irish Home Rule party, however, examples of colonial politicians achieving direct representation are rare. Dadabhai Naoroji, who was three times President of the Indian National Congress, sat as a Liberal Member of Parliament from 1892 to 1895. As a Conservative Member of Parliament from 1895 to 1905, Mancherjee Bhownaggree advocated the cause of the disadvantaged

The South African coloured and African delegation to Britain, 1909. While white political leaders were taking the draft constitution for the new Union of South Africa to Britain for ratification, a delegation from coloured (mixed-race) and African political organizations also came to appeal to British justice against some parts of the draft, such as the provision that non-whites could not be members of the new Parliament. The delegation was headed by W.P. Schreiner, a liberal-minded white politician. It was unable to obtain concessions.

Indians of South Africa. Shapurji Saklatvala moved from the prosperity of his family's Tata Iron and Steel Works to, in turn, membership of the Liberal, Labour, and Communist parties, being elected to Parliament as a Labour candidate and later as a Communist in the 1920s.

Otherwise, there are many more instances of nationalist leaders attempting to influence Parliament by petitioning Secretaries of State and lobbying Members of Parliament, often in the hope that all would be well once they had got round obstructive administrators. For example, in 1914 J.W. Dube led a deputation from the African National Congress to protest – without success – against legislation passed in South Africa restricting the purchase of land by black Africans. Similarly, in 1918 Zaghlul Pasha came to London at the head of a delegation of Egyptian nationalists campaigning for the end of the British protectorate. During the 1930s leaders of the Indian National Congress established a close rapport with Labour politicians, notably Attlee, Stafford Cripps, and Harold Laski, and in the 1950s and 1960s Labour Members of Parliament promoted the cause of Afro-Asian nationalism through the Movement for Colonial Freedom.

By setting standards, no matter how loose and ill-defined, Parliament scrutinized the activities of the British overseas and justified imperial rule to the world at large. The concept of trusteeship was first enunciated in relation to Asia during the parliamentary impeachment of Warren Hastings, who was eventually acquitted of the charges of tyranny, rapacity, and corruption alleged to have been perpetrated whilst he was Governor-General of India from 1774 to 1785. Thereafter Members of Parliament regularly proclaimed their obligations as trustees for dependent peoples until the ending of the African empire when Enoch Powell (see page 332) declared, 'We cannot, we dare not, in Africa of all places, fall below our own highest standards in the acceptance of responsibility.'

The prestige attached to the so-called 'Westminster model' was demonstrated by the ease with which it was exported overseas. British people, anxious to secure imperial unity, promoted such exports, but they were eagerly received by nationalists seeking freedom from imperial subjugation, for whom a parliament on British lines was the embodiment of freedom – even though the written constitutions, federal structures, and one-party states that sprang up in the former colonies could hardly be regarded as mere clones of Britain's parliamentary system.

Lord Curzon as Viceroy of India. Curzon has been described as 'the greatest administrator that India has ever known'. He had an ambitious vision of how British India should develop, even if he saw little role for Indian political participation in its development.

'English supremacy should last until the end of time'

For two centuries, possession of empire was justified by British politicians on either authoritarian or libertarian grounds and sometimes on both. Those who saw the virtues of empire as authoritarian maintained that it committed the rulers, or 'guardians', to service and bound the ruled to obedience; while those who saw the empire as libertarian claimed that it provided subject peoples with freedom from oppression at the hands of 'lesser breeds without the law', such as their own 'self-appointed' leaders or foreign adventurers or unbridled British colonialists. Witness, for example, the claims that British rule was preferable to that of the French, Dutch, Germans, or Belgians, and that the empire would free Asians from oriental despotism, Africans from barbaric customs, Maoris from settler rapacity, and white settlers from international aggression. 'There has never been anything so great in the world's history', declared Curzon (Viceroy of India, 1898–1905), 'than the British Empire, so great an instrument for the good of humanity.' This flourish was echoed by highly individualistic Dominion premiers. One, Alexander Mackenzie (Prime Minister of Canada 1873–78), was 'anxious that … English supremacy should last until the end of time, because it means universal freedom, universal liberty, emancipation from everything degrading'. Another, William Hughes (Prime Minister of Australia 1915–23), maintained that 'without the Empire we shall be tossed like a cork in the cross-current of world politics. It is at once our sword and our shield.'

The main British political parties had different interpretations of empire. Conservatives stood for empire as authority, order, and good government; Liberals looked beyond the provision of good government for its own sake to the evolution of colonies into self-governing societies and of the empire into a Commonwealth of Nations. Planning the anglicization of India through English education in the 1830s, the politician and historian Thomas Macaulay foresaw the moment when

Britain would transfer power while, seventy years later, the Liberal Prime Minister Henry Campbell-Bannerman reiterated the pledge that 'good government could never be a satisfactory substitute for self-government'. In spite of distinctive differences between authoritarian and libertarian interpretations of the imperial mission, however, all governments were as reluctant to end their empire as they had originally been to acquire it. In so far as they were in fact able to control political developments in their dependencies, they measured out concessions on scales calibrating the material progress, social stability, and political 'maturity' of subject peoples. Liberal, Conservative, and Labour governments all preferred the prospect of 'freedom through empire' to that of 'freedom from empire'.

FREEDOM FROM IMPERIAL RULE

However skilfully the images of empire were projected, there were always those who disbelieved them. 'Lies are one of the central pillars of the British Empire', said Jayaprakash Narayan, a prominent member of the Indian National Congress. For those who chafed at the flummery accompanying the iron fist of foreign rule and denounced the humbug of imperial rhetoric, offers of freedom within the empire were far less attractive than the possibility of enjoying freedom without it. Indeed, the goal of those who, like Gandhi, preferred to be seen as rebels rather than subjects was national freedom.

The British empire was to be succeeded by a series of nation states, based in nearly every case on the colonies that the British had created. The inevitability of the triumph of colonial nationalism can be taken too easily for granted. At the time, few British people anticipated such a conclusion. Their idea of what constituted a 'nation' was usually based on the German, Italian, or even Irish nationalism of the nineteenth century – movements through which a people who shared a common language, set of historical traditions, or sense of ethnic identity either recovered or won their independence. By these criteria, however, most of the colonial populations clearly did not constitute nations. In Africa very different peoples had been brought into a new colonial territory by the random processes of European treaty making. India was a subcontinent full of peoples of different languages and religions, whose boundaries had been fixed by the limits of British conquest. The ultimate destiny of the peoples of the colonies of settlement seemed to lie in closer relations with their fellow Britons at home, not in separate nationhood.

Yet British colonial rule provided the basic elements of unity – a single government and, in the case of non-European peoples, at least for an elite, English as a common language. Thus colonies created by an alien power became the focus for the loyalties and aspirations of the often very mixed populations brought together within their boundaries. Peoples' ambitions to control their own affairs came to be directed at taking over the colonial states through which they had been ruled. There were strong pressures either to fragment these states into smaller units of ethnically similar peoples or to merge them into larger entities, such as movements for African unity or for the unity of Muslims. But, with a few exceptions, most notably the partition of India in 1947, nationalisms based on colonial territories have been embodied in nations.

Freedom for settlers

The British overseas were self-consciously British. Although they were on their guard against infringements of their rights and freedoms from imperial interference and centralization upon London, they expected, and regularly called upon Britain for, military or economic protection. The early British settlers remained tenaciously loyal to the mother country. Whatever their reasons for emigration, British settlers in Australasia persisted in regarding Britain as home up to the early twentieth century. White farmers in East and Central Africa from around 1900 onwards combined allegiance to the Crown with criticism of British governments who fell short of the expatriate's expectations of Britishness. Gradually, however, these cultural and kinship ties with Britain weakened in the face of the other factors promoting separate Dominion identities (see pages 269–73).

Affray between British troops and French Canadians, November 1837. During the 1830s French-speaking Canada was troubled by political conflicts between the local politicians and the British Governor and by the economic difficulties of the farming community suffering from a recession. In 1837 and 1838 some of the farmers took up arms. In this encounter more than seventy rebels were killed at the village of St Eustache.

The Irish, the French Canadians, and the Afrikaners in South Africa, on the other hand, mounted far more significant resistance to the imperial connection. The identity of each of these communities was shaped by non-British traditions and sharpened by antagonism towards British rule. In 1837 some French Canadians rose in national revolt against the colonial regime. In the decade after 1836 the Afrikaners attempted to trek beyond British jurisdiction and in 1881 and 1899–1902 they fought two nationalist wars against imperial Britain. Ireland was not merely an occupied dependency; it was itself a mother country – scattering throughout the empire and the world beyond a diaspora of settlers who expressed intense sympathy for Ireland's struggle for independence, a struggle whose aims and ideology resembled those nationalist movements in continental Europe seeking the unification of Italy or liberation from the Habsburg empire. When, after the Anglo-Irish war of 1919–21, the Irish Free State was created and granted Dominion status on a par with, say, Canada, it would not act as other Dominions. Irish nationalists did not regard Commonwealth membership as full freedom; rather, as one Sinn Féin leader, Michael Collins, admitted at the time, it amounted to freedom to achieve full freedom. The subsequent history of Ireland's membership of the Commonwealth, until it withdrew to become a fully independent republic in 1949, can largely be written in terms of Irish attempts to remove the residual monarchical and imperial accretions of Dominion status.

Resistance by non-Europeans

As regards non-European responses to imperial rule, the British at the time generally held in contempt those 'uncivilized' peoples who, like the Australian Aborigines and the Khoikhoi of the South African Cape, were displaced by European occupation of their lands. They were also scornful of opponents whose appeal lay in the resurrection of a legendary, pre-colonial, golden age – as seemed to be the case with the Maori 'king movement' and the Indian Rebellion of 1857. Furthermore, until they were forced to negotiate with them in order to secure British interests, they discounted leaders of political parties as self-serving troublemakers. Colonial societies, their argument ran until at least the 1940s, were not nations but collections of peoples or tribes; they were best administered by British rulers in collaboration with their natural leaders – that is, chiefs and princes. Self-appointed nationalists were seen as a special-interest group who, having become uprooted from their own societies, then misapplied to those same societies foreign ideas learned in English-medium schools and universities or, alternatively, mischievously whipped up the atavistic fears of their uneducated countrymen. Not only did colonial administrations choose not to recognize the possibility of connections between 'sporadic' protests, which they managed to subdue, and nationalist movements, to which they were eventually obliged to transfer power; they also disparaged the significance of any kind of opposition (using such pejorative terms as 'dacoity', 'banditry', or 'mutiny') and constructed a demonology of principal opponents. Winston Churchill sneered at Gandhi as the 'naked fakir'; Sir Charles Arden-Clarke, on assuming the governorship of the Gold Coast (Ghana) in 1949, referred to Kwame Nkrumah as 'our local Hitler'; and Sir Patrick Renison (the penultimate Governor of Kenya, 1959–62) persisted in calling the detained Jomo Kenyatta, shortly to be the first President of an independent Kenya, 'a leader unto darkness and death'.

Since the end of empire, however, historians have dug deeper into the origins of colonial nationalist movements to discover long histories of popular protest and connections and overlaps between 'traditional' resistance, which did not explicitly aim at creating a nation, and 'modern' nationalism, which did. Three cases illustrate this: the Maori 'king movement', the 1857 Indian Rebellion, and the 'pacification' of Burma after 1886.

Maori nationalism was provoked by land disputes and sustained by racial conflict. The Treaty of Waitangi (1840) was intended to settle differences between settlers and Maoris over the possession, enjoyment, and sale of land; instead it ushered in more than thirty years of armed conflict. Dispossession of land and consequent spiritual deprivation led to the formation of a Maori nationalist movement at a meeting of chiefs at Manawapou in South Taranaki in 1854 (the same year, it may be noted, that the first settler Parliament was convened in Auckland under the new constitution). Led by Potatau I, the consequent 'king movement' was partly an attempt to recreate a traditional order out of the chaotic remnants of tribalism and partly a response to, if not deliberate imitation of, European political organizations. The 'king movement' enabled the Maoris to mount a rearguard resistance to European advances, but prolonged war broke both their will and capacity for further resistance, and it was in vain that Wiremu Kingi wrote in 1860 'though my people and I may die, we die for New Zealand'.

The Indian Rebellion of 1857 was more a civil rebellion than a military mutiny, but, though extensive, it lacked cohesion and common purpose. All kinds of strands – Hindu regeneration, Islamic revivalism, Mughal restoration, peasant millenarianism – were worked into the ideology of revolt with the result that it is not possible to conclude that those who joined the revolt were simply representative of backward-looking 'traditional' India; after all, reform and change were sweeping through mainstream Hinduism and Islam at that time. Nor was it the case that those who acquiesced in British rule were exclusively forward-looking collaborators, committed to 'modernist' goals; on the contrary, many Indian professionals in the British camp felt humiliated by their association with the British regime. In short, the widespread yet fragmented nature of the rising is largely explained by reference to local circumstances and the realistic appraisal of individual self-interest. Nor, finally, is there a complete break between Indian resistance before 1857 and Indian nationalism of the late nineteenth and twentieth centuries, since there were in fact echoes of 1857 in peasant movements during the 1920s and 1930s.

Chief Wiremu Tamihana. The chief and his rifle symbolize Maori resistance, provoked by loss of land and of control over their own affairs in the face of the ever-increasing European presence in New Zealand. Resistance led to a series of wars from 1844 to 1872 in which some 2,000 Maoris and 560 British people were killed.

Burma presents a third example where 'traditional' forms merged with 'modern' nationalism. Although the British swiftly occupied Mandalay in 1885–86, deposing King Thibaw and annexing Burma to the Indian Raj, it took another five years of campaigning to subdue the country, and at one point the British deployed an army of 32,000 troops and 8,500 military police against guerrilla forces. Royal misrule had been the principal justification for British action, but the collapse of the Konbaung dynasty signified for the Burmese the end of a Buddhist World Age and spawned rival claimants to the throne. By destroying Burmese cosmological order, the British in effect provoked armed resistance in which Buddhist monks (*pongyi*) played a leading part. The British underplayed the significance of these disturbances, yet the *pongyi* continued to fan rural rebellion, notably during the economic depression of the 1930s when Saya San, a former monk armed with amulets and magic spells, aroused villagers to revolt in the Irrawaddy delta (1930–32) with promises of the restoration of a golden age of prosperity and monarchical rule. Here, as in India in 1857, however, there is no stark demarcation between traditional and modern protest. The main causes of rural unrest in 1930–32 were taxes, usury, and depressed rice prices; the main targets of rebellion were colonial administrators and Indian moneylenders. Moreover, Saya San himself was not merely a purveyor of reactionary superstition but had experience in more modernist anti-colonial movements, with their urban, secular, and radical features, which, like many other nationalist movements elsewhere in the empire, were strongly influenced by the Indian National Congress.

The growth of modern nationalist movements

Although there is significant overlap between 'modern' and 'traditional' nationalist movements, modern nationalists are distinguished by their readiness to work for change, their acceptance of the institutions and framework of the colonial state, and their adoption of ideologies and political techniques from outside. The first modern nationalist movement to arise in the non-European empire, and one that became an inspiration for many others, was the Indian National Congress. Founded in 1885, the Indian National Congress was a broad-based organization embracing a number of political associations which were rooted in the provincial politics of the subcontinent – such as the British Indian Association (founded as early as 1851), the Deccan Association, the Madras Native Association, and the Bombay Presidency Association. Before the First World War, Congress was elitist, urban-based, and 'loyalist'. Though B.G. Tilak, a powerful nationalist leader in western India from the 1890s to the First World War, adopted militant tactics, Congress on the whole sought partnership with the Raj and eschewed populist social and religious causes. It also lacked mass support, organization, and a clear ideology, being a loose association of individuals who were influential in provincial politics but had different views of what constituted the 'nation' and how nationhood could be achieved. In spite of its ultimately successful opposition to

Opposite: Indian Congress poster called 'The Right Path of Liberty'. This poster uses Indian idioms to rally support for nationalism. Indians of all communities are shown marching towards freedom. The bridge on the road to freedom is broken and Gandhi and Nehru among others are in a dungeon. The Hindu deity Krishna, however, tells mother India that with a little more sacrifice the road will be mended.

Gandhi

As early as 1909 Gandhi stated his principles. In a tract called *Hind Swaraj*, or Home Rule for India, he wrote:

1. Real home rule is self rule or self-control.
2. The way to it is passive resistance; that is soul-force or love-force.
3. In order to exert this force, Swadeshi [self-sufficiency] in every sense is necessary.
4. What we want to do should be done, not because we object to the English or because we want to retaliate but because it is our duty to do so. Thus supposing that the English remove the salt tax, restore our money, give the highest posts to Indians, withdraw the English troops, we shall certainly not use their machine-made goods, nor use the English language, nor many of their industries. It is worth noting that many of these things are in their nature harmful; hence we do not want them. I bear no enmity towards the English but I do towards their civilisation.

Gandhi remained true to these principles throughout his life. He was, first and foremost, a moralist and a religious and social reformer. Politics was a means to the moral and religious transformation of India. It was never an end in itself. The India that he hoped to see would be regenerated along the lines of what he believed to be its own traditions. It would not become a 'modern', 'developed', secular, industrial society with centralized institutions. His visionary India was one of small communities, such as villages, held together by the freely accepted obligations of their members to one another.

Such an India could not come about under colonial rule: the British must therefore be opposed. But to oppose them with violence would be to commit a crime. They must be opposed with love and truth. Mass movements must be strictly non-violent *satyagraha*s, demonstrations of the force of truth. Unjust laws must be broken, but those who did so must accept punishment or violence without hitting back.

Even if politics was only a secondary activity for him, Gandhi had great talents as a political organizer and as a director of mass campaigns. He showed this in the series of demonstrations, beginning in 1919, which culminated in the Non Co-operation Movement of the following year, in the Civil Disobedience Movement of 1930–31 and 1932–34, and the Quit India Movement of 1942. For him the campaigns themselves were probably more important than any objective they might attain. He was vague about the goals – he sought truth, not political settlements, and truth was hard to find. He very much disliked the terms of partition on which Indian independence was finally established and kept away from the final negotiations in 1947. Nor, had he lived beyond his assassination in 1948, would he have had much taste for the modern industrial India that the Congress governments were trying to bring about after independence.   [PJM]

Gandhi spinning.

Curzon's partition of Bengal (1905) and the constitutional concessions of the Morley–Minto Reforms (1909), Congress had little impact upon either Indians or the British before 1914.

The First World War and its aftermath, however, transformed Congress, which by the early 1920s had acquired a constitution, organization, rural support, and a compelling ideology of *swaraj* (home rule) under the inspiration of Mahatma Gandhi. The political advantage swung in Congress's favour: in 1937, following the first general elections under the 1935 Government of India Act, Congress formed governments in seven out of eleven provinces (adding an eighth in 1939) and, having rejected constitutional offers made by Churchill's envoy, Stafford Cripps, in 1942 and the Cabinet Mission in 1946, won the independence of India (separate from Pakistan) on 15 August 1947.

From the First World War onwards, therefore, Congress forced the pace of political change and constitutional advance in India. Moreover, the aims, methods, and achievements of Congress inspired nationalist movements elsewhere in the empire (for example, the National Congress of West Africa founded in 1918) while, after independence, Jawaharlal Nehru, as India's Prime Minister and a prime mover of the non-aligned movement, supported campaigns for the independence of Britain's African territories.

But an account of the end of empire that is presented simply in terms of the ultimate triumph of nationalism over imperialism would neglect the complexities of the relationship between the two. The first qualification to note is that nationalist movements developed within the imperial system. In so doing, they did not merely feed off the injustices and hardships attributed to alien rule. They were also nurtured by the experiences and facilities provided by the colonial state, which inspired political aspirations and protest, moulded political identity, and supplied the means to articulate ideas and mobilize support. The spread of printing, the expansion of education from primary to tertiary level, and the growth of roads, railways, cheap post, and the press – all of which took place under colonial rule – contributed to national consciousness, political leadership, and mass mobilization.

The second point to bear in mind is that all colonial nationalisms were riven with fissures. They were both shaped and fragmented by local circumstances, factional struggles, cultural or religious revivalism, and political rivalry between ethnic groups. Side by side with the nationalist struggle for independence occurred equally vigorous struggles between nationalists over the spoils of the colonial state. In Malaya, for example, communal rivalry between Malays and Chinese was as influential as the Communist emergency in the events leading to independence in 1957; in the Gold Coast the paramountcy of Nkrumah's Convention Peoples Party was contested on the eve of independence (1957) by the peoples of Ashanti and the Northern Territories; the Greek Cypriots' campaign for *enosis* (union with Greece) aroused the hostility of Turkish Cypriots; in the Indian subcontinent the success of the Hindu-dominated Congress contributed to Hindu–Muslim communalism and

Opposite: A burnt-out post office, Cyprus, 1955. Britain had ruled Cyprus with its Greek majority and Turkish minority since 1878. By the 1950s there was a strong movement among the Greek Cypriots, led by Archbishop Makarios, for Enosis, or union with Greece. Britain was unwilling to concede this because of what was thought to be the strategic importance of British bases on Cyprus and because of the need to maintain good relations with Turkey. In 1955 a terrorist movement called EOKA began a campaign of bombing and assassinations. The British replied with military repression and the deportation of the Archbishop. In 1960 it was agreed that Cyprus should become independent but not united with Greece, while Britain would retain bases on the island.

provoked the counter-nationalism of the Muslim League. Ghana, Malaya, and Cyprus became independent as unitary states but the British failed to prevent the partition of the Indian subcontinent. Communalism and counter-nationalism, which had originated outside the imperial experience but were aggravated by it, prevented nationalist unity and contributed to succession struggles in one dependency after another when it became clear that the British were preparing to leave.

Thirdly, the very significance of nationalist movements for bringing about the end of empire has itself been questioned. How important were they when weighed against other pressures bearing down on Britain? Until local crises blew up, policy towards specific colonies was mainly determined by Britain's economic and international needs, while plans for individual territories were shaped by reasoned assessments for the security, economic viability, social cohesion, and political maturity of each. Increasingly, however, events forced the British to compromise – ultimately to abandon – staged progress, measured programmes, and long-term planning. But even then the authorities were influenced more by the dangers of lawlessness in a colony than by the force of nationalists' demands. For example, in 1946 Lord Wavell, the penultimate Viceroy of India, suggested British withdrawal from India, not because of overwhelming nationalist pressure (on the contrary, Congress and League were in political deadlock), but because government was on the verge of collapse. Since both Congress and the League hoped to inherit the imperial legacy intact and not in disarray, they swiftly came to the conference table when the British Prime Minister, Clement Attlee, instructed Mountbatten to prepare for Indian independence by a date no later than 1 June 1948.

Violence and end of empire

Left to themselves, the British would probably have proceeded slowly – worrying about whether colonies were important from a British point of view and setting a leisurely programme for them to evolve towards independence. But outbreaks of violence and disorder increasingly forced the pace. In short, governments reacted to events on the ground, as was revealed in the case of Palestine in 1945–48 (see page 82). Despairing of a settlement between Zionists and Arabs and unwilling to partition the territory between them, the Labour government returned the responsibility for the mandate to the United Nations and evacuated Palestine in May 1948.

In general, violence was not deliberately instigated by nationalists. Even Archbishop Makarios and Jomo Kenyatta, both of whom were detained by the British, were only indirectly linked with the EOKA insurgency in Cyprus and the Mau Mau violence in Kenya respectively, and in Malaya the nationalist leader Tunku Abdul Rahman was openly hostile to the violence accompanying the Communist insurrection. But nationalist movements did benefit from unrest since the British did not want to hold out for long against violence. In the short term,

emergencies such as those in Cyprus, Kenya, and Malaya had a stultifying effect on constitutional reform, but in the longer perspective they may well have had the result of foreshortening colonial rule, even though 'moderates' and not the 'men of violence' profited from the outcome. The link between violence and decolonization was more direct in the case of the Gold Coast: the Accra riots of February 1948 are usually regarded as a turning-point since they opened the way for Nkrumah's ascendancy and invited a more radical policy from Britain. Nonetheless, in terms of casualties and destruction, these riots, which arose from frayed nerves and frustrations and not from premeditated plans, were on a small scale compared with instances of violence elsewhere in the empire during the postwar period.

At the ceremony inaugurating Ghana's independence on 6 March 1957, Nkrumah and his comrades led the assembled crowd in shouts of 'Freedom! Freedom! Freedom!' What sort of freedom was attained when the British empire came to an end? Some would say that very little changed, at least immediately.

Indeed, the process of decolonization has been interpreted as imperialism by other means or as the process whereby Britain replaced formal by informal empire, and attempted to substitute economic, diplomatic, and cultural influence for direct colonial rule. Certainly, British governments made every effort to retain former dependencies within the sterling area, the new multiracial Commonwealth, and Britain's network of global defence, while in each new state former colonial officials stayed on as expatriate advisers in key positions. In so doing, the British laid themselves open to charges of 'neo-colonialism'. In addition, an imperial legacy of international frontiers, government institutions, economic programmes, law, and language, all inhibited any fresh start – not that many successor regimes wished to embark on revolutionary courses in the honeymoon period following the end of empire. In one country after another, however, free speech was stifled, the economic infrastructure eroded, parliaments and the democratic processes succumbed to military regimes, and intricate constitutions were torn apart as pre-colonial loyalties and patterns of political behaviour were reasserted, and the goals of national unity fell victim to civil war, shifts in world prices which undermined their economies, population growth, and famine. When it came to the exercise of actual power, nationalists, like imperialists before them, encountered constraints and experienced reversals. These post-colonial developments suggest, perhaps, that the imperial legacy was skin-deep and that the breadth and depth of the imperial impact on the non-European world may well have been exaggerated in the past both by apologists for empire and by their nationalist critics.

Empires in the Mind

The growth of the British empire and the expansion of British influence spread British ideas and beliefs throughout the world. This has had far-reaching consequences. In many instances this movement of ideas was incoherent, spontaneous, or unconscious: expatriate traders, for example, built square brick houses with verandas, in which tea was taken, gin drunk before dinner, and ladies were expected to retire together afterwards. Elsewhere the diffusion of Britain's customs, factual knowledge, and beliefs was more purposeful: Scottish mission-aries taught English literature and sciences to generations of Indians and Africans, while colonial administrators nurtured attachment to regularity and honesty in the payment and collection of government taxes.

Movement and influence, however, were never in one direction only. British scholars genuinely tried to understand and interpret alien societies, both to their own compatriots and to indigenous peoples themselves. Anglo-Indian contacts, for example, were enriched by a long tradition of linguistic and historical work. Polo, introduced to Britain early in the 1870s, was exchanged for cricket. Although the pronounced self-confidence of the British people in the superiority of their own culture for much of the imperial period restricted their willingness and ability to learn consciously from the peoples of the empire, their unconscious absorption of the exotic went on continuously. The rhododendron, introduced from the Himalayas, flourished in Britain and blighted many a garden; wardrobes have embraced colonial ostrich feathers as readily as the cummerbund and kaftan. Meanwhile the English language has absorbed myriad usages from its imperial connections – such as 'bosh', 'cheroot', and 'gong' – just as it has from its continental European ties. Imperial borrowing has been especially marked in respect of India and the Far East. This reflects not only a long history of British connections since the founding of the East India Company in 1600, but also the immense scale of

The first baby show in Mauritius, 1 August 1924. The baby show was a British institution that was readily adopted in colonial societies. Here the Governor, Sir Henry Hesketh Bell, presides.

commercial, administrative, and other ties after 1820, and the significance in British life of British people who have lived in India.

Adoption and usage, of course, do not necessarily mean that people fundamentally change their view of the world. However, even the casual appropriation of material things from their original location, or the continuous, habitual employment of words and customs in a new environment, reflects a broadening of experience within an imperial setting. But while interchange and interaction between Britain and its colonies were inescapable, empire also fostered intensely narrow outlooks. Dislike and fear of the unfamiliar are universal sentiments and travel does not necessarily open the mind to new ideas: the conditions of empire readily bred on all sides intolerance, nationalism, racialism, or the exaggerated attachment to the comfortable and familiar. The possession of empire often prompted Britons to clarify their ideas about themselves, reinforcing their sense of superiority to all those – white as well as black – with whom they came into contact. Less easily appreciated is the extent to which colonial rule influenced the outlooks of colonial subjects in the same way.

The subject matter for this chapter fits no clean-cut mould or neat patterns. The history of the British empire should not be seen as resulting in either the spread of western 'civilization' and enlightenment on the one hand, or the imposition of alien customs to the wholesale detriment of indigenous cultures on the other. It involves both these processes. Imperialist and colonized were each capable of openness and insularity, of giving and taking, of actions and attitudes both coherent and chaotic. Misperceptions, ignorance, and limited power on all sides frequently ensured that hopes and intentions were remote from what actually happened.

THE SPREAD OF ENGLISH

A striking feature of Britain's two imperial centuries has been the global diffusion of spoken and written English. Although the growth of the United States has undoubtedly assisted this process in the twentieth century, it was Britain's increasing presence overseas that provided the main impetus until the 1930s. Britain's economic weight in the world throughout the period of empire made English a natural language of commerce and the fact that the government and administration of large parts of the world were conducted in English created powerful incentives for non-English-speakers to acquire the language of their rulers. There were, nevertheless, various routes by which the dominant position of English was reached, not all of them easily negotiated.

English by migration
The most straightforward cases were those of the Australian colonies and New Zealand where most of the white immigrants were English-speaking and British colonial authorities were established soon after annexation. The indigenous populations in these colonies were relatively small and in many areas were quite

soon outnumbered. The extermination of many of Australia's Aborigines and military conquest of the Maoris left both communities shrinking under the colonial impact, and their isolation long seemed to leave them no real hope of modifying British cultural and linguistic hegemony.

Circumstances were very different in Upper and Lower Canada and at the Cape of Good Hope in South Africa. Both colonies were spoils of war, which, when acquired, already contained fairly large white populations – the one French-speaking, the other Dutch/Afrikaans. An influx into Canada of English-speaking loyalists fleeing the American War of Independence, together with later immigrants, especially from Scotland and Ireland, began to transform the population balance of Canada from the 1820s; at the Cape, however, the local Dutch population for long outnumbered the British. In both cases, population imbalance bred discrimination and conflict – the French resenting their minority position, the Afrikaners their subordination despite their numerical strength. For both peoples, the survival of their language became a crucial issue and they campaigned vigorously to ensure that French and Afrikaans had at least equal status with English. In South Africa the language question contributed not only to the revolt of poor and ill-educated Afrikaners, like those at Slachters Nek in 1815, who felt that even 'Hottentots [were] preferred to the Burghers'. Others thereafter worked constantly for the preservation of the Afrikaans language in church worship and its use in public life – thereby nurturing an Afrikaner communal identity which by the late nineteenth century was of great political importance.

Street signs in Hong Kong, 1908. This picture shows the use of both English and Chinese for signs. English, the language of trade and government, was taught in most of the seventy government-supported schools. But only 6,000 children out of an estimated school population of 500,000 attended such schools. The rest, if they got any education at all, were still being taught in Chinese.

English by government action

In colonies in Asia and in tropical Africa English was initially the language of no more than small groups of British administrators, traders, or missionaries. Many Asian and African people were, however, willing to learn English in order to do business with or to gain employment under their new rulers and to acquire a share of their knowledge. British colonial regimes were at first uncertain whether to reinforce the more or less spontaneous spread of English by deliberate government policies. In India, for instance, government business was transacted in Persian (the official language of the Mughal empire) during the early years of British rule, and government funding was given to institutions where the ancient learned languages, Sanskrit and Arabic, were studied.

By the 1820s, however, the use of English was being vigorously promoted in most colonies. The colonial authorities saw it as the vehicle of an authoritative, essentially superior culture; they believed that its official propagation was not only morally justified but administratively useful. This view persisted into modern times, in spite of shifting attitudes towards empire. A common language was widely believed to make government easier, to promote a sense of unity, and to reflect shared values. As John Barrow, who had served at the Cape of Good Hope, wrote in 1819, '... let but all official documents be in the English language and the next generation will become Englishmen'.

In India after 1825 the 'anglicists', who wanted the government's support to go exclusively to the learning of English, prevailed over the 'orientalists', who believed that western knowledge could best be diffused through Indian languages. As a result, the study of Sanskrit, Arabic, and Persian was no longer officially promoted. Thomas Macaulay, Liberal politician and famous historian, in a recommendation to the Governor-General in 1835, expressed his single-minded conviction that:

> The claims of our own language it is hardly necessary to recapitulate. It stands pre-eminent even among the languages of the West ... In India, English is the language spoken by the ruling class ... [and] by the higher class of natives at the seats of government. It is likely to become the language of commerce throughout the seas of the East. It is the language of two great European communities which are rising ... in the south of Africa [and] in Australia; communities which are every year becoming more important, and more closely connected with our Indian Empire.

The spread of English aided both the forging of control by British authorities and the creation of colonial communities. In the Gold Coast (Ghana), the adoption of English effectively drove out the earlier fragmentary use of Portuguese, Dutch, and Danish, and offered a bridge linking members of the several different language groups in the region. In colonial Sierra Leone English had a vital role in linking peoples speaking an estimated 200 different languages. Through the use of English, colonial people found that the imperial authorities and a wider world

The adventures of a 'Baboo'. 'Baboo' or Babu was properly a term of respect, signifying mister or master. But, as a contemporary put it, British people in India often used it with 'a savour of disparagement, as characterizing a superficially cultivated but too often effeminate Bengali'. This stereotype was exemplified in a book published in 1902 called *A Bayard from Bengal*, which mocked the attempts of an imaginary Bengali Babu to adjust to life in Britain and in particular ridiculed his pedantic and unidiomatic English. The story to which this was an illustration was entitled 'How Mr Bhosh delivered a damsel from a demented cow'.

might be made to listen to what they were saying: using English enabled people to communicate with and often to oppose the colonial system. English was the convenient common language for nationalists in their political battles.

Divisive consequences

Nevertheless, there were limits to the unifying potential of English, since in the colonies it took many different forms. British people took with them overseas the varied accents and dialects of the British Isles. In due course these mingled with the languages appropriated and adapted by Africans, West Indians, and Asians. Many forms of pidgin and creole developed. These days such inventiveness is appreciated, but by the beginning of the nineteenth century it was already commonly accepted in Britain that English as used outside the British Isles was inferior, tainted with slang, and imperfectly known or understood.

Gradually, a standard variety of English became the language of government authority and higher education in British colonies. This standardization reinforced social, cultural, and racial exclusiveness. When British governors such as Sir Frederick Lugard and Lord Curzon castigated educated Africans in Lagos and Accra or 'baboos' in Calcutta for pretentiousness, they were criticizing linguistic style as much as the uses (frequently critical of the British) to which the language was put. Kipling created a 'baboo' – that is, a western-educated Bengali – in *Kim* and makes him speak in what British people took to be a characteristic way: 'Ah! Thatt is the question, as Shakespeare hath said. I come to congratulate you on your extraordinary effeecient performance at Delhi ... Well, there I hear what you have done so well, so quickly, upon the instantaneous spur of the moment. I tell our mutual friend you take the bally bun, by Jove!'

The spread of more than a smattering of English was always restricted in Asian and African colonies by the lack of mass literacy. For the educated and ambitious, avoidance or rejection of English under colonial rule was difficult. It was and remains the chief vehicle of international communication and an important unifying factor in culturally-divided societies. Even so, it was often used grudgingly or half-heartedly. Gandhi spoke for many in asserting that to

> ... give millions a knowledge of English is to enslave them ... Is it not a painful thing that, if I want to go to a court of justice, I must employ the English language as a medium; that, when I become a Barrister, I may not speak my mother-tongue, and that someone else should have to translate to me from my own language?

For him and many others English served utilitarian ends. But British nationalism needed to be countered with another rooted in its own linguistic heritage and vernacular languages were increasingly adopted during the colonial period as the true expression of national identity.

THE DEVELOPMENT OF NON-EUROPEAN LANGUAGES

The spread and transformation of English was not the only linguistic result of empire. Still more striking was the development of standardized forms of non-European languages, many of which, above all in Africa, had no written form until well into the nineteenth century. S.W. Koelle, a German from Wurtemburg working with the Anglican Church Missionary Society and author of the *Polyglotta Africana*, commented in 1854 how 'Africa is still an unknown country in many respects. Its numerous languages are a wide field, the cultivation of which would be sure to reward the professional philologist with many interesting discoveries.'

From the mid-eighteenth century onwards, in first one then another part of the empire, scripts (that is, the hand-written characters), dictionaries, and grammars in the indigenous languages were being put together for the first time. Although, for some, the scholarly study of non-European languages had its own intrinsic attractions, the dominant impetus behind these compilations was to provide vernacular translations of the Bible. British Christian missionaries, in particular, made a critical contribution here, and in 1804 the British and Foreign Bible Society was formed to support this work. On the river Niger by mid-century, agents of the Church Missionary Society such as Heinrich Schon and the African Bishop Samuel Adjai Crowther, together with numerous Sierra Leoneans, were laying the foundation for transcription, translation, and literacy in West African languages such as Yoruba, Hausa, Kanuri, Igala, and Igbo. Similar activity elsewhere brought Bemba, Fante, Herero and, in the South Pacific, Samoan into the world of modern literacy. The first substantial Chinese–English dictionary, compiled by Robert Morrison of the London Missionary Society, was published in six volumes between

Wiliam Carey (1764–1834) and his chief pundit Mritunjaya by Robert Home, Calcutta, 1811. Although Mritunjaya was an orthodox Hindu scholar or pundit, he worked with the Christian missionary Carey in making translations from Hindu texts. Carey's translations helped to establish the standard written forms of several Indian languages.

1815 and 1822. In India the Baptist William Carey, with Indian help, produced an astonishing range of translations: according to a recent historian of the Baptist Missionary Society, he was mainly responsible for six complete and twenty-nine partial translations of the Bible, grammars in seven Indian languages, and the compilation of dictionaries in Bengali, Sanskrit, and Marathi.

The consequences both of the spreading use of English and this linguistic work were far-reaching. In many respects the benefits they brought are incontestable. Communication between previously somewhat isolated communities became much easier, as did the transmission of precise knowledge to other contemporaries and to successive generations. In many societies individual memory and local oral tradition ceased to be the sole repositories of information. However, there are many today who, recognizing the intimate connections between language, ideas, and cultures, would argue that the transcriptions and translations made by British people inevitably had British preconceptions imposed on them, and that these indelibly marked the outlook and thought-patterns of non-European societies. Scottish missionaries in the Niger delta, for example, struggled with the local Efik language, which lacked the means to express concepts such as 'resurrection', 'temptation', individual responsibility, and human sinfulness. Examination of their sermons has shown how they responded both by using Christian concepts to describe Efik religion and by redefining Efik terms to make it possible for them to explain Christian beliefs. The result of this stretching of language is likely to have been that elements of non-Christian beliefs were mixed with Efik Christianity and, conversely, that Efik people who were not converted still absorbed something of Christianity.

Although the precise nature of such influences is controversial, there can be little doubt that, by encouraging the use of certain indigenous languages rather than others, missionary preferences and the needs of early colonial administrators strengthened the political and cultural position of classes or societies that were already quite prominent. For example, in East Africa, around Lake Victoria, British religious and political alliances meant that Luganda was formalized and established as the principal language of church and state before 1914, thus enhancing the influence of the Ganda people and their kingdom of Buganda at the expense of other groups such as the Acholi in the north. As a cause of social and political rivalries, this has had lasting consequences for Uganda's history.

LITERATURE

Since 1969 a prize for a new novel written in English by an author who is either British or a citizen of a Commonwealth country has been awarded annually in London. Over the first twenty-four years of what has now become a very prestigious prize, the Commonwealth in one form or another has been very well represented: among prizewinners have been two Australians, two South Africans, an author of Indian origin and another who has spent much of her life there, a writer from New

Zealand, one from Nigeria, and one from Sri Lanka. It would not be difficult to draw up a list of other Commonwealth novelists writing in English, arguably of equal distinction to those who have won the Booker Prize.

Writers from Commonwealth countries or from what were then colonial territories have been producing novels in English of the highest quality, at least from the beginning of the twentieth century, long before the institution of the Booker Prize. Obvious examples are the work of the South Africans, Olive Schreiner and Alan Paton, of Doris Lessing, who was brought up in Southern Rhodesia (Zimbabwe), of the Indians, R.K. Narayan and Mulk Raj Anand, of the Australian, Patrick White, of V.S. Naipaul from Trinidad, Wole Soyinka and Chinua Achebe from Nigeria, or the Kenyan, Ngugi wa Thiong'o.

For many Commonwealth writers, most obviously Australians, New Zealanders, and English-speaking Canadians and South Africans, English is a language passed down to them by their English-speaking ancestors. For writers from Africa or South Asia English may be a second language and they may have a choice as to whether they write in English or their mother tongue. For others, such as those from the Caribbean, English is their first language, but it is an English that may have

The colonial past in Chinua Achebe and V.S. Naipaul

Chinua Achebe.

Novels offer valuable insights into the way in which colonial life was experienced by those ruled by the British. Points of view vary. The view of their societies' colonial past taken by two distinguished writers, Chinua Achebe, a Nigerian, and V.S. Naipaul, who was brought up in Trinidad but has lived most of his adult life in Britain, shows something of the range of conflicting interpretations.

Achebe's first novel, *Things Fall Apart* (1958), is set in southern Nigeria in the nineteenth century. The first part of the book describes the workings and beliefs of Igbo clan society before the intrusion of colonial rule in a sympathetic if not wholly uncritical way. Before the coming of the British, people lived within a stable framework: 'A man's life from birth to death was a series of transition rites which brought him nearer and nearer to his ancestors.' This part of the book has a clear didactic purpose. 'I would be quite satisfied', Achebe has written, 'if my novels ... did no more than teach my readers that their past – with all its imperfections – was

not one long night of savagery from which the first Europeans acting on God's behalf delivered them.' The second part of *Things Fall Apart* deals with the disruptive effects of missionary Christianity and colonial rule. The central figure of the book, who sees himself as the embodiment of old Igbo virtues, is driven to suicide. But his young son finds 'the poetry of the new religion, something felt in the marrow. The words of the hymn were like the drops of frozen rain melting on the dry palate of the panting earth.' In an autobiographical essay Achebe wrote that, although he was brought up as a Christian, he felt 'a fascination for the ritual and life' of that part of his family which was not Christian, and he evidently moved easily between the two worlds. The colonial encounter was profoundly disruptive, Achebe believes, but a new generation of Nigerians could take Christianity and the English language from this experience and make them their own.

For V.S. Naipaul the colonial order ripped people out of their pasts and put them down in places like Trinidad, where significant variations from the English of the British Isles. The following poem by Louise Bennett is characteristic of popular English usage in Jamaica.

Rainy Day

I yuh want it an no need it
Curb yuh wanti-wanti ways,
Puddung wanti-wanti money
Fe de needy rainy days.

No might-be bout de rainy day,
No few a we, no some;
But ina everybody life
It mus an boun fe come.

Teday, tomorrow – nex week –
Dis yah mont or tarra 'ear,
De rainy day deh pon de way
Fe ketch yuh unaware.

Sometime him creep up sofly like
A puss an stir up strife.
Sometime him drop like atom-bomb
An worries up yuh life.

But me gwine fe trick de bugga,
Day by day me dah prepare,
dah save up lickle money an
Me ready fe him, me dear.

Wen rainy day strike me, ah gwine
Fe bring him to disgrace,
Jus wave me bank-book an bus out
A laugh eena him face.

they created nothing of value of their own. Naipaul's family had been induced to go to Trinidad with other Indian labourers imported to work on the sugar plantations. The culture that had once tied the indentured servants to India had withered. People of Indian origin mixed with ex-slaves from Africa and a small European elite who were equally rootless. For Naipaul Trinidad is one of the 'dark places of the earth', disfigured by grinding poverty. In his great novel, *A House for Mr Biswas* (1961), set in Trinidad, Naipaul describes how his hero

> ... visited the eastern sections of the city where the narrow houses pressed their scabbed and blistered facades together and hid the horrors that lay behind them: the constricted, undrained back-yards, coated with green slime, in the perpetual shadow of adjacent houses and the tall rubble-stone fences against which additional sheds had been built: yards choked with flimsy cooking sheds, crowded fowl-coops of wire-netting, bleaching stones spread with sour washing: smell upon smell, but none overcoming the stench of cesspits and overloaded septic tanks: horror increased by the litters of children, most of them illegitimate, with navels projecting inches out of their bellies, as though they had been delivered with haste and disgust.

Trinidad was a place that the young Naipaul was determined to leave as soon as possible. 'In Trinidad', he writes in the semi-autobiographical *Enigma of Arrival*, 'feeling myself far away, I held myself back as it were, for life at the center of things.' All his reading made him see London as the 'center of things'. The London to which he came as a young man in the 1950s greatly disappointed him. But there he has remained, casting from time to time a baleful eye on ex-colonial territories where he sees none of the vigour of tradition and the adaptation of colonial imports that Achebe finds in Nigeria.   [PJM]

V.S. Naipaul.

Those who choose to write in English rather than their mother tongue can still make important statements about the aspirations of their own societies. Yet their audience among their own people will inevitably be limited and many have always considered it more appropriate to write in their own language, even if they were using a foreign literary form like the novel or borrowing foreign poetic metres. Rabindranath Tagore, who was knighted by the British and awarded a Nobel Prize for Literature on the basis of a translation of his work, is a conspicuous example. While possessing a perfect mastery of English, he still wrote nearly all his poetry, songs, stories, and novels in Bengali. In so doing he did much to develop Bengali as a literary language and powerfully shaped Bengalis' consciousness of their culture, their identity, and even of the landscape of Bengal. More and more major African writers are choosing to do the same thing – to write in an African language in addition to or instead of the ultimately alien English.

EDUCATION

The diffusion of English and the promotion of indigenous languages, in making it possible for very different peoples to communicate with each other on a far wider scale, laid the foundations for Britain's empire as the world's greatest-ever educational enterprise. To describe empire in these terms is not to pass judgement on the value or nature of the schooling, educational systems, or scholarship promoted by imperial and colonial interests. It reflects instead the fact that in generating and communicating knowledge about the world, in supporting formal instruction and the spread of literacy, in widening horizons and taxing imaginations by compelling attention to the alien or unfamiliar, British expansion as an agent of formal and informal education was unparalleled.

Scholarship – knowledge for rule?
While many, perhaps most, Britons took little interest in empire either at first or second hand, in all periods others can be found who were distinctly curious in a comparatively disinterested and scholarly way. This tradition of enquiry was sustained and extended throughout the nineteenth and early twentieth centuries by the great learned societies. The Royal Society was joined by others like the Bengal Asiatic Society (1784), London's Royal Geographical Society (1830), and many more specialized bodies in anthropology, geology, ethnography, or folklore. As the nineteenth century progressed, bodies like these organized expeditions and research, helped to raise funds, and disseminated information and results – mingled with speculation – in their reports or public journals. As President of the Royal Society, Sir Joseph Banks not only fostered Pacific exploration, but in 1788 helped to found the Association for Promoting the Discovery of the Interior Parts of Africa (commonly known as the African Association) as general interest in that continent began to revive. From the 1840s to the 1860s Sir Roderick Murchison provided comparable driving force at the Royal Geographical Society, backing William Baikie in exploring the Niger and David Livingstone the Zambezi river.

Alongside the work of these societies, there continued that of individual scholars who pursued their studies often as a direct offshoot from their own careers, sometimes in an essentially amateur and unpaid fashion, and occasionally as professional academics. Among East India Company officials, and, later, members of the Indian civil service, were some prolific writers on the history, languages, society, and customs of the subcontinent. Sir William Jones, a judge of the Calcutta Supreme Court from 1783 who was celebrated both for his comparative linguistic work and his translations of Indian literary or legal texts, was one of the first in a long line which included well-known figures like Sir Henry Maine, the great scholar of law and ancient societies, as well as many lesser-known district commissioners. The output of missionaries, too, was by no means confined to hagiography and hallelujahs; their writings included not only instructive autobiographical memoirs, such as those of John Williams on the Pacific published in 1837, but also linguistic, theological, and medical works.

The direct experience and professional work of such groups was of continuing importance to academics, especially in Britain's own universities – to a philologist and interpreter of Hindu civilization like Professor Max Muller in Oxford, or to armchair anthropologists like the Cambridge fellow J.G. Frazer, author of *The*

Meeting of the Royal Geographical Society, 28 April 1902. This was one of a number of learned bodies concerned with collecting and disseminating information about territories of potential interest to Britain as well as about the empire. From its origins in 1830, the society had an imperial purpose: geographical knowledge would promote 'the welfare of a maritime nation like Great Britain, with its numerous and extensive foreign possessions'. In the late nineteenth century the society was much involved with the exploration and 'opening up' of Africa.

Golden Bough. For example, Francis Galton, for his work on heredity and race, pressed the Reverend Charles Robinson of the Church Missionary Society to send him finger and palm prints from northern Nigeria.

In recent years, however, the extent and even the possibility of dispassionate, objective scholarship in both the natural sciences and humane learning has been called into question, especially in relation to empire. In *Orientalism* (1978) Edward Said set out an argument that has become very influential. Said claims that European outlooks and motives for study were fundamentally and inescapably shaped by the ambition to dominate and control the non-European world. He sees European literature and comment about that world 'as part of the general European effort to rule distant lands and peoples'. They embody 'a Western style for dominating, restructuring, and having authority over' non-Europeans. The findings of scholarship, the conclusions of commentators however well- or ill-informed, novels as much as travel writings: all, he believes, were shaped by the purposes they were to serve, dominant among them being the construction of empire.

What can be said in support of this view? There can be little doubt that, as British acquaintance with the non-European world grew in the nineteenth century, so did a readiness to be highly critical and even totally dismissive of alien cultures as well as a view that Britain had a mission or national duty to spread the benefits of its civilization, economy, and religion as widely as possible overseas. Critical stereotypes and assumptions of British superiority were used for at least 100 years to justify colonial rule in various forms. Between 1890 and 1914, for example, both Lord Cromer and Sir Alfred Milner defended at length a continued British presence in Egypt on grounds of the inability of Egypt's own ruling classes to maintain a stable and prosperous state. In East and Central Africa only the combination of colonial rule and white-settler farming was thought capable of attaining similar goals, until the 1930s depression raised some uncomfortable doubts.

British knowledge was not only used to justify colonial rule and expansion; it could also be used directly to service the needs of Britain and of colonial authorities. Colonial governments therefore became steadily more involved in the acquisition of useful knowledge. Just as Banks presented schemes for scientific investigation in ways that he knew would appeal either to government or to private commercial interests, so Murchison secured official support for ventures such as the Palestine Exploration Fund, which satisfied not only geologists' curiosity but that of the British government about strategic resources such as coal and metals. The development of physical and later social anthropology in nineteenth- and twentieth-century India, for example, was closely bound up with the colonial government's desire to fit its subjects into clear categories. From the 1880s the British government's interest in scientific research as the ally of imperial development grew considerably. It supported the opening of the Imperial Institute in 1893, which among other things aimed to promote scientific research into the natural resources of the empire and their commercial applications. Kew Gardens, with its similar role in respect to plants and the development of agricultural science, was drawn much closer to the Colonial and India Offices in the 1890s; backing was also given to the setting up of schools of hygiene and tropical medicine in London and Liverpool. After 1940 colonial needs and the evolution of official policies for 'colonial development and welfare' only accentuated the conjunction of academic ambition and state requirements – in agriculture, forestry, veterinary science, and engineering.

Clearly, the acquisition of knowledge about the empire was used for and, to some extent, encouraged by official administrative needs. However, it is quite another thing to argue that the scholars themselves were driven, directly or indirectly, by a British 'effort to rule'. Said's arguments can lead one to ignore that academic research is done for its own sake and that the knowledge acquired can be used for all sorts of purposes.

Training for empire

The spread of 'imperial' knowledge in a formal fashion through schools or training institutions in Britain itself was at first exceedingly slow and patchy. Early attempts to link education and government were made by the East India Company. On Governor-General Wellesley's initiative, Fort William College was set up in Calcutta in 1800, so that young civil servants might acquire the rudiments of Indian adminstration, history, and languages; in Britain, the company founded what became Haileybury College for the same purpose in 1805. However, these steps were unusual and, at least in India itself, short-lived, although Oxford University not only took Indian studies seriously but also taught Indian civil service probationers from the 1880s onwards. Throughout the nineteenth century it was far more common for those in authority to rely on informal or unofficial means of education, gleaned as a result of the accidents of domestic upbringing and schooling. Promising recruits to the colonial service and, equally, to business or missionary work, were usually left to gather local knowledge only as they felt inclined to do so.

The coincidences of curiosity, antiquarianism, occasional sympathy, and above all personal experience thus determined most expatriates' knowledge of their field. Not until the 1930s, for example, did hazy reliance on qualifications of birth, character, and availability give way to a more systematic selection and training of colonial civil servants. This became the norm only after 1945, as summer schools, one-year so-called Devonshire training courses, and other schemes were started to make professionals of those running – and soon running down – the remaining colonial empire.

Outside government, things were little different. Colonial clergy in the Church of England were often those unable to secure a living at home, rather than interested men keenly seeking an Australian or Rhodesian parish. The Church

Missionary Society, despite its size and organizational pre-eminence, was typical in its failure to offer instruction to its volunteers in either languages or non-Christian religions until shortly before 1914. Commercial firms, too, were unlikely to foster a wider learning about colonial societies among their employees. Even the most successful entrepreneurs, like William Mackinnon and Alfred Jones, the Indian and West African shipping magnates, were often 'self-made' men, their knowledge bounded by its severely practical bent. Wider perspectives might have saved Mackinnnon when he turned from involvement in India towards East Africa in the 1880s and 1890s: his miscalculations meant that his Imperial British East Africa Company, despite its official privileges, was rapidly bankrupted.

From the 1930s to the 1950s, British merchant houses and plantation owners in Malaya as elsewhere remained remarkably self-confident in their traditional enclaves and markedly insensitive to much of the political change going on around them. Official efforts to encourage indigenous enterprise and to head off the prospect of nationalization after independence were often bitterly resisted by the rubber and tin industries.

There was perhaps still less incentive for the British to consider the character and development of immigrant settler communities in, say, New Zealand or the Canadian provinces. Viewed ambivalently, with both satisfaction as outliers of 'Greater Britain' and disdain as inferior 'little Englands' on the make, white colonists, in the eyes of the British, scarcely seemed to display an individuality worth examination.

Schools

The British empire was a great educator, but it is wrong to assume that colonial subjects were educated in a uniform way for imperial purposes. Most people, if they belonged to those small minorities who had a formal education, acquired it

Lowest class at Government High School, Peshawar, North West Frontier Province of India, c.1908. The great majority of the population of this part of India were Muslim Pathans. Levels of literacy and educational provision of any kind were very low. The youngest boys of a fortunate minority are here being taught to read and write in Urdu.

The pre-university class, Belleville High School, Ontario, c.1913. State-supported high schools, such as this one, were part of a generous level of educational provision available to the people of the Canadian province of Ontario.

themselves with little or no colonial supervision. Before the establishment of colonial rule, the Islamic societies with which the British came into contact had educated their children and the professionals they required in their Koranic schools and universities. They continued to do so under British rule. However, the expansion of British settlement and rule inevitably entailed the spread of British models and changes in existing practices among non-Europeans, both to provide for the functioning of colonial society and to enable individuals to come to terms with the colonial world.

In the English-speaking colonies of settlement, even more than in Britain itself before 1870, the availability of education was to start with very haphazard. New Zealand offers a good example. Where white farming was thinly spread and parents themselves often had virtually no education, family needs for labour, lack of money to pay the fees so often required, and distance all limited schooling in the countryside. Even in towns, like Otago or Nelson, where either individual initiative and the presence of the churches meant that schools were more common or some public provision was made, large numbers escaped the educational net. However, a non-denominational elementary school system was established by the New Zealand Parliament in 1877; by the 1890s, with the aid of public funds, 80 per cent of children aged five to fifteen were being taught a standardized curriculum much on British lines. Education beyond the primary stage was freely available in 1900 to only about 3 per cent of those up to eighteen, although by 1939 some 65 per cent were in secondary schools of some kind. For Maoris a parallel system of Christian denominational and government Native Schools was thought to suffice; most of these schools were primary schools, descended from the missionary schools of the 1830s, and, until changes began in the 1930s, they attempted to fulfil whites' expectations that Maoris' future lay in agriculture and rural employment.

In the non-white colonies the concern to link British culture and formal schooling was often strong. Impetus came from several directions, not least from the Christian churches and missionaries, most of whom regarded the promotion of education and Christianity as inseparable. Especially in its Protestant varieties, Christianity was regarded as a religion dependent on literacy, which alone made it possible for converts to read and study the Bible. Inevitably, however, this involved the risk that non-Europeans would exploit the mission-school education for other ends. This is precisely what happened. Indeed it was rarely for specifically religious purposes that local African rulers allowed the settlement, for example, of Wesleyan Methodists on the Gold Coast in the 1840s, or Scottish Presbyterians around Lake Nyasa in the 1880s. Education was regarded as the key to the white man's advantages, and was valued because it brought the means of coping with white society – English, reading, writing, jobs on ships or in trading firms, medicine, and better commerce. In India mission schools found themselves the target of violent Muslim or Hindu protest when conversions occurred, but popular when offering Wordsworth and chemistry. To prevent trouble, colonial officials generally did their best to discourage attempts by mission schools to convert their pupils to Christianity. As long as the progress of Christianity and British culture were seen as linked, missionary teachers were prepared to accept restrictions on direct proselytization. But the specifically Christian content of mission education was limited less by official policy than by the known wishes of parents whose children went to the schools. Most non-Christian parents would not pay for openly Christian education. There is no disguising the fact that the spread of education and ideas was fundamentally affected by what colonial peoples wished to take. The limits to the 'imposition' of any colonial education are not always sufficiently recognized.

Eventually the relative importance and independence of mission schools – whether the barest of African bush schools or grandly maintained institutions like Wilson's High School run by the Scottish churches in Bombay – began to change. Church schools first lost their pre-eminence in India, especially in the major towns, where the demand for both English-language and vernacular education greatly outstripped what the missionaries could provide and private secular schools run by Indians therefore mushroomed. Gradually, in colonies everywhere, the oversight and financing of education passed into state hands. Mission schools, which were recognized as performing essential functions, came increasingly to rely on government grants for their expansion since the missions' own funds were inadequate. General taxation alone could ultimately provide the necessary resources, but public inspection was then essential to ensure both that funds were properly spent and that appropriate standards were maintained.

Universities – an empire of learning

The university 'is the roots and the trunk, the pursuit of knowledge the sap, and the schools the branches, foliage and flowers'. This image of the university, painted in about 1940 by a Governor of Uganda addressing trainee teachers at Makerere College, is not one that will find universal acceptance. Nevertheless, just as higher education was regarded as the goal of able students, so universities were seen as essential hallmarks of any advanced or well-established society, repositories of its best learning and research and possessing great potential influence. Colonial communities therefore began very early to exploit the two alternatives open to them. They sent their children to Britain's (or, from the late nineteenth century, the United States's) colleges, universities, Inns of Court, and medical schools; and they took steps to establish their own.

The two processes were very closely linked, and in starting to expand their own institutions Britain's colonies hardly lagged behind Britain itself. Fourah Bay College in Freetown (1827) and Cape Town's South African College (1829) were contemporary with London's own University College (1826) and King's College (1829). Like their British counterparts, these two colleges served as feeders to the better endowed universities such as Oxford and Cambridge. New Zealand's foundations, from Otago University (1869) to Victoria University College (1898), mirrored in various ways the establishment of Britain's own Victorian civic universities, serving the needs of growing business and professional classes.

The British university model was overwhelmingly influential and colonial foundations tended to be highly derivative. Architecture, collegiate arrangements, and academic flavour often echoed those that the founders or professors had themselves attended. In endowing a scholarship scheme whereby young colonial men (plus some Germans and Americans) could go to Oxford, Cecil Rhodes was intent on exploiting such ties in order to give 'breadth to their views for their instruction in life and manners and for instilling into their minds the advantages to the Colonies as well as to the United Kingdom of the retention of the unity of the Empire'.

Whether colonial universities founded on British lines would instil a sense of the 'unity of the empire' in their students was debatable. Higher education everywhere necessarily encourages critical scrutiny of all opinion or argument, and especially of received wisdom. As a result, Indian university students, for instance, were particularly prone to political sedition. In 1909 Lugard's plans for a university in Hong Kong met widespread opposition, not least from those who feared the creation of a 'merely Utilitarian University' likely to become 'a hotbed of revolutionary intrigue'. As Lord William Cecil also told him, '... two ideas will probably fill your University. Number one, China for the Chinese and death to the foreigner; number two, the equality of man and its two developments, socialism and anarchism ... to foster a crowd of bomb-throwing patriots in your midst will be extremely unpleasant.'

In the flurry of African foundations after 1945, arrangements under which colonial universities, such as Nigeria's Ibadan University College (1948) or the University College of Rhodesia and Nyasaland (1954) in Salisbury (Harare), taught for the degrees of the University of London, again seem designed to create imperial look-alikes. In practice, however, the recruitment of expatriate British academic staff and the early training of local researchers overseas, especially in the United Kingdom, was a fairly short-lived phase. Continuing links with British academic life helped to develop a university system that combined a liberal, critical tradition with both world-wide connections and local peculiarities: on balance, this has done far more since 1960 to diversify the world of learning than to foster in ex-colonies a specifically British or imperial cultural dominance. Institutions such as Makerere's Institute of Social and Economic Research have not only pioneered research into Africa's own problems but have also been able to win funds to support it from bodies such as the Ford and Rockefeller Foundations. Like so many other British colonial institutions, universities adapted to the societies in which they were implanted and took on the character of those societies.

In Africa, the Gold Coast illustrates the general pattern of education in colonies with a non-European population. The colonial government introduced a poll tax in 1852 to foster expansion of its own schools, and began to make annual grants to the Wesleyan and Swiss Basel missions in 1874. A general system of government-financed primary schools and grant-aided mission schools subject to regular inspection was established in 1882. By 1919 the Gold Coast had 19 government and 194 inspected schools taking in over 27,000 pupils, a more than five-fold increase since the system was started; there were also many other missionary schools that received no government funds. These were nevertheless tiny figures in absolute terms – about 3.9 per cent of the 693,185 children under sixteen offically recorded in the 1921 census – and the increase in educational provision had many drawbacks. Trained teachers, especially indigenous Africans, were very few; syllabuses, weighted to literary subjects, were often unimaginative transpositions from Britain; schools were very unevenly scattered, 77 per cent being concentrated in the colony's east and central provinces; and the only secondary schools were two each in Accra and Cape Coast. However, the 1920s witnessed reforms and a major expansion which included technical schools and teacher training. Pushed forward by an energetic Governor, Gordon Guggisberg, and by the demands from educated Africans, this expansion culminated in the founding of Prince of Wales College at Achimota. This decade also set the pattern of colonial schooling throughout Britain's African territories until the next surge after 1945, which was intended to provide the immediate foundation for Africanization of the public services and political independence.

Patterns of colonial education thus varied immensely. In the relatively wealthy colonies of settlement the goal of universal education was early and widely accepted and most children benefited. Among New Zealand whites, for example, the literacy rate was high (82 per cent in 1891) even if, to some observers, the standard of taste was less so. By contrast, in India, although there was a substantial growth in the percentage of literate people and numbers of colleges and schools in the 1930s (despite a rising population), by 1941 still only 27.4 per cent of men and 6.9 per cent of women were literate, and a majority of villages were without schools. In 1938 5.8 per cent of the Gold Coast's budget went on education, but for every seventy primary schools there was still less than one secondary institution. Government efforts to educate were sincere but, almost everywhere, these efforts were limited by a combined inability and refusal to provide more funds at the expense of other objectives.

Throughout the empire the content of education involved more or less unhappy compromises. Colonial governments wanted an employable, contented population and feared the extensive, unregulated schooling of indigenous peoples. Missions wanted education shaped by religious priorities. White settlers regarded more than a minimum of schooling for the non-European population as insupportable extravagance, while the indigenous people themselves saw education as the means to social or economic advancement, an escape from manual labour. Kenya in the mid-1920s came to illustrate the tensions: the Native Industrial Training School had the support of the settlers, anxious to make Africans useful labourers in the white economy; many officials favoured the Jeanes Schools, training Africans to improve conditions in their own tribal reserves; the Alliance High Schools represented the culmination thus far of the Protestant missionary tradition of Christian education; and in reaction against all three, the Kikuyu began to found their own independent schools to instil their own values. For the most part, the only non-European people who got the education they either wanted or could best use were members of the colonial elites, and while this education was usually one that now seems unduly theoretical and literary, it was attractive enough to outrage Indians when Lord Curzon tried to reform the universities. Technical or 'industrial' education at any level found little popular or official support.

RELIGION AND EMPIRE

Religion was central to the colonial encounter. The British claimed to be a Christian people and clergy and missionaries were a very important part of any British presence overseas, while the peoples of the empire had strong religious convictions of their own. Religion was therefore the vehicle for much of the interchange of ideas within the imperial framework.

The propagation of Christianity

At the end of the eighteenth century there were two major developments that would affect the religious life of the empire – the revival of government concern for religious provision to white colonists and the formation by evangelical Protestant lay people of overseas missionary societies committed to converting the non-Christian world.

The missionary societies were of various denominations – Baptist (1792), the Church Missionary Society (Anglican, in 1798), and later various Scottish and Methodist bodies. They all shared a common conviction that world-wide conversion was both possible and a duty – not only a divine promise but a divine command. At the end of the eighteenth century the selection of areas for missionary work depended chiefly on an awareness and contacts developed through British exploration and trade. The London Missionary Society (1795) was excited by the prospects both in the Pacific and, a little later, at the newly conquered Cape of Good Hope, which it saw as its launching-pad into Africa. The famous Baptist trio, William Carey, Joshua Marshman, and William Ward, initially discouraged from working in East India Company territory, settled in 1800 just outside Calcutta at Serampore. Even a century later, missionaries still tended to move well ahead of any British and other colonial frontiers into the 'regions beyond'. By the 1880s areas well outside the orbit of British influence and control, like the Congo and inland China, were attracting extensive missionary attention.

The connection between missionary ideas or commitment and the extension of empire has provoked plenty of debate. Non-conformist societies in particular tried to steer clear of any 'political' involvement in their work; but the manner in which missionary attitudes merged with support for colonialism or the extension of powerful British influences goes far beyond such a superficial neutrality. As white

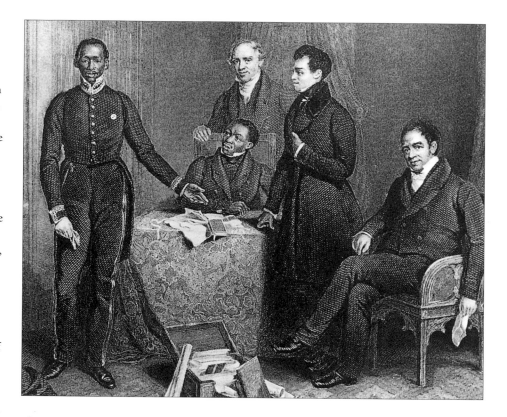

Dr John Philip's delegation to London, 1836. Philip, a Scot with the London Missionary Society, exemplifies the involvement of missionaries in the politics of southern Africa. He served at the Cape from 1819 to 1845. During that time he constantly lobbied the colonial and the British governments on behalf of the Khoikhoi within the colony and the African and mixed-race communities on its frontiers, protesting about forced labour, wars, and the seizure of land. The delegation he brought to London in 1836 included a Xhosa called Dyani 'John' Tshatshu and a Khoikhoi called Andries Stoffels. Both of them gave evidence to a House of Commons committee on the treatment of Aboriginal peoples in the empire. Thomas Buxton, who was keenly interested in the welfare of such people, described an occasion on which they dined with him. Tshatshu 'was dressed in a fanciful uniform, with a gold-laced coat, something like a naval officer. He is rather a fine-looking well made man, but his hair is like a carpet.' After dinner both men sang: Tshatshu in 'caffre', while Stoffles 'sang a war song in Hottentot'.

settlers or planters maltreated non-Europeans or obstructed missionary preaching as subversive of hierarchy and social order, so missions turned inevitably to imperial authorities to defend their rights. This often involved an expansion of colonial power. Imperial restriction of planter power over their slaves in the West Indies, the extension of imperial frontiers at the Cape to preserve both indigenous communities and a sphere for missionary enterprise, the imperial annexation of New Zealand: all were demanded by the missions. In Africa, from the start of the second wave of mission expansion in the 1840s to the conclusion of colonial partition round about 1900, missions grew steadily more prepared to request colonial or imperial protection, and began in the late 1880s and 1890s to advocate the break-up of societies that were particularly resistant to their message, like the Ijebu in Nigeria or the Ndebele in Rhodesia. Elsewhere the missionaries only arrived for the first time in the wake of conquest, like the Church Missionary Society in the Punjab early in the 1850s.

Missionary aggressiveness was bred in part by the profound conviction of Christianity's absolute claims. It also fed on the developing nineteenth-century view that most non-European religions and cultures were worthless, and it sometimes reflected missionaries' frustration and bitter experience of slow progress towards their goal. However, this aggressiveness was by no means universal even before 1914, and should not be allowed to obscure the fact that missionary attitudes towards Britain's colonial expansion were often profoundly ambivalent.

This can be seen clearly, for example, in the long-running debate within the church about missionary strategy: could Christianity be most effectively spread in association with western culture and commerce, or was more to be achieved by preaching a purely religious message detached from Britain's cultural baggage? Much evangelical opinion, especially after about 1885, tended to favour the latter approach. This view was partly based on current theological thinking which emphasized the benefits of rapid, world-wide evangelization rather than a more thorough conversion linked to social transformation. However, it was also fostered by the periodic upsurges of evangelical criticism of British expansion and colonial practice. The fraud and corruption so often a feature of unregulated commerce, the damaging effects of trade in alcohol or weapons, the support of British authorities for indigenous beliefs and practices (such as the levying of pilgrim taxes for the upkeep of Indian temples) at the expense of Christian teaching, the frequent hostility of British officials towards missionaries: all these were very irksome.

From the 1890s onwards it became common for missionaries to take a more sympathetic and constructive attitude towards other religions. As Mary Kingsley (who made journeys through West Africa in the 1890s) and professional anthropologists called for a better understanding of the value and integrated nature of indigenous cultures, so missionaries began to explore the possibility that Christianity represented the natural complement to or even fulfilment of existing beliefs. They accepted more readily the need to work with the grain of local cultures, rather than aiming at their complete displacement. People could perhaps be converted to Christianity without being subjected to colonial rule. As Chauncy Maples of the Universities Mission to Central Africa put it in 1882, '…the European missionary must become an African to win Africans. He must, so far as is consistent with his Christian principles, assimilate himself to them.' J.N. Farquhar's influential work, *The Crown of Hinduism* (1913), put a similar point in theological terms, representing missionary Christianity in various ways as the 'fulfilment' of Hinduism.

Not surprisingly, this mixture of explicit support for colonial expansion with principled detachment, a willingness to criticize British actions, and appreciation of non-western ways, frequently produced confused consequences. By the 1850s missionaries had generally accepted that their goal was to establish local churches which would be self-governing, self-financing, and capable of their own missionary expansion. White missionaries would be freed to move on, and non-European communities, transformed by Christian teaching, would run their own affairs. Practice rarely matched up to the theory. There always seemed reason to delay the withdrawal – insufficient local resources, perhaps indiscipline and immorality among local Christian laity, too few teachers or ministers of the right calibre – and missionary control therefore persisted. A natural human reluctance to abandon one's life's work, the influence of racial stereotyping, and missionary bureaucracy all played their part in prolonging a measure of colonial control in the church as in politics and commerce.

Samuel Crowther. Crowther had been sold into slavery from what is now Nigeria at the age of twelve. He was taken off the slave ship by the navy and brought to Sierra Leone. From Sierra Leone he went to London to be ordained into the Church of England in 1842. He went back to the Niger as Bishop of the Church Missionary Society's mission. He later resigned in the face of accusations of laxity in tolerating heathen practices. To some Africans he was a victim of racial prejudice.

This unwillingness to relax control was also the product of uncertainty about religious conversion. Were the signs of conversion to be found in regular church attendance and the adoption of western dress, in the outward abandonment of non-European ways? Ex-slaves and their descendants in Sierra Leone (see page 45) with weakened traditional attachments found this kind of conformity relatively simple; Chinese and Indians did not. Or was conversion to be judged by states of mind and ethical intentions, with only occasional conformity to western living patterns being expected of converts in a crucial area like monogamous marriage? What lapses undermined one's fitness to be a teacher, catechist, churchwarden, or even priest? Was the priority given to the long-drawn-out process of complete conversion a distraction for missions, would a greater emphasis on the preliminaries of evangelization instead serve just as well – covering a far wider territory and giving more hearers the chance of conversion if they so chose? Missionaries debated such questions unceasingly, and as a result were occasionally involved in very bitter conflicts like that between the Church Missionary Society and the first Anglican African Bishop, Samuel Crowther, on the Niger in the 1880s and 1890s, which led to the Bishop's resignation. The absence of easy answers and a proper concern for standards of Christian behaviour, not least among Protestants who thought that Roman Catholics baptized too readily, often kept missionaries *in situ* and converts in their place.

Why did people convert to Christianity? Missionary Christianity, for all its narrowness even in the eyes of many European contemporaries and despite the restraints it involved, was also a vital liberating force. Converts were often drawn from the most marginal members of society – slaves, victims of war and famine, debtors, the ill and outcast – who clearly found in the church a new community which gave order and meaning to their existence. In the words of one of Crowther's early assistants, recruited from the liberated slave community of Sierra Leone, '… when I heard that the Gospel is being carried just to the fore of my birthplace I resigned my office as Government messenger and voluntarily offered myself to the Niger … in the teaching of my brethren the unsearchable riches of Christ Jesus'.

Undoubtedly Christianity was widely linked to white power, and as colonial rule took root so it seemed important to acquire white beliefs. Conversion has therefore sometimes been attributed to a natural process of adjustment in which Africans, for example, substituted a new over-arching Christian God for their traditional local spirits, a God in tune with the enlargement of scale and outlook introduced by colonial contacts. Rather more persuasive, however, are recent writings that show how Christian beliefs were attractive because they addressed important aspects of everyday life inadequately dealt with by traditional religion. In particular, Christianity offered answers to questions about evil in the forms of poverty, disease, or other misfortunes, it appeared to face up to the fact of death, and it elaborated on the nature of an afterlife. These answers were often the more

The baptism of the Maori Te Puni. Christian missions came to New Zealand from 1814, long before the establishment of British rule. Maoris showed interest in Christianity and, allowing for the uncertainties of knowing what 'conversion' might mean, the missions claimed many converts. In the first half of the nineteenth century New Zealand seemed to be a particularly fruitful mission field.

persuasive when, as was most often the case, they were conveyed by indigenous teachers or catechists, rather than the white missionaries who established the first mission stations.

The attractions of conversion therefore ranged from the purely material offerings of food, jobs, or even land tied to church or mission station, via its connection with education and the prospects of personal advancement, to the psychological reassurance or intellectual consolations of belief itself. By the twentieth century, Christianity had attracted large numbers of adherents in nearly all British territories. Even in India by 1911 Christians were almost 3.9 million strong, 1.2 million of them in Madras where they made up almost 3 per cent of the population: throughout the period to 1947 they could not be ignored in the constitutional negotiations that led ultimately to independence. In Britain's African territories Christians were far stronger in both numbers and influence and the great majority of nationalist politicians were educated in mission schools. The fundamental egalitarianism of much in the Christian message was no more lost in colonial Africa or India than it had been a century before when West Indian slave owners did everything they could to restrict missionary activity. It is therefore not surprising to find in the twentieth century that, as numbers of colonial Christians grew and the resources of the missionary societies shrank in relation to the size of their religious, educational, and humanitarian tasks, the self-government in religious affairs so long promised to local Christians rapidly became a reality.

Missionary activity also took place in the colonies of settlement – among New Zealand's Maoris, Australian Aborigines, and Canada's native Indians. However, this evangelization soon became a responsibility of the local white settler churches. As a result, it became a far more localized and restricted activity than the global missionary work of the British-based societies, and was heavily overshadowed by the many other challenges involved in establishing viable Christian churches in recently-settled territories.

Among these difficulties was the hotly-debated question of whether colonial taxes and other resources should be used to support an established church. In Canada in 1791 and New South Wales in 1825 attempts were made to endow

David Livingstone in Britain.

David Livingstone: 'light of Africa'

David Livingstone was a Scot who went to South Africa as a missionary in 1840. He made a series of journeys into Central Africa in the 1840s and the 1850s, which took him north to the Zambezi and then east and west to the Indian and Atlantic Oceans. He was given an ecstatic reception in Britain on his return in 1856–57 and became the model of a Christian hero in the eyes of the public. He returned to Africa in 1858 'to try to make an open path for commerce and Christianity' with an expedition along the Zambezi, which lasted until 1863. He was again rapturously received in Britain before setting off in 1865 with another expedition to search for the sources of the Nile. In 1871 he was 'found' by H. M. Stanley, but died in Africa in 1873. He was seen as a martyr who had sacrificed his life for the cause of Africa.   [PJM]

Livingstone the missionary. The Victorian imagination was fed innumerable accounts and visual images, such as this one, of Livingstone's saintliness.

an established Anglican church with land and educational responsibilities, and later in New Zealand specific denominational settlements were founded in Christchurch (Anglican) and Otago (Presbyterian). However, none of these experiments lasted. The British government's support for establishment was fitful, even in Roman Catholic Quebec, and in any case the tendency in Britain itself from the 1830s was to disentangle church from state. In the colonies themselves the variety of denominations all lacking clergy and endowments, plus the indifference of many settlers, made state support for any one church too invidious and divisive to last. Although compromises were attempted in some colonies to provide state grants to the most important denominations, these too foundered. By the 1870s there was no longer any state support for church schools in Canada, Australia, and New Zealand, and churches were completely separated from government at least in legal and financial matters. Lack of official support and limited endowments compelled all the churches to depend heavily on voluntary support: alongside issues such as denominational schools, missions to the local heathen hardly appealed to settler congregations.

This separation between church and state had happened much more rapidly than in Britain itself, reflecting not just the competition between the various denominations but also the widely secular and materialistic outlook of settler society. Even if not opposed to organized religion, many immigrants' religious leanings cooled owing to the absence of churches and ministers on the spot. Anglicans and other groups slowly built up their organizations but never found it easy to hold their own against indifference or apathy. In Australia, however, Roman Catholics, overwhelmingly Irish and working-class until the 1940s, did rather better than their rivals. This Catholic presence, resolutely anti-English and determined to maintain its own educational values, injected a continuing religious dimension into Australia's colonial and later federal as well as state politics. Linked as it was to the interests of organized labour, this alliance of class, sectarianism, and nationality was obnoxious to more conservative Protestant interests, as conflicts over employment, welfare, and foreign policies showed, especially during the World Wars of the twentieth century.

The growth of independent African churches
Reactions to Christian ideas have taken many forms besides the clear acceptance or rejection of missionaries' teachings. This has been most obvious in colonial Africa, where at times Africans' deep attachment to biblical ideas has been associated with rejection of the western churches' formalized rituals, organization, and theology.

In places where the missionary or colonial presence was unusually oppressive and unyielding, too oblivious to the particular religious needs of local people or their ambitions to run their own churches, the result – often reflecting the influence of American revivalist inspiration in Britain and Africa in the nineteenth century –

was the powerful development of independent African churches. Sometimes these were straightforward secession movements from existing churches. The Niger Delta Pastorate, for instance, led by James Johnson in reaction against the Church Missionary Society's overbearing treatment of Bishop Crowther in 1891, was committed above all to African leadership, while retaining Anglican practice in most other respects. The Niger Delta Pastorate was itself the victim of further schism in 1901, when the Bethel African church broke away. Similar divisions took place in the Baptist and Methodist missionary-led churches of the Gold Coast and Sierra Leone.

In contrast to the 'Ethiopian' churches as they were known, were other more radical or 'Zionist' movements, often with greater mass appeal. These were built around particular charismatic individuals or Christian 'prophets', and incorporated many more explicit references to traditional African religious beliefs. Nigeria again provides examples, in the shape of the movement of Garrick Braide (c. 1915–18), regarded by his followers as a prophet, Elijah II, whose words were the words of God. Much more extensive was the Church of the Lord (Aladura) after 1930. Members of this church worship God in many sacred places, rather than in conventional churches, and use the objects of daily life in their worship in which God is praised 'with claps, jumps, bows, Hallelujah, Hossana, Hurrah, laughter, singing, dancing, organ and drumming'. But the most striking proliferation occurred in Central and South Africa, where there were estimated to be some 130 such churches by 1925 and ten times that number by 1946.

To western missionaries, white settlers, and colonial administrators, such developments appeared irrational and threatening, voicing as they so often did challenges to political and social authority as well as to Christian norms. Independent church movements were dismissed as 'syncretist' – new religions comprising confused and inconsistent or possibly dangerously heretical selections from opposed religious traditions. Their prophets were sometimes imprisoned and their followers excommunicated. Eventually, however, it came to be recognized that even orthodox Christianity was constantly evolving and that both western and African understandings of Christianity were broadened by the interaction that took place within the context of colonialism. As a result, bodies like the World Council of Churches or the Roman Catholic church have had to take account of African as well as western European theology.

Indian responses to Christianity

The extensive mingling of Christianity and existing religions, which was so marked in Africa, did not occur to the same extent in British India or China. The greater resilience of Indian customs and the self-confidence of religions such as Islam or Hinduism meant that although, as in African territories, indifference and even outright hostility towards Christianity were common, conversion and acceptance of Christian beliefs were comparatively rare. Instead, especially among the elites,

Indian responses were to reform and redefine their own religious or educational systems in the light of the inspiration and criticisms that British religion and secular culture could offer.

The first major evidence of this reformation among Hindus was the 'Bengal renaissance' in Calcutta, especially between 1813 and the early 1830s. During this period leading wealthy Bengali families such as the Debs and the Tagores, who established Hindu College in 1816, shared the belief of British orientalists employed by the East India Company that British-style education should provide the stimulus for reinvigorating Bengali culture from within. This conviction led to the founding of the Calcutta School Book Society of 1817, the Calcutta Public Library in 1818, and the fusion under the company's auspices of Hindu College with a new Sanskrit College in 1823. It also encouraged both British and Indian scholars to conduct research and to recover old Hindu texts and traditions: such research promoted the ideal of a 'less corrupt' Hinduism derived from evidence of an earlier golden age.

A 'purified' Hindu culture, incorporating modern rationalism or scientific knowledge, was intended by the Indian reformers both to provide an answer to mounting British Christian and secular criticisms of Indian society as corrupt and degenerate, and to overcome the pervasive crisis of confidence felt by many Hindus in the face of British achievements. The leaders of the renaissance were offering a justification for change and a guide to the direction that reform might take. Local societies like the Brahmo Samaj (Society for the Transcendent Deity), started by Raja Rammohun Roy in 1828, became the means by which such reforming ideas were kept alive even after the triumph in British administrative circles of militant westernizers and, later still, of those sceptical of any fundamental changes ever taking place in India.

Raja Rammohun Roy. The Raja was a Brahmin, deeply learned in European and Muslim culture as well as in the Hindu tradition. He promoted social and religious reform in British India and was the first Indian intellectual to make an impact in Britain, where he died on a visit in 1833.

There were similar developments in Indian Islam, in response to the widespread socio-economic changes accompanying the expanding British presence in the century from 1760 to 1860. In centres such as Peshawar, Delhi, and Lucknow, as well as others in the Punjab and eastern Bengal, individual teachers and learned families associated with particular mosques or *madrasa*s (colleges) re-examined Koranic traditions and engaged in debates with missionaries, often in public, as in the famous exchanges with Carl Pfander of the Church Missionary Society at Agra in 1854. Christian advocates found these encounters difficult. Not only were Muslim teachers by the 1850s making effective use of the missionaries' own vernacular translations of Christian texts – for example, to point out illogicalities in the doctrine of the Trinity; they were also acquainted with recent western biblical criticism. This enabled the Muslim teacher Wazir Khan, for instance, to use textual evidence and Roman Catholic commentaries on Protestant translations to show how unreliable and corrupt the Christian scriptures were. Thus evangelical argument was undermined and the errors of Christianity appeared to be demonstrated.

Such intellectual exchange and evolution was often restricted to quite limited circles of scholars, their patrons, and pupils, isolated even within the towns they inhabited. It is therefore important not to exaggerate their direct influence. However, there were some potentially practical implications for ordinary people. The religious revivals encouraged by both Hindu and Islamic reformers frequently carried social and political messages – being critical, for instance, of caste hierarchies or the rights of landlords against tenants. Throughout the colonial period there were frequent connections between social protest and religious inspiration. In this respect there are striking similarities between Indian and African responses to colonialism. Religious beliefs had a very important role at every level, from the highest to the lowest, in African and Indian society. Either through the selective use of some Christian ideas or through reinterpreting their existing religious traditions, colonial communities could bind themselves together. Religion not only helped to give African and Indian people their sense of identity; it also often gave them criteria with which to criticize and resist colonial regimes. For example, John Chilembwe, who rebelled against colonial rule in Nyasaland (Malawi) in 1915, had built up his own Christian missionary institution. Hinduism and Islam in many different forms were essential elements of Indian resistance to the British from the Indian Rebellion of 1857 to twentieth-century nationalism. By contrast, for the white settler colonies of the British empire, apart from French-Canadian Quebec, religion has played at most a superficial and probably a negligible role in questions of identity.

THE MEDIA

Technological advances in communications were inseparably tied to British expansion. The nineteenth century saw the development of railways, steam shipping, and overland and submarine telegraphs. In the twentieth century, telephones, radio, air communications, and – overlapping with the end of empire – television and satellite transmission were added. The development of photography from the 1850s and, later, cinematic film expanded communication still further. To all these changes the British made major contributions, driven on time and again by the needs of running an empire and of protecting their global trade, as well as by the demands of colonial peoples.

Printing and publishing

Of primary importance to the movement of ideas was the expansion of printing and publishing. Far more than the learning and diffusion of languages or the invention of written scripts, printing had unprecedented consequences for both the scale on which ideas and information could be disseminated and the frequency with which this could be done. Printing made possible the long-term or even permanent influence and availability of published material, irrespective of its content. According to one Victorian, 'The hand that rocks the cradle, Is the hand that rules the world'; but the hand that printed pamphlets ran it a close second. Aware of this, governments, scholars, teachers, missionaries, and propagandists of all kinds aimed to control printing presses in their own interests.

British activity in Bengal provides excellent illustrations of the readiness with which printing was seized on for the spreading of new ideas and knowledge. In 1778 Charles Wilkins set up the first vernacular printing press in India and brought out Nathaniel Halhed's *Grammar of the Bengali Language*. Within two years he was handling not only all printing of the government's official vernacular documents, but also the first English-language newspaper, *Hicky's Gazette*. In 1800 Baptist missionaries arrived at Serampore and immediately established their own press, greatly extending vernacular printing, serving the new Fort William College and the Asiatic Society, and publishing classics of Indian literature. 'The Press is humming,' Carey wrote in 1802. 'My Bengali Grammar and Colloquies and Bashoo's History ... are sold off ... We are printing the Hitopadosha from Sanskrit into Bengali and the Mahabarat ...' Within a few years Fort William College had a printing capacity sufficient to support its own programmes in Urdu, Persian, and Arabic. By the early 1820s Bengali intellectuals and businessmen had branched out into publishing vernacular journals and newspapers, and bookshops were becoming a feature of Calcutta's life.

Even where government played no role, the combination of missionary work, education, and printing, which then spilled over into wider publishing including newspapers, was a common one. The Glasgow Missionary Society began work in the eastern Cape of South Africa in 1820: translations immediately followed and a press arrived on 16 December 1823. 'On the 17th we got our Press in order; on the 18th the alphabet was set up; and yesterday [the 19th] we threw off 50 copies ... Through your instrumentality a new era has commenced in the history of the Kaffer

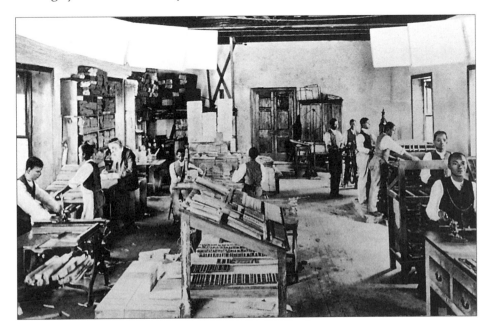

The press at Lovedale, eastern Cape, South Africa. In addition to their school, the Scottish missionaries at Lovedale developed a press for printing books in English and in Xhosa. By 1939 the Lovedale press had been responsible for 238 separate titles in Xhosa. This made Xhosa, together with Swahili, one of the most extensively published African languages. Both owed much to the patronage of British Christian missionaries.

[Xhosa] nation.' By 1845 a periodical in English and Xhosa, *Ikwezi* (The Morning Star), had been started. A printing department was established at the great Scottish mission station of Lovedale in 1861, and again English and Xhosa translations followed in large numbers. The mission's monthly Xhosa newspaper, *Isigidimi Sama-Xosa* (The Xhosa Messenger), eventually succumbed in 1894 to the rival vernacular competition of *Imvo*, a weekly paper edited by J.T. Jabavu, previously a Lovedale pupil.

Printed material of all kinds soon spread beyond any possibility of tight control by cautious political and religious authorities. Newspaper printing and publishing were not just good business propositions; they were quickly hitched to the ambitions of regional and national political interests. In South Africa Robert Godlonton built up the *Graham's Town Journal* to give coherence and leadership to settler interests in the eastern Cape – above all in their prolonged battle for separation from the control of unsympathetic authorities in distant Cape Town. Where Godlonton ultimately failed, another forceful newspaper proprietor like George Brown of Toronto's *Globe* was able to play a critical role in rallying opinion behind Canada's Confederation in the 1860s. Everywhere nationalist critics of colonial rule set up their papers. By 1914 a clutch of West African English-language newspapers – the *Gold Coast Nation*, the *Gold Coast Leader*, and most significantly the *Gold Coast Independent* – were educating and mobilizing a readership with interests in African history, culture, and economic and political advancement. These were the forerunners of the far more outspoken nationalist papers of the 1940s and 1950s, like Accra's *African Morning Post* or Lagos's daily *West African Pilot*.

The power of unrestricted print loomed large in many minds, and governments frequently if vainly tried to contain the flood. Sometimes their methods were blatantly restrictive, as was reflected in the government of India's Vernacular Press Act (1878) and its successors, and the Defence of India Act (1915). The latter led to a host of restraints, including 289 newspapers and 389 presses being required to deposit special securities against good behaviour during the First World War. Prosecutions for sedition or refusals of registration were commonly used against African newspapers. At other times more subtle methods were used. In the battle for support during 1898–99, ahead of the South African War, the Cape's Governor, Sir Alfred Milner, engineered the appointment of W.F. Monypenny to edit the Johannesburg *Star* – to mobilize opinion hostile to President Kruger and the Boers and to serve as a source of 'independent' comment which Milner could then use to influence his superiors in London.

Such details illustrate the endlessly ambiguous impact of growing literacy, knowledge of other languages, and printing, on imperial and colonial relations. On the one hand, the powers of colonial governments to administer and control were greatly enhanced; on the other hand, the ability of ordinary people to question and subvert traditional attitudes or imperialist assumptions similarly increased.

Technological change reinforced the competition for information. Players in the empire's games of persuasion – newspaper proprietors, politicians, businessmen, and missionaries – constantly tried to outbid each other, with the consequence that ideas and information were transmitted ever more rapidly, and attitudes were more readily affronted or adjusted. The fact that steamships, postal or railway systems, and submarine telegraphs were developed to assist commercial rivalries did not lessen their impact on assumptions and outlooks. By 1907 the Gold Coast's telegraph system was widely established inland as well as on the coast, and within a decade annual private use had risen fourfold to 165,000 telegrams. Publicity became even cheaper and easier by the 1930s when British newspapers reached Calcutta or Adelaide by air in days rather than after months at sea, and regular airmail became the norm.

Film and broadcasting

In 1926 the imperial conference of Dominion prime ministers agreed that 'the Cinema is not merely a form of entertainment but ... a powerful instrument of education ... and even when it is not used avowedly for purposes of instruction, advertisement or propaganda, it exercises indirectly a great influence in shaping the ideas of the very large numbers to whom it appeals'. With such views gaining ground, it is not surprising that the 1930s in particular were years of important changes in the projection of western images to the colonial world. It is tempting to see symbolic links between King George V's apparent concern that American films were undermining white prestige and his agreement in 1932 to begin what became the practice of royal Christmas broadcasts. His concern with the impact of both film and radio shows how even the most traditional sections of British society were alive to the great significance of the new technology's impact on imperial ideas and attitudes. The royal

King George V broadcasting. The King's Christmas broadcasts were aimed at audiences throughout the empire and the Commonwealth as well as in Britain.

interest was enough to add another patriotic programme to those already regularly arranged by the BBC for Empire and Armistice Days; no such counter-action was contemplated in response to the film makers' peddling of stereotypes that discredited black and coloured colonial people.

Branches of the imperial government also began to experiment with the new technology. The Colonial Office supported the making of educational films to back up programmes promoting hygiene and other aspects of colonial welfare. The Empire Marketing Board, in a brief life from 1926 to 1933 devoted to the advancement of trade within the empire, created as many as 100 films to extend its range of advertising, and set up its own library to lend out documentary films with titles such as *Solid Sunshine* (about New Zealand butter) and *Wheatfields of the Empire*. On the fringes of government, the expansion of the BBC's Empire Service went ahead steadily after its creation in 1932 – with its somewhat fuzzily-defined aim of promoting internationalism and imperial unity under Britain's leadership – and overseas the Dominions set out to weld their own populations more closely together by developing national broadcasting services.

During the Second World War governments took control of all communication to an unprecedented degree. The needs of the war gave still greater impetus to developing new techniques for transmitting ideas and opinion. Government propagandists seized on radio and cinema film to mould perceptions of the war – its progress, its aims, and Britain's enemies. For British home audiences and for Dominion and colonial listeners, the Empire Intelligence Section of the BBC was set up in January 1941 and worked closely with the Ministries of Education and Information, paying particular attention to broadcasting for schools. Figures like the well-known historian W.M. Macmillan were roped in to provide news and comment that would underpin an essential wartime solidarity. While being asked at first to help specifically with material for the West Indies, Macmillan was told how 'these newsletters that we do for different parts of the Empire, are directed at the average native listener, if there is such a person, and not at all at the European population'.

As with all changes brought about by colonialism, the impact of broadcasting was two-sided. The results, which reached far beyond any 'average native listener', included a massive extension of technical equipment and know-how to those previously without it, and this was incapable of being withdrawn once peace came. 'Wireless sets' were made widely available to assist the diffusion of wartime propaganda. Illegal transmitters were operated – for example, by members of India's Congress Party. In wartime broadcasts colonial governments were led to make pledges to libertarian and welfare policies which raised the future expectations of their citizens. Thus ideas about the scope and purpose of colonial government were created which altogether changed the environment in which authorities had to work after 1945. Pledges easily made and broadcast were far less easily redeemed.

By the 1950s the British government was as likely to feel constrained as it was strengthened by the spread of radios and transmitters. Certainly Oliver Lyttelton, Colonial Secretary from 1951 to 1954, was aware of being restricted. Colonial populations were far more familiar than before with developments taking place elsewhere in the world, with the result that, for example, it was very difficult for Britain to allow decolonization to proceed at widely different paces in its East and West African territories. Moreover, instances of discreditable colonial activity were far more likely to be exposed, and the possibility of suppressing colonial unrest was correspondingly reduced. Lyttelton and his colleagues found it hard to cope with what they regarded as misrepresentations of British policy – for example, in British Guiana (Guyana) and Kenya – transmitted by countries critical of or actively hostile to Britain, such as Egypt, India, or Russia.

IMAGES OF THE COLONIAL WORLD

Aspirations to order were deeply embedded in British thinking about empire. Colonies, their peoples, and resources were listed, mapped, and classified in innumerable publications. The reality was rather different. It was an empire so diverse and about which so much information – capable of being interpreted in so many different ways – was available that it burst out of all attempts to force it into categories. Nevertheless, at least two forms of categorization had a very powerful influence on interpretations of empire. For much of the nineteenth century the empire was seen as an empire of races; in the twentieth century it came to be seen as an empire or a Commonwealth of nations.

Races

British disdain or contempt for the religious beliefs and the social and political customs of other societies was nothing new in the later eighteenth century. However, those who then proclaimed British superiority – in morals, law, religion, or political institutions – did so not in relation to race as such but in relation to a host of circumstantial influences, such as the debilitating effects of tropical climates, the degrading consequences of 'oriental despotism', or the necessity for all societies to pass through a fixed sequence of historical stages before approximating to the British model. Fundamentally, human nature was supposed by most British people to be everywhere the same – broadly amenable to reason and capable of progress through the assimilation of higher ideas and institutions together with the reform or abandonment of corrupt and inhuman practices. Throughout the late eighteenth and early nineteenth centuries this basic assumption – that there was a single human race – was common to administrators confident in their ability to reshape Indian society, to evangelicals convinced of the possibility of worldwide conversion to Christianity, and to admirers of 'noble savages' as well as opponents of slavery. All aimed for the liberation of individuals from unnatural or archaic restraints, which prevented them from leading a free and independent existence and were to the detriment of society at large.

The effect of Christianity on the people of the Cook Islands. These engravings of the 1870s illustrate assumptions about the underlying similarities of human beings throughout the world. Once purged of heathen beliefs, the islanders of the Pacific would become like British people: industrious, respectable property owners.

Kipling was the son of Methodists, born late in 1865 in Bombay where his father taught at the government's art school. After going away to school in England, he returned to his parents in Lahore where in 1882 he started work as a newspaper reporter on the *Civil and Military Gazette*. In 1887 he took a similar position with the Allahabad *Pioneer*, and in 1889 left India for England. Already well-known for his verse and short stories, he rapidly became perhaps the most celebrated British literary exponent of imperial, military, and patriotic themes. His books such as *Plain Tales from the Hills*, *Barrack-room Ballads*, *The Jungle Book*, and *Kim* were widely popular, as too was his occasional verse. They helped to win for him the Nobel Prize for Literature in 1907, and did much to shape the attitudes of a conservative British public towards empire and its purposes in the years before the First World War.

In some ways Kipling's popularity was – still is – surprising. There have always been those who have found themselves repelled by the bitterness, vulgarity, obsessive detail, chauvinism, and contrived dialogue that marks much of his writing, notwithstanding its technical facility. Reams of his sharp-edged satire are aimed at those in authority, especially members of the Indian civil service with their elaborate social rituals, personal patronage, and administrative absurdities, and there is an evident pleasure taken in their blunders and disgrace. For him the empire survived despite the best efforts of the public schools. Yet even those who caught Kipling's affection seem often to be patronized

and caricatured, notably Tommy Atkins with his dropped consonants and earthy appetites.

from *The Ladies* (v. 2)

> Now I aren't no 'and with the ladies,
> For, takin' 'em all along,
> You never can say till you've tried 'em,
> An' then you are like to be wrong.
> There's times when you'll think that you mightn't,
> There's times when you'll know that you might;
> But the things you will learn from the Yellow an' Brown
> They'll 'elp you a lot with the White!

Kipling also maintained a great reservoir of contempt for the intellectuals, politicians, and all other classes, especially those at home in Britain, whose narrow outlooks failed to comprehend what empire meant, what it required of its rulers, and what it cost those who kept it going.

from *The Supplication of Kerr Cross, Missionary* (vv. 1, 6, 10)

> Father of Mercy, who hast made
> The sun by day, the moon by night,
> To show the course of British Trade
> And cheer the Gospel-teaching white,
> Tho' we attack with fire and sword,
> The heathen press us hard, O Lord!
>
> A minister of Christ, I kneel
> Before Thy altar to beseech
> One seven-pounder – rifled – steel –
> Ten-grooved and loading at the breech:
> Thereto, for Thou dost all things well,
> Much ammunition – shot and shell.
>
> Creator of the countless suns,
> We spread the message of the Cross,
> Grant that we smuggle safe those guns
> And horribly avenge our loss!
> So shall we teach, by death and dearth,
> Goodwill to men and peace on earth.

from *Chant-Pagan: English Irregular, discharged* (v. 1)

> Me that 'ave been what I've been –
> Me that 'ave gone where I've gone –
> Me that 'ave seen what I've seen –
> 'Ow can I ever take on
> With awful old England again,
> An' 'ouses both sides of the street,
> An' 'edges two sides of the lane,
> And the parson an' gentry between,
> An' touchin' my 'at when we meet –
> Me that 'ave been what I've been?

To a certain extent, Kipling's appeal lay in his endlessly reiterated faith that all these defects and frailties could be remedied, especially by hard work; his writings are dotted with reminders of higher goals and references to the enduring if not virtuous common sense of modest men. Nevertheless, these are constantly clouded by elements of coarseness and caricature, by mention of past failures and likely lapses deserving ridicule or reprimand.

from *Recessional* (vv. 4, 5)

If, drunk with sight of power, we loose
Wild tongues that have not Thee in awe,
Such boastings as the Gentiles use,
Or lesser breeds without the Law –
Lord God of Hosts, be with us yet,
Lest we forget – lest we forget!

...

For heathen heart that puts her trust
In reeking tube and iron shard,
All valiant dust that builds on dust,
And guarding, calls not Thee to guard.
For frantic boast and foolish word –
Thy mercy on Thy People, Lord!

However, while he sometimes encouraged cynicism and mockery of the pillars of empire, there is wide agreement that Kipling's influence nurtured a potent brand of imperial patriotism. England's greatness, he believed, lay in its achievements overseas, its true qualities and character comprehensible only to those who knew their empire. In the empire were to be found the examples of progress – the roads and bridges (Kipling was more doubtful about the benefits of western education) – achieved by the power, energy, respect for law, discipline, and expertise that were so lacking at home. Empire was not only the expression but the nursery of the capacity to govern.

In later life Kipling was an increasingly dispirited man, more and more painfully aware of the inability of governments and voters to rise to the effective defence either of empire or of the idealized visions of England he had fostered in writings such as *Puck of Pook's Hill* and *A History of England*. The waste of the First World War (including the death of his son for whom he had secured a special commission) after all his warnings, together with the interwar Irish and Indian settlements, confirmed his worst premonitions of imperial decline. He died in January 1936 and was buried in Westminster Abbey.

The village club. Kipling told his readers not only about the doings of their kith and kin in the empire but also about Indian people. In one of the stories in *The Jungle Book* the boy Mowgli, who has been brought up by wolves, goes back to the village in which he was born. Kipling's depiction of the ways of the village is informative if patronizing in tone.

'Subadar-Major Sher Bahadur Khan'. This is one of a series of illustrations to a book called *The People of India* by Henry Risley, organizer of the Indian census of 1901. Risley believed that the people of India were divided into many different races and he used photography to demonstrate their differences. Sher Bahadur Khan, from Baluchistan in what is now Pakistan, came from 'a fine manly race', who 'fight well under an officer they trust'. The Indian martial race theory was also applied to Africa.

This universalist outlook changed gradually during the nineteenth century. The pace of Britain's own material development quickened, and Britons' sense of a widening gap between the standards of their home country and those of non-European societies, as well as their greater familiarity with the latter, heightened criticism and contempt for 'inferior' cultures. This criticism was at first usually combined with a continuing belief in the uniformity of human nature, and created in many minds the paradoxical combination of complete dismissiveness of non-European cultures with enhanced optimism about the prospects for changing them.

However, the expectations for a rapid transformation – held in the 1830s for India by Alexander Duff, the Scottish missionary, or by Thomas Fowell Buxton contemplating Africa and the West Indies – were quickly disappointed. India's reform and conversion did not take off; the regeneration of Africa did not follow rapidly on slave trade suppression and the introduction of new 'legitimate' commodities; and West Indian society after emancipation sank into poverty and disenchantment. The shock caused by the Indian Rebellion of 1857 and the Jamaican Rebellion of 1865 was very great, and these rebellions were widely interpreted as rejections of British policies and values. As a result, the capacity of non-Europeans to match British standards was seriously questioned.

Other developments also raised doubts about a common humanity. Some ethnic groups – North American Indians, Maoris, and Aborigines – were clearly declining in numbers and even dying out, prompting questions about the qualities required for survival. The Victorian passion for measurement and statistics was extended to embrace the human physique, to skull size and the brain's volume, with the result that phrenologists and anthropologists began to define not only criminal types at home but racial categories overseas. Increasingly, the idea took hold that cultural attainment and racial attributes were interdependent, a notion illustrated in the identification of colonial 'martial races' – natural fighting men such as the Pathans, Sikhs, Hausas, and Zulus – and the steady subdivision of population groups in the Indian census.

Many facets of imperial experience seemed to provide support for the watershed in evolutionary thinking marked by Charles Darwin's book *The Origin of Species* (1859). Darwin's hypothesis was that evolutionary change had taken place through the natural selection of random variations which had given particular individuals or species significant advantages over their competitors. Darwin himself was reluctant to apply these ideas to human societies but others were not slow to argue that racial variety rather than uniformity was the natural outcome of the evolutionary process.

As 'race' thus assumed a reality, and appeared to provide a ready answer to account for disappointed expectations and otherwise obscure facts or inexplicable developments, it also served imperial purposes. Conquest and rule by Britain, even at its most benign, required justification: to electorates at home carping at the costs, to sharp-eyed humanitarians critical of abuses of power and trust, and to colonial subjects. More than any 'civilizing mission', ideas of natural racial superiority, of an undeniable, scientifically established racial hierarchy, provided a seemingly irrefutable defence of Britain's imperial position. Their value as supports to imperial institutions and practice made concepts of 'race' intellectually even more irresistible.

'Racialist' attitudes, with their elements of hostility, unthinking abuse, and aggression, existed before 'races' were 'scientifically' identified or classified. But as 'race' became more widely accepted, so races became more rigidly defined. This was due in part to the changing nature of colonial communities. The increasing numbers of whites in the nineteenth-century empire, higher chances of survival even in the 'white man's grave' of the tropics, the arrival of white women and families, and the growing segregation of residential areas, all produced greater physical separation to match the intellectual. The aloofness and separation between races in the colonial world were also increased by the transmission from Britain of ideas about social status: as class distinctions and antipathies burgeoned in mid-Victorian Britain, so the mixture of class and race inflicted double jeopardy on colonial subjects. The powerful impact of such attitudes was further enhanced by the extent to which many colonial inhabitants themselves began to accept the white person's representation of reality including its stereotypes of non-whites.

'Niggers are tigers, niggers are tigers' was the rhythmic refrain with which the Poet Laureate, Alfred Tennyson, reportedly tried to persuade his dinner companions in 1865 as to the basic cause of Jamaica's troubles. 'Wild and savage' non-whites were of course considered unfit for self-government and social advancement beyond a certain level. Protests by British people in India in 1883 at the extension of the powers of Indian judges to try Europeans outside the major towns demonstrated this view that non-whites could not be trusted with authority over whites. Thus the definition of race penetrated British assumptions and colonial practice. It also shaped official plans for the future. In the 1890s Harry Johnston, Commissioner for British Central Africa, was convinced that the development of East Africa would depend on Indian trade, immigration, and enterprise.

> ... I think the admixture of yellow that the negro requires should come from India, and that Eastern Africa and British Central Africa should become the America of the Hindu. The mixture of the two races would give the Indian the physical development which he lacks, and he in his turn would transmit to his half negro offspring the industry, ambition, and aspiration towards a civilized life which the negro so markedly lacks.

Racial stereotyping reached its peak at the end of the nineteenth century and discrimination was common or even institutionalized in varying degrees throughout the empire – nowhere more so perhaps than in South Africa. But challenges now came from several directions. The most effective were based on a reassessment of the value and importance of indigenous non-European cultures.

This new perspective originated mainly in the shift of anthropological interest from physical features and artefacts to social organization. It was given greater force by the writings and political lobbying of Mary Kingsley, the West African traveller. Kingsley and a few others rejected the attempts at partial Europeanization by missionaries and 'the stay-at-home statesman [who] thinks that Africans are awful savages or silly children, people who can only be dealt with on a reformatory penitentiary line'. These were half-baked approaches, doomed to failure, she felt;

Mary Kingsley in the 1890s. Mary Kingsley travelled in West Africa in 1893–94 and 1894–95, publishing an account of her journeys in 1897. For her Africans were 'a great world race ... one that has an immense amount of history before it'.

racial and cultural differences were not to be decried but welcomed, and Africans' undoubted capacity for development positively encouraged. Despite Mary Kingsley's scorn for the 'official class' of her day, it, too, was having to accept that lack of resources often left administrators no alternative but to understand and make use of indigenous authorities or institutions if their pretensions to effective colonial rule were to have any substance.

Preoccupation with the supposed limitations created by race – the assumption that people never change – thus began to give way to a new belief in the potential ability of non-European cultures to develop and adapt. The language used reflected this more flexible approach and after 1914, for example, it became more common to speak of 'more' or 'less' advanced peoples. At least in official pronouncements, the identification of race with culture slowly disintegrated. This had the result for colonial policy that, early in the 1940s, the older notion of Britain's 'trusteeship' on behalf of its colonial subjects gave way to the very different terminology of 'partnership' with them.

Nations

The concept of race was one that British people applied to those they ruled. Belief in a hierarchy of races, with the British at the top and the peoples of the empire in various degrees of inferiority below them, justified British claims to power. In this scheme of things, the British themselves were a race, usually referred to as the 'Anglo-Saxons', a race in which Scottish, Welsh, and most especially Irish Celts had at best a doubtful place. To most British people, however, the British constituted not a race but a nation with many different elements. Nations unified peoples; races divided them. There was a hierarchy of races, but all nations were increasingly regarded as equal, especially in the rhetoric that emerged from the First World War and the creation of the League of Nations of which all nation states were equal members. If colonies constituted nations, then they were the equals of the British nation and the legitimacy of British authority over them was undermined. Not surprisingly, British opinion often asserted that colonies were simply collections of separate races. The leaders of colonial opinion increasingly denied this and did their best to encourage the peoples of colonies to believe in a common nationhood. In most cases the unit for the new nation was taken to be the colonial territory that the British had united under a single rule, but other criteria were also put forward. In the 1940s, for example, M.A. Jinnah worked to convince the Muslims of British India that they constituted a nation, the future Pakistan, and were therefore separate from the Hindus, Sikhs, Christians, and peoples of other religions who had been their fellow subjects under the British. Unlikely as many claims to nationhood might seem to their British rulers, they could not resist them indefinitely. Unwittingly, through the development of language, education, religion, and the media, colonial rule had established the conditions in which nations could be created.

CHAPTER 8

Thomas R. Metcalf

Imperial Towns and Cities

Arriving at the Indian port of Madras in 1780, the artist William Hodges wrote:

> The English town, rising from within Fort St. George, has from the sea a rich and beautiful appearance; the houses being covered with a stucco called chunam, which in itself is nearly as compact as the finest marble, and, as it bears as high a polish, is equally splendid with that elegant material. The stile of the buildings is in general handsome. They consist of long colonades with open porticoes, and flat roofs and offer to the eye an appearance similar to what we may conceive of a Grecian city in the age of Alexander. The clear, blue, cloudless sky, the polished white buildings, the bright sandy beach, and the dark green sea, present a combination totally new to the eye of an Englishman, just arrived from London.

This vision, with its evocation of a classical past set on the shores of a distant India, announced the conquests of a new Alexander. In the 1780s the British empire, despite the loss of the thirteen American colonies, was set to embark upon a world-wide expansion across the face of Africa, Asia, and Australia. In the process an array of new towns sprung up – as ports and capitals, agricultural and mining centres, holiday resorts and military outposts.

Fort St George, Madras, at the end of the eighteenth century. In Madras, first ceded to the East India Company in 1639, Fort St George from the beginning marked out the source of British authority. Rebuilt and enlarged during the mid-eighteenth-century wars with the French, with impressive moats and bastions, the fort contained barracks, a parade ground, St Mary's church, offices, and council chambers for the company's officials.

VARIETIES OF COLONIAL TOWN

Though sharing some features with the burgeoning British provincial cities thrown up by the industrial revolution, colonial cities were distinct, unique, urban centres – integral elements of the empire that created them.

Towns with mixed populations

Early colonial port cities were bridgeheads in an alien world in which indigenous people were brought under British rule. No matter where they were, they reflected the power and authority of the imperial regime. Frequently this was accomplished by the location at their centre of colonial government buildings. These often sheltered within the walls of a fort whose guns, overawing the indigenous people and keeping European rivals at bay, were the indispensable foundation on which colonial towns grew up. Calcutta, from 1773 the capital of Britain's Indian empire, began as a fortified centre for British trade on the banks of the Hugli river. In similar fashion, the Dutch fort at Cape Town, first built in 1666 and taken over by the British after 1795, provided a secure footing from which British power subsequently spread to encompass all of South Africa. Penang too, off the west coast of Malaya, established by the East India Company in 1786, began with the construction of Fort Cornwallis, around which the colonial government offices clustered.

Colonial authority also made its presence felt by laying down where people should live. From a very early date Madras, for example, was divided into a 'white town' and a 'black town'. Initially the area just outside the fort walls, this first 'black town' was demolished in the 1770s to expand the buffer zone around the fort and a new 'black town' was established to the north, separated from the old by a wide strip of marshy land. In Calcutta too, by the mid-eighteenth century there was a clear demarcation between a 'white' and a 'black' town. The former spread out to the east and north beyond the city's vast *maidan* or park – initially laid out to secure a clear field of fire for the fort's guns. This European district included the city's commercial centre, together with the growing residential area to the east of the *maidan* around Chowringhee. By 1773 visitors to Calcutta had already begun commenting on the city's 'spacious and showy houses'. Thirty-five years later, in 1809, the traveller and writer Maria Graham described the city as a 'great capital'. On landing, she wrote, 'I was struck with the general appearance of grandeur in all the buildings; not that any of them are according to the strict rules of art, but groups of columns, porticoes, domes, and fine gateways, interspersed with trees and the broad river crowded with shipping, made the whole picture magnificent.' Immediately to the north of the British settlement there grew up a 'black' town with shops, bazaars, and the houses of Indians, including substantial mansions for the wealthy merchants. On the outskirts were to be found the sprawling huts of the remaining villagers and the working poor of the city.

'Native Shop in a Calcutta Bazaar', *c.*1859. The densely populated 'black' or Indian town of nineteenth-century Calcutta covered a large area to the north of the spacious European core of the city. Segregated living in the early port cities was less rigid than it was to become later in the nineteenth century.

'White' and 'black' towns were not only physically separated but were also very different in appearance. The Calcutta town plan, for instance, provided in its European core for extensive open spaces and ceremonial vistas; after 1802 these radiated out from the new Government House at the head of the *maidan*. The British residential suburbs were planned on an extensive scale. In Madras, as the white population, growing in numbers and wealth, began to desert the fort in search of spacious garden living, there grew up as early as 1780, thinly spread to the south and west of the urban centre, some 200 houses set on estates ranging from eighteen acres to fifty and more. In the Indian sectors, by contrast, dwellings were crowded together along narrow alleyways, with even substantial residences focused, as was traditional, on interior courtyards rather than set on garden plots. Europeans frequently commented on the 'narrow filthy streets and crooked lanes' of these neighbourhoods, together with the smells that assaulted them on those rare occasions when they picked their way through these streets.

Another distinctive feature of these colonial port cities was their integration into the world capitalist system. Their original siting, as well as the pace and pattern of their growth, was determined by the requirements of the export trade to Europe. Calcutta's location on the Ganges estuary enabled the city to funnel to itself all the trade of a vast hinterland extending 1,000 miles into the interior. Cape Town's situation at the southern tip of Africa – like Singapore's at the southern tip of the Malay peninsula, or Colombo's on the island of Ceylon (Sri Lanka) at the midpoint of the Indian Ocean – enabled the city to serve both as a centre for international trade and a refreshment station for travellers on long inter-continental journeys. Yet each drew to it as well the produce of the interior: the meat, and then the wine and wool of the Cape, or the coffee, spices, and tea of Ceylon.

In the late eighteenth century Indian cities such as Madras and Calcutta prospered by supplying the English demand for the luxuries of sophisticated Asian economies, and benefited from long-existing, indigenous trading networks. By the 1790s the East India Company's Bengal exports, largely of fine hand-loomed textiles, were worth some £2.5 million annually, and Calcutta had become the second largest city of the British empire. After 1820, with the growth of the industrial revolution, such commodities could no longer compete with machine-made goods and the commercial role of the East India Company was replaced by that of private merchants. Organized into agency houses, these free traders developed a new export trade in an ever-widening range of commodities, from cotton and jute to tea and tin, to feed the insatiable demands of Britain's industries and its increasingly prosperous consumer economy. This trade further encouraged the growth of interior centres of wholesaling and warehousing and so generated new colonial towns, such as Mirzapur and Cawnpore (Kanpur) on the banks of the Ganges. On India's west coast too, especially after the completion of the Indian railways and, in 1869, of the Suez canal, a resurgent Bombay prospered as, so the city's motto described it, *urbs prima in Indis*. Facing out towards Europe, Bombay saw itself, as the American visitor J.H. Furneaux wrote at the end of the century, as 'the connecting link between Europe and Asia, the point where two civilizations meet and mingle'. Unlike such comparable Victorian British cities as Manchester and Glasgow, the colonial cities remained mercantile and commercial in character. Confined by imperial free trade, and the interests of Britain's industrialists, they rarely developed any substantial manufacturing sector. Bombay's cotton textile industry, for instance, was a product of Indian capital and entrepreneurship, not British, and it secured a footing only by selling yarn to China and undercutting Manchester in the cheapest cloths.

With the security provided by the British colonial administration, and drawn by the opportunities for trade, people of many ethnic and occupational backgrounds flocked to the growing colonial cities. Traders came to do business with the British; the poor sought work in domestic service, as manual labourers in the docks or in building work, or as porters and carriers. From the outset these were cities populated by migrants. Some remained permanently in the cities; others returned home with their savings. In India the migrants were usually drawn from the rural hinterland, often travelling huge distances to the cities. Elsewhere migrants also came from overseas. Singapore, established in 1819 on a nearly uninhabited island, became from the 1830s and 1840s a city almost wholly Chinese, as it remains to the present day. Penang also attacted Chinese merchants and traders, as well as Indians from across the Bay of Bengal. By the later ninteenth century, both cities were prospering – not just as transshipment centres for goods going between Europe and India on the one hand and East Asia and Australia on the other, but also as outlets for Malaya's tin and rubber. By the 1920s Singapore's trade had reached some £200 million, and its population exceeded 400,000. Yet, despite these close links to the mainland, both cities had only tiny Malay populations. The colonial cities of the West Indies were also peopled wholly by outsiders. Founded in 1692, Kingston, Jamaica, was inhabited by white merchants and sugar planters, slaves brought by force from West Africa, and a free 'coloured' or mixed-race community produced by widely-accepted interracial sexual liaisions. With slave emancipation in 1833, and the end of a protected market for Jamaican sugar in Britain a decade later, the economy stagnated and the white population, in the late eighteenth century a quarter of Kingston's total, rapidly declined. The city nevertheless grew as emancipated slaves and impoverished peasants drifted in from the countryside. By 1940 Kingston was almost wholly a black and mixed-race town, with only a tiny white administrative elite.

Most striking, perhaps, was the diversity of peoples to be found in Cape Town. Though set among a pastoral Khoikhoi people, the town drew its settlers from lands as far removed as Holland and Britain on the one side, and Madagascar and Indonesia on the other. Until 1833 many were slaves brought from the East Indies and employed as skilled artisans and craftsmen. As a result Cape Town developed a unique Malay Quarter. Over time, the freed slaves, as they mixed with the settled Khoikhoi and local whites, created the distinctive Cape Coloured community. By the mid-nineteenth century the population of Cape Town, some 20,000 in all, was split almost evenly between whites and coloureds, now regarded as separate racial groups. By contrast, in West Africa – commonly regarded as the 'white man's grave' – the white population was at all times minuscule. Black Africans from hinterland regions always made up the bulk of the population of such towns as Accra on the

The Malay Quarter, Cape Town, *c*.1900. The Malay Quarter was named after the descendants of slaves from Asia brought to the Cape by the Dutch East India Company before the British conquest. Many of these ex-slaves were Muslims, as the mid-nineteenth-century mosque indicates. In the nineteenth century white working-class people also lived in the Malay Quarter. Cape Town was one of the most ethnically diverse of the earlier colonial port cities, most of which attracted a diversity of people.

Gold Coast (Ghana) and Lagos in Nigeria. Nevertheless, these cities drew enterprising traders from as far away as Lebanon in the Middle East, as well as African elites from neighbouring colonies such as Sierra Leone.

The segregation of peoples, practised in colonial cities from the outset, was much more vigorously enforced in the nineteenth century. As the South African colonial frontier marched inexorably eastwards, new towns, among them Port Elizabeth, Durban, and Pietermaritzburg, grew up. In these areas the British encountered black Africans – Xhosa, Zulu, and others – who, as their tribal structures were broken by incessant warfare and the demands of white settlers for land, sought work in the new towns. This, for the whites, presented at once opportunities – for cheap labour was always in demand – and perceived dangers. The martial Zulus were always feared, and whites believed that large urban African populations, living in squalor, would bring with them disease which would spread to their own community. As the Cape Prime Minister W.P. Schreiner put it in 1901, as Africans had begun to drift even into Cape Town, there were 'some 10,000 raw natives', living 'all over the place', and learning 'all sorts of bad habits'. But, as he realized, 'We could not get rid of them: They were necessary for work.' Hence, from 1902 onwards – elaborating upon precedents established long before in India – towns in South Africa were rigidly segregated. The urban core was meant to be an area of white (and coloured) residence only; Africans were confined to 'locations' just outside the city and their access to the urban areas was restricted by pass laws. Similar patterns of urban segregation subsequently developed in the colonial towns of East and Central Africa, among them Nairobi in Kenya and Salisbury (Harare) in Rhodesia (Zimbabwe).

In India too, as the British established commercial and administrative centres in the interior, they redoubled their efforts to keep the indigenous population both securely under control and at arm's length. To the fear of disease – arising, they believed, from the 'insanitary conditions' in which the Indian urban population lived – was added, after the Indian Rebellion of 1857, apprehension for their own safety, for the massacres by mutinous sepoys of the unsuspecting British in Delhi, Cawnpore, and other Indian towns had left an enduring legacy. Hence, as the British consolidated their authority following the uprising, they constructed new urban centres adjacent to, but separate from, such older-established cities as Allahabad, Lucknow, and Lahore. These 'civil lines', as the new European areas were called, were laid out on a spacious pattern, with regular, broad roads lined with trees framing bungalows set in large compounds. Nearby, frequently, was a military cantonment which could provide aid to the civil inhabitants in case of need. By contrast to the areas of European settlement, drainage and sanitation were only fitfully and spasmodically supplied to the 'native' city, and its congested mass was opened up, largely for military purposes, only by forcing arrow-straight roads through its heart. The boundaries between the two portions of the urban area were usually marked out by barriers that restricted movement – railway lines, city walls, or open fields. Of course, as in South Africa, separation was never complete, for servants and Indian sepoys always lived in the 'British' areas, while the British inevitably shared air, food supplies, water (and hence disease) with their Indian neighbours.

In West Africa no part of the population was immune from the hazards of the tropics until the end of the nineteenth century. A visitor to Bathurst in The Gambia in 1863 commented on the hospital:

> The place is murderous. There is a sick ward upon the ground floor! – One night on the ground floor is certain fever in most parts of tropical Africa – and that ground floor is, like the latrene and other offices, frequently under water. In the first story the beds are crowded together, each patient having 800, whereas 2,000 feet of air should be the minimum ... On the second floor are the quarters of the medical officers, within pleasant distance of an atmosphere wraught with smallpox and dysentery, typhus and yellowjack. This caution of a hospital is built to 'accomodate' 23, at times it has had 32 ... I was not astonished after going the rounds to hear of 92 deaths out of 96 admissions and that at times *El Vomito* improves off everybody...

White settler towns

The colonial towns in Canada, Australia, and New Zealand, which were inhabited exclusively by whites, did not take on the dual nature so common elsewhere. Nevertheless, their character was stamped in fundamental ways by their colonial origin. Cities such as Sydney and Melbourne in Australia, for instance, where the

indigenous people posed no threat, were not focused on a fort. The imperial government still proclaimed its presence, however – above all by a commanding residence for the colonial Governor. In Sydney, Government House, an ornate Tudor Gothic structure, was set in a vast park called the Domain, with a sweeping view of the harbour. Melbourne's Government House, built in the 1870s from the colony's gold wealth, in an elaborate Italianate style with a massive tower, overlooked the town from its site high on a hill nearby.

Colonial towns of European settlement were also, for the most part, like their counterparts in Asia and Africa, established as ports, their primary function that of funnelling commodities from the interior onto ships bound for Europe. The major cities of all Australia's colonies, from Brisbane around to Perth in the west, each with its own hinterland, were pre-eminently centres of finance, wholesaling, and warehousing rather than manufacturing. Only in the second half of the nineteenth century did some Australian industries develop in the face of British competition. By 1881 about 25 per cent of Melbourne's male work-force was engaged in manufacturing, but such activity never dominated the city, nor was it significant in Sydney, which continued to be sustained by its role as an exporter of wool.

Mid-nineteenth-century Adelaide. Aborigines are among those strolling through the spacious streets of the carefully planned centre of the town.

Simla: summer capital of British India

To escape the heat of the plains, every year from 1864 the government of India, including the Viceroy himself, migrated to Simla, set on a network of wooded ridges, 7,000 to 8,000 feet above sea level. The officials left Calcutta between March and May and stayed at Simla until October or November. Public buildings and residential bungalows sprouted wherever there was level ground on the ridges. During the summer season Simla developed an elaborate social life.

Right: Picnic at Simla, 1891.

Below: Simla with Christ Church in the foreground.

Towns in these colonies of settlement were further set apart from the towns of Victorian Britain by their carefully laid-out plans. Based on precedents established in Kingston, Jamaica, and the North American colonies, these plans usually involved a grid of streets and blocks subdivided into rectangular building plots. Grid plans were imposed across Ontario from the 1780s, where they defined the layout of such cities as the provincial capital, Toronto. Adelaide in South Australia, one of the most successful examples of such planning, was laid out by its developer, Colonel William Light, in the 1830s on a grand set of interlocking squares before any settlers were allowed to take up residence. Similar smaller-scale plans, with their parkland character, shaped subsequent town development throughout the region.

Inevitably, in towns planned on such a regular and ambitious scale, the population density was bound to be low. The pattern continued: as the towns filled up, they spread into the countryside. By the late nineteenth century suburban sprawl in Australia's towns far exceeded that of any urban centre in Britain. Melbourne, for instance, had an overall density of only three people to the acre in 1888. A number of factors fostered such patterns of growth. Buoyed by an exuberant and optimistic outlook and with ample land available, colonial cities often developed suburban rail networks well beyond the settled area, and these, by facilitating access to the city centre, encouraged further settlement along them. The medium-sized town of Christchurch, New Zealand, for instance, constructed some fifty miles of tramways. Much of this expansion was propelled by successive bursts of land speculation, in which developers bought large areas in anticipation of future growth. Most striking perhaps was the development of Melbourne, which, sparked by the gold rushes, mushroomed to a total population of over 450,000 by 1890. During the decade of the 1880s, especially, as a speculative mania gripped the city, over half of Melbourne's private capital investment was devoted to residential development, with the result that the terraced houses of the inner suburbs were abandoned for distant villas on individual plots. Though the anglicized

The suburbs of Johannesburg, c.1907. Johannesburg was a spectacular example of the way in which colonial cities spread over a huge area. By 1907 suburbs extended up to six miles away from the city centre, from which richer Europeans had moved to escape crowding and squalor or the locations into which African workers were beginning to be segregated.

professional and business elites remained apart from the working classes – the distinction marked out in Melbourne by the contrast between those served by trams and those whose homes were located along surburban railway lines – there were no tenement dwellings, and social stratification never began to approach that of contemporary Britain. Instead of the contrasts of a city like London, where the desperate poverty of the city's East End was balanced by the elegant town houses of Mayfair, cities in these colonies of white settlement were characterized by the bland uniformity of rows of suburban cottages.

Mining towns and hill stations

Two exceptional kinds of colonial town, apart from the usual commercial and administrative centres, grew up during the last half of the nineteenth century – the mining settlement and the holiday resort, or hill station. Mining towns often sprang up almost overnight, as word of mineral discoveries spread around the world. Some 250,000 'Diggers' poured into Australia in the wake of the 1851 gold strikes, swelling towns like Ballarat and Bendigo into major urban centres. Often, after brief bursts of prosperity, their population drained away and such towns became little

Street scene in Johannesburg, *c.*1906. The gold of the Rand attracted a wide range of European, Asian, and African immigrants, hoping to make their fortunes. Here the Europeans walk on the pavement, the Africans in the street.

more than urban shells. But a few, sustained by lasting mineral deposits, survived into the twentieth century. Of these by far the most important were the two South African cities of Kimberley, which grew up in the 1870s around the diamond fields, and Johannesburg, founded in 1886 atop the gold-bearing reefs of the Witwatersrand. As the richness of the gold deposits of the Rand became apparent, Johannesburg grew with astonishing speed. Within a decade the few diggers of the original mining camp had given way to a city of 100,000 residents; by 1914 there were 250,000 inhabitants, and the city had taken on the appearance of a major industrial metropolis in a countryside dominated by Afrikaner farmers. Like other colonial towns, Johannesburg was overwhelmingly a city of migrants, drawing to itself wealthy capitalists – mostly from Britain but also from other European countries – who alone could develop the deep-level ores, skilled Cornish working-class miners, and unskilled black labourers from throughout southern Africa. A city predominantly male, its white residents lived in boarding houses, while the Africans were pushed into the conformity of mine compounds.

Far different were the hill stations. 'There in the sight of the snows', wrote one visitor to an Indian hill town in 1912, 'are collected in the midst of the green and the trees and the flowers, all of the fair women of Anglo-India who have been driven up by the summer heat.' While sharing some features with English resorts such as Brighton and Bath, the colonial hill station was set apart by its position as an arcadia meant to recreate an imagined England. Such towns as Ootacamund in the Nilgiri hills of south India, with Darjeeling, Mussoorie, and Simla to the north, perched high above the plains on Himalayan ridges, were initially established in the 1820s and 1830s primarily as sanatoria for European troops. Soon, however, they became attractive to a larger British population. As the separate civil lines in the plains secured some sense of distance from the feared 'native' city, so too, to a far greater extent, did the hill station, seen as a retreat where climate and isolation together shaped a sense of 'home'. As the Viceroy Lord Lytton wrote after a visit to Ootacamund, 'The afternoon was rainy and the road muddy, but such beautiful *English* rain, such delicious *English* mud.'

Yet the hill station was an integral part of the larger colonial fabric. Its imposing Gothic viceregal residence looming above its twisting paths, Simla was for nearly eighty years, from the 1860s to the 1940s, summer capital of British India and headquarters of the British Indian army. Although the Indian hill towns were the most well-known, similar hill resorts grew up elsewhere as the empire spread throughout the tropical world. Malaya's Cameron Highlands, for instance, around a famed golf course, drew planters, merchants, and officials alike. In these towns, with their ample numbers of English women and children, the colonial British could reaffirm their sense of themselves as a community at once fit to rule and bound together by common values. Sites of childbirth, education, and courtship, the cottages, schools, and bandstands of the hill towns were a necessary complement to the forts of Calcutta and Penang.

Much of the appeal of the bungalow was its adaptability to the tropical climate. In its Indian form, the bungalow's thick walls and high ceilings secured interior ventilation and shade, while an encircling verandah provided a way to enjoy the cool of morning and evening. Yet more was at stake than mere comfort, for other building forms, such as the enclosed courtyard of much Indian urban building, with cool basement and flat sleeping roof, were equally suited to the country's severe climate. The bungalow's attraction was in large part the way it advanced a political purpose – that of social distancing. Its setting, in a spacious compound, with a curving entry drive and access controlled by walls, gates, and watchmen, announced the superiority of the British Raj and helped contain the pervasive British fears of disease and contamination from too close a contact with 'natives'. The watchman turned away all unauthorized visitors at the gate. Others – such as tradesmen and supplicants for favour – were allowed onto the verandah, where the memsahib examined goods, perhaps dispensed tea, while the sahib conducted whatever business might be necessary. Only social equals were allowed into the interior. Access to the interior of British residences, like membership of the club, was, in the colonial period, a very sore point for Asians and Africans who saw these exclusions, rightly, as markers of racial discrimination.

During the colonial era, the bungalow provided an arena in which the Englishwoman played a central role. Although meant, in the colonies as in Britain, to embody the virtues of purity and domesticity assigned to her by the Victorian gender code of 'separate spheres', the colonial woman was at the same time often obliged to be active and resourceful. In frontier towns in places like New Zealand, where the males were often absent in the 'bush', she was responsible for sustaining much of the society's cultural life, while in India she had to take on in the private sphere the task that confronted her husband in the world outside: ordering rationality in a land where disorder and disease were perceived as raging unchecked. Above all, like a general, she had to discipline and control servants. As Flora Annie Steel wrote in *The Complete Indian Housekeeper* (1904), 'An Indian household can no more be governed peacefully, without dignity and prestige, than an Indian Empire.'

As the bungalow spread throughout the empire, its form

underwent modification. In areas of largely European settlement, where social distancing was less urgent, as well as among the less well-to-do, the bungalow was frequently reduced in size and set on smaller plots. The verandah, for instance, was often compressed onto one side of the structure. At the same time, however, the bungalow in colonies of settlement was frequently distinguished by an exuberance of ornamentation never found among the standardized forms of its Indian counterpart, used by a transient population of officials. The material form of the bungalow also varied with its location. In Australia, for instance, where labour was scarce, in place of the plaster and whitewash of India, bungalows were often constructed of preformed cast or wrought iron, with corrugated iron roofing. Ordered from catalogues, these elements might even be imported, like the pieces of a jigsaw puzzle, from one of several Glasgow engineering firms. Where wood was readily available, as in Queensland, it might be used instead. Bungalows of this sort were inexpensive; they could easily be set up and as easily disassembled and moved to a new site.

In its Australian form – frequently raised on stilts, enshrouded in lattice screens to secure ventilation without sunlight – the bungalow was essential for the creation of comfortable, white, working-class communities, above all in the hot interior and along the subtropical Queensland coast. Whether associated with European towns in Australia or those of colonial India, with a hard-working Digger or with an administrative elite, the bungalow always defined a style of life set apart from that of England. Hence, when the bungalow eventually made its way to Britain, where neither climatic nor political needs dictated its use, it did so as an exotic architectural form, mainly in seaside and holiday resorts, where it signified an ideal of leisure.

Above: A bungalow in Queensland, Australia. The design of this bungalow, set on stilts with lattice screens, is characteristic of such buildings in the tropical north of Australia.

Left: The verandah of a bungalow in India in the nineteenth century. The verandah is kept cool by a punkah, or fan, fixed to the ceiling and swung by a cord. Its decor is almost a caricature of what is assumed to have been the taste of the British in India, with a plethora of sporting trophies, the crossed lances for pig-sticking, the topees on the hat stand, and cane-backed chairs.

Opposite: A bungalow in India, c.1896.

COLONIAL ARCHITECTURE

As the colonial town developed a distinctive character of its own, so too did the buildings erected within it.

Colonial buildings

Some buildings derived their distinctive form from their purpose. Despite its apparent similarity to such structures as Buckingham Palace in London, a colonial Government House, never the residence of a royal dynasty or the focus of national sentiment, announced instead the authority of the imperial regime. The Governor, commonly an English aristocrat sent out for a short term, was always the British monarch's representative in the colony. Hence the imperial authorities frequently adopted an impressive grandeur for this structure.

Other structures, although they adopted standard European architectural forms, took on an enhanced meaning in the colonies. Many colonial churches, for instance, were modelled on the prototype of St Martin-in-the-Fields, London. In part this was due to the ready availability of published plans of that church, which as a result could easily be duplicated anywhere. Yet that church, by its position at the very heart of the empire in Trafalgar Square, could in some measure be said to represent the empire. For the British colonial population, needing reassurance in an unfamiliar land, the soaring spires of such colonial churches as St John's, Calcutta (1787) spoke, perhaps, not only of God but of the power of the English as they set out to mark their presence, and the superiority of their faith, on the territories they ruled over.

Subsequently, in the Victorian era, colonial cities often endeavoured in their building to assert their growing wealth and prosperity. In towns of European settlement, especially, civic pride and confidence prompted the construction of an ornate and elaborate architecture. The rivalry between Sydney and Melbourne produced, in both cities, some of the most impressive Victorian Gothic buildings to be found anywhere in the world. Even a small town like Natal's Pietermaritzburg, after it began to share in the wealth of the Rand, erected an array of commercial and civic structures designed to demonstrate its new prosperity. By contrast with the colony's Government House, an inconspicuous rambling structure from Natal's impoverished early years, the 1890s Town Hall, burned to the ground immediately after its completion and at once rebuilt in an ornate Gothic style, still looms over the town's central square.

In the major colonial cities domestic architecture took a variety of forms. During the late eighteenth century the wealthy nabobs of Calcutta, for instance, built large, high-ceilinged town houses, of several storeys, their windows shaded by green shutters, set back in large plots. Where space was at a premium, as in sea-girt Bombay, all but the highest government officials lived in multi-storeyed blocks of spacious flats from the mid-nineteenth century. Rows of terraced houses, one and two storey, housed the middle-class European residents of the major colonial cities.

The inner suburbs of such cities as Melbourne still contain row upon row of such houses, usually with a small verandah on the front. The most distinctive colonial architectural form however was the bungalow residence. Originally a thatched-roofed hut of Bengal (hence the name), the bungalow was first developed as a colonial residence in India, as British rule spread from Calcutta and Madras to the country towns of the interior; it then spread throughout the empire, from Australia to Africa.

Changing styles in colonial architecture

The architectural style of colonial civic buildings drew largely upon British forms, together with, in some areas, those of India. (Almost no attempt was made to adopt the indigenous building styles of Africa or other parts of the empire.) To some degree colonial buildings reproduced overseas the predominant European style of the time. During the eighteenth century this was the baroque classicism associated with Sir Christopher Wren. Subsequently, in the early nineteenth century, when the Doric neoclassicism of the Greek revival came into favour, this in turn shaped much colonial building, from Cape Town to Calcutta and beyond. The use of such classical forms was, however, in the colonies never merely a matter of fashion – styles were always shaped to fit the distinctive requirements of the colonial environment. In part, this involved a process of exaggeration designed to enhance an effect of magnificence. Unlike the English country house on which it was modelled, the Calcutta Government House was raised for visibility on a high basement platform; and its grand staircase was placed on the outside so as to make possible a ceremonial entrance. In such buildings the British sought also to link their empire with the empires of antiquity. The Government House state dining

Government House, Calcutta. Lord Wellesley's Government House was built on the model of Kedleston Hall in Derbyshire. It was completed at great expense in 1803. Criticism of its costliness was countered by arguments that India was 'a country of splendor, of extravagance, and of outward appearances', which ought appropriately to be 'ruled from a palace, not from a counting-house; with the ideas of a Prince, not those of a retail dealer in muslins and indigo'.

The state opening of the Parliament Building at Ottawa, 1868. Ottawa was chosen in 1857 to be the capital of the new Dominion of Canada in 1867. A Gothic style was chosen for the new Parliament. In making this choice, Canadians were following contemporary British taste and marking their difference from the classical public buildings of the United States. The smoke is rising from a *feu de joie* to celebrate the opening.

room incorporated a nave and pillars on the model of a Roman atrium and contained life-sized marble busts of the twelve Caesars. In similar fashion, the 1808 Banqueting Hall in Madras was set on a high podium with double-storeyed columns and decorated with emblems of conquest. Britain's empire, so these structures proclaimed, was one with that of Alexander and of Rome. Furthermore, as this architecture, in the British view, incorporated an aesthetic perfection that stood above the vagaries of time, so too did it proclaim overseas the superiority of the western culture that had created it. Indeed, its very character, as an architecture shaped by principles of proportion, order, and balance – 'eternal principles of ordered beauty', as the architect Herbert Baker described them – exalted, so the British imagined, those ideals of law and order that they saw at the heart of their own imperial enterprise.

How far such claims evoked a response among the colonized peoples is difficult to judge. Certainly India's princely and mercantile elites saw in these classical

buildings symbols of the modern world they sought to enter, and so endeavoured to emulate them in their own building. Pachiappa's Hall (1840) in Madras, modelled on the Athenian Temple of the Winds, was built from the bequest of an Indian merchant to house the first English school in the city. When used for domestic building, in both India and West Africa, European architectural forms were usually confined to the exterior of structures whose interior was designed to accommodate extended families and the seclusion of women. In towns inhabited by non-English-speaking whites, such as Montreal, Quebec, and Pretoria, a shared European heritage encouraged an appreciation of classical (and Gothic) forms, though Afrikaner and French Canadian builders frequently adopted continental European styles – from the Netherlands, France, or Germany – to assert a sense of difference.

As the Gothic revival came into prominence in Europe, its forms too found a footing in the colonial town. With its medieval and ecclesiastical associations, however, Gothic architecture was less well suited to the representation of empire than was classical architecture with its suggestion of an imperial Rome. Gothic, however, could be used to assert colonial nationalism, as in Ottawa, whose Gothic Parliament announced at once Canada's enduring link with Great Britain and its difference from the United States with its classically styled capital city. Gothic found favour too in commercial towns such as Bombay and Melbourne, whose elites sought to appear 'modern' by surrounding themselves with the architectural styles of contemporary Europe. But the widest use of this style was in the design of churches. Even in Calcutta, with its deeply set traditions of classical design, the cathedral (1847) was constructed in a Gothic style. The colonial church must be, as the architect Swinton Jacob wrote, 'in keeping with a style, with which all our feelings of devotion are associated'. As a result, church buildings, even those meant for convert communities, rarely incorporated indigenous elements into their designs. Only the exceptional church, like those in Zanzibar and Mombasa in East Africa, incorporating minaret-like spires and slitted windows ending in cusped arches, sought to reach out to indigenous peoples with familiar forms.

From the mid-nineteenth century, alongside Gothic, classicism was giving way to adaptations of Indian styles. After the Indian Rebellion of 1857, the British were determined to portray themselves not as mere foreign conquerors, like the Romans, but as legitimate, even indigenous rulers of India. As such, they sought to use an 'oriental' architectural form, appropriate to 'the east'. They believed that their Indian subjects consisted of two distinct communities – Hindus and Muslims – each with its own architectural form, which expressed the 'traditional', unchanging values of that community. Of the two they inclined more towards what they regarded as the predominantly Muslim 'Saracenic' style, which was both more congenial to western canons of taste and had the great advantage of being associated with the authority of the Mughal emperors, whose successors the British conceived themselves to be. The result was a series of buildings in the Saracenic

The last, and greatest, British imperial architectural enterprise was the creation of New Delhi. Constructed over a span of nearly twenty years after 1912, this new Indian capital, designed by Edwin Lutyens in collaboration with Herbert Baker, combined the regularity of French *beaux-arts* design, with its boulevards radiating from monumental plazas, and the ideals of the garden city, which sought a pleasing variety of structures set amidst gardens and greenery. New Delhi was, however, never meant to evoke only western associations. The city's location, adjacent to Shah Jahan's seventeenth-century capital, together with the use of red sandstone as a building material, announced the continuing British endeavour to lay claim to India's past, in this case the 'historic associations' of Delhi. Furthermore, the Viceroy, Lord Hardinge, and with him Herbert Baker, were committed to creating an 'orientalized' city, 'imbued with the spirit of the East', and so appealing to 'Orientals' as well as Europeans. For Baker this meant grafting onto the 'elemental and universal forms' of classical architecture a number of 'characteristically Indian' features. In keeping with this ideal, Baker's Secretariats took their basic form from Wren's baroque classicism as well as his own earlier work at Pretoria in South Africa, yet incorporated such visibly Indian elements as *chattris* (free-standing kiosks), pierced-stone *jaali* screens, and even miniature elephants set around the base of the domes.

Lutyens adamantly opposed such ornamentation and disdained what he saw as the 'childish ignorance' of basic principles pervading India's historic architecture. Nevertheless, in the Viceroy's House, in stunningly imaginative fashion, he too assimilated a number of Indic elements – including a unique black dome derived from the ancient Buddhist stupa at Sanchi –

into the fabric of a structure shaped by a European classical idiom. The mammoth size and seemingly endless ranks of columns of this vast palace, one might argue, almost designedly obscured what by 1920 had become ever more obvious – Britain's waning authority over its premier dependency.

Above: Indian Arch and Processional Way, New Delhi. A processional King's Way leading up to the government buildings of New Delhi was spanned by an arch 139 feet high to honour the dead of the First World War.

Left: The Secretariat Building, New Delhi, by Herbert Baker.

Opposite: Viceregal Lodge, New Delhi, by Edwin Lutyens.

Design for the Mayo College,
Ajmer, 1879. This building
was a pioneer exercise in the
'Indo-Saracenic' mode, using
what was believed to be 'the
indigenous ancient style' for
modern purposes.

style. Such buildings were dominated by supposedly Mughal arches and domes, but in reality they were an architectural pastiche, in which a variety of forms were mixed together. In his design for the Muir College, Allahabad, for instance, William Emerson combined 'an Egyptian phase of Moslem architecture' with 'the Indian Saracenic style of Beejapoor and the north-west', and then confined the whole in 'a western Gothic design'. Other structures were no less eclectic.

The use of the mixed Indo-Saracenic style was not simply an exercise in antiquarianism. Unlike the French in Morocco, the British never sought to preserve intact whole 'native' towns. Their objective, in the colonial cities of India, and subsequently in the new Malayan capital of Kuala Lumpur, was always to give a 'traditional' appearance to structures meant for 'modern' purposes. Hence the style was applied to buildings such as railway stations, banks, colleges, museums, law courts, and the other requirements of the colonial state. In Malaya, where there existed little indigenous monumental architecture, Saracenic forms had the additional purpose of affirming an Islamic identity for the colony, whose sultans presided over a Muslim peasantry presumed to pursue 'traditional' ways.

In the first decade of the twentieth century a revived classicism in Europe prompted a return to classical forms, with their claims to universality and absolute value, in the empire as well. The Viceroy of India, Lord Curzon, defiantly insisted that the Victoria Memorial in Calcutta should be constructed in a Palladian or Italian Renaissance style, while in South Africa, where after the South African War the British embarked on a far-ranging 'reconstruction' to make its society more British and to develop its economy, the young English architect Herbert Baker designed an array of classically inspired monuments, from the Rhodes Memorial in Cape Town (1902) to the Union Buildings in Pretoria (1910). Although the Union Buildings were erected to house the representatives of a new self-governing and Afrikaner-dominated South Africa, nevertheless this structure, with the other classical monuments of the Edwardian era, served important imperial purposes. Above all, by their prominent display around the world of familiar forms long associated with empire, these buildings reassured an anxious British public, beseiged by European rivals as well as colonial nationalists, that theirs was still an empire on which the sun never set.

Imperial building continued into the interwar period, above all in Kenya, where Baker designed the Nairobi Government House and other structures in a classicism that incorporated the central features of his Pretoria and Delhi designs. But such building could not long be sustained. A defiant colonial nationalism repudiated the assumptions underpinning both the classical and the Indo-Saracenic (rarely used by Indian leaders such as Nehru when they assumed power). At the same time the burgeoning modernist movement insisted on the stripping away of all architectural decoration. The architecture of the post-colonial city can be found in Le Corbusier's Chandigarh, the new capital of the Punjab in post-independence India, or among the towering glass and steel skyscrapers of contemporary Singapore.

LIFE IN THE COLONIAL TOWN

Diversity was always a feature of colonial towns, where people of all sorts, many from distant places, were brought together. As Calcutta, for instance, grew in the later eighteenth century, it drew enterprising Bengalis from older, now decaying, towns throughout Bengal. By the early decades of the nineteenth century Calcutta was not only a colonial city, but the focus of Bengali life and culture; its wealthy elite built ornate urban mansions, patronized local festivals, and saw themselves as members of a new 'respectable' class, known as the *bhadralok*. Over time this Bengali elite largely abandoned trade for the settled life of the *rentier* landlord and urban professional.

On the opposite side of India, in Bombay, the city's prominent merchant families came not from its immediate hinterland, but from the province of Gujarat several hundred miles to the north. Most enterprising were the Parsis, Zoroastrians displaced centuries before from Persia (Iran), who brought skills in ship building and overseas trade with them from Surat to Bombay. Working closely with the British, for whom they acted as commissariat agents and dealers in European goods, the Parsis, themselves highly anglicized, dominated the urban life of Bombay throughout the nineteenth century and laid the foundations of its modern industrial economy. Parsis also migrated northwards to Karachi after the annexation of Sind in 1843; there, working with the minority Hindu Sindhi trading castes, they prospered in the trade up the Indus to Punjab and Afghanistan.

Some merchant communities, exceptional in their mobility, ranged far from their homelands to take advantage of the trading opportunities and political order provided by the British empire. Enterprising Gujaratis established themselves throughout the western Indian Ocean, where they dominated trade in colonial towns from Durban and Zanzibar to Mombasa and Aden; from these centres they moved on into the interior, especially of East Africa. In their wake came such

A Parsi family in Bombay, 1867. The Parsi community, conspicuous for its commercial acumen, its deep involvement in education, and its munificence in charity, contributed much to the development of Bombay.

Some British people persist in believing that 'the women lost us the empire'. The assumptions behind such propositions are that race relations in tropical colonies were poisoned by the presence of white women, who forced white males to stop sexual relations with 'native' women and instead to cocoon their wives and children, as well as themselves, in a world where contact with non-European people, domestic servants apart, was reduced to a minimum. Within the fastness of this enclosed world, white women were said to live artificial and trivial lives, cut off from all meaningful contact with the mass of the people amongst whom they lived and forcing their men to do the same. Such assertions are not only trite attempts to explain a great process of historical change; they also reflect a high degree of male prejudice. Studies of British women in colonial territories reveal lives that were often much fuller than stereotypes imply. They also suggest that the stereotypes reflect the expectations of white men, rather than the reality of women's lives.

Throughout the whole colonial period white women were always very much outnumbered by men in the tropical empire. Until well into the twentieth century, West African colonies were

Left: A female doctor on the Church Missionary Society's Niger mission. Medicine and teaching were the obvious outlets in the colonies for the professional skills of British women.

Opposite: Going visiting by rickshaw in Ceylon (Sri Lanka).

thought to be entirely unsuitable for women. Even in Northern Rhodesia (Zambia), considered a relatively salubrious part of Africa, there were more than twice as many men as women until the Second World War. British women went to India in small numbers in the eighteenth century. Numbers increased over the next century, but in 1901, with a very big garrison of largely unmarried British soldiers, the proportion of women to men was still only 38 to 100. In 1921 there were twice as many men in Malaya as women.

In colonial situations where few European women were available, sexual relations between British men and 'native' women were common. In the early twentieth century a Colonial Office official in London believed that 'cohabitation with native women is extremely common throughout West and East Africa: indeed I am informed that of the unmarried white officials, there is only a small percentage who abstain entirely from the practice'. In India before the mid-nineteenth century a high proportion of army officers and civil servants kept Indian mistresses. Books of guidance for young men going to India assumed that they would do precisely that. Critics of what was alleged to be the prudery of later generations have assumed that liaisons were conducive to good race relations. Some well-documented instances do indeed leave no doubt of deep mutual affection, but in many cases such relationships were highly exploitative of the women involved, since offspring were usually not recognized and the man abandoned the woman when he returned to Europe.

In the mid-nineteenth century in India and the early twentieth century in Africa official policies and social attitudes turned strongly against cohabitation, while more European women ventured into the tropics. Some were said to go to India on speculative voyages in search of rich husbands as part of what was rudely called 'the fishing fleet'; but most marriages probably took place in Britain, wives then accompanying their husbands back to their postings. Colonial wives were commonly believed to live over-secluded and trivial lives. To some degree convention did indeed force this upon them: they were excluded from work outside their homes, their children were sent to Britain at a very early age, and British males were fiercely protective of their womenfolk. In India unfounded fears of rape dating from the time of the 1857 rebellion reinforced this seclusion. But women could break out of a tightly constricting domesticity. As in Britain, women took part in charitable and philanthropic work and in the late nineteenth century women were beginning to do in the tropics what was regarded as appropriate professional work at home – nursing and teaching. Women were not admitted into administrative posts in the colonies until after the Second World War, but this does not mean that individual women had not been able to exert a significant influence on colonial policies long before that: Mary Carpenter visited India in 1866 to press for more opportunities for Indian women to obtain education; Eleanor Rathbone campaigned in the 1920s and 1930s for an extension of the franchise to Indian women; Flora Shaw (later Lady Lugard) became colonial editor of *The Times* in the 1890s; Margery Perham travelled all over Africa and acquired a position of unrivalled authority on African affairs in the last years of empire. [PJM] professionals as M.K. Gandhi, freshly trained at the London bar, who first gained a reputation as a lawyer for his fellow Gujaratis in Natal. In similar fashion, merchants and traders from south China spread outwards from Hong Kong and Shanghai to dominate the cities of colonial Malaya, the Dutch East Indies, and the Philippines.

But it was the poor and disadvantaged who formed the bulk of the population of all colonial towns. Sometimes they too had travelled great distances, as with the Irish – some transported convicts, others respectable artisans and smallholders – who made up a disproportionate share of the population of such cities as Melbourne and Sydney and gave Australia's cultural life an enduring populist character. Prostitution drew European women to bustling colonial cities – in 1895 some 97 brothels employing 1,000 women were counted in Johannesburg; while domestic service, as nursemaid and governess, provided 'respectable' positions for white women. As such employment often came to an abrupt end with marriage into settler families, domestic work was usually left to 'native' cooks, washermen, and 'houseboys' – Indian and African. The numbers of domestic servants grew rapidly as colonial towns throughout Asia and Africa attracted a more stable European population; together with self-employed hawkers, coolies (carriers), and rickshaw-pullers, peons (orderlies), and servants of all kinds, they formed a large floating class of urban labourers dependent on the colonial presence.

Divided societies

The mixed populations of colonial towns presented perennial problems of urban order, and, more generally, of social organization. The response of the British colonial authorities was, wherever possible, to leave the various communities to regulate their internal affairs and develop their own institutions. This solved their immediate administrative problems but accentuated the differences between communities. Chinese society in mid-nineteenth-century Singapore, for example, was kept in order by the organized clans that ran the government opium monopoly, while in Calcutta from the late eighteenth century the new merchant elites took the lead in organizing multicaste factions, called *dals*. These *dals* helped resolve disputes about caste, inheritance, and marriage among their adherents, and provided centres of cultural activity for them. Among the merchant communities of western India, caste associations, together with sectarian leaders such as the Aga Khan, performed much the same function. Such internal cohesion was often facilitated by the residence of the various ethnic groups in compact neighbourhoods. From the outset Singapore was laid out with Chinese, European, and Muslim Malay settlements, arrayed side by side along the waterfront, while an Indian quarter grew up behind the city.

Frequently, the British took an even more active role in demarcating ethnic communities by appointing leaders and enforcing subordination to them. Penang, for instance, had its 'Kapitan China', who was responsible for keeping the local

Chinese in order. The British always preferred to work with, and through, so-called 'natural' leaders. As urban municipalities were instituted from the 1850s, the British secured the representation, whether by appointment or election, of leading members of those constituencies that, in their view, deserved inclusion. The designation of separate communities could be carried to absurd lengths. In Karachi, for instance, when the municipal commission was set up in 1861, its eleven seats were apportioned among some ten communities, comprising various Muslim, Hindu, and European trading and merchant groups; fifteen years later seventeen 'native communities' were represented.

Clubs and associations

The separation of communities was reinforced by the creation of exclusive institutions, many of which secured privileges for their members. Most famed were the restrictive clubs in colonial towns throughout the empire, which brought together European residents but excluded 'natives'. A sanctuary and a haven, as well as an arena for sport and gossip, the club was central to the lives of the British overseas. Even towns wholly European in population possessed exclusive associations, like the Melbourne Club, retreat of the oldest settlers and wealthiest merchants, together with ethnic organizations, such as the militantly Protestant Orange Order, and various Hibernian lodges, which kept alive memories of Ireland from Canada to Australia. Scots too cherished their clans and tartans and celebrated the ties that bound them to their homeland.

The Bengal Club, Calcutta. Founded in 1827, the Bengal Club was the oldest one in British India. As was the case in all colonial clubs, Indians, like other 'natives' were excluded from membership until well into the twentieth century and it was said to be difficult for a European 'to obtain an entrance unless you had been a long time in the city and had a certain standing'.

Voluntary associations could, however, build bridges between communities as well as strengthening their sense of separateness. Many of these linked the colonial society with that of Britain, and expressed the enduring power of British values and culture. The universities of both Sydney and Bombay, arrayed in a European Gothic architecture, taught a British curriculum in which the histories of Australia and India were conspicuously absent. Mechanics' institutes, horticultural societies, libraries, and museums flourished in all colonial capitals, and joined together to share specimens, displays, and staff with each other and with scientific bodies at 'home'. Such organizations involved a tiny cultured elite, but colonial exhibitions and fairs, following upon the triumphs of the Great Exhibition of 1851, drew multitudes of visitors. Melbourne entertained some two million at its 1888 Centennial Exhibition, even though the city's population at the time was barely a quarter of that figure, while the Calcutta Exhibition some five years before recorded a total attendance of one million visitors. Besides catering to a popular thirst for diversion, such fairs enabled fledging towns to proclaim their 'progress' in wealth and sophistication, and encouraged a new-found sense of colonial national pride among visitors and organizers alike. Other ritual occasions brought all residents together. Everyone in Melbourne, high and low, turned out, as they still do, for the annual running of the Melbourne Cup race. In similar fashion, cricket matches throughout the empire generated passionate enthusiasm even across racial lines.

Many associations, of varied character, cut across ethnic and communal divisions. A few, above all Masonic lodges, brought Briton and 'native' together on a basis of relative equality; others linked members in related occupations, such as chambers of commerce; while yet others, such as the British Indian Association of Bengal, though always careful to protect their members' interests, pursued questions of social and political reform.

Two lives

Male members of the indigenous elite in the cities usually had occupations where they spoke English, wore European clothes, and worked under the supervision of European superiors. Sometimes, as in much of Africa, urban Europeanized employment and education were complemented by conversion to Christianity. Outwardly, the Igbo clerk of Lagos, much like the Bengali babu of Calcutta, might seem to be no more than a caricature Englishman, and he was often despised by the English for his threatening mimicry. Yet the cultural life of the anglicized elite of the colonies was complex and multi-faceted. While outwardly co-operating with the British within the urban framework, colonized peoples were able to preserve for themselves an autonomous space even within the intensely western atmosphere of the colonial city. For example, much African Christianity took the form of African-led 'Ethiopian' or charismatic churches (see pages 209–10), while the richly-textured life of the joint family by no means disappeared when transplanted from the 'bush' to the colonial city. Indian businessmen in similar fashion brought brides

A husband killing his wife, Kalighat painting *c.*1880. This painting by a popular Indian artist reflects the tensions in the life of the urban elite in colonial Calcutta. The ideal was for the man to live separate lives: in his working life he assumed western dress and manners, while – as here – resuming his dhoti to enjoy domestic tranquillity with his wife who lived in seclusion from the outside world. In this case, based on a famous murder trial, the ideal has broken down completely. The wife has been unfaithful and the husband has abandoned his western restraint to exact bloody revenge.

to Nairobi from far-off Gujarat, while in Calcutta the Bengali office worker made of his house a retreat from the snubs of the colonial master. Central to the creation of this private realm was the role of the woman. Educated but not anglicized, a companion for her husband but still remaining in seclusion, the Indian wife was meant to embody in her behaviour an idealized 'Indian' personality. Even though these ideals were often derived from Victorian notions of 'respectability', they nevertheless enabled the Bengali male, abandoning his coat and tie in favour of a flowing dhoti, to assert within his home an enduring independence of the colonial order.

THE CITY UNDER STRAIN

Despite all of the forces – both institutional and cultural – that drove apart the residents of colonial cities, by the end of the nineteenth century a sense of participation in a shared urban life had begun to emerge, as communities, while preserving their own sense of identity, also co-operated to make the city work. But in the early twentieth century nationalist pressures and the growth of towns meant that this balance between separateness and common endeavour became increasingly difficult to sustain. Nationalism demanded a more active confrontation with the imperial regime, and so turned its residents against the cosmopolitan values of the colonial city. Gandhi, with his simple ways and focus upon values shared with the peasantry, sought to be everything that the colonial city was not. Even in fiercely anglophile Australia, by the 1890s, in opposition to the anglicized city, writers had begun to idealize the 'bush' as the home of uniquely Australian virtues such as 'mateship' and a rugged self-reliance. Nationalism also led to ethnic conflict: in East Africa, Malaya, Fiji, and elsewhere newly dominant indigenous elites constructed an image of the nation that excluded those immigrant communites, largely Indian and Chinese, who had established themselves in towns and cities during colonial rule (see pages 293–94). After independence Indians were forcibly expelled from Uganda and often restricted in their rights elsewhere.

Orderly co-existence was also threatened by the uncontrolled growth of towns and the inadequacy of urban facilities. With the control from the 1920s of famine and most epidemic disease, former small colonial towns exploded into metropolitan centres, inundated by job-seekers from the countryside and often surrounded by rings of slums and shantytowns. Occasional efforts at town planning, such as those of Patrick Geddes, who drew up plans for thirty cities in India in the years after 1914, did little to stem the tide. The failure of effective town planning was due, in part, to the British tradition of municipal self-government: even when the imperial authorities kept a tight hold on power at the centre, the encouragement of voluntary associations and ethnic segregation meant that colonial cities were always ill-planned. The old towns had worked because communities could look after their own members. But this system could not cope with the huge increases in population, and demand for services, that accompanied independence. By the 1960s more than three-quarters of Calcutta's residents lived in slums, sheltering in cardboard and tin shacks, while a municipal sewage system designed for 600,000 was being used by five times that number.

Colonial city to national city

Yet, against all odds, some sense of corporate existence did survive and the colonial city became, after independence, the national city. In New Delhi the names of streets honouring British viceroys were changed, and the statues of British royalty were removed, but the new bureaucrats moved easily into the offices and bungalows vacated by the old. In Calcutta the old British commercial companies retained their predominance even into the 1960s. Altogether, the transition to independence only made visible a process that had been under way for decades. Although founded by the British, and brought together under one imperial flag, these cities had over time become deeply embedded in the life of the territories where they were located. It is important not be misled by the spectacular architectural remains of the British, nor to fall prey to Raj nostalgia. Calcutta is now, as it has been for 200 years, the city that shapes and defines the culture of Bengal; while Singapore is both Chinese and, unlike its twin, Hong Kong (set to revert to China), an independent city-state, uniquely a product of its commercial and colonial heritage. Even those cities peopled by settlers of British origin diverged, as they grew, from each other as well as from those of the old homeland. Staid, tidy, conservative Toronto denoted a distinctively Canadian style, while brash, sprawling Sydney remains a quintessentially Australian town. Everywhere these one-time colonial cities – throbbing, vital, and full of entrepreneurial energy – embody much of the hope for the future of Africa, Asia, and Australia.

CHAPTER 9

*Ged Martin and
Benjamin E. Kline*

British Emigration and New Identities

British emigrants travelling to
Australia in the age of the
1850s gold rushes. In this
romanticized painting, the
group crowd round a primrose,
a last link with home. Scenes
like this would have been
enacted on many emigrant
ships crossing the Atlantic to
Canada as well as going to
Australasia.

The British empire was built on waves of migration overseas by British people. For many – such as soldiers, administrators, and businessmen – residence abroad was temporary. In some colonies, most obviously in Southern Rhodesia (Zimbabwe) or Kenya, permanently resident British communities were established and these survived as important minorities after the indigenous people of the colony had won independence. In Australia, Canada, and New Zealand, however, people of British origin came to constitute the majority of the population, while in parts of South Africa, although never more than a numerical minority, they exercised a dominant influence which lasted down to the great changes of the 1990s.

The process by which new societies emerged out of the British diaspora may look deceptively simple. It may be tempting to think of the British empire as a vast mincing machine. At one end, it devoured refugees from the Scottish Highlands,

Irish peasants fleeing from famine, Welsh and Cornish miners, and an occasional eccentric English aristocrat. These people were flung across the oceans on tiny ships and churned out as new peoples with entirely fresh identities. In fact, the processes were far from straightforward.

British people and British traditions and ways of doing things were exported into alien environments, sometimes already occupied by other Europeans and always inhabited by indigenous peoples, who were subordinated or pushed into the margins of society. Complex processes of adaptation within the imperial framework eventually produced new societies distinct from one another and from their British roots.

Even when they constituted the great majority of the population, as in South Africa, indigenous peoples were rarely given a significant role in shaping the identities of the new settler communities, although their presence might have an important effect on the way immigrant societies saw themselves. Yet even among immigrants of European origin, identities had to incorporate a wide diversity of human material. The British element of the population consisted of people of many different religious and political beliefs and social backgrounds, drawn from all parts of the United Kingdom. In Canada there was an old-established French community and in South Africa Afrikaners remained the majority of the white population. In Australia and New Zealand new immigrants were to be overwhelmingly British until well after 1945, but some Canadian provinces and the South African mining cities began to attract a sizeable inflow from continental Europe from the end of the nineteenth century.

ANATOMY OF A NEW SOCIETY

For all their obvious differences, the communities of British origin in Australia, Canada, New Zealand, and South Africa had important similarities which have left an enduring mark on them. They had relatively small populations, they were physically far removed from Britain, and they were young societies with short histories.

Colonial molehills

The British were an emigrating people. Huge numbers – over twenty million between 1815 and 1914 – left the British Isles, Ireland included, for destinations outside Europe. Yet this vast outflow did not involve the permanent transfer of population to the British colonies of settlement on anything like the same scale. In the first place, a majority of the emigrants who left Britain in this period, 62 per cent, were destined for the United States, not for any British colony. Of the rest, 19 per cent went to Canada, over 10.5 per cent to Australia and New Zealand, and under 3.5 per cent to South Africa. Secondly, many immigrants into British colonies did not stay there. About half the emigrants from England and Wales between 1861 and 1900 are thought to have come back.

In the early phases of white settlement overseas men tended heavily to outnumber women. The cargoes of convicts shipped to Australia were overwhelmingly male. By 1861 there was still a large majority of men in the white populations of the antipodes: 140 men to 100 women in Australia and 160 men to 100 women in New Zealand. Even in the early twentieth century men outnumbered women in both countries; in Britain, by contrast, there were 94 men to every 100 women.

The white population in early colonies of settlement was predominantly a rural one. Most of the female population lived on farms. There they generally brought up large families, and their lives were dominated by domestic and agricultural work.

The Australian poem *The Shearer's Wife* described a life of unremitting toil.

> Before the glare 'o dawn I rise
> To milk the sleepy cows an' shake
> The droving dust from tired eyes.
> I set the rabbit traps, then bake
> The children's bread.
> There's hay to stook an' beans to hoe,
> Ferns to cut in the scrub below.
> Women must work, when men must go
> Shearing from shed to shed.

For later generations of Australians and New Zealanders, a rural society largely composed of males has left a potent legacy for the way in which they see themselves. Male virtues of physical hardness, being able to turn one's hand to anything, and comradeship or 'mateship' have been assumed to be characteristic of Australia and New Zealand as a whole, long after most people had moved to the cities.

Admirable as pioneer societies might seem in retrospect, contemporaries viewed them with misgiving. Pioneer men were thought to be drunken, dissolute, and erratic workers – in urgent need of being tamed and turned into industrious citizens. Women were thought to be the best agents for taming men. In a famous phrase in 1847 Caroline Chisholm urged that if the British government really wanted to see 'a well-conducted community spring up' in the Australian colonies it should employ '"God's police" – wives and little children – good and virtuous women'.

Australia quickly became a highly urbanized society and by the end of the nineteenth century most women in New Zealand also lived in the towns. There women could live out the ideals of domesticity that were firmly established in Britain. Work and home should be kept separate. The ideal woman did not 'work': she devoted all her attention to the needs of her husband and her children. Indeed with rather higher living standards and better housing in colonial cities it may have been possible for the British ideal to be more completely realized. Colonial women in Australia and New Zealand had more opportunities to be home makers, even though they generally lacked the squads of domestic servants of middle-class Britain.

In spite of the cult of domesticity and of women as the dependants of men, female access to higher education, involvement in public affairs, and voting rights came as early in these colonies as in most European societies. In 1893 New Zealand was in fact the first country in the empire to concede the vote in national elections to women, even if the assumption behind some of those who supported the change was that it would give married men two votes.   [PJM]

Opposite: Bark hut, *c*.1900. Pioneer settlers' first homes in the Australian bush were likely to be extremely primitive.

Below: Women in a New Zealand town voting for the first time in 1893. Votes for women were taken as evidence that New Zealand was putting its turbulent pioneering past behind it. Female suffrage would, it was thought, increase the influence of 'the settler and the family man as against the loafing and single man'.

A 'bull dance' at Barberton, Transvaal. The disproportion between men and women, characteristic of the earlier stages of colonial settlement in general, was particularly marked in mining communities. Barberton in the Transvaal was the scene of a brief gold boom in 1884.

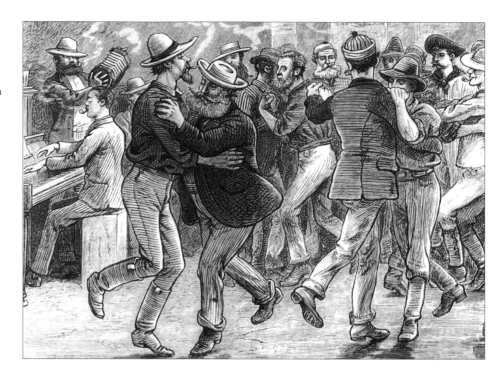

Statistics indicating with any reliability how many emigrants remained permanently in the colonies, rather than returning to Britain, are only available from 1876. These show that in the thirty-eight years to 1914 Canada gained just under one and a half million British immigrants, although some of them went on to the United States, along with many native-born Canadians. Australia and New Zealand added 800,000 British people to their permanently resident population and South Africa 136,000, most of them in a spurt just after the South African War (1899–1902). Seen from the British perspective, these were not enormous figures: the permanent gain to New Zealand's population for the hundred years from 1860 to 1960, overwhelmingly from Britain, was no more than 650,000. At all events, in 1901 there were still eight times as many people packed into the British Isles as scattered across the wide spaces of Canada. The mountains of British emigration had produced a range of distant colonial molehills. Critics of empire asked what was the use of the colonies; enthusiasts backed endless schemes to shift surplus people from Britain.

Since the overwhelming need of early colonial societies was for male labour to work the land or extract minerals, men were more likely to emigrate than women and early settlers did not always form families and make a long-term addition to colonial populations. Male convicts sent to Australia outnumbered women by about four to one: in rural New South Wales in 1838 the ratio was seventeen to one, giving a highly charged quality to the evolving culture of masculinity in the bush. In pioneer communities all around the empire the gender ratio was invariably massively unbalanced. Vancouver in 1891 had 187 men for every 100 women, and it was another fifty years before the sexes were roughly in balance. In Australia women did not catch up in numbers with men until after the Second World War and it took a further generation for them to mount an effective challenge to the dominant male culture.

Thus, overall, we have a paradox: massive numbers leaving a Britain still teeming with people, but individual colonies with very small populations. A friendly observer commented in 1852 that 'the Cape of Good Hope ... is not equal in population to Leicestershire, and is far inferior in its wealth; Australasia, including New Zealand, may rank with Norfolk; and the rest, all taken together, are hardly equal to a couple of medium English counties'. Australia's population boomed in the 1850s but it took all six colonies combined to reach one million by the end of the decade. A population explosion in Upper Canada (Ontario) helped bring about the political revolution that created the Canadian Confederation in 1867, but even in 1861 the province had fewer than one and a half million. Not until the eve of the First World War did Canada overtake Greater London in population, while Australia was still trailing Britain's capital in the 1950s. New Zealand passed the million mark in 1908 and clocked up two million in 1952.

These tiny, scattered, white settler communities overseas only took root because, outside South Africa, they faced relatively small numbers of indigenous people, sometimes semi-nomadic and all vulnerable to European disease and demoralization. Current estimates point to three-quarters of a million Aborigines when the First Fleet arrived in Australia in 1788 – hardly a vast population for a continent, although it was still a demographic catastrophe that their numbers fell to 10 per cent of that level in the 1920s.

In the vast area of what is now modern Canada, the native population at the time of first contact with Europeans has been estimated at around 350,000, while in New Zealand there may have been 100,000 Maoris when Cook sailed by in 1769. In

'Natives in Sydney', c.1830. During the first half of the nineteenth century the Aborigines were generally pushed away from the areas of European settlement, often with a violence that went largely unrecorded, by the demand for more and more land on which to graze sheep. A few Aborigines, however, found their way into the towns, where their vulnerability to alcohol attracted much attention.

Australia, Canada, and New Zealand indigenous peoples up to the end of the nineteenth century were assumed to be on the road to extinction: the Maoris hit a low point of 42,000 in 1896 (but recovered to ten times that number by the 1980s). There is much guesswork in these figures. What is clear, however, is that white colonization required the conquest or subjection of indigenous people in South Africa and the North Island of New Zealand, whereas in Australia and Canada the smaller, more thinly spread populations suffered severely from disease and could be displaced more easily.

In all the colonies of settlement British immigrants also encountered other people who had migrated from Europe. By contrast with the United States – in theory at least the classic 'melting pot' – in the colonies people of British origin were rarely numerous enough to absorb non-British immigrant communities. In 1942, for example, when Churchill wished to send South Africa's Prime Minister Smuts to negotiate with President Roosevelt as 'one Dutchman to another', he was indicating that, to this way of thinking, the Afrikaners had remained Dutch and had not become British South Africans. Throughout the nineteenth century, English had to compete with Dutch and above all with the language that became increasingly formalized as Afrikaans. Of the four original colonies that constituted the Union of South Africa of 1910, English-speakers were only an overwhelming majority among Europeans in Natal. In the Orange Free State they were few and far between. In the Transvaal, from the end of the nineteenth century, they dominated the big cities but the countryside and small towns remained solidly Afrikaner. In the Cape the Afrikaans- and English-speakers were more evenly balanced but there was a clear Afrikaner majority.

A high birth rate enabled French Canadians to maintain a four-fifths dominance of the population of their own province of Quebec and a share of the total Canadian population of around one quarter until the 1970s, when a dramatic fall in family sizes began to threaten their position. But in 1900, with little more than five million people spread across a vast country, there did not seem to be much prospect that the English-speaking community would absorb the French-speaking Acadians of New Brunswick, the Gaelic-speaking Scots of Nova Scotia, or the Ukrainians and Icelanders who were opening the west. One politician had argued in 1890 that it was 'expedient in the interest of national unity in the Dominion that there should be community of language among the people of Canada'. If a single language was the hallmark of a national identity, then it was hard to see how Canada would ever qualify.

A far-flung empire

No empire had ever founded so many far-flung colonies. British Columbia was probably the most remote colony of British settlement, five months sailing time round Cape Horn even in the 1850s. In a modern world of air travel and satellite communications, it is hard to recapture just how fragile and slow were the ships that carried emigrants to the far-away colonies. When John Dunmore Lang left Leith in Scotland in 1822 for Hobart in Tasmania, he boarded a sailing ship no larger than a modern Sydney harbour ferry and it took six and a half months to sail round the world. The first steamship to cross the Atlantic from Nova Scotia to Britain, the 343-ton *Royal William* in 1833, carried seven passengers and took twenty-five days – ten of them becalmed while the engines were repaired.

Distance encouraged self-reliance and self-determination in small colonial communities. Colonies separated from Britain by vast extents of ocean inevitably had freedom to develop in ways of their own without effective control from London. Their remoteness from Britain – and their low place in official priorities – logically pointed to giving the colonies of settlement some form of local self-government as soon as possible. Distance not only restricted contact between colonies and Britain; it also cut them off from one another. Bringing together a series of isolated colonies separated by great tracts of the virtually uninhabited landmass of Australia was, for instance, a slow and difficult process. When Australians formed their Commonwealth in 1901, a loose federal bond seemed to be the only possible basis for any kind of union. The Dominion of Canada was intended by its founders in 1867 to be tightly centralized, but within twenty years the problems of distance were becoming apparent and the Canadian constitution was taking a decisive shift towards a truly federal structure.

The conquest of distance through new technologies in the second half of the nineteenth century enabled dispersed colonies to unite into larger blocks and pulled all the colonies back into closer relations with Britain. The development of railways helped to close the distance between colonies, and the need to promote and plan railways was a strong incentive for colonies to form political unions. Indeed the needs of the railways were an important element in the moves towards federation in Canada, Australia, and South Africa. The first railways were little more than toys within the existing colonies. By the 1870s, however, they were being pressed beyond the then limits of settlement. British Columbia was joined by rail to eastern Canada in 1885; Western Australia was linked to the rest of the continent in 1917. Many of the projects for long-distance railways had to be sustained by the new colonial governments. The Canadian Pacific Railway Company, for example, received massive subsidies in cash, land, and existing public works, such as bridges, from the government of Canada. It still had to be rescued from the verge of bankruptcy in 1884 and 1885 and to be given additional cash in 1897. When Canada's second transcontinental railway went bankrupt in 1917, it was taken over outright by the government.

The instantaneous telegraph conquered distance overland more dramatically than the lumbering train. The Governor of New South Wales congratulated Victoria and South Australia on 'the shortening of the distance between us', when the wire got as far as Adelaide in 1858; to plug Western Australia into the system required a line of 1,800 miles in length through desert scrub.

Laying a submarine cable, Botany Bay, 1876. This line, linking Australia to New Zealand, was part of a network extending to Britain through Asia. Important messages could now reach Australia almost instantaneously instead of taking some five weeks by fast mail steamer.

Of the technological developments that brought the colonies closer to Britain, the long-distance submarine cables were at first the most spectacular, enabling messages to be flashed across the world. Canada was joined to Ireland from 1866, Australia to the wider world in 1872 – prompting the Prime Minister of New South Wales to predict that the cable would be the means of 'uniting us hand-in-hand, as it were, to the parent land'. Appeals for troops to participate in the British campaign in the Sudan in 1885, sent by telegraph to New South Wales, or for aid in the South African War, sent by the same means to Canada in 1899, had a very powerful effect by creating an immediate sense of an imperial crisis to which there must be an immediate response. As the twentieth century opened, it seemed that even the cable was unnecessary: in 1901 Marconi sent the first 'wireless' message from Cornwall to Newfoundland. Radio brought the empire even closer together. Although Canada, Australia, and New Zealand had all followed the British example and established a state radio network, in the Second World War the New Zealand Broadcasting Corporation lacked the resources to run its own news service, and simply rebroadcast the overseas bulletins of the BBC. This underlined the New Zealand sense of closeness to Britain, especially in the terrifying British peril of 1940 when Britain was threatened by invasion after the defeat of France.

Innovation in shipping meant that economic ties between the colonies could be strengthened as well as emotional and cultural ones. The great improvement in the capacity of steamships from the 1870s ensured that bulk items could be moved cheaply over any distance. Refrigerated ships were especially important for tying Australia and New Zealand more closely to Britain. The first refrigerated shipment from Australia was despatched to Britain in 1879. In 1882 the celebrated voyage of the *Dunedin* launched frozen meat exports from New Zealand. New Zealand became Britain's overseas farm, sending four-fifths of its exports to Britain.

In the early nineteenth century the links of empire had been attenuated by distance and time. Isolated communities of recent British immigrants had to fend for themselves far removed from British influences. As these communities grew and became more rooted in their new homes, technological change dramatically reduced their isolation. Thus the evolution of a sense of identity with the lands in which Canadians, Australians, New Zealanders, or English-speaking South Africans had grown up was being counterbalanced by closer links with the Britain they or their ancestors had left.

Compensating for a short past

How they interpret their past is one of the most important ways in which societies define themselves. For the people who were not of British origin, the past in the colonies was supremely important. Cut off from their European past, Afrikaners

Mythological origins

Colonial identities were complicated by the invention of myths, which tended to create stereotypes of the Scottish, Irish, and English immigrants. The most powerful myth was that of the victim in the 'old country' who made good in the new. But it was not true that all Scottish Highlanders were 'cleared' from their homely glens by cruel lairds to make way for sheep, as legend had it: on the contrary, early-nineteenth-century commentators used words like 'craze' and 'mania' to describe the headlong rush of Scots across the Atlantic. Nor were all Irish emigrants refugees from starvation. Emigration cost money: after all, somebody had to pay the fare. Very poor people were indeed shipped to the colonies, sometimes by well-meaning landlords who wished to give them a fresh start and sometimes by harsh government agencies who sought to be rid of them. Yet many Irish immigrants were actually from the middling ranks of society, people with a little property or savings which gave them enough capital to start a new life.

New Zealanders cherished a myth that they were not simply 'British' but 'best British', a sly slander against the convict origins of Australia. They chose to forget the description of the first white New Zealanders – the human flotsam engaged in catching whales and seals or trading with the Maoris who gathered around the Bay of Islands in the 1830s – as 'extremely immoral and addicted to low vices'.

Many Australian pioneers had good reasons of their own to explain away their country's origin as an outdoor prison, claiming that convicts were victims of unjust laws – in a country cursed with rabbits, it was easy to present poaching as a service to the community – or martyred for their radical political views, as was the case with a small number of early Scots and Irish prisoners. However, the evidence suggests that most of those transported were persistent urban thieves.

Historians have sometimes connived in this myth-making, since their motive for writing history was often a patriotic desire to show how their countries had travelled the road – in the title of one Canadian history textbook – *From Colony to Nation*. Central to such an approach was the assumption that Canada, for example, was made up of communities of people called 'Canadians', and there had been a steady linear progress from colonial origins to national independence and distinct identity.

The Highland clearances. From the mid-eighteenth century onwards there was a long process of emigration from the Scottish Highlands to overseas destinations, especially to Canada.

Although most emigrants left to better themselves, coercion by landlords to clear land for sheep in the 1840s and 1850s created a powerful folk memory of brutal clearances.

defined themselves through their versions of the sagas of the treks, French Canadians through an inevitably idealized interpretation of the history of New France before the British conquest. For most British people in the colonies of settlement, on the other hand, the past in these countries was too short for the formulation of powerful local traditions or myths to replace those they brought with them from Britain.

The history of the new countries overseas has been packed into a short span of time: the first white child to be born in Australia lived until 1883, the year in which the Royal Theatre in Sydney introduced that symbol of modernity, electric lighting. Because the colonies had such a short past, they tended to invert their historical perspective and focus on their glorious future instead. When New Zealand's Governor Sir George Grey returned to Britain in 1854, he was struck by the way in which people there 'lived for the present'. In a colony, 'whatever you do or plan is calculated with a view to what it will or ought to be in twenty or fifty or a hundred years hence'. He once promised a twelve-year-old boy 'that New Zealand was going to be a great country and that everyone would have a chance to get on'. The lad never forgot that encounter: 'I had no boots on at the time,' he recalled. 'There is always something better to be done, something greater to be attained,' the French Canadian leader George Cartier exclaimed in 1864. With an enthusiastic vagueness of vocabulary, a Sydney newspaper celebrated the centenary of settlement in 1888 with the assurance that 'Australia can march forward to the second anniversary without a cloud to dim the horizon of the future.'

In South Africa, however, there were anxieties as well as optimism. 'South Africa is a country of black men, and not of white men,' wrote Anthony Trollope in 1878. 'It has been so; and it will continue to be so.' The Afrikaner Smuts no doubt spoke for many English-speaking South Africans when he saw only 'shadows and darkness' in the 'political future' of South African race relations, and he abdicated responsibility for 'the intolerable burden' 'to the ampler shoulders and stronger brains of the future'.

The Voortrekker Memorial. Those who left the Cape to go into the interior in the 1830s and 1840s became heroes for Afrikaners and were revered as the founders of the nation. They had, it was believed, defied British oppression and had defeated godless Africans to found the new republics. In 1949 a memorial was dedicated to the Voortrekkers with a frieze of panels 320 feet long commemorating their exploits.

THE MIXING OF THE BRITISH

Serving with the allied forces in 1944, an aristocratic Scot 'was attracted by the individualist personalities of the Australians'. Canadians, on the other hand, although 'brave, friendly and resourceful' had 'a rubber-stamped outlook'. Perhaps, far from home, Australians and Canadians were simply acting out the roles expected of them. If there was indeed such a difference, we might begin to account for it by examining the ingredients each colonial society received from Britain. The census of 1901 gives a revealing snapshot. In the British Isles themselves, 75 per cent of the population lived in England, 5 per cent in Wales, and 10 per cent apiece in Scotland and Ireland. Overseas, however, the picture was different. People from England made up not three-quarters, but just over half of the British-born in Canada, Australia, and New Zealand, while the Welsh were rarities everywhere. On the other hand, Scots formed 15 per cent of the British-born in Australia, 21 per cent in Canada, and 23 per cent in New Zealand. The Irish score was 27 per cent in Australia, and 21 per cent in Canada and New Zealand. English people very much predominated among the British-born South Africans at the first Union census of 1911: they contributed over 70 per cent of the total with some 20 per cent Scottish and only 8 per cent Irish.

Clearly, Scots and Irish people made as large a contribution to the overseas empire, outside South Africa, as did the English. Yet national origin was not the only way in which people labelled themselves. 'Scots' and 'Irish' meant many

The Welsh and the empire

In 1901, 5 per cent of the population of the British Isles lived in Wales. Yet overseas, the Welsh constituted less than 1 per cent of the British-born in Australia and New Zealand, and in the Canadian census they suffered that statistical indignity of being lumped in with the English.

From the nineteenth century, a combination of opportunities elsewhere and obstacles within the empire explain why so few Welsh people went to the colonies and why the Welsh impact on the colonies was very much a story of individuals. The great surge of emigration from the British Isles in the late nineteenth century coincided with the development of the south Wales industrial area, creating opportunities within the country in what some called 'American Wales'. When people flowed out of Wales – over 400,000 left between 1921 and 1940 – they headed either for the new car factories of the English Midlands or to long-established outlets in the United States, such as the mines and steelworks of Pennsylvania.

Attempts to form Welsh-speaking settlements in the colonies were few and unsuccessful. A shipload of 180 people from Cardigan went to New Brunswick in 1819 – hardly enough to establish a New Wales. It was probably language difficulties that prompted one official to dismiss them as 'sluggish, avaricious and petulant', unusually contrasting them unfavourably with the 'industrious' Irish.

In 1856 the Reverend Michael Daniel Jones of Bala asked the Colonial Office if it would hand over first Vancouver Island – and then the whole of British Columbia – for a Welsh colony, with free steamship passages and immediate self-government. 'The Welsh are a moral, industrious and thriving people,' he wrote, 'and make the very best of emigrants, and are truly loyal.' A wary official feared 'mischief' in the notion of a colony 'where they may speak Welsh and "govern themselves"', and the Colonial Office remained unmoved even by the argument that a Welsh colony on the Pacific seaboard would defend British North America against a Russian invasion. Jones eventually established his colony in Argentina, further reducing the likelihood that Welsh-language communities would form within the empire. Still, in 1899 at least one place in Canada had regular chapel services in Welsh – the coal-mining town of Nanaimo on Vancouver Island. Michael Daniel Jones would have been pleased.

different things. Nova Scotia's Cape Breton Island and New Zealand's Otago settlement were both Scots, but the first was dominated by Gaelic-speaking Highland Catholics, and the second by Free Church Presbyterians. The majority of Irish who went to Canada were Protestants, while the Australian Irish were mainly Catholic.

The Irish

Were the Irish 'British'? Irish Protestants did not doubt it but Irish Catholics were less enthusiastic. It may not have been an accident that, for example, Protestant Irish preferred to live under the British flag in Canada while Irish Catholics chose the republican freedom of the United States. The 1916 Easter Rising in Dublin inflamed Irish feeling around the empire. Archbishop Mannix of Melbourne, a Corkman by birth, provocatively announced that 'Irishmen are as loyal to the Empire to which, fortunately or unfortunately, they belong, as a self-respecting people could be under the circumstances.' When Bishop Liston of Auckland – Dunedin-born of Irish Catholic parents – attacked British policy in Ireland in 1922, New Zealand's Prime Minister Massey – a Protestant from County Londonderry – had him prosecuted for sedition.

But Catholic and Protestant were not the only ways in which the Irish defined themselves. Among Canada's Irish, for example, local loyalties persisted. In nineteenth-century Newfoundland 'dadyeens' from County Cork engaged in faction fights with 'yellowbellies' from Wexford. Ulster Protestant Timothy Eaton was always ready to find jobs for new arrivals from his native Ballymena in the department store empire he founded in Toronto in 1869. On the other hand, the Charitable Irish Society, founded in Halifax, Nova Scotia, in 1786, symbolized the breaking down of barriers by alternating its presidency between Catholic and Protestant.

The Scots

Individual Scots and their descendants filled important posts throughout the colonies. In Canada, confederation in the 1860s was the product of a fragile alliance between John A. Macdonald, born in Glasgow, and George Brown, reared in Edinburgh. Macdonald effortlessly emerged as the first Prime Minister, his twenty-year ascendancy broken only by the single term of Alexander Mackenzie from Perthshire. Speysiders George Stephen and Donald A. Smith masterminded the Canadian Pacific railway. So dominant were the Scots that others sought to join their ranks: General Sir Arthur Currie was the grandson of an immigrant called Corrigan who had the wit to notice that people with Scottish surnames did better in Canada than Irish Catholics.

To be Scots (or 'Scotch') in Canada was usually to transcend local loyalties within Scotland itself. Gradually, however, Canada's Scottish identity came to be interpreted in a curious way. The dominant English-speaking influences from

Lowland Scotland became blended into the Canadian mainstream, leaving the atypical Highland communities of Glengarry County and Cape Breton to be identified as essentially 'Scottish'. Nova Scotia adopted a version of the flag of St Andrew as the provincial flag in 1929, and tourists were greeted with bagpipes. Politicians named Macdonald and MacKinnon solemnly discussed whether government employees in Cape Breton – now 'the Cape Breton Highlands' – should be made to wear kilts or merely dressed in tartan trousers. Tourism equated a Scottish heritage with a Highland Gaelic identity. The irony of this was that a century earlier Lowland Scots had shown an embarrassed ethnic prejudice against Highlanders and 'the gibberish of Gaelic', even urging that emigrant ships should be used to inculcate 'Lowland accomplishments of knife, fork and spoon' among their half-savage brethren. Now the kilt and the bagpipes became the badges of being Scottish.

Throwing the hammer at the Highland Games in Australia. The Highland tradition tended to take over other Scottish traditions among the Scots in British communities overseas.

Scots were also widely identified with Highlanders in other British colonies of settlement. The reality was more prosaic. Poor Scots, commonly regarded as resilient and industrious colonists, were a significant element in nineteenth-century British emigration to Australia, New Zealand, and South Africa, but Scots were also prominent in business and in education and in the religious life of colonies. Scots were dominant in Australian banking and shipping and in the pastoral industry which provided the wool for the British market. William Pember Reeves, New Zealand's first national historian, noted the same thing in his own country. 'Scots are more prominent than other races in politics, commerce, finance, sheep farming' and, he added, in 'the work of education.' This was particularly marked in South Island, where the Free Church of Scotland had settled Otago, bringing with them their commitment to parochial schools and higher education. Scottish merchants were important at the Cape Colony in South Africa, but Scots also provided missionaries and clergy, not only for their own people but also for some congregations of the Afrikaner Dutch Reformed Church whose Calvinism was close to their own. Scots were heavily represented among teachers in schools and colleges throughout South Africa.

The English

A specifically English contribution to empire is difficult to disentangle because of the extent to which the terms 'English' and 'British' have been regarded as interchangeable. While the Irish, Scots, and Welsh communities overseas celebrated their separate traditions, the English could call on no characteristically English traditions since all things British were English. Nineteenth-century Westminster politicians invariably referred to the island group as 'England', even if, like Palmerston or Gladstone, they were themselves of Irish or Scottish background. And when Hitler invaded Poland in 1939, the Conservative L.S. Amery – for whom the British empire was an obsession – called across the House of Commons to Labour's Arthur Greenwood, 'Speak for England!'

The extent to which many things of specifically English origin had come to be applied to the United Kingdom as a whole and had therefore become 'British' left little that was distinctively English to export to the colonies. Even the common law of England had become British by the nineteenth century. Admittedly the Anglican church called itself the 'Church of England' in Canada until 1955 and in Australia until 1981. In 1940 the education board in the New Zealand province of Canterbury, which had originated as a colony founded by Anglicans, decided that children should start the school day by singing *There'll always be an England*, to the disappointment of those who argued for *God defend New Zealand*. Yet the majority of colonists of English origin gave the Anglican church only nominal allegiance and it faced competition from other Christian churches on a larger scale than in England itself.

There were those who tried to foster a distinctively English class system in the colonies. Some commentators were concerned that the 'wrong' social patterns were developing – too much democracy, too many opportunities for new wealth to command power and respect. As one Anglican bishop put it, a colony without a class structure was a 'hop-ground left without poles'. The colonial theorist Edward Gibbon Wakefield argued that colonial land should be sold at a 'sufficient price', an undefined level that would ensure that only the right sort of monied people became landowners and would finance the immigration of the poor to work as labourers. His *Art of Colonization* (1833), with its call for the creation of hereditary titles in the colonies, helped inspire William Charles Wentworth, the leader of the rich sheep farmers of New South Wales, to propose in 1853 an order of baronets, from whom the colony might establish its own House of Lords. This scheme faded, like the earlier British plan to create a titled aristocracy in Canada in 1791.

The kennels at Cannington Manor, Canada. 'You will still fancy yourself in England, only without England's worries', a prospective emigrant was assured by the founder of Cannington Manor, which drew to the Canadian West an assortment of ex-public-school boys, who lounged about the prairies in the 1880s wearing striped blazers.

The 'real' British

The Scots took the lead in proclaiming the new societies to be 'British'. 'A British subject I was born,' Canada's Prime Minister Macdonald announced in 1891, 'a British subject I shall die.' Robert Menzies, who dominated Australian politics from 1949 to 1966, described himself as 'British to the bootstraps'. Among the honours acquired by this grandson of a Scot from Dumfries was the English feudal title of Lord Warden of the Cinque Ports and two knighthoods, one from Scotland's Order of the Thistle and the other, near the end of his life, from the new Order of Australia. Pride in being 'British' did not mean that Canadians, Australians, and South Africans were trapped in the 'cultural cringe'. Rather they were implying that a process of amalgamation was taking place overseas which had not happened in the home islands. In 1930 the historian W.K. Hancock boldly proclaimed – from temporary exile in Oxford – that 'if such creature as the average Briton exists anywhere upon this earth, he will be found in Australia'.

THE EMERGENCE OF NEW IDENTITIES

Gradually, this sense of being 'British' was supplanted by pride in being a Canadian, an Australian, a New Zealander, or a South African. It is easier for historians to note that this happened than to explain the how and why: two years after Sir Robert Menzies had retired in 1966, the new Prime Minister, John Gorton, was describing himself as 'Australian to the boot-heels'. In 1952 Menzies wept at the death of King George VI. Forty years later, Australian Prime Minister Paul Keating coolly argued that Australia should amicably dispense with the Queen.

New forms of English

The emergence of new forms of English in each of the former colonies was one sign of a distinctive identity. Canadian English was marked by the frequent insertion of the interrogative 'eh?', in contrast to the American 'uh?': humorists even pointed out that the country's first Prime Minister was Sir John Eh? [A.] Macdonald. In New Zealand the final syllable became stressed in adverbs, as in 'quick-lee'. In South Africa the Dutch/Afrikaans accent influenced Transvaal English, although it was less evident in the English of the eastern Cape and Natal. Australian English was particularly vigorous in creating and adapting words; Canadians tended to defend themselves against Americanization by keeping closer to British usage, notably in terminology ('railway' not 'railroad') and spelling. Terms such as 'larrikin' (Australian for an unruly young man), 'riding' (Canadian for a parliamentary constituency), and 'robot' (South African for a traffic light) testify to vigorous creation of vocabulary. Indigenous languages have also made their contributions, especially to the names of plants and animals, and there are occasional echoes from the Celtic world: the Irish took the expressive word 'aindeisoir', meaning a 'wretched person', to Newfoundland where it took root as 'hangashore', a wimp who would not go fishing.

A sense of place

A people's sense of identity is shaped in part by their sense of the country in which they live. British societies overseas tended to identify less with towns than with the rural landscape. In the early nineteenth century landscapes were depicted in European and especially in English terms, rather than as uniquely Australian, Canadian, New Zealand, or South African. By 1900 generations of colonial artists had tried to reproduce the distinctive features of their own landscapes and thus to establish the identity of their own countries (see pages 305–10).

Nationhood through war

In the twentieth century war sharpened a sense of national identity in the Dominions but in an ambivalent way, for the wars were fought alongside Britain, not to gain national independence. Some of those who enlisted in the New South Wales detachment to the Sudan in 1885 and the Australian and Canadian contingents to the South African War seem to have seen fighting for the empire as a huge and sometimes even as a drunken lark. Men even showed outward insouciance in volunteering for the First World War: as he left Halifax for France in 1915, one Canadian soldier called it 'the greatest adventure of my life'.

Shortly before her tragic death in 1939, the writer Robin Hyde wrote that her generation of New Zealanders had 'ceased to be "forever England". We became, for so long as we have a country, New Zealand.' Yet when the war against Hitler broke out on 3 September 1939, New Zealand's Labour government abandoned its attempts at an independent external policy and ranged the country at Britain's side. Prime Minister Savage – Australian born of Irish Catholic extraction – simply stated: 'Where she goes we go; where she stands we stand.'

War itself cost the Dominions dear in blood. Canada lost 60,000 people in the First World War; in proportion to population New Zealand's casualty rate was higher even than that of Belgium. These sacrifices created pride. In April 1917 the Canadians captured the apparently impregnable Vimy Ridge on the Western Front in France, in a new kind of scientific warfare in which infantry advanced behind the protection of a carefully targeted artillery barrage. 'We went up Vimy Ridge as Albertans and Nova Scotians,' wrote one soldier. 'We came down as Canadians.' Their pride carried a high price: over 3,000 Canadian soldiers did not come down from Vimy Ridge at all.

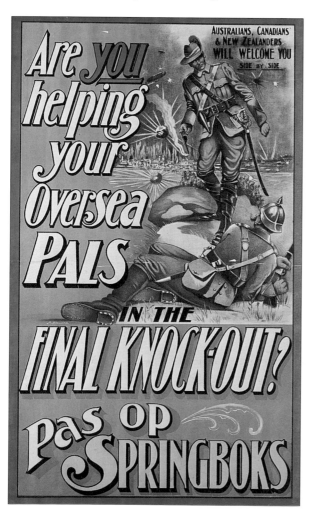

'Watch out for the Springboks'. This poster is an appeal to white South Africans to match the contributions of Australians, Canadians, and New Zealanders to the First World War. It suggests something of the pride and even competitiveness that citizens of the Dominions showed in making their own contributions to the common British cause. Thus a war fought for Britain actually strengthened colonial peoples' sense of their own identity.

For Australians, the devastating losses inflicted on the Australian and New Zealand troops by the Turks at Gallipoli in 1915 had been the national baptism of fire, creating the Anzac legend of the brave Digger. Yet it was a complex form of identity, which tended to obliterate the part played by the New Zealanders – whose initials gave them claim on Anzac too. Moreover, the celebration of the hopeless courage of the Australians at Gallipoli combined loyalty to the empire with protest against the British, whose incompetent military leadership had botched the operation. One of the many curious aspects of the Anzac legend was that it saw the quintessential assertion of the Australian identity in an event that took place thousands of miles from Australian shores. By contrast, white South Africans experienced little of the bloodshed that had helped to forge nationhood elsewhere: most of their troops fought in Africa.

The First World War also opened deep internal wounds throughout the empire. In 1914 an Afrikaner rebellion in South Africa strained the fragile reconciliation among white South Africans that had followed the South African War of 1899–1902. About half of the Afrikaner population remained opposed to active participation in the war. In Australia the issue of conscription pitted Catholics and Protestants in poisonous acrimony and almost ruptured the partnership of French and English in Canada in 1917.

Nationhood through sport

If war was seen as a game, sport was a surrogate form of conflict. The term 'test match' was an Australian invention – the 1882 touring team displayed 'general over-anxiety' at carrying the responsibility of representing the colonies against the motherland. Australia passed its test: Spofforth ripped the English batting apart, taking fourteen wickets for ninety runs, to clinch the first Australian test match victory on English soil by seven runs. One spectator died of excitement, and the *Sporting Times* even announced the demise of English cricket: 'The body will be cremated and the Ashes taken to Australia.' Australia had asserted its identity not on the battlefield fighting for independence, but on the cricket pitch struggling for self-esteem. For New Zealanders, self-assertion came through rugby, especially when the All Blacks took the British Isles by storm in 1905.

Emblems of identity

Three of the Dominions were the outcome of movements for intercolonial union – Canada in 1867, Australia in 1901, and South Africa in 1910. In each case, the process was more a marriage of convenience or a business merger than the product of a forest-fire of local nationalism. In Australia it was necessary to overcome the jealousy that New South Wales felt for the upstart 'cabbage patch' of Victoria. In 1888 politicians in Sydney had attempted to rename their colony 'Australia' both to clinch its primacy and to throw off echoes of its past. (A Melbourne newspaper unkindly suggested 'Convictoria' as an alternative.) New South Wales reluctantly agreed to join the federal Commonwealth, but only on condition that it would have the new Australian capital. Victoria in turn insisted that the chosen site must be at least 100 miles from Sydney. A decade of wrangling preceded the selection of Canberra, and it was not until 1927 that the capital was actually moved to the bush metropolis – 'seven suburbs in search of a city', as the process has been called. South Africans simply cut their capital into three, locating civil servants in Pretoria, Parliament in Cape Town, and the courts in Bloemfontein.

Other symbols of national identity emerged slowly and often controversially. It took two years of passionate argument before South Africans in the 1920s and Canadians in the 1960s could decide whether to include the Union Jack in their flag. *O Canada* was officially adopted as a national anthem only in 1967: there are entirely different versions in French and English, one calling Canada 'land of our altars', the other 'our home and native land' – a curious definition in a country where one citizen in every six is an immigrant. For Afrikaner nationalists, flags and anthems were weapons of triumphalism, not symbols of healing. In 1957 the Strijdom government finally got rid of the Union Jack flying alongside the national

Labels and legitimacy

The most basic requirement of a new identity is a label. Labels do not emerge ready-made; they evolve over time and are often highly contentious. Some names were imposed, others adopted by the people concerned – labelling has always been a weapon in the struggle for legitimacy between newcomers and indigenous peoples. As a result, terms that one set of people have regarded as simple classifications have been rejected by others as insults, and the history of the empire is littered with discarded labels now regarded as offensive: in South Africa, for instance, 'kaffir' for blacks, 'boer' for Afrikaners, 'coolie' for Indians, and 'rooinek' for English-speaking whites.

In colonial societies in the past people often felt they had a choice of labels: a family in the Australian outback mining town of Charters Towers in 1882, for example, might feel themselves to be 'British' in demanding the exclusion of Chinese from their gold field, or 'Australians' when they rejoiced in the feats of the 'demon' bowler Spofforth against the England cricket team, or 'Queenslanders' when debating whether there should be a federal council spanning the whole continent. Being Catholic or Protestant would probably also matter to them, as would their origins – especially if their parents had been free immigrants and not convicts, although this would probably have been a less sensitive matter in Queensland than in New South Wales and Tasmania. If born in Australia, the husband might well be a member of the Australian Natives Association – Charters Towers had led the way three years earlier in forming the first branch outside Victoria. A few decades earlier, he would have been nicknamed a 'cornstalk', a sarcastic reference to the way in which Australian children, like colonial wheat, grew fast and gangly; but labels could change with great rapidity and by 1882 'cornstalk' had become a caustic term for the New South Welsh. If the family were new immigrants, they might be irritated by children chanting 'jimmy-granate, pomegranate' – and hence 'Pom'.

flag and the singing of *God Save the Queen* – as part of a campaign to cut the links of English-speaking South Africans with what was left of the empire prior to the achievement of a republic and departure from the Commonwealth in 1961. In December 1993, as the last white Parliament voted itself out of existence, opposition Conservatives defiantly sang the national anthem, *Die Stem van Suid Afrika* (The Voice of South Africa): its message had always been that one South African voice should drown out all others.

Perhaps it is fitting that Australia should bring the story of anthem politics full-circle back to sport. After the 1972 Olympic Games, Australian athletes complained that *God Save the Queen* had been played at medal ceremonies to honour their victories. The government of Gough Whitlam agreed that before the next Olympics Australia must have a distinctive anthem of its own. In keeping with Australian democratic spirit, a national referendum chose *Advance Australia Fair*, despite a strong vote in Canberra for *Waltzing Matilda*. Alas, the new anthem was not played at the 1976 Olympics, for Australia's athletes were unable to gain a single gold medal.

By 1954, when Elizabeth II became the first sovereign to set foot on Australian soil, the Dominions had made the transition to full independence. The Balfour Declaration of 1926 had turned George V, King of the British empire, into a series of monarchs, one for each of the Dominions. For a week in September 1939, George VI had been at war with Hitler in his capacity as King of Britain, Australia, New Zealand, and South Africa, but carefully neutral in his role as King of Canada. These subtleties meant little to ordinary people. Elizabeth II was at pains to stress that she had come 'to meet my Australian people as their Queen'. For her Australian people, she was simply *the* Queen, and millions of them turned to cheer her. One historian only appreciated the full emotional impact of the 1954 first tour on learning that her aunt had been inspired to buy a corgi. A conservative politician called on Australians to use the Queen's visit to 're-affirm our faith in ourselves as British people in the first place, our faith in our country in the second place, and our faith in our democratic systems ... in the third place'.

The emphasis in the tripod of identity is significant: in 1954 Australia could still be claimed as first and foremost 'British'. Perhaps the need for such a strident reaffirmation was in itself a sign that Australia was evolving, but crucial and shattering changes were taking place at the centre of what was left of the empire. In 1956 Britain failed in the assertion of its old-style imperial role in the Suez crisis, and rapidly granted independence to its colonial territories, while seeking a new role in Europe. Hardly anyone talked of Britain as 'home' any more. By 1969 even the doubting poet Earle Birney wondered whether Canada was 'still the case of a high school land deadset in adolescence?' It was not so much that the people of the old Dominions had decided that they were no longer 'British' but rather that Britain itself had kicked away the emotional underpinning and left Australians and Canadians to define themselves in a post-imperial world.

IDENTITY BY SEPARATION

To understand how people came to see themselves as Australians, Canadians, New Zealanders, or English-speaking South Africans, we must appreciate that they passed through an intermediate phase in which they defined themselves as 'British' in a way that both represented a merging of different traditions from the British Isles and asserted equality of self-respect with fellow 'Britishers' who had not emigrated. This pride in Britishness inevitably meant that there would be little incentive to form an identity that included non-British people. Indeed maintaining Britishness among non-British populations implied separation and exclusion.

Separate from 'the natives'

Until very recent times, Australian Aborigines and native Americans were presumed to have no part in the shaping of Australia or Canada. They were not regarded as full citizens. At worst, Aborigines in particular were considered to be scarcely human; at best, they were objects for special protection. The expansion of European society in New Zealand was made possible by the crushing of Maori resistance, but since then Maoris have been included as full members of a New Zealand 'nation' with formal recognition of voting rights from 1867. New Zealand whites have even adopted some Maori traditions as national symbols, as in rituals before rugby matches. White New Zealanders took some pride in this inclusiveness, even if their critics insisted that Maoris were only included after defeat and dispossession. A degree of racial inclusiveness was also accepted by some British settlers at the Cape in South Africa. The first Parliament for the Cape Colony was elected in 1854 on a franchise that was based on the ownership of property, not on colour. It therefore included some voters who were African or of mixed race. This franchise was to last until 1956, when an Afrikaner Nationalist majority in the South African Parliament abolished it. A kind of liberalism associated with the Cape had a long life, even if the number of non-whites admitted to full citizenship was always small. To assume, however, that the racial exclusiveness that was elevated in the twentieth century into the apartheid system was an Afrikaner imposition on the unwilling English-speakers would be a serious distortion. The liberalism of the Cape had as much to do with the Afrikaners, who were always a majority among the whites, as with English-speakers. In Natal the British settlers effectively excluded African voters and in the Transvaal the English-speaking mine owners became very much the beneficiaries of apartheid through their need for cheap labour.

Separate from other European settlers

The institutions of Canada after 1867 and South Africa after 1910 were devised to meet the needs of both English-speakers and of French Canadians or Afrikaners. In general they seem to have been successful in creating a Canadian or a South African state to which the great majority on both sides of the language divide could commit

The All Blacks performing the traditional haka, before the start of a rugby match. Sport has helped in the integration of whites and Maoris in New Zealand: Maoris have played a prominent part in New Zealand rugby teams, while whites have adopted the haka, or Maori challenge, as a national ritual.

their loyalty. Whether loyalty to the state produced a merged identity is another matter. An unofficial geographical segregation, which has confined the French to Quebec or kept the English out of rural Transvaal or Orange Free State, did not help. Intermarriage was not very common. Most English-speakers did not prove very adept at learning French or Afrikaans. Although British influences on English-speaking Canadians and South Africans have waned in the twentieth century, this has not led to extensive mixing of the English-speaking communities with those who speak French or Afrikaans.

Separate from Asians

To Australians in particular, but also to New Zealanders and those who lived in Western Canada and in the province of Natal in South Africa, the vast populations of India and China and the military power of Japan seemed to be the main threat to their sense of identity. In resisting immigration by Asians or other non-European peoples, the white populations of the British colonies explicitly defined the values they wished to protect. Confronted with people from Asia or Polynesia, British settlers usually slammed the door – but sometimes sought to use them as a labour supply. The Chinese were seen as a threat to the numerically small colonial communities: by the late 1850s, for example, they were 15 per cent of the male population of gold-rush Victoria. White colonists used violence and the law to discourage them from making permanent homes in Australia. The gold fields of British Columbia also attracted Chinese, about 7,000 by 1860. In the 1880s more were brought in to work on the railways. By 1911 there were 27,000 Chinese in Canada. With remarkable inconsistency, white colonists then criticized the Chinese communities for the very features that white prejudice had forced upon them. Chinese were attacked as cheap labour – because white employers invariably paid them at low rates. Overall only 3.5 per cent of the Chinese in Canada were women, while the Victorian Legislative Council claimed that there were just four Chinese women alongside the 40,000 men. But discriminatory immigration taxes made it almost impossible for Chinese men to bring their wives. As a consequence, male Chinese were seen as a sexual threat, and the social institutions to which unattached Chinese men were drawn – the counterparts of such bodies as the Protestant Orange Order – were damned as secret societies and opium dens. All Chinese immigration to Canada was stopped between 1923 and 1947, while Canadians of Japanese origin were forcibly shipped out of British Columbia in 1942 as a wartime security measure.

The fact that Asian entrepreneurs concentrated on a few areas of commerce aroused charges of unfair competition. In Sudbury, Ontario, a steam laundry appealed for business against Chinese rivals in 1903, urging townspeople not to patronize 'a class of people who send every cent to their native land and invest nothing in the towns in which they do business'. Since the Chinese had hardly been made welcome, this was a trifle unfair. In any case, Sudbury had only a few dozen

Chinese residents, even in 1921 when the local council debated whether the spread of Chinese restaurants constituted a 'Yellow Peril'. The following year, unemployed miners demanded free meals from the Chinese, and the council tried to ban the employment of white waitresses. 'We obey law, we make no noise, we have feelings like other men, we want to be brothers with Englishmen – why not be so?' bewildered Chinese had asked on the Australian gold fields in the 1850s. The Chinese of Sudbury made the same point in 1941, buying newspaper space in support of the war effort to carry pictures of the allied leaders – Churchill and Chiang Kai-Shek.

If cheap Asian labour was seen as a threat in some parts of the empire, in others it was encouraged. From 1860, the British authorities in India permitted the shipping of indentured labour to the Natal sugar plantations. They were to work on three-year contracts, after which they would return home. Europeans considered Africans to be unsatisfactory workers because they 'leave their employer whenever their caprice prompts them to return homeward' and generally disliked 'steady and systematic toil'. In a strange country, Indians would have no choice. The Governor of Natal hoped that the introduction of indentured labour would quieten the

This *Punch* cartoon of 2 June 1888 was prompted by a conference of the then separate Australian colonies to co-ordinate action against Asian immigration and enforce exclusion. The conference had been prompted by outbursts of hostility against Chinese, including riots in Brisbane and on the gold fields. The caption to the cartoon reads: 'Mrs Australia (to John Chinaman) "Outside, Sir! Outside! I've had quite enough of you! No admittance, not even on business!"'

'continual cry' of the settlers to compel Africans to work for them, but critics condemned 'a new system of slavery'. The introduction of Chinese labourers into the South African gold mines in 1903 provoked an outcry – part humanitarian, part racist.

Assumptions that indentured labourers would return to their homeland proved unfounded: about three-quarters of the Indians in Natal remained after their contracts, becoming farmers, labourers, miners, shepherds, fishermen, and hawkers. From about 1880 other Indians came as 'passengers' – free immigrants who opened shops, provoking claims of 'unfair competition'. When Natal gained self-government in 1893, white politicians tried to deprive Indians of the right to vote and imposed discriminatory taxes to get rid of them altogether. A young London-educated lawyer, M.K. Gandhi, became their leader, developing tactics that he would later use to drive the British from India.

India was a convenient source of labour supply because it was under British rule. However, being part of the empire did not entitle the people of India to the right to free movement within it, as 376 would-be immigrants, mainly from the Punjab, discovered when their ship, the *Komagata Maru*, anchored in Vancouver harbour in May 1914. There they remained for two months, blocked by a local campaign to exclude them from Canada. As a local newspaper put it, all arguments based on 'the brotherhood of man and fellow-British citizenship' crumbled against the overwhelming fact that there were 300 million people in India. Even a trickle of immigrants would be enough to overwhelm the 450,000 British Columbians who wished to remain safely under 'Anglo-Saxon British rule'. *The Komagata Maru* sailed back to Calcutta, to add to the grievances of Indian nationalists.

Gradually, however, in both Australia and Canada, as people identified less strongly with Britain, they became more tolerant of other racial groups. The Pacific War was a warning that Australia must 'populate or perish', and the government embarked on a campaign to attract 'new Australians' from Europe. Immigration minister Arthur Calwell hoped that British immigrants would outnumber the rest by ten to one, but for the first time newcomers from Britain fell short of a majority in the postwar decade, as Australia acquired visible communities of Italians, Greeks, and Croats. Gradually the 'White Australia' policy went too, being finally pronounced dead in 1973. Canada also widened its immigrant entry, adopting a non-discriminatory policy in 1962. Canada's 1976 Immigration Act gave priority to refugees and to family reunion, both tending to increase the number of people arriving from Asia. Meanwhile, the province of Quebec sought to compensate for its falling birthrate by actively recruiting immigrants from French-speaking countries in Africa and the Caribbean. On a smaller scale, New Zealand's ethnic mix began to change as a result of the backwash from its own Polynesian sub-empire – with immigrants from Samoa and the Cook Islands making Auckland a cosmopolitan city. All three countries welcomed wealthy entrepreneurs who might stimulate their economies, regardless of skin colour.

NO LONGER FAWNING CUBS

Since the Second World War ties with Britain have weakened and the allure of British power has become a thing of the past. No one now thinks of the old Dominions as fawning cubs of an imperial lion. By whatever mysterious process, new countries have emerged from the imperial mincing machine in Canada, Australia, and New Zealand. No one now doubts that, for example, the people who inhabit Canada are Canadians, even if the exact definition of identity remains a mystery. It was not that the New Zealander Robin Hyde was wrong in 1939 when she saw her generation as the one that had ceased to be 'forever England' overseas. Rather she was half a century too early.

In South Africa, too, links with Britain have been eroded. South Africa was even outside the Commonwealth from 1961 to 1994. In other respects, however, the story of South Africa has been rather different. Under the doctrine of apartheid, in

'South Africans third'

The attitudes of the white population of the province of Natal in South Africa were summed up in 1929 as being 'Natalians first, Britishers second and South Africans third.' Much of Natal is indeed cut off from the rest of South Africa by the Drakensberg mountains, while being open to the outside world by sea. It is a rich territory of grasslands with a sub-tropical coastal belt. Early nineteenth-century Natal, when the British first arrived there, had a large African population. The raids of the powerful Zulu state to the north had, however, effectively depopulated big areas in the south, leaving good land apparently vacant for white settlement. Afrikaners trekking away from the Cape moved in for a time, but withdrew when Britain annexed the area in 1843. British settlers followed annexation and Natal's population has remained predominantly British in origin. By the end of the nineteenth century white farmers were raising sheep and cattle and growing maize and wattle in the inland areas and sugar plantations had been established on the coastal belt. Railways had been built linking the mining towns of the Transvaal to Durban, which became the most important port in South Africa.

But although Natal was a viable colony of white settlement, its European population was vastly outnumbered by Africans and was even outnumbered by the Indians who had been brought in to increase the colony's labour force. In 1911 there were estimated to be just under 100,000 Europeans (mostly living in the cities of Durban and Pietermaritzburg), compared to nearly one million Africans and 133,000 Indians. Conscious of their lack of numbers, whites segregated themselves from the other communities.

From the mid-nineteenth century, African people moved back into the areas devastated by the Zulu. There were far too many for the British to try to integrate them into the society of the new colony, even if they were willing to do so. Africans were assigned 'reserved' land in which to live under 'tribal' law, administered by chiefs. The number of Africans living under Natal's rule greatly increased in 1897, when Zululand was annexed. The population of the African reserves became a pool of labour for the white farms, for Durban, and for the mines of the Transvaal, but whites regarded the large African population within the colony's boundaries with apprehension. A rising in Zululand in 1906 seemed to confirm these fears and it was repressed with severity.

Indian workers had first been brought into Natal in 1861 to work on the sugar plantations. They became a settled population, competing with whites as farmers, traders, and skilled workers. Such competition was resented and laws were passed to encourage Indians to leave the colony once they had finished their contracts and to restrict the areas in which they might live and the occupations they could pursue. Indians, like Africans, were effectively excluded from having any part in the political life of the colony.

The British population of Natal faced an unresolvable dilemma: in order to impose their policies of control over Africans and Indians, they needed autonomy from outside interference, but they lacked the numbers to stand completely on their own. They cherished their sense of identity with Britain and, until the Zulu War of 1879, needed the British army to protect them from the Zulu, but they resented any British interference. Economically they were which most English-speakers must be said to have acquiesced, the ostensible aim was not one but several countries – a white South Africa and black 'homelands'. In the 1990s there was a spectacular change of direction and a new South Africa emerged in which all its peoples became equal citizens. English-speaking South Africans ceased to be partners in a white-dominated state and became a minority in a black-dominated one. The extent to which the new South Africa will be able to create a new sense of identity which will encompass all sections of its population, white as well as black, is as yet unclear.

Going to a Christmas picnic. Self-consciously British people in South Africa maintained British traditions.

tied to the Transvaal and as British influence weakened in the early twentieth century, the whites of Natal were well aware that they could not distance themselves too far from the rest of South Africa. Yet the predominantly English-speaking population very much disliked the prospect of domination by an Afrikaner majority in any united South Africa. In 1909 Natal entered the Union of South Africa after vain attempts to negotiate autonomy for individual provinces. Under the Union the whites of Natal protested against measures that weakened the British link with South Africa, such as replacing the Union Jack with a national flag in 1926-27 or proclaiming South Africa a republic in 1961. The Afrikaner-dominated Union governments did, however, formalize and enforce the segregation against Africans and Indians that Natal had practised for so long. In 1994, when Africans and Indians voted for the first time, Natal still expressed a sense of difference from the rest of South Africa: nearly half of the votes were cast for the Inkatha Freedom Party, a party based on a sense of Zulu identity.   [PJM]

P. J. Marshall

CHAPTER 10

The Diaspora of the Africans and the Asians

New societies were created in British colonies in the West Indies, in East Africa, in South East Asia, and on Pacific islands largely to meet the insatiable demand of British people for the produce of the tropics. At the end of the nineteenth century a British population of some 40 million people was consuming a yearly average for every man, woman, and child of about 85 pounds of sugar, 6 pounds of tea, and three-quarters of a pound of coffee. Other Europeans and North Americans, if not quite so addicted to sugar and tea as the British, also consumed these items in great quantities. This gigantic flow of produce from the tropics to Europe was made possible by huge movements of labour. People were moved from Africa, India, or China to sugar and coffee plantations on islands and coastal tracts from the Caribbean to the Pacific, or to the hills in India or Ceylon (Sri Lanka), which in the nineteenth century were cleared for more coffee and above all for the new tea gardens that replaced China as the world's main supplier. Others worked on rubber plantations in Malaya or in railway building in East Africa. Only a minority of those who emigrated great distances for work ever returned home. The rest put down roots in the countries to which they had been moved.

The legacy of Europe's appetite for tropical produce and of the success with which the British empire supplied this appetite has been a great mixing of peoples. Governments that succeeded the British have had to build nations out of very disparate elements: Africans and Indians in Guyana, Trinidad, or Mauritius; Indians added to Sinhalese in Sri Lanka or to the indigenous population in Fiji; Indians and Chinese added to Malays in Malaysia.

WAVES OF MIGRATION

Some of the great movements of labour within the British empire were directly organized by the British but, alongside officially sponsored migration, enormous numbers of Asian people made their own way to British colonies in search of work.

Africans

Until the abolition of the trade in 1807, the slave labour force in the British West Indies was renewed and expanded by a very vigorous British slave trade. From 1807 until 1833 the British plantations were still worked by slaves. In old-established colonies, like Jamaica or Barbados, where the black population at last began to maintain its numbers as the death rate fell, cutting off further recruitment of slaves did not seriously restrict the production of sugar and other crops. Sugar production could be extended to the island of Mauritius in the Indian Ocean, which the British captured together with a large slave population from the French in the Napoleonic

War. Other potentially valuable acquisitions from the war, however – Trinidad and British Guiana (Guyana) – could not be fully developed without new imports of slaves.

Slavery was abolished in 1833 and in 1838 the system of apprenticeship, by which ex-slaves were still compelled to work for their masters, also came to an end. Planters and British officials assumed, however, that the ending of slavery would make no real difference to the economy of the British sugar colonies. They believed that the former slaves would continue to work on the plantations – no longer under compulsion but to earn wages. On smaller islands in the West Indies, such as Antigua or Barbados, this is what happened. There was little if any spare land and virtually no alternative employment. Black people of necessity therefore continued to work for the planters, so long as sugar remained a viable crop economically. There was no need to recruit new labour from other sources and so the population of these islands has remained overwhelmingly of African origin.

Slave laws

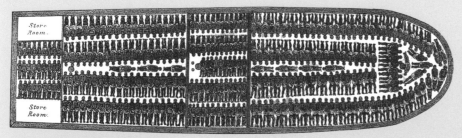

Plan of the main deck of a slave ship. Such plans were published by campaigners against the slave trade in the late eighteenth century to show the horrors of the 'middle passage'.

Slavery, the treatment of a person as property, was a status uniquely applied to blacks in the British world. It had no basis in English law, but was defined in a series of local laws made in individual British colonies – laws that the British Privy Council could have revoked at any time had it chosen to do so, but never did. Slaves were subject to virtually whatever discipline and punishments their masters chose to enforce. Local laws reinforced the masters' power and gave the slaves very little protection from them. In Barbados a master was liable to a fine of £15 for wilfully killing a slave: murder of a slave by a white was not a capital felony in Barbados until 1805. Colonial slave codes were all broadly similar. The main Barbados law, for instance, began:

> Whereas the plantations and estates of this island, cannot be fully managed and brought into use without the labour and service of great numbers of Negroes and other slaves; and forasmuch as the said Negroes and other slaves are of barbarous, wild and savage nature, and such as render them wholly unqualified to be governed by the laws, customs and practices of our nation.

It prescribed 'a moderate whipping' for absence from a plantation without leave. Runaways were to be taken 'alive or dead'. Those absent for more than thirty days were liable to the death penalty. A slave who 'offered violence to any Christian … shall be severely whipped, his nose slit or be burned on some part of his face with a hot iron'. Death was the punishment for serious offences, such as theft.

A branding iron. Slaves were branded with the marks of their owners.

Sugar and slaves

In the eighteenth century sugar and later tea were the two imported items that featured in almost every British person's diet, however poor that person might be. As well as sweetening tea and other drinks like coffee, sugar was extensively used in all sorts of cooking and in the making of punch. Nearly all the Caribbean colonies were dominated by the production of sugar, introduced into Barbados in the 1650s and spreading in succession throughout Britain's West Indian acquisitions. Sugar shaped colonial society. The white population became a limited garrison of owners, managers, overseers, and bookkeepers on the plantations, with small communities of professional people in the towns. Black slaves constituted the vast bulk of the population. Except in Barbados, whites rarely amounted to 10 per cent of the total population.

The plantation, a combination of farm and factory, was the unit of sugar production. The main farming operation was the cultivation of sugar cane, the field gangs of slaves being

Plantation buildings on Trinity estate, Jamaica, 1825. This plate from a series reflects both the desire of Jamaica planters to show themselves, like English country gentlemen, as the proud owners of rural estates, and the size and complexity of a sugar plantation. The mill for crushing the cane on the Trinity estate was powered by water brought from a considerable distance by an aqueduct.

In the larger colonies of Jamaica, British Guiana, Trinidad, and Mauritius, however, much land was available. If, as was often the case, planters tried to maintain tight control over their labour force and to keep wages at a low level, the ex-slaves could move away from the plantations to set up their own homesteads and villages on vacant land. There they could run their own lives and try to make a living as peasant farmers cultivating small plots. If they continued to work on the plantations, they did so on their own terms to earn extra money. Within a few years of the ending of slavery, planters in British Guiana and Trinidad were complaining that a labour force that they had never regarded as adequate had been depleted by up to a half and that the high wages they were paying to the rest were making their sugar uncompetitive. The Mauritius planters also immediately reacted to the end of slavery by looking for another source of labour.

employed on preparing the ground, planting the cane, keeping it clear of weeds, and cutting it at harvest time. The factory operations took place in the sugar mill – driven by oxen, or by wind or water power – where the cane was crushed, and in the boiling house, where the sugar was made from cane juice. A typical Jamaica plantation in the later eighteenth century might consist of about 600 acres, of which under half would be planted with cane, employing about 200 slaves, and worth £20,000 in contemporary values.

Conditions for slaves were particularly bleak in the Caribbean. In the late eighteenth century an average of up to 15 per cent of the slaves were likely to die on the voyage across the Atlantic. During the first three 'seasoning' years on the plantation about 20 per cent of newly landed slaves might die from the new diseases, diets, and ways of life. Slaves were, however, less vulnerable to the great waves of 'fevers' of African origin, malaria or yellow fever, which devastated the white population of the West Indies. Studies of plantation records suggest that slaves who had survived the seasoning might have a working life of up to twenty years. This would take people imported from Africa as young adults into their forties, before they would be considered too debilitated to work in the field gangs – planting, hoeing, and cutting cane. The records also reveal unmistakably that the slave population of the West Indies (as opposed to that of the North American colonies) had a very low rate of reproduction. On one Jamaican estate only 410 children were born alive between 1762 and 1831 to a slave population of 504 women. Undernourished and overworked women seem to have conceived few children, still births were very frequent, and the survival rate for young children was pitiably low. Primarily as a result of this low fertility, which lasted well into the nineteenth century on most West Indian islands, there was a constant shrinkage in the slave population, unless it was supplemented by new imports from Africa. The annual average 'wastage' of the slave population of Jamaica in the eighteenth century is usually estimated at 3 per cent.

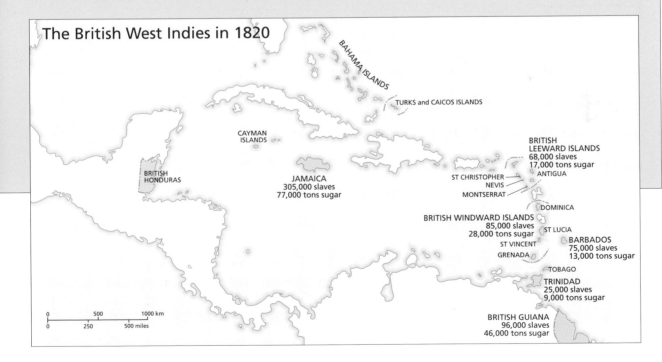

The British West Indies in 1820

The search for new supplies of labour began with Africa. A resumption of the British slave trade was inconceivable. Attempts were, however, made to persuade Africans to go voluntarily to the West Indies. The British African colony of Sierra Leone was the main recruiting ground. Slaves seized by the Royal Navy from foreign ships that were still slave trading were released there and efforts were made to persuade such people to enlist for the West Indies. The response was not enthusiastic. Over a period of twenty-five years some 36,000 'free' Africans embarked for the West Indies – a total that did little to solve labour shortages.

Indentured Indians

India with its vast population living under British rule seemed to be a much more promising source of labour than West Africa without the slave trade. From the 1830s until well into the twentieth century labour for overseas destinations could indeed be readily recruited in India. The pressure of people on available land and employment was already forcing sections of the Indian rural population to leave

Indentured labour – a new system of slavery?

To many contemporaries the indentured emigration of Indians to British sugar colonies from the 1830s looked suspiciously like the slave trade thinly disguised. A critic of the system believed that some recruits were duped into signing contracts that they did not understand. Once such a person had been ensnared, it was supposed that he became resigned to his fate, 'like an animal who has been caught in a trap and has given up the useless struggle to escape'. On the estates planters exercised rigorous control over their indentured labour. There were many complaints of excessive workloads for which inadequate pay was awarded and which were enforced by harsh punishments. Indian workers in Mauritius lamented their decision to emigrate:

> Having heard the name of the island of Mauritius
> We arrived here to find gold, to find gold.
> Instead we got beatings of bamboos,
> Which peeled the skin off the backs of the labourers.
> We became kolhu's [the sugar mill's] bullocks to extract
>   cane sugar.
> Alas! we left our country to become coolies.

To articulate Indian opinion, indentured labour was an abusive system and degrading to Indian people. With Gandhi very much to the fore, campaigns were directed against the system and in 1917 the British government of India responded to pressure and refused to sanction further emigration of indentured workers.

Indentured emigration was certainly a harsh system. Yet the Indian emigrant showed remarkable tenacity in the face of adversity. While there were no doubt many hapless victims of recruiting agents' wiles, others seem to have taken a deliberate decision to emigrate and to turn the opportunity to their advantage. In spite of the often poor conditions in which they lived and worked, mortality among the emigrants was lower than mortality in India itself. Workers were able to save money – either to send back to India or take with them when they returned. Emigrants leaving Trinidad in the late nineteenth century were taking with them sums of between £20 or £50 in contemporary values, considerable savings for a peasant family. Some of those who remained in the colonies were able to buy plots of land or to set up small businesses.

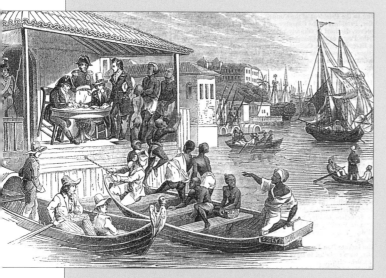

Indians arriving in Mauritius. Mauritius was the destination for the largest numbers of indentured Indians: some 450,000 of them went there between 1834 and the early twentieth century.

their villages in search of work, especially in heavily populated and generally impoverished parts of what is now eastern Uttar Pradesh in the Ganges valley of northern India or in the largely Tamil-speaking districts of south-eastern India. Life was normally hard in both these areas, but bad harvests or personal misfortune left many people with no alternative but to leave their communities. Few overseas emigrants were taken straight out of the villages; they had normally left home to look for work in towns or other parts of the countryside, where they could sometimes be induced to accept contracts to go even further afield. The recruits from northern India would eventually be shipped out of the port of Calcutta; the Tamils left from Madras.

The poor worker, or the 'coolie' as he was dismissively called, could not of course afford to pay his passage to the West Indies or Fiji. The planter, usually with a subsidy from the colonial or the British government, had to find the money. Planters and governments expected a return for their money. This was embodied in arrangements called indentures. An indenture was in theory a voluntary contract: the emigrant committed himself to work, usually for a period of five years, in return for a free passage. He was paid wages and government officials were supposed to ensure proper treatment in the way in which he was recruited, in his passage to the colonies, and in his employment there. After his contracted period of work had expired, he might remain in the colony or, after a certain period, apply for a free passage back to India.

Indentured emigration from India began to Mauritius in 1834. It was adopted in British Guiana in 1838 and in Trinidad and Jamaica in 1845. Indentured Indians arrived in Natal, South Africa, in 1861 (see pages 276–77). In 1879 the first Indians were shipped to Fiji. From 1896 indentured labour from India was taken to East Africa to build a railway. Indentured servants were also part of a much larger movement of Indian people to Malaya.

'Free' Indians

Indentures provided the framework within which people could make long and expensive journeys across the world. Many Indians, on the other hand, making their own arrangements for travelling, migrated over shorter distances – crossing the straits to Ceylon, the Bay of Bengal to Burma or Malaya, or the Arabian Sea to East Africa. They were 'free' emigrants in the sense that they travelled without officially recognized contractual obligations or government regulation. Some went as traders or to practise skills or professions, but many, like the indentured emigrants, went as labourers in the Ceylon tea gardens, the Burmese rice mills, or the Malayan rubber plantations. Many of these people had to pledge their future labour in return for the cost of the passage, but the contracts were usually for short periods. There was, in fact, much coming and going, many people spending quite short periods abroad: seasonal labour in Ceylon could, for instance, supplement what a family earned from its own land in India. Since the colonial authorities had

Thomas Stamford Raffles. Raffles was responsible in 1819 for the settlement of the island of Singapore, which quickly attracted many Chinese people to live under British rule and was to grow into the second great Chinese city of the British empire (Hong Kong being the first). Presciently, Raffles hoped that it would be come 'a great commercial emporium and a fulcrum whence we may extend our influence politically as circumstances may hereafter require'.

no official concern with these movements, statistics are scarce. Indications suggest, however, that the numbers were very large. Over a long period in the nineteenth and twentieth centuries, it has been estimated that over four million Indians may have gone to Malaya, of whom three million probably returned to India.

Chinese

Certain coastal regions of southern China had very old-established links with South East Asia, which far predated British interest in the area. When the British settled on the Malay coast from the end of the eighteenth century, they traded with Chinese merchants and attracted Chinese inhabitants to their enclaves. Chinese people soon became the largest part of the population of the new British settlement at Singapore, founded in 1819. From the mid-nineteenth century there was a great increase in the number of Chinese coming to Malaya and northern Borneo owing to the disruptions caused by civil war in southern China and the new opportunities offered by an increasingly assertive British presence in the region. Tin mining, for instance, was very much a Chinese enterprise. From 1901 to 1904, 653,077 Chinese immigrants passed into Malaya through Singapore. In 1880 Malays had constituted 80 per cent of the population; by 1911 the volume of largely Chinese but also of Indian immigration meant that the proportion of Malays had fallen to 51 per cent.

Chinese immigration was entirely a Chinese affair. New immigrants travelled on junks and later on steamers from the ports of southern China. Conditions were often appalling – in 1863 a junk arrived with only 120 of its 300 passengers still alive. Since the main demand in Malaya was for men to do manual labour, most of the immigrants were single males, who often stayed for relatively short periods before returning with their savings to China. In 1921 there were still twice as many Chinese males in Malaya as females.

The insatiable demand for labour of the Caribbean planters led to schemes for shipping Chinese to the West Indies under indenture contracts. Some 17,000 Chinese were enrolled in this way. For a brief period in the aftermath of the South African War, indentured Chinese also went to the Transvaal where labour was urgently needed to get the gold mines of the Rand back to full production. As the African labour force had been dispersed by war, 54,000 Chinese were recruited in northern China and served in the Transvaal from 1904 to 1907, when they were repatriated, after much criticism of the scheme.

MAKING PLURAL SOCIETIES

The need for labour for plantation agriculture, mining, or construction work had been met by drawing people out of Africa, India, or China and scattering them into British colonies across the world. Most of the British who were concerned with these movements of population seem to have taken an entirely short-term view of them. Urgent labour needs must be met from whatever might be the best source

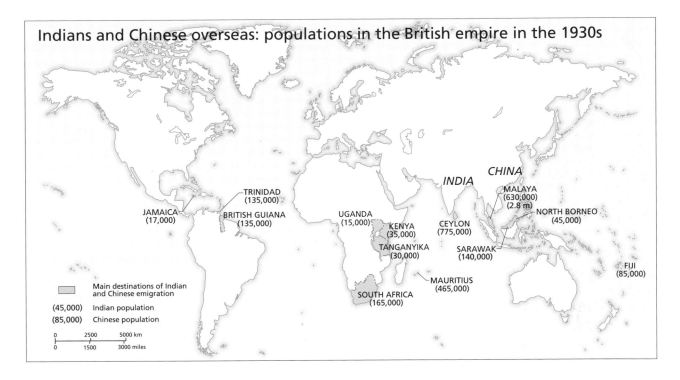

Indians and Chinese overseas: populations in the British empire in the 1930s

available. Long-term consequences need not be considered: the immigrants would do the job required of them and then would presumably go home. For the most part, this is not what happened. Slaves never went home. A majority of the indentured immigrants also remained in the colonies to which they had been carried. Although many of the 'free' Indian and Chinese immigrants were no more than temporary residents, many of these, too, sank permanent roots in their new abodes.

Waves of migration produced what are often called plural societies – that is, societies with sharp ethnic divisions and very little cohesion or sense of unity to transcend their divisions. In such a society the different elements of the population largely keep apart from one another and do not recognize a common identity.

The British empire created plural societies extending from Trinidad in the Caribbean to Fiji in the Pacific. In each case the pattern was roughly similar. At the top was a small white elite, usually British but predominantly of French origin in Mauritius and partly French in Trinidad. Below the whites and separate from them and from one another were layers of immigrant peoples – ex-slaves from Africa and indentured labourers or free migrants from Asia. In Mauritius and most Caribbean colonies indigenous populations had died out; in Ceylon, Malaya, East Africa, and Fiji indigenous peoples constituted another separate layer of society. In some cases the ethnic mix was very diverse indeed. British Guiana, for instance, was known as a land of six peoples: its original native Americans, the British, Portuguese brought in from Madeira, ex-slaves from Africa, Indians, and Chinese. Each of these groups kept itself apart from the rest.

With the ending of slavery, the British had turned to Indian and Chinese labour to develop the resources of tropical colonies. By the 1930s a hundred years of labour migration had produced substantial communities of Indians and Chinese permanently resident in many parts of the empire.

In British colonies with plural societies segregation was effectively practised, if not legally enforced. Whites kept very much to themselves. The other communities tended to live in separate villages or separate quarters of the towns, where the British treated them as distinct entities. In Fiji, for instance, Indians and Fijians had different systems of law and government. In Malaya separate government departments were responsible for the Indians and Chinese.

White elites

Small white elites retained their dominant position until well into the twentieth century. Plantations require a large investment of capital (see pages 131–32). This increasingly came not from individual planters but from companies, either based in Britain or operating from cities like Calcutta, Sydney, or Singapore. Planters or, more usually, the managers of plantations owned by a company were commanding figures. They were responsible for extensive tracts of land, a large labour force, and complex machinery for processing the crop, often in very remote situations. They had to be resourceful and had a reputation for also being somewhat tyrannical. One manager of a Malayan rubber plantation prided himself on being 'very much the king of his district'; 'because one was an Englishman one did not have any difficulty in exerting one's authority; it was accepted straightaway'.

British-owned tea gardens in Ceylon or rubber plantations in Malaya remained generally profitable until the end of empire, but the history of sugar – the crop that

Fiji: 'benevolent apartheid'

Fiji, a cluster of 320 islands in the South Pacific, is a prime example of a country whose ethnic diversity, leading to antagonism, grew out of British colonial rule.

In 1874, the year in which it became a British colony, Fiji had a population of perhaps some 150,000 Fiji islanders. There was also a group of about 1,500 Europeans who had recently settled there, largely to grow cotton. British annexation was intended, among other reasons, to bring the activities of these people under control.

From the beginning of their rule the British imposed on themselves a duty to protect Fijian society, as they understood it, from disruption. As late as 1959, the British administration restated the need to 'intervene to reinforce the moral and customary sanctions which in earlier times bound Fijians together in a communal fold'. Most of the land was to be guaranteed to Fijians and could not be sold to others. Under an extreme system of indirect rule, the chiefs were to exercise authority and administer Fijian law with as little interference as possible – no elected element was introduced into Fijian government until the 1960s.

In 1874 the danger to the stability of Fiji was thought to

come from the desire of the Europeans for land and labour with which to cultivate cotton and later sugar. To provide them with a labour force, Indian indentured servants were brought into Fiji in 1879. Fiji became a major sugar producer and 60,965 Indians in all were shipped there. They inevitably became a settled community, whose numbers grew to exceed those of the Fijians by the end of colonial rule. Under a system that has been called 'benevolent apartheid', the two communities lived largely apart from one another: the Indians in their villages under direct British rule; the Fijians in theirs under their chiefs.

Relations between the British and the Fijians were based on a genuine feeling of mutual esteem. Fijians converted to Christianity in large numbers; they provided very brave soldiers for the British army in the Second World War; and they took to rugby with enthusiasm. Touring British officials noted the frequency of pictures of the British royal family in Fijian huts.

Relations between Indians on one hand and the Fijians and the local Europeans on the other were, however, less cordial. Both Fijians and Europeans feared the Indians' increasing numbers, their economic enterprise, and their political shaped so many plural societies – was an increasingly difficult one. Most of the old West Indian plantation colonies of the age of slavery fell on hard times in the nineteenth century. British Guiana, Trinidad, and Mauritius, however, did relatively well until about the 1880s, and it still proved remunerative to open up new sugar plantations in places like Natal or Fiji. By the end of the nineteenth century sugar prices were falling sharply everywhere, as tropical cane sugar was challenged by a huge output of sugar beet in continental Europe.

White political power reflected white economic power. From the middle of the nineteenth century the British government was no longer willing to allow white minorities to exercise the kind of untrammelled power over the rest of the population that the West Indian planters had enjoyed through their assemblies (the local parliaments elected by whites) and London resumed its authority over all the colonies except for Barbados. Nevertheless, rule from London still left local whites with much influence. The other layers of society were only effectively able to claim political rights in the twentieth century.

African creoles

'Creole' is a term applied to people born in a colony, but who are not part of its original population. It can be applied to white settlers and to people of mixed race, but by far the largest part of the creole population of the British West Indies and Mauritius was African in origin, the descendants of slaves.

ambitions. With what has been described as a 'mixture of pride and self-pity', Fijians repeatedly asked the colonial administration for protection against the Indians. The Fijian Council of Chiefs resolved in 1933 that Indians 'should neither directly nor indirectly have any part in the control or direction of matters affecting the Fijian race'. They were assured that their lands would be sacrosanct and that in any move towards representative government, their interests would be guaranteed: there would be separate Fijian and Indian electorates. Independence was granted to Fiji in 1970 on this basis. The following exchange is reported to have taken place at the London conference to settle independence. The Indian Speaker of the Fijian Parliament told the British minister, Lord Shepherd: 'Surely Britain had kept the races apart for the last 90 years, and now it must take some responsibility to bring them together. It cannot just leave us to our own devices.' 'My dear chap,' Lord Shepherd replied, 'if I had to assume responsibility for the sins of my British forefathers for the past 300 years, I would hardly be sitting here as a minister of the Crown. Indeed, I would be in sackcloth and ashes doing penance in some monastery.'

Wairaka village, Fiji, 1910. Fijians are carrying the baggage of a visiting European woman.

Even before the abolition of the slave trade, a creole culture and identity had begun to emerge among slaves in the West Indies. It was a mixture of diverse African and European influences. Slaves had been taken from very different African societies extending over a huge area from Senegal to the Congo. The degree to which they were exposed to contact with Europeans varied from the domestic servants or craftsmen, who must have seen a great deal of them, to those who worked in the field gangs and lived apart from them. Most slaves probably spoke a creole language, which had a vocabulary that was largely English combined with African grammatical structures. Some words of African origin spread throughout the islands, such as 'buckra' from an Efik or southern Nigerian word meaning 'he who governs' – hence a white man. But in general the creole or *patois* varied from island to island: in Mauritius and in Trinidad and one or two other West Indian islands the vocabulary was largely French. Slaves expressed themselves independently of their masters through music and dance. African musical instruments and African dances were easily adapted to the Caribbean, but European influences were also absorbed. The Trinidad calypso is thought to have African origins with French and Spanish elements. Africa and Europe also came together in slave religion. Myalism, a set of beliefs derived from several African religions but also showing Christian influences, long outlived the ending of slavery in Jamaica. Sixteen Yoruba (Nigerian) deities have been identified with Christian saints in Trinidad.

Conscious efforts to instil British culture and values into black West Indians began in the last years of slavery. This was a task undertaken by Christian missionaries. In Jamaica, in particular, Baptists established a powerful influence among the slaves and were very actively engaged in helping the ex-slaves to set up village communities away from the plantations. Baptist villages were given appropriately British names, such as Birmingham, Victoria, or Wilberforce, and the missionaries tried to instil a Christian and very British order into them. Inhabitants were told that:

> It is essentially necessary that you keep your houses clean, have their walls, or plaster, washed with white lime water, twice or at least once a year ... have a neat white-pine or cedar table, with a few good chairs in your room, so that you and your family may be comfortably seated at meals; have a clean table-cloth, plates, knives and forks on your table, and accustom your children to come to meals with their hands and faces clean; always implore the blessing of God before you eat your food; maintain family prayers in your houses ...

Missionary schools spread after the abolition of slavery and by the end of the nineteenth century there were a few secondary schools and colleges in the towns.

A section of the creole population was deeply influenced by British values. People of mixed race, a particularly influential community in Jamaica, generally adhered to them. So did a small number of ex-slaves who were able to use education

Missionary village, St John's, Antigua, in the 1840s. Missionaries encouraged black people who had left the plantations after the abolition of slavery to settle in villages under their influence.

as a ladder for advancement. There were, however, few opportunities for such people. A predominantly agricultural economy, dominated by whites and generally in decline in the late nineteenth century, offered few rewards for the educated. Some did, however, become journalists, lawyers, or teachers. The outlook of such people was intensely British, an enduring feature of the West Indian middle class. E.R. Braithwaite, a West Indian working in Britain after the Second World War, wrote of his childhood in British Guiana in the 1930s:

> I had grown up British in every way. Myself, my parents and my parents' parents, none of us knew or could know any other pattern of living, of thinking, of being; we knew no other cultural pattern, and I had never heard any of my forebears complain about being British. As a boy I was taught to appreciate English literature, poetry, prose, classical and contemporary, and it was absolutely natural for me to identify with the British heroes of the adventure stories against the villains of the piece who were inevitably non-British and so to my boyish mind more easily capable of villainous conduct.

The mass of creole blacks were much less accessible to British influences. They had been freed from slavery, but they remained either as rural workers or as struggling smallholders. The missionaries complained that they were losing their hold over most of the people by the middle of the nineteenth century. Spoken English only slowly replaced creole in the West Indies, while a French-based creole remained the language of the majority of the population in Mauritius. Literacy made little progress.

Indian communities overseas

Everywhere that Indians went in the nineteenth century they tended to live separate lives in isolation from other communities. Emigrants maintained their sense of a Hindu or a Muslim identity with the utmost tenacity. Those who had gone to Ceylon or to South East Asia were able to keep in close contact with their homeland; those who had travelled great distances as indentured labourers tended to lose contact. Gradually, however, their sense of what it meant to be an Indian was adapted to their surroundings and they too became something of a creole community: caste divisions among Hindus were observed much less strictly; the extended family gave way to a nuclear one; western modes of dress were widely adopted; and local usages developed in the Hindi spoken in different colonies.

Chinese communities overseas

Most of the Chinese of British South East Asia not only lived in isolation from other communities but were sharply divided among themselves. They preserved the dialects and local allegiances of the coastal provinces of southern China from which they came. They formed themselves into 'pangs', or guilds, based on a common place of origin or occupation. In Malaya secret societies, such as the Triad of Heaven and Earth Society, were easily transplanted, their rivalry leading to much violence before effective British action was taken against them at the end of the nineteenth century. The British treated the Chinese in Malaya very much as a distinct community, leaving them largely to their own devices until 1877, when a separate government department was set up for them under an official called the Protector of Chinese.

Most Chinese in South East Asia evidently saw themselves as a transitory community whose members would eventually return to China. Chinese customs were strictly preserved and few learnt English. Some, called the Straits Chinese by the British, had, however, become permanently resident over a long period and in British settlements, above all in Singapore, a few Chinese associated closely with the British. Conspicuous among these was Hoo Ah Kay (nicknamed 'Whampoa') who lived in Singapore from 1830 to 1880 and was said to be 'almost as much an Englishman as he was a Chinaman'. Hoo Ah Kay spoke excellent English and sent his son to school in Britain; but he himself always wore Chinese dress and was outraged when his son cut off his pigtail and converted to Christianity. The rich Chinese of Singapore were munificent in their charity, especially in founding schools, and they lived in loyal harmony with their colonial rulers. They were, however, a tiny minority in a largely unassimilated population.

TOWARDS INDEPENDENCE

In the twentieth century the dominance of white interests was slowly eroded and the British government yielded to pressure from other communities for political representation. In the aftermath of the Second World War power was gradually transferred to the elected representatives of these communities, who became the rulers of independent nation states in the 1960s. The new governments had inherited states from British colonial rule, but whether they had inherited nations was much more doubtful.

Late colonial rule

The very diverse elements living under British rule in colonies with 'plural' societies had shown little inclination to coalesce into a whole in the nineteenth century. During the twentieth century the tendency to stress separate identity became, if anything, more marked. In imperial China the overseas Chinese, for instance, had officially been illegal emigrants, who had defied the Emperor's instructions by going abroad and thus had severed their links with their homeland. In Malaya many Chinese involved themselves closely with the reform movements in China under the Chinese Republic and from 1948 a section identified with Chinese Com-munism to the extent of taking up arms in rebellion against British rule. Indians throughout the empire tended to renew their contacts with India: religious observances, for example, became stricter and more 'orthodox'. Black people through-out the Caribbean participated in more self-confident assertions of a common Afro-American identity: in 'black power' movements, emanating from the United States, or in affirmations of African roots such as Rastafarianism – a movement originating in Jamaica, which rejects what is seen as white or Christian domination and looks forward to an eventual return to Africa. Heightened self-awareness among the immigrant communities was matched by similar movements among indigenous peoples: Sinhalese in Ceylon, Malays, Fijians, and Africans in the colonies of Kenya, Uganda, and Tanganyika (Tanzania).

Under colonial rule all the communities of a plural society were subject to a colonial power that none could control. When the colonial rulers divested themselves of their authority, the communities inevitably competed for shares of it. Such competition could lead to rivalry and even to violence.

The transfer of power in Ceylon set a pattern that was frequently to be repeated. Many Sinhalese had been unwilling to accept that the Indian workers on the tea gardens were citizens of Ceylon. Immediately after attaining independence in 1948, the new government introduced a bill to deprive all but long-term

Marcus Garvey. Garvey, a Jamaican, campaigned for the union of all peoples of African origin. He founded the Universal Negro Improvement Association in 1914 and took it to the United States. He declared himself to be the Provisional President of Africa and dabbled in plans to resettle black people from the Americas in Africa.

Indian residents of citizenship and therefore of the vote. Relations between the Sinhalese and Indian or Tamil communities in Sri Lanka, as Ceylon has been called since 1972, subsequently deteriorated to the point where a Tamil separatist movement using violence erupted in the 1970s.

Malaya attained independence in 1957. In 1963 a union of Malaya, Singapore, and the British Borneo territories of Sarawak and North Borneo was created. The new Malaysia was a multi-ethnic country containing Malays, Chinese, Indians, and Borneo peoples, such as the Ibans or Dyaks. Within two years the predominantly Chinese city of Singapore seceded and became an independent state. Within the rest of Malaysia tension continued between Chinese and Malays, who insisted on their special status in the new nation: its national language and main medium of education were to be Malay and policies were initiated to give Malays a greater stake in the national economy, and therefore by implication to reduce that enjoyed by the Chinese.

In Fiji the indigenous population was also accorded a special position in relation to the immigrant Indian community: Fijians were guaranteed their share of the islands' land, which amounted to 83 per cent of it, and the provisions of the independence constitution of 1970 made it extremely difficult for the slightly more numerous Indian community to win political power away from the Fijians. Nevertheless, a perceived threat to Fijian dominance in 1987 was countered by a military coup by Colonel Rebouka of the Fijian army and the introduction of a new constitution even more weighted in favour of Fijians.

In what became Kenya Indians and British settlers arrived more or less simultaneously in the early twentieth century and competed for supremacy. Serious consideration was given to making British East Africa virtually an Indian colony of settlement, administered from India. But British settlers eventually prevailed – Indians were excluded from holding land and whites were given the bulk of political representation.

Kenya was not, however, to develop into the 'white man's country' that the settlers envisaged. In 1923 the British government proclaimed that African interests would be paramount in Kenya, as they were in the other colonies of East Africa – Uganda and Tanganyika – in which Indians had also taken up residence. In the long run Indians would have to concern themselves not with the privileges of white settlers but with the policies of the African politicians who had taken their countries into independence in the 1960s. In 1972 disaster struck the Indians of Uganda when the military dictator, Idi Amin, ordered the expulsion of what was by then largely a community of professional and business people, shopkeepers, and skilled workers.

New nations

Whatever immigrant communities may have thought of British rule, independence for Ceylon, Malaya, Fiji, and the East African colonies took them out of the frying pan of white dominance into the fire of the resentment felt against them by indigenous peoples. In Mauritius and most of the ex-colonies in the Caribbean, however, the lack of indigenous populations meant that the immigrant peoples were free to try to create new nations among themselves.

In most Caribbean islands the population was relatively homogeneous, being overwhelmingly of African origin. Common West Indian feeling did not, however, extend much further than a single university and a single cricket team. It is some indication of the extent of popular identification with particular islands, rather than with the West Indies as a whole, that attempts to launch a West Indian Federation aroused little enthusiasm and were abandoned in 1962. In Mauritius people descended from Indian immigrants comprised about 67 per cent of the population at independence in 1968. Although there was tension between Indians and creoles of African origin, the claims of the strong Indian-dominated Mauritius Labour party to govern the new nation could not be thwarted. In British Guiana and Trinidad Indians and creoles were much more evenly balanced. Politically, however, creoles prevailed in both territories at independence. In the new Guyana relations between the communities were particularly embittered.

To build and sustain a nation whose people are sharply divided along ethnic lines is a difficult task in any circumstances. The task that the British handed down to some of their successors was daunting in the extreme. The British encouraged emigrants to move from one continent to another in order to cultivate crops whose economic viability, as in the case of sugar, had often disappeared long before the end of colonial rule. In ruling such colonies the British were most unlikely to have followed Machiavellian strategies of deliberately fomenting divisions, but they saw no need to encourage integration. Communities were treated as separate entities. For long it was assumed that the Indians and the Chinese were no more than temporary sojourners. For high-minded reasons the British often saw it as their duty to protect what they regarded as vulnerable indigenous communities, such as the Fijians, the Malays, or the Dyaks, from being displaced by the Indians and Chinese, and accordingly gave them special privileges.

The English language and British education did something to bring together elites from the very diverse colonial populations, but the masses remained largely untouched by such things. When they were drawn into politics, they naturally identified with the aims and culture of their own communities and saw other communities not as fellow citizens, but as rivals for the very limited range of jobs or other opportunities that poor ex-colonial economies could afford. In times of tension, rivals easily turned into enemies.

Yet if the hands dealt by the British to the peoples of the colonies dominated in the past by sugar, tea, coffee, or rubber have not been easy ones to play, new nations have nonetheless been built. Inter-community violence has been only part of the story; people brought together by the British have also learnt to live together and to accept common loyalties.

CHAPTER 11

John M. MacKenzie

Art and the Empire

Many peoples use art as a way of coming to terms with their environment, with religious or political ideas, and with social relations. This is particularly true of imperial systems. Members of the dominant group invariably use art as a device to explain and justify their power, to express the mystique of rulers, and to illustrate their knowledge and command of the natural world. Those who find themselves incorporated into empires often pass through phases of adapting their art to that of their political masters, rediscovering the wellsprings of their own art – sometimes as a conscious act of resistance, and, finally, reflecting through their art a new national consciousness.

The history of art in the British empire illustrates all of these developments. The British visual arts were unquestionably stimulated by imperial rule: the experience of warfare and of economic and political power, and the encompassing of almost the entire world and its peoples within a new global order led to a remarkably innovative drive in artistic technique, taste, and sensibility. Europeans who established themselves as permanent settlers in British North America, Australasia, and South Africa embarked upon a search for distinctive artistic expression appropriate to their sense of national identity in the twentieth century.

Empire may have stimulated British art, but it disrupted the artistic life of the societies conquered by the British. For most of the nineteenth century, the British showed little appreciation of or interest in any art that seemed to differ widely from their own or other European traditions. Indigenous artists could not therefore expect much support or encouragement from their new rulers. At best, what they produced might be collected and displayed as a tool of anthropology rather than for any aesthetic merit. Yet indigenous art survived, whatever Europeans might think of it, as a sort of underground river which was to break surface in the twentieth century. Then so-called 'ethnic' art began to attract the serious attention of European artists and to influence their work. At the same time artists in Asia, Africa, and the Pacific, as well as drawing on their own artistic traditions, were taking an increasing interest in European forms and techniques and allowing their work to be influenced by them. Thus, within the framework of empire the once rigid divide between western and 'ethnic' art began to break down.

ART AND IMPERIAL EXPANSION

From the sixteenth century, art was the handmaiden of the exploration of the wider world in the dynamic expansion of Europe. We know, for example, that artists were appointed to Sir Humphrey Gilbert's expedition to Newfoundland in 1583 and Sir Walter Raleigh's to Virginia in 1585. The greatest flourishing of the arts of exploration, however, came with the remarkable series of voyages undertaken by Captain Cook in the late eighteenth century. There were artists and draughtsmen

Kangaroo. This sketch was done by Sydney Parkinson, an artist on Captain Cook's first voyage, at one of the expedition's landings on the eastern coast of Australia in 1770. It is one of a huge series of studies which recorded species of animals, birds, fishes, and insects unknown to Europeans before the Pacific voyages. Kangaroos puzzled Cook's crew: 'What to liken him to I could not tell', wrote Sir Joseph Banks.

on all three of Cook's voyages – across the Pacific (1768-71), to the southern Pacific and the Antarctic (1772–75), and to the northern Pacific and the Arctic (1776–79) – and they produced several thousand drawings and paintings (both oils and watercolours), most of which still exist. Of those that were lost, some survive through contemporary engravings. Constant reproduction of the art of the expeditions, together with imaginative reconstructions by later artists, made these voyages the great epic of exploration for many generations. Cook's voyages set a pattern for artists to travel with expeditions and to record their findings – a pattern that was to last until the photographer replaced the artist late in the nineteenth century.

This extraordinary outburst of artistic endeavour can be explained by the fact that the voyages were an inseparable part of the scientific revolution of the eighteenth century. Both the Royal Society and the Admiralty collaborated to ensure that research in a whole range of subjects was pressed forward by Cook's explorations. The distinguished scientist Sir Joseph Banks, who was present on the first voyage, regarded drawings as more valuable than words in recording and classifying natural history specimens and other peoples, as well as environmental, astronomical, and meterological phenomena. The role of the artists and draughtsmen, therefore, was to record the botany, zoology, and ethnography of the regions visited. They also provided aids to navigation by drawing coastal profiles and they contributed to cartography and to the study of planetary and weather patterns.

But good artists are generally free agents. Employed to keep an empirical record of all that was seen and discovered, they could not suppress their imaginative and technical faculties. The three principal artists on the voyages – Sydney Parkinson, William Hodges, and John Webber – all far exceeded their briefs. Together with their draughtsmen, they produced more than enough empirical work to satisfy their masters, but they also responded to the excitements of different climates, environments, and peoples to create some remarkable landscapes, portraits, and depictions of events during these great voyages.

Hodges was perhaps the finest of them. He turned what had long been the duty of the seamen in unknown waters – that is, to draw profiles of coasts indicating landmarks with bearings and distances – into a striking art form. He almost certainly painted his major pictures not from sketches, as had previously been the practice, but from direct observation – from the stern windows of Cook's great cabin or ashore in the Pacific. In these remarkable pictures he succeeded in capturing the extraordinary meteorological and light effects of the Antarctic and he experimented with ways of reproducing the nature and intensity of tropical light. In the succeeding voyage, Hodges and Webber produced some sympathetic depictions of the indigenous peoples and animals of the Pacific. Sometimes birds, mammals, or humans were painted as 'specimens' rather than as specific examples, but at other times their subjects were highly individualized, full of character and personality.

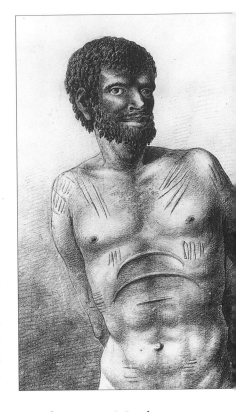

Man of Van Diemen's Land. This drawing was made by John Webber, artist on Captain Cook's third voyage, during a brief stop on the coast of Tasmania in January 1777. Cook recorded that the Aborigines were 'quite naked and wore no ornaments except the large punctures or ridges raised on their skin'. The tendency in portrayals of Pacific peoples by Cook's artists was to present them in what was thought to be a sympathetic light, sometimes as noble savages approximating to classical ideals.

The *Resolution* in the Antarctic by William Hodges. In December 1773 and January 1774 Cook sailed close to the Antarctic ice cap, enabling Hodges to record meteorological and light effects never before depicted by Europeans. In this picture he recorded an iceberg and the glow in the background known as 'ice blink'.

Much of the art of the Cook expedition conveys the delight with which artists tried to depict what was startlingly new to them and tried to interpret the peoples of the Pacific in what Europeans thought of as a sympathetic manner. The work of the artists was, however, an integral part of the extension of European power into the area in ways that were to have very serious consequences for its peoples. Coastal profiles and cartography made it easier for Europeans to return, to settle, and to impose their authority. Even Cook's relatively brief encounters with the coasts of New Zealand, Australia, and the Pacific islands initiated their peoples into market relations and began the spread of European artefacts and even animals. Moreover, the drawings and paintings of the expeditions do not depict their darker side – moments of violence and the spread of sexually transmitted diseases.

Yet the achievements of these artists were outstanding: not only did they make significant contributions to the vast range of scientific materials that emerged from the Cook voyages; they also explored new subjects and fresh techniques in painting, and in so doing influenced major changes in taste that helped to break with the dominant eighteenth-century conventions - the decorative style known as rococo or the strict adherence to Greek and Roman ideals of neoclassicism. As well as occasionally working in oils, they extended the range of watercolours, demonstrating the great value of this relatively recent medium in offering the opportunity for swift and vivid illustration of unfamiliar scenes. They also helped to create a new school of imperial history painting, particularly when they worked up events (such as Webber's painting of the death of Captain Cook in Hawaii) into oils on their return. Following the pattern set by the Cook voyages, artists continued to serve expeditions until well into the nineteenth century. David Livingstone's journeys through Africa were seen as a triumph of exploration to

Tipoo – the British Hannibal

Tipu Sultan, known to the British as 'Tipoo', ruler of Mysore, became a popular legend and an almost demonic figure as the opponent of British expansion in India – the struggles of Britain against such a foe were considered a very appropriate theme for history painters. The state of Mysore was involved in four hard–fought wars against the British. By the 1780s Tipoo came to be regarded as an implacable and cruel foe, at whose hands British prisoners had suffered grievously. To many, he was the modern Hannibal opposing the new Rome. In 1792 the British celebrated the magnanimity with which they believed he had been treated after defeat; in 1799 they celebrated his destruction. Tipoo and the Mysore Wars were frequently protrayed on the London stage. As late as 1833 an Indian visitor to Britain found that children ran after him shouting 'Tipoo! Tipoo!'. [JMM/PJM]

'General Sir David Baird discovering the body of the Sultaun Tippoo Saib'. This vast canvas was completed in 1838, forty years after the event in 1799 it commemorates. Baird finds Tipu's body in a dark corner, close to the grille of the the prison in which Baird himself had been incarcerated by Tipu some years before.

match Cook's voyages. For the first part of the Zambezi expedition of 1858–63, Livingstone too took an artist with him – Thomas Baines, who painted the landscapes and peoples of central Africa.

HISTORY PAINTINGS AND THE MYTHOLOGY OF EMPIRE

In the eighteenth century there was a strict hierarchy of seniority or respectability in painting. At the head was 'history' painting which was concerned with the portrayal of classical events or scenes from mythology and the Bible. It had been extended to cover Celtic images and moments from the remote British past, but later in the century imperial events were to transform history painting into a field that could concern itself with contemporary times.

Painters began to discover in moments of high imperial drama scenes that could be recreated, embellished, and heightened in a myth-making form. The geographical remoteness of the empire provided an acceptable alternative to the chronological remoteness of the old themes of history painting and the exotic surroundings – the landscapes, buildings, and animals – offered stimulating contexts. Above all, the larger-than-life events could readily be incorporated into heroic myth.

'The remnants of an Army' by Lady Butler. This picture depicts the return to the British-held fortress of Jalalabad in 1842 of Dr Bryden, sole survivor of the army that had occupied Kabul, the capital of Afghanistan. Painted in 1879, a year of serious losses in another Afghan war and in the Zulu War, this picture was clearly designed as a warning against the sacrifices of heroic endeavour inadequately planned and supported.

Occasionally artists were present at the events they painted, but generally they were not. The paintings were mostly based on a combination of published or oral accounts and the re-imagining of events in epic terms. Except in the case of peripheral detail, artists were seldom accused of inaccuracy because spectators, including those who had been present at the events, were happy to be conspirators in the poetic truth of the heroic moment.

The first such moment to receive this treatment was the death of General Wolfe on the Heights of Abraham in 1759, the symbolic sacrifice for the British capture of Quebec. The treatment by the American artist Benjamin West (who later became President of the British Royal Academy) hit the artistic headlines when displayed at the Academy in 1771. West was much criticized for putting actors in a history painting into modern dress, but nonetheless the form took hold of the artistic and public imagination. Subsequent history painters were able to create a more distancing effect by placing some of the figures – Indians, Africans, or other non-European people – into exotic dress.

The conventions of the imperial history painting had been swiftly established. The paintings portrayed symbolic moments in the imperial endeavour, most of which could be endowed with powerful moral overtones: the sacrificial heroic death, the magnanimous gesture, or the key turning point that indicated a supposedly more civilized future. They focused imperial endeavour on the heroic individual, creating highly personalized myths that continued to resonate with the public throughout much of the imperial period. These subjects were taken up again and again, both by a succession of artists and by engravers and illustrators of children's and popular works. In the late nineteenth century history paintings became models for tableaux vivants, in which live people re-enacted, in frozen dumb-show, these striking moments. Thus some of them reached iconic status, providing images that many members of the British public could call to mind and help them to justify imperial rule.

This tradition of history painting, with further subjects derived from naval battles and events such as the death of Nelson in the Napoleonic Wars and the Indian Rebellion of 1857, carried on throughout the nineteenth century. By the late nineteenth century, paintings of imperial campaigns had become almost commonplace, partly stimulated by the appointment of war artists and correspondents. Battle paintings ceased to be true history paintings. Henceforth they purported to be factual representations of actual events rather than embodiments of high moral sentiments.

Many of the images produced by the imperial artists of the nineteenth century reached a wider public through engravings in the illustrated journals. The *Illustrated London News*, founded in 1842, *The Graphic* (1869), and other illustrated newspapers contained large numbers of imperial images. In key years like 1879 – a year of war in South Africa and Afghanistan – the *Illustrated London News* seemed to contain little else. As well as the warfare and disasters of empire, significant events, such as the visit of the Prince of Wales to India in 1875–76, were commemorated in special editions. The iconography of contemporary history had by this time become a demotic art form.

'The Death of General Gordon, Khartoum, 26 January 1885' by G.W. Joy. The artist presents a wholly mythic representation of the event; Gordon was almost certainly cut down in much less heroic circumstances. Here the followers of the Mahdi are frozen in awe before hurling their spears at the man who became the subject of the last and greatest heroic myth of empire.

BRITISH PAINTING IN INDIA

The elite that dominated British India was an opulent one with sophisticated tastes. It provided patronage for professional British painters on a scale that no other colonial community could match and included its own amateur artists of considerable ability. The pictorial record of British India from British sources is thus a very rich one. All these professional and amateur artists interpreted what they saw in terms of their own culture, their individual feelings, and their understanding of the relationship between their own society and the one in which they lived. In doing so, they helped British people at home to envisage the imperial order in India and in representing the Indian world in their own terms they expressed their sense that they understood that world, felt at home in it, and could dominate it.

Portraiture

In the second half of the eighteenth century a remarkable group of portrait painters moved to India. These painters looked for patronage among the European community in the major cities. To make a living, they painted portraits of East India Company officials, from the Governor-General downwards, or moved to Indian courts to paint princes, their relatives, and palace officials. But they also painted pictures for their own pleasure – of Indians, Indian landscapes, and exotic curiosities.

There are a number of reasons why these portraitists did well in India. The British were increasingly aware of being involved in grand designs – commercial, military, and political – in the subcontinent. Public buildings, if they were to

The Palmer family by Francesco Renaldi, Calcutta, 1786. A British officer, Major William Palmer, was painted with the two Muslim ladies with whom he lived and with his three young children by his 'senior wife', who sits on his right. The celebration of such relationships in paint would have been entirely unacceptable to later generations in British India.

emulate the style of those at home, required paintings: the dignity of law courts, for example, would be enhanced by portraits of judges and chief justices. Many officials and officers sought to commemorate their period in India. Others wished to give presents to friends or family. Societies commissioned paintings of leading patrons and portraits of the leading grandees were painted to be presented to the royal court, leading aristocrats, or major institutions at home.

The courts of the Indian princes were lucrative sources of work for similar reasons. There was a genuine fascination with the novelty of western art – its realism, perspective, and handling of colour – but, like the British, the indigenous rulers sought to enhance their style and importance through grand images. Moreover, a convention of present-giving developed whereby the Governor-General and other leading officials like the British Resident presented portraits of themselves and often received images of the Prince in return.

Such portraiture was not merely an extension of European styles and conventions into a new environment. The subjects of paintings were, it is true, often placed in stylized architectural settings – against classical columns, a grand balcony, or hanging drapes – which could equally have worked in Europe. But others appeared against identifiable Indian scenes, featuring indigenous vegetation, backgrounds symbolizing the profession of the sitter (for example, a sepoy camp behind a British officer), or local buildings, both European and Indian. Even more interestingly, British subjects were sometimes painted with their Indian servants or with the 'bibis' (the concubines many men acquired in India) and their children. These portraits gave the artists further opportunities to dwell upon the beauty of carpets, clothing, jewellery, hookahs and other examples of Indian crafts, garden pavilions, and the like. By these means, the Indian portraits, like landscapes painted in the colonies, extended the range and taste of eighteenth-century art.

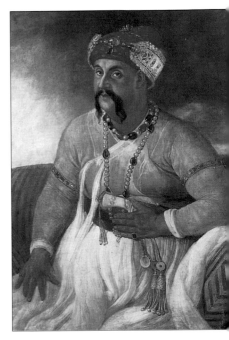

Above: Shuja-ud-daula by Tilly Kettle, 1772. Shuja-ud-daula was the Wazir of Oudh in northern India. In the court of the wazirs eastern and western cultural tastes mixed: Indians were painted by British artists, while British connoisseurs made collections of Indian miniatures and manuscripts.

Left: Aurangzeb's mosque at Benares by Robert Smith, c.1830. All parts of the empire, especially India, became the setting for the work of amateur artists. For some, sketching and painting were simply a recreation. Others had a more direct professional interest. Army oficers had to study the lie of the land, often making maps and sketches. Revenue officers, surveyors, and engineers also had to record land, people, and projects. Colonel Robert Smith was the finest artist among the Indian engineers.

Indian portraits also acquired political significance. The paintings of Warren Hastings, Governor-General from 1774 to 1785, were generally informal or, when he was painted with his family, were in the style of the English country parkland group portrait. Later in the century, however, portraitists were very much aware of painting a magnificent British court, almost seeking to match its Indian counterparts. Lord Mornington, later the Marquess Wellesley, was convinced that India could only be ruled from a great palace and in the grandest style. The many portraits he commissioned sought to convey this sense of a British court transplanted to the east and Wellesley was depicted in quasi-monarchical stance, magnificently robed and adorned. Later in the century the regal style became the standard for all the portraits of viceroys, now often accompanied by their vicereines, splendidly attired and bejewelled.

From the 1840s painted portraits began to be replaced by photographs. Paintings were now restricted to the most senior of the British rulers in India and their function was almost exclusively a ceremonial and political one.

Indian landscapes

India extended the range of British landscape as well as of British portraiture. While some portraitists also painted landscapes, other painters arrived with the intention of specializing in that field. These landscape painters generally painted not only scenery, but also Indian architecture, palaces, forts, temples, and village scenes. In such paintings human figures often become incidental – providers of scale, indicators of the exotic, but not individually realized personalities.

At the end of the eighteenth century Indian landscapes were painted according to the conventions of European landscape art, especially those of the 'picturesque'. Picturesque art placed its emphasis not on realistic representation, but on the creation of an arranged landscape that fulfilled certain expectations. Thus a variety of elements, often derived from on-the-spot sketching, would be brought together in a satisfying composition that met both a somewhat restrained sense of what was judged to be sublime and also the painter's idea of what India should look like. Picturesque conventions were to be remarkably durable in representations of India, lasting until the final quarter of the nineteenth century. India as depicted by the artists of the picturesque had some of what Europeans would have regarded as its exotic elements taken out of it. Indian architecture, for instance, was either shown in conventionally picturesque ruins or had its (to European eyes) startling lack of symmetry reduced to symmetrical forms. Nevertheless, these painters were enthralled by Indian vegetation, by the details of buildings and their sculpture, as well as by aspects of Indian ceremony. Through the publication of their works as engravings in major books of illustrations, they made available to a wider public some understanding of the appearance of India and above all of its architectural inheritance. They were the forerunners of the major nineteenth-century projects for discovering, drawing, and photographing the Indian architectural and

India 'is as clearly reflected as the moon in a lake'

British conceptions of a picturesque India owed much to the work of Thomas Daniell and his nephew who went to India in 1786. After seven years of journeyings, often far beyond the area under direct British rule, they brought back some 1,400 drawings of buildings or landscapes. Between 1795 and 1808 the Daniells brought out six sumptuous volumes of aquatints, a process of making engravings that reproduced the qualities of watercolours. Their aquatints were much admired. To the great painter J.M.W. Turner, through them 'The East is as clearly reflected as the moon in a lake.'   [PJM]

'Coaduwar Ghat' by Thomas Daniell.

sculptural traditions which helped to uncover the sequence and history of the more distant Indian past. The convention of the picturesque finally lost its hold on British representations of Indian scenes late in the nineteenth century, when it was replaced by what purported to be a more realistic style, often stressing what seemed to be an exotic India.

THE ART OF THE SETTLER COMMUNITIES

The colonies that came to be known as the Dominions produced artistic traditions with intriguing parallels, despite their physical remoteness from one another. The artists of each of these territories ultimately strove for a distinctive national visual language; before they could achieve this, however, they had to pass through phases of imitation and experimentation.

'Under southern sun', by Charles Conder, 1890. This painting is characteristic of the way in which the unique features of the Australian landscape – the light and the vegetation – were rendered in a manner based on impressionism by members of the Heidelberg school.

In the initial stages of settlement painting usually imitated – and sometimes extended – British models. The exotic was often viewed as repellent, so colonial scenery was rendered in a more familiar, almost English, form. Each colonial 'school' (New Zealand is perhaps an exception) started with gentler landscapes – the Maritimes or the shores of the St Lawrence in Canada, the coastal regions of south-eastern Australia, the long-settled agricultural lands of the Cape. Later, a combination of exploration and economic change produced efforts to portray strikingly different and dramatic landscapes. In Canada, it was the rendering of snow, of vast landscapes, higher mountains, and raging torrents – all of a power scarcely known in Europe. Artists in Australia, New Zealand, and South Africa could find no European parallels at all. They had to find their own means of representing the strength of light and the effects of luminosity of the southern hemisphere, the strikingly different geologies, and the unique flora and fauna. In Australia, the eucalyptus presented a specific artistic problem, as did the contrasting colours of downs, desert, and rocks. For New Zealand artists, the challenge lay in the striking geomorphology of its mountain landscape. South Africa offered problems of harsh light effects, brilliant colours – particularly in geology, in the seasonal flora of the Cape interior, and in the apparent vast monotony of the interior veld.

While artists were struggling to record the characteristics of the lands in which they lived, they also tried to portray the distinctive patterns of social life in each of the colonies and to depict their indigenous peoples. Here artistic conventions passed from crude anthropology to a tendency to romanticize and finally to a greater realism. It is perhaps not surprising that until the mid-twentieth century, such colonial art concentrated on landscapes and ethnographic subjects. In the search for the unique national form, painters were less likely to adopt urban or industrial subjects which were more difficult to distinguish from their European prototypes. Even though the white populations of all of these territories rapidly became highly urbanized, the physical image presented to the outside world was of vast open spaces, overwhelmingly different terrains, striking indigenous peoples, and farming or ranching on a scale unknown in Europe. Social realism, the recognition of the urban, industrial, economic, and social realities of these territories, an art with a grittier political content: all this had to wait until after the Second World War.

Colonial art was often highly conservative, only interacting with European movements after a considerable time-lag and at one remove. Until the 1880s British movements were most influential (although both Canada and South Africa inevitably drew some inspiration from France and the Netherlands). For the next thirty years French influence was supreme and young artists headed for Paris to study. By then artists were trying to concentrate the essence of the colonial landscapes in colour and symbolic form. Impressionism and post-impressionism and Japanese techniques found their Canadian, Australasian, and South African

adherents, who all adapted these movements to local conditions. As these modernist movements developed, wider European fashions took hold, while since the Second World War American styles have produced echoes around the world. During the twentieth century artists in the Dominions also began to draw on the traditions and motifs of the indigenous peoples of their countries in their attempts to engender a unique local art.

Portraying Canada

The longest settler experience of art was in Canada where the French tradition went back to the seventeenth century. At the end of the eighteenth century British army topographers and watercolourists were working in Canada as in every other part of the empire. At this stage their work was imitative of British conventions rather than distinctive. By the late nineteenth century many Canadian patrons were looking for powerful and 'typical' landscapes which somehow conveyed the grandeur of the imperial and settler enterprise. In Canada, these were supplied by, among others, the artists who were associated with the Canadian Pacific railway. Sir William Van Horne, the company's chief executive, was himself a major patron of Canadian art, but he also recognized the value of such painting for advertising purposes. Canadian art was also heavily influenced by Europe at the end of the nineteenth century: in 1893 no fewer than twenty-five Canadian artists were studying in Paris.

A scene in the interior of the Cape Colony by Thomas Baines. Baines came to the Cape in 1842 and travelled extensively throughout southern Africa recording a great variety of people and landscapes. As a war artist, he depicted the dramatic mountain scenery of the eastern Cape (see page 31).

Above: 'Aboriginal head –
Charlie Turner' by Tom
Roberts, 1890 (The Art Gallery
of New South Wales). Roberts
included Aborigines in his
depictions of scenes and
people whom he regarded as
most characteristic of
Australia.

The Canadian painters were influenced by the Barbizon movement, stressing ordinary agricultural activities, and by impressionism. But the emergence of a genuinely national Canadian school had to wait until 1913 when the celebrated 'Group of Seven' came together in Ontario. Amidst some controversy and conservative criticism, they achieved their first exhibition in 1920 and were well represented at the Wembley British Empire Exhibition of 1924. This group, sometimes known as the 'Algonquin school' because of their devotion to painting the landscapes of the great Canadian shield, maintained the landscape tradition, in a country now heavily urbanized, but brought to it influences derived not only from aspects of impressionism, but also from Japanese art. Trees were rendered in spare and symbolic ways; features of the terrain were reduced to their essence.

Portraying Australia

From the 1790s, convict and free artists depicted Australia as a land Europeans could find perfectly sympathetic. Lachlan Macquarie, the influential Governor of New South Wales from 1810 to 1821, encouraged the building of Georgian architecture and the artists painted the grander houses in their almost English parkland. Here was a tamed and elegant landscape on the fringes of a vast, unfamiliar, and remote continent.

The discovery of gold in Australia in the mid-nineteenth century galvanized the economic life and rate of settlement of Europeans and quickly introduced artists to new interior landscapes, to fresh social contexts, and to characteristic colonial types – the Diggers and other inhabitants of the gold-rush townships. Aborigines attracted relatively little interest from European painters – they were sometimes included as decorative figures in landscapes. However, in the late nineteenth century, when it was commonly supposed that Aborigines were a dying race, portrait studies of individuals were seen as 'historical documents' of a people who were disappearing for ever.

Ironically, Australian art only aspired to be truly Australian once it was influenced by artists who had been trained abroad. In the late 1880s and 1890s a group of artists established the Heidelberg school on the outskirts of Melbourne. They introduced impressionist principles, attempting to portray the higher, brighter tones of the powerful light of Australia and to render the design and colouring of the eucalyptus tree; they also emphasized the dignity of the lives of ordinary people (see 'Shearing the rams', page 127). With their art, an Australian national school and a recognizably appropriate and distinctive landscape style had come of age.

Australian art found more successful national vehicles when it set out to blend the starkly opalescent hues of its environment with the rediscovery of the art of its indigenous peoples. A new school of Australian painters, of whom Sir Sidney Nolan is the best known, set about juxtaposing symbols of European material life with antipodean landscapes and indigenous motifs, mostly conveyed in the shrill colours of the Australian interior. Some of these painters have also attempted to present a colonial past as dominated by resistance. Nolan, for example, has done this through his sequence of paintings of the Ned Kelly legend.

Portraying New Zealand

In New Zealand, paintings done in the early nineteenth century idealized the Maoris through an approach to the grandeur of their physiques, which drew its inspiration both from the classical approach to human form and from a romantic vision of individuals within their landscape. Theirs was again a romantic vision which had little relation to the social and economic reality of Maori life in the period.

As white settlement developed in New Zealand in the 1840s, surveyors and explorers produced notable watercolours of New Zealand landscapes. These acted as practical aids to their survey of economic resources and as propaganda for the company and settlement opportunities. But they also showed the artists' fascination with the land around them. Artists soon developed an obsession with the stunning scenery of the west side of the South Island. As in Australia, the discovery of gold in New Zealand in 1861 produced a considerable quickening of both economic and artistic activity. Enhanced commercial contact with the outside world brought more artists and European influences to the colony. Although much of their art was to remain allusive – likening the New Zealand landscape in turn to Scotland, Switzerland, Norway, and California, artists struggled to find a local 'feel' for their paintings, particularly emphasizing the translucent light effects of the southern hemisphere and the distinctive alternation of brightness and shade. By the end of the century, New Zealand artists, like their counterparts elsewhere, were leaving to be trained in Europe and among them – in a country that had female suffrage earlier than anywhere else in the empire – was a remarkable group of women artists.

Portraying South Africa

Of all Dominion art, that of the Europeans in South Africa was the most conservative. The reason for this was that, for much of the nineteenth century, artists from the Afrikaner community continued to draw upon the traditions of Dutch painting. Indeed Cape paintings in the sumptuous Amsterdam style continued to find favour well into the twentieth century. French impressionism only became influential in the 1920s and modernists movements in the 1940s – in each case several decades after their arrival in Canada, Australia, and New Zealand.

Moreover, art in South Africa seemed to be little influenced by economic change and urbanization for the first half of the twentieth century. As elsewhere, the prime focus of South African art was to render the essence of its landscape and meteorology, its botany and zoology, in terms of its own values of light and colour, and to portray its indigenous peoples in supposedly traditional settings. The Zulu people, who were seen as representing the essence of a black military tradition,

Opposite below: 'Hannah and Mary, girls of the Waikato' by Joseph Merrett. Merrett's work of the 1840s reflects a sympathetic view of New Zealand Maoris before the wars of the mid-century.

Below: 'Basuto woman' by Constance Greaves. Greaves painted many 'native studies' from 1930 until her death in 1966. Her intention, she said, was to make an accurate record of the appearance of African people.

fearsome yet dignified, were depicted in the same romantic convention as had been applied to studies of Maoris. Other Africans were either ignored or were shown as long-suffering servants and agricultural employees. It was not until after the Second World War that a more realistic and fully urban art began to emerge. This came about partly because the artistic centre of gravity shifted from the Cape to the Transvaal and partly because artists became much more aware of the black presence in the white economy.

International recognition

'October on the North Shore, Lake Superior' by Arthur Lismer, 1927. Lismer was one of the Group of Seven painters, who applied impressionist and symbolic approaches to their depiction of the Canadian landscape.

Despite the dominance of European influences, the art of the Dominions was, from at least the middle of the nineteenth century, something more than simply the pale imitation of European movements, although, ironically enough, national styles have usually emerged as a result of European training and the application of radical techniques learnt from Europe.

International recognition came slowly. Exhibitions held in Europe, the United States, and the Dominions themselves in the late nineteenth and early twentieth

centuries enabled Dominion artists to appear on the world stage. There were disputes between artistic establishments on the one hand and radical younger figures on the other as to what were the appropriate images of their territories that should be presented to the world. At first, images of the imperial order were projected through these exhibitions but, as national sentiment strengthened, so the paintings exhibited begain to reflect distinctive forms of Dominion nationalism.

Some art from the territories of white settlement appeared at an exhibition in London in 1862 and large numbers of paintings from the empire were exhibited at the 1886 Colonial and Indian Exhibition in London. At the American exhibitions in Philadelphia (1876), Chicago (1893), Buffalo (1901), and others it was the art depicting Canadian Indians, New Zealand Maoris, and other indigenous peoples that created the greatest sensation. The largest exhibit of paintings from all of these territories was at the Wembley British Empire Exhibition of 1924, when, in each case, there were major disputes between conservatives and radicals as to which examples should be shown. The Canadian Group of Seven was well represented, as was the work of the Australian Heidelberg impressionists and the New Zealand painters, many of the latter working in Europe. These shows enabled the artists of the Dominions to meet one another and be judged by critics in Europe whose views were often more favourable than those of critics in the Dominions who still looked for the sumptuous quasi-realism of Victorian taste. By 1924 the painting of the Dominions had reached maturity.

THE MEETING OF INDIGENOUS AND WESTERN TRADITIONS

For much of the nineteenth century British opinion had tended to denigrate the art of non-Europeans. It was seen as 'ethnic' – wholly separate from the history of the 'progressive', 'advanced', arts that had evolved in the west. Even Chinese art, which had so intrigued eighteenth-century connoisseurs, fell into disrepute for a time. James Mill, in what was for long accepted as the authoritative *History of India*, pronounced in 1817 that Indians were 'entirely without a knowledge of perspective and by consequence of all those finer and nobler parts of painting which have perspective for their requisite basis'. According to the great critic John Ruskin, Indians could 'not produce any noble art, only a savage or grotesque form of it'.

British opinion tended to make a sharp distinction between 'art', in which Indians were generally judged to be seriously deficient, and 'crafts', at which they excelled. The design and decoration of Indian textiles, earthenware, and toys shown in London in 1851 at the Great Exhibition drew much admiration. Ruskin shared this admiration, as did William Morris, who praised Indian decorative arts for being 'at once beautiful, orderly, living in our own day, and, above all, popular'. If Indians were at least allowed to be skilled at crafts, most of the peoples of Africa or the Pacific were regarded as having neither arts or crafts. Their artefacts were seen as bereft of aesthetic value. It was assumed that their carved figures had religious significance and were thus idolatrous to Christian opinion. Missionaries

From 'Company painting' to national art in India

In the second half of the eighteenth century, Indian artists created works now known as 'Company paintings' which attempted to adopt western perspective and subject matter, while maintaining certain of the conventions and colour schemes of Mughal and other indigenous art. These artists, who worked in a number of Indian cities for many decades, produced a vast number of paintings for European clients which have only been recognized as a major school in comparatively recent times. Parallel movements developed in Burma, Ceylon (Sri Lanka), and the Chinese ports.

In the course of the nineteenth century Indian artists increasingly tried to emulate European art, particularly after western-style art schools were founded in the principal Indian cities. To give young Indians 'an idea of man and things in Europe', copies of European masterpieces were provided for their enlightenment. The teaching of the art schools culminated in the work of the Indian 'orientalist', Ravi Varma, who came from South India and whose work achieved great popularity, extolled as matching Europeans at their own style. By the time of Varma's death in 1906, however, many were beginning to reject his slavish attachment to European models. The resurgence of a distinctively Indian art was now seen as an essential component of the *swadeshi* or boycott of foreign goods movement which became a central plank of Indian nationalism.

Indian magazines and art journals were founded to discuss what was an appropriate national art. A fresh appreciation of Indian crafts had been stimulated by British commentators in India, as well as by enthusiasts in Britain. E.B. Havell, a British art historian working in India, urged Indians to rediscover and reinterpret their ancient arts and instituted the sale of all the western art from the Calcutta art gallery. Writers like A.K. Coomaraswamy, who was of mixed Sinhalese and German parentage, insisted that a non-materialist and mystical vision was the distinguishing characteristic of the art of the east.

While Bombay artists tended to continue to aspire to a western realistic tradition, artists in the Punjab and particularly in Bengal started to strike out on new courses. The great Bengali philosopher and poet Rabindranath Tagore was himself an artist who broke completely with realism. Rabindranath's nephew, Abanindranath Tagore, was the founder of a new Calcutta school and influenced an entire generation of painters. They returned to the fundamentals of Indian design, Indian history, and what they saw as India's spiritual life. No fewer than fifty-six of their paintings were exhibited at Wembley in 1924 and by the interwar years a fully fledged Indian national tradition had emerged in Bengal.

Above: 'Portrait of a woman' by Ravi Varma.

Below: Painting by Rabindranath Tagore, c.1930.

Collecting and empire: from cabinet of curiosities to museum of art

From very early periods British travellers had been expected to bring home 'curiosities', and miscellaneous objects picked up overseas were displayed in cabinets. Fragments of Indian sculpture began to appear in British collections from the seventeenth century, but the major accumulations of non-European material were first made in the late eighteenth century with the initial British conquests in India and the great Pacific voyages. Robert Clive brought from India 'a chest full of shawls, pictures, swords and other curiosities', while Warren Hastings made a impressive collection of Mughal paintings and illuminated manuscript books.

At the end of the century the East India Company set up what was called the Indian Museum for books and all sorts of 'curiosities'. Those who went with Cook on his three voyages collected objects on a massive scale. These Pacific 'curiosities' were eventually distributed widely: many went to the British Museum, some to Oxford, and some to Dublin. Private collectors also snapped them up. In the British Museum a 'South Seas' room was opened in 1808 with other galleries to 'illustrate the particular customs of particular nations' – largely furnished by the collection made in the eighteenth century by Sir Hans Sloane, who had spent his early life in the West Indies.

For much of the nineteenth century the purpose behind the Indian collections was practical rather than aesthetic. Little was done to acquire painting or sculpture. When the Indian Museum was refurbished in 1858, it was 'to illustrate the productive resources of India and to give information about the life and manners, the arts and industry of its inhabitants'. The collection was eventually distributed between the South Kensington (later the Victoria and Albert) Museum and the British Museum. From early in the twentieth century both museums began to display Indian art – sculpture and paintings - in the way in which they displayed European art.

The art of the Pacific and of other 'primitive' peoples was not generally treated in the same way, and indeed was not recognized as being 'art' at all, until rather later. The most ambitious attempt to display such objects in the late nineteenth century had a very different purpose. This was the museum opened in Oxford in 1884 to house the collection of Arthur Pitt Rivers. Since about 1851 Pitt Rivers had been assiduously collecting material from all over the world. He had very strong views as to how this should be displayed. It must not be distributed according to the geographical areas from which it originated, but to demonstrate Pitt Rivers's tenaciously held theories about the evolution of cultures. The layout of the museum would enable the visitor to trace how simple objects, produced by simple societies (for Pitt Rivers the Australian Aborigines, many of whose artefacts he had collected, were the great exemplars of a simple society), were replaced by more complex ones appropriate to more 'advanced' societies. He made it a condition of his donation that his layout must be adhered to forever. [PJM]

Interior of the Pitt Rivers Museum, Oxford.

'Fishermen drawing nets' by Walter Battiss. An example of an artist who draws on indigenous traditions, Battiss adapts the pigments, figures, and motifs of the San ('bushman') paintings.

described figures from the Pacific as 'so ridiculously fantastic, so monstrously uncouth, so frightfully distorted'. Such things could be collected and displayed merely to illustrate the life of 'primitive' people, as a tool of what was coming to be known as anthropology.

By the end of the nineteenth century, however, European connoisseurs were beginning to give serious attention to non-European art. Enthusiasm for the bronzes of Benin in Nigeria spread to African carving and sculpture in general. In 1910 a group of artists and intellectuals published a letter in *The Times*, praising the Indian 'school of national art' for 'its vitality and its capacity for the interpretation of Indian life and thought'. Some British artists derived inspiration for their work from non-European art. Japanese prints were very much admired and were very widely imitated.

Post-impressionists like Georges Braque and Pablo Picasso became enthralled by the representational, geometric, and spiritual character of the African mask and sought to incorporate some of its characteristics in their art. Examples of African sculpture and metal work, which had often been looted in colonial campaigns and then relegated to the ethnographic departments of western museums, came to have a new significance for western art.

In the search for uniquely national forms, the artists of the Dominions began to draw upon the motifs, pigments, and spiritual concepts of indigenous art. By the middle of the twentieth century, this fusing of local symbols with European techniques had become standard throughout the territories of white settlement. Part of this revolutionary interest lay in a renewed fascination with design and motif. In New Zealand there was a fresh concern with the magnificent carvings of Maori canoes, or in the gloriously carved and decorated churches produced by Maori builders and artists in the mid-nineteenth century, such as that at Otaki, completed in 1851. By the middle of the twentieth century New Zealand art was attempting to fuse international movements with Maori motifs.

'Composition' by Louis Maqhubela, 1970. Maqhubela was prominent among the group of African artists living in the townships of Johannesburg, who were influenced by western art.

Something of the same development occurred in Australia, where Aboriginal art remains a living tradition. Today Aborigine painters still decorate rocks with modern versions of the art of their ancestors; others transfer Aboriginal designs onto various fabrics. In Canada, the art of the Indian totem of the north west coast and of Inuit sculpture and design has similarly entered the artistic mainstream.

In South Africa, the great tradition of rock painting by the San people ('Bushman' painting) was rediscovered in the interwar years. Soon African artists were beginning to be accepted and encouraged on their own terms. By the 1950s an entire school of artists had emerged in Johannesburg, associated with the Polly Street Art Centre. They developed a tradition known as 'township art' which placed African designs and ways of looking at the world into new contexts, sometimes influenced by the social and economic realities of the urban setting. Africans were thus feeding back into a European tradition fresh insights derived from the long-standing abstract core of African art.

PAINTING AND NATIONAL IDENTITY

If imperial art had so often expressed the power of dominant peoples, the nationalist responses of the twentieth century inspired a new confidence both on the part of the displaced white societies, whose arts had so often seemed borrowed and second-rate, and more particularly in the achievements of indigenous cultures. In the ex-Dominions attempts at fusion produced syncretic forms of art which pointed the way to distinctive cultures which could secure international recognition and avoid what has often been called in Australia 'the cultural cringe'. In India and Africa the development of an art confident in its integrity as the expression of the traditions of its own society constituted a vital part of a political re-awakening. In the evolution of national art forms throughout the former British empire, the old distinction between the European mainstream and 'ethnographic' traditions are being broken down. In this, as in many other respects, the British empire has provided the setting in which connections have been made and controversies worked out.

The Imperial Experience

PART III

CHAPTER 12

P. J. Marshall

Imperial Britain

Between 4 and 5 per cent of the present population of Britain are either immigrants or the descendants of immigrants from former British colonial territories in the Caribbean or in South Asia. Movements of people from these parts of the world to Britain in any large quantities is a recent phenomenon, dating from the 1950s. Even on the dubious assumption that people from so wide a range of different countries and different backgrounds should be treated as a single group, this is still a relatively small minority by comparison with, for example, those in France or the United States. Nevertheless, since the 1950s people from the Caribbean or South Asia settled in Britain have been regarded as a 'problem'. It is often argued that this problem is an inheritance of empire. The presence of these people in Britain and the reception that they have met with here can be explained by Britain's imperial past. 'The empire' is said to be 'striking back'; its legacy is haunting contemporary Britain.

This is perhaps the issue on which the significance of the imperial past for contemporary Britain attracts most discussion. It is, however, only one of a wide range of such issues. Questioning the consequences of empire for Britain is, moreover, a preoccupation of previous generations as well as our own. Assessments have tended to vary as different generations of British people interpret the state of Britain in their own time. For confident mid-Victorians, empire and its values were seen as an expression of British greatness. For less confident generations at the end of the nineteenth century or the beginning of the twentieth, a remodelled empire was seen as embodying the greatness that Britain might attain. Since the Second World War British people have generally believed that their position in the world has deteriorated markedly. When the imperial past is assessed now it is usually used to explain some aspect of decline. Did commitment to empire make the British insular and unwisely self-sufficient – ignoring dangers in Europe in 1914 or the 1930s, or opportunities in Europe through the moves towards European integration in the 1950s? Did Britain develop institutions appropriate to an imperial state, but ill-equipped for the modern world? Did the British economy become increasingly dependent on easy access to empire markets and resources and thus ill-fitted to compete with advanced economies in Europe, North America, and Japan? Did the need for colonial administrators entrench values in British education that continue to produce an elite without technological capacity or entrepreneurial drive? In short, did empire leave the British with insufferable pretensions, while it sapped the economic and military base with which to support such pretensions, or did it uplift the people of Britain, as was commonly claimed in earlier periods, and make Britain a great power in the world? Underlying these specific questions are more general ones: what effect did empire have on the sense of Britain's identity, institutions, and economy, and on British society as a whole?

A London school with children from immigrant communities, most of them from countries that were once within the British empire.

AN IMPERIAL IDENTITY?

In the eighteenth century Britain was coming to be defined for many of its citizens by possession of an empire. In 1774 Edmund Burke told the electors of Bristol that their city was 'but part of a rich commercial *nation*, the interests of which are various, multiform, and intricate'. But, he added, 'We are members of that great nation, which however is itself but part of a great *empire*, extended by our virtue and our fortune to the farthest limits of the east and of the west.' Nearly 200 years later Winston Churchill used very similar language. 'Britain cannot be thought of as a single state in isolation. She is the founder and centre of a worldwide empire and Commonwealth.'

Empire and Britishness

In its origins the empire overseas was English. From the middle of the eighteenth century onwards, it was, however, most unusual for anyone to write about 'the English empire' or 'the empire of England' or to use any similar form of words. The term was unequivocally 'the British empire', and so it remained. As with so much of the imperial strand in the British past, the Britishness of the British empire both reflected developments in Britain itself and helped to shape them.

In the late eighteenth century, some merging of identities between the peoples of the United Kingdom of Great Britain and Ireland was producing a new sense of 'Britishness'. At the same time there were major changes in the empire overseas: the creation of an English-speaking majority in Canada, the beginnings of white settlement in Australia, and the conquest of India. This fresh wave of expansion was very much a joint enterprise of all the peoples of the British Isles, rather than of the English alone, as had generally been the case for early American settlement. That the empire ceased to be an English empire and became a British empire was no doubt only to be expected from the merging of the peoples of the United Kingdom. But empire did more than reflect the Britishness of the British in Britain; it helped to focus and develop it.

In part, empire contributed to Britishness because access to it and its rewards demonstrated in a tangible sense the advantages to be reaped from being a part of the United Kingdom and working within its institutions. The pattern of successful Scottish participation in empire set in the later eighteenth century continued into the twentieth century. The Scots maintained a very large stake in the administration of India, whether posts were filled by nomination of the directors of the East India Company or by competitive examination. Scottish business concerns were also very active in India, as they were in Australia, Canada, and tropical Africa, and especially in the great shipping enterprises that spanned the empire in the nineteenth century. Scots continued to migrate throughout the empire in very large numbers: the Scottish element in the influx of people in all the colonies of settlement was very much greater than the Scottish proportion of the population of the United Kingdom as a whole (see page 265). It is perhaps not surprising that attempts to arouse public opposition to the South African War got relatively little support in Scotland. Pro-Boer anti-war sentiment in Ireland, by contrast, was very strong. This of course reflects a frustrated Irish nationalism, which no amount of employment opportunities in the empire could have propitiated. Nevertheless, Ireland got relatively little out of the empire for most of the nineteenth century. Irish Protestants had always been well represented in imperial service, but Irish Catholics only began to obtain posts beyond those of the rank and file of the army late in the century.

The empire's contribution to Britishness, however, went much further than providing material incentives for adhering to the United Kingdom. Empire helped to define Britishness. The rancorous controversies between the American colonies and authority in Britain in the 1760s and early 1770s had been about Englishness. Americans had claimed the 'rights of Englishmen' emanating from Magna Carta and the common law. Ministers and Parliament had disputed their interpretation of Englishness. The empire that grew after the loss of America was very much a British one. Amalgamation of people from all parts of the British Isles in new lands overseas was eventually to produce new identities – a sense of being distinctly an Australian or a Canadian or a New Zealander. But these new identities took some time to grow. In the meanwhile those living in Australia or Canada or New Zealand were still emphatically British. The elements from the different parts of the United Kingdom were too evenly balanced for immigrants from any one part to be able to impose their identity on the others. In 1915 a Canadian historian could still write that 'the average Canadian' thought himself 'both a Canadian and a Briton', because 'the Empire is not an English Empire, and the English are only one of many peoples in it'. Those who had settled the empire generally experienced a greater sense of undifferentiated Britishness than those who stayed at home and emigrants who returned to Britain no doubt brought that sense of Britishness with them.

Varieties of Britishness

There was, however, no single model for the Britishness embodied by the empire. Different ideals for Britain were reflected in different interpretations of what the British empire stood for. In the late nineteenth century, self-confessed 'imperialists' had strong views about Britain as well as about the empire. For them society rested on hierarchy and obedience to one's superiors and on the individual's qualities of manliness and resourcefulness. To go with this, they had a view of gender relations in which the role of women was to sustain their menfolk in a life of patriotic service and to produce children for the empire. Fictional representations of empire, in Kipling, G.A. Henty, Rider Haggard, and other stories for boys and girls, were filled with ideal personifications of the qualities they admired: brave soldiers, dutiful administrators, rugged pioneers, and stoical but submissive women. Such a view of empire and, with it, of Britain's national identity was very widely propagated for a time by publishers, in schools, and in popular entertainment.

The imperialists' view of national identity was, however, always contested. Max Beerbohm drew a series of cartoons in 1901, contrasting 'The real John Bull' of the imperialists' imagination with John Bull 'in his second childhood' making a fool of himself over the South African War. One of the cartoons shows a drunken John Bull celebrating the relief of Kimberley, Ladysmith, and Mafeking. By the 1920s the cult of manliness, associated not only with imperialism but also with a kind of militarism that was being brought into discredit by revulsion at the carnage of the First World War, looked increasingly out of fashion. It was criticized and ridiculed at many levels, from E.M. Forster's *A Passage to India* to Noel Coward's 'mad dogs and Englishmen' or the sayings of David Low's cartoon character 'Colonel Blimp'. Scepticism about the beliefs of old-style imperial enthusiasts did not, however, necessarily lead to the complete rejection either of the empire or of an imperial identity for Britain. When Mrs Moore, in *A Passage to India*, mused on her misgivings about her son, an Indian administrator who felt that British officials were 'not out here for the purpose of behaving pleasantly', she was expressing aspirations for the British empire to be a 'different institution', not for the ending of empire.

Colonel Blimp. David Low worked on the *Evening Standard* from 1927 to 1950. 'Colonel Blimp', his unregenerate Tory figure, was a strongly traditional imperialist.

The imperial identity that prevailed from the 1920s onwards was essentially that on which so many Victorians had always prided themselves. Britain stood for freedom both as a nation and in its imperial role. Even when freedom had to be withheld from people for whom it was considered inappropriate, the British remained a free people themselves while exercising a humane trusteeship over others to whom freedom would be granted in the future, although this future might be remote. Liberal or self-confessedly progressive and enlightened sections of British opinion for long had little difficulty in accepting an imperial identity, even if British confidence in their role as promoters of freedom was built on a profound disdain for other Europeans, presumed to be incapable of such an imperial role, and on a very paternalistic attitude to non-Europeans, who required the tutelage of the British before they too could attain freedom.

The extent to which British people as a whole accepted any sort of imperial identity is a controversial issue. Popular attitudes to empire are difficult to gauge. There is, however, little evidence of overt hostility to it at any time. The mass of British people from the eighteenth century onwards seem to have had at least a rudimentary awareness that Britain was a great imperial power and to have accepted that without question. Few members of the British working class evidently saw subjects of the empire as fellow victims with whom they should identify. Much effort was devoted at various times to trying to turn popular acceptance of empire into positive enthusiasm for it. The mass signings of anti-slave trade and anti-slavery petitions are evidence of some success. So too are the records of attendance at missionary rallies and of money subscribed to mission societies. At the end of the nineteenth century dissemination of material about the empire was on a vast scale. The bulk of the British working population had probably by then come to accept that Britain's position in the world was enhanced by empire and to take some pride in it. Reasons for being proud of the empire no doubt varied. For some it was pride in freeborn Englishmen spreading freedom and the Gospel throughout the world. Popular support for missionary societies was at its height at the very end of the century. Others seem to have taken a more secular, chauvinistic view and seen empire as an expression of Britain's supremacy over its foreign rivals. In both cases, pride in empire was underpinning a sense of British national identity. Pride in Britain's religious mission and pride in Britain's armed might were not necessarily incompatible. General Havelock, avenger of the Indian Rebellion of 1857, and General Gordon are famous examples of Christian military heroes. Nevertheless, those who gloried in battles and those who gloried in the gathering in of souls were probably subscribing to different versions of a British imperial identity.

IMPERIAL INSTITUTIONS?

The extent to which Britain's imperial identity reshaped British institutions varied widely.

Parliament

Parliament was referred to on many occasions as the Imperial Parliament, but it remained in all essentials the Parliament of Great Britain. From the time of the American Revolution onwards, schemes were floated for incorporating members directly elected by the peoples of the colonial territories into the Parliament at Westminster. This was never done and there is no evidence that it was ever much desired either by colonial or by British opinion. In the eighteenth century considerable numbers of people with colonial backgrounds, such as West Indian planters, got themselves elected for British constituencies. Reform of the British electoral system to make it more representative of British opinion greatly reduced such opportunities but did not eliminate them altogether. Robert Lowe, a major political figure of the age of Gladstone and Disraeli, was an Australian by origin. Max Aitken, the future Lord Beaverbrook, was Canadian and Bonar Law, Prime Minister in 1922–23, spent his first twelve years in Canada. A small number of Indians also sat in the House of Commons (see pages 171–72). But if colonial voices could usually be heard in it, there is no sense in which the British Parliament became the kind of parliament representing the whole empire that imperial reformers advocated in the early twentieth century.

Parliament's unrepresentative nature did not of course prevent it from sometimes taking an active role in ruling the empire. It renounced its powers to tax the colonies after the American Revolution, but it remained a law maker for the whole empire. However, this power was used sparingly. The colonies generally developed within a constitutional framework laid down by acts of Parliament, but wherever possible Parliament tended to leave local legislatures to settle local issues.

The British state

Possession of a great empire did not bring about major changes in the way in which Britain was governed. The administration of the empire at home had to fit into the traditions of the British state, rather than the other way round. The Colonial Office developed like any other nineteenth-century ministry. Considering the size of its responsibilities, it was a very small operation. By 1900 some twenty clerks were trying to deal with an annual inflow of 42,620 dispatches from the colonies.

Government overseas could be conducted on very different principles to government at home; the two worlds were kept largely separate. In many senses the British government of India was the antithesis of the government of Great Britain. In India British rule was an autocracy which had its professional agents in the districts, the collectors and magistrates; in Britain public servants accountable to Parliament had to rely on self-appointed or elected local representatives to carry out their policies. In India the colonial government assumed responsibility for building roads and railways, providing irrigation, and setting up schools and colleges; in Britain most of these things were done by private initiative. British opinion viewed the government of India with a mixture of admiration and misgiving. From the eighteenth century, fears had been expressed that for Britain to maintain in India or anywhere else in the empire a centralized, despotic government, which rested on military force, would ultimately endanger freedom in Britain itself. Richard Cobden, for instance, feared in 1858 that 'our national character is being deteriorated and our love of freedom in danger of being impaired by what is passing in India. Is it possible that we can play the part of despot and butcher there without finding our character deteriorated at home?'

Although Cobden's fears were to be echoed at other times, notably during the South African War, a majority of British people at any time would probably have answered Cobden's question with a firm 'no'. The British were confident that they would not be corrupted by empire. There was no real danger of their becoming an authoritarian imperial people and losing their own taste for liberty, as the Romans were supposed to have done, by ruling over the peoples of the East. The British would not only maintain their own freedom and their free institutions, but, as they had repeatedly shown, they would export them wherever new communities of British origin got established overseas. Autocracy was thought to be necessary in India because of the state of Indian society and Indians' long subjection to 'oriental despotism'. But exercising autocratic power over Indians and other non-European peoples, far from corrupting the British, reaffirmed their national character. They could wield an autocratic power that was very different from the despotism, as they liked to conceive it, of others. They saw their rule not as that of the tyrant, according to his own whim, but as regulated by law and principles of equity. Empire over those considered not fit for freedom themselves helped to define the British people's belief in their own identity as a free people and strengthened their confidence in their unique destiny.

The armed forces

For more than 200 years the British armed forces were very closely associated with empire. The Victorian army was essentially an army for defending the empire. Mr George, the old soldier in Dickens's *Bleak House*, called his daughters 'Quebec' and 'Malta' as an indication of the amount of time he had spent overseas. The great commanders of the late nineteenth century, Wolseley, Roberts, and Kitchener, all made their reputations in imperial wars. Indeed these were the only wars in which reputations could be made. The Royal Navy was not concentrated in home waters nor was the army tentatively prepared for continental war until early in the twentieth century. Nevertheless, for all their length of service overseas, the British armed forces, even the officers of the Indian army, always seem to have identified themselves with Britain, not with the colonial territories in which they served. In the last stages of the British empire there was nothing comparable to the resistance to the decolonization of Algeria offered by sections of the French army.

The churches

The experience of empire was of great importance for the religious life of Britain. The British Protestant churches acquired a world-wide and in some senses an imperial identity, which helped to reinforce ideas of the uniqueness of British freedom. British denominations spread throughout the world with the dispersal of British people by emigration. From the late eighteenth century, British missionary societies began their great offensives to convert the heathen. The whole world was their target, but British missionaries felt a special obligation for the spiritual welfare of those placed under British rule. They saw their obligation in terms of bringing freedom. British Protestants were God's chosen agents for spreading true freedom throughout the world. Catholic missions in the past, they maintained, had been

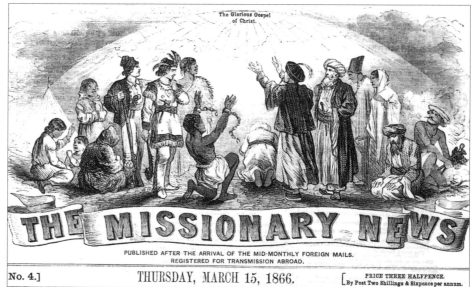

agents for the slavery of superstition. The heathen would be freed by true conversion from the slavery of sin and the shackles of idolatry. In the words of Bishop Heber's famous hymn:

> From Greenland's icy mountains,
> From India's coral strand ...
> They call us to deliver
> Their land from error's chain.

The involvement of ordinary British people in missions – as attenders at meetings, readers of tracts and, above all, as subscribers of money – was very great and grew throughout the nineteenth century. By 1900 there were 154 mission societies in Britain and in the previous year £2 million, or 2 per cent of the national budget, had been collected on their behalf.

The monarchy

Like the churches, the monarchy became very much identified with empire. Towards the end of his very long reign (from 1760 to 1820) George III came to be seen as the embodiment of Britishness, a King equally of his Welsh and Scottish subjects (if not necessarily of his Irish ones), as of his English subjects. The engrafting of an imperial role onto the British role of the monarchy developed under Queen Victoria. She was very much the Queen of British people living in the colonies of settlement as well as of those at home. As the monarchy lost most of its active functions in British politics, it became an acceptable link for a freer association of Britain and these colonies.

After each retreat of the British government or the British Parliament from the affairs of colonies, the monarchy remained, increasingly assuming the role of a separate King or Queen of, for example, Canada or Australia, as well as being the sovereign of Great Britain, but also acting as a symbol of the free association of the Commonwealth. In 1926 the Balfour Declaration described the Commonwealth as 'united by a common allegiance to the Crown'. When Commonwealth membership was redefined in 1949 to include republics, George VI was described as 'the symbol of the free association of [the Commonwealth's] independent member nations, and as such the Head of the Commonwealth'. For a time, George VI and, later, Elizabeth II, were able to identify the monarchy with the aspirations of new Asian, African, and Caribbean states as well as with the older Dominions. The Commonwealth gave the British monarchy a much enhanced role from the 1930s at least until the 1970s.

While the monarchy was acquiring a role as a symbol of an empire based on liberty and free association, it was also reinforcing rather different ideas about empire. In 1876 Queen Victoria was given a new title, 'Empress of India' – a change intended to symbolize the hierarchy of authority on which British India rested. Indian princes and dignitaries were to be placed directly under the British Crown

(Opposite margin)
Top: Lord Wolseley. Garnet Wolseley fought all over the empire from the 1850s to the 1880s.

Middle: Lord Roberts. Frederick Roberts was Commander-in-Chief in India from 1885 to 1893 and took command in the South African War from 1899 to 1900.

Bottom: Lord Kitchener. Horatio Herbert Kitchener was conqueror of the Sudan and victor at Omdurman in 1898. He succeeded Roberts in South Africa and became Commander-in-Chief in India from 1902 to 1909.

Opposite: *The Missionary News*, 15 March 1866. Missionary magazines and newspapers began to be published early in the nineteenth century. They had a very wide circulation. *The Children's World* of the Church Missionary Society, for instance, was selling over 700,000 copies a year at the end of the century. Missionary newspapers were major retailers of information about the peoples of the world, even if, as this example shows, in a very stereotyped form.

as inheritors of the authority of the Mughal Emperor. Ceremonies were devised at which homage was expressed. Great assemblages and durbars were held to enable Indian princes to pledge their loyalty to the Crown.

The use of the monarchy to project ideas of freedom and of authority at the same time may seem in retrospect contradictory. Most contemporaries would not, however, have seen the contradiction. For them this would merely have reflected the diversity of the empire: some parts of it were ready for freedom; others were not and must be governed in accordance with what were assumed to be their traditions under firm, benevolent British rule. Even so, different images of the monarchy coexisting at the same time reveal a point of fundamental importance about Britain's imperial identity. There was no single identity. Different people engrafted different ideas of empire onto their own conceptions of Britain.

AN IMPERIAL ECONOMY?

Questions about the extent to which Britain benefited economically from the possession of an empire are likely to produce different answers at different times from the late eighteenth century to the 1960s. The divisions used in chapter 5 (pages 108–13) are helpful ones and will be used here: 'the end of mercantilism' lasting until about 1850, which is also the period of Britain's industrialization; 'the era of free trade' from 1850 to 1932, the age of Britain's mature industrial economy; and 'a return to protectionism' from 1932 to the 1960s.

The industrial revolution

There can be no doubt that colonial trades were very rich ones in the late eighteenth century. By the 1770s Asia, Africa, and America were taking over 30 per cent of British exports and providing more than 50 per cent of its imports. The white populations of the Americas were very important consumers of British manufactures. A big proportion of colonial imports into Britain – especially Virginian tobacco, Indian calico, and West Indian sugar – was subsequently re-exported to Europe. The British had become the main middlemen between tropical producers and European consumers, much to the profit of shippers, merchants, brokers, and the customs revenue of the government. Great fortunes were also made by men who had participated in· the conquest of Bengal. Robert Clive, for example, was worth more than £400,000 at the end of his Indian service.

What effect did this new wealth have on the British economy as a whole? It is sometimes seen as central to the industrial revolution. Those who give empire a crucial role in the industrial revolution generally use two lines of argument: British industry needed a heavy investment of capital, much of which came from the profits made in the colonial trades or from the plunder of wealth overseas, especially in India; and it needed new markets which the empire provided within the restrictive mercantilist system.

Although great wealth was accumulated in the eighteenth-century empire, it was not on the whole reinvested in industry during that period: the fortunes of the merchants and the nabobs (men who had been enriched in India) went on houses, estates, and general high living. Early industrialization drew most of its capital from within the British domestic economy. However, the late eighteenth-century empire did provide protected markets whose increasing demand for British goods encouraged manufacturers to invest in new technology, such as mechanical means of spinning cotton thread and weaving cotton cloth. In this sense, theories that industry in Britain was built on slavery have some force. Slave labour in the West Indies increased the output of sugar, which in turn led to an increased demand for food supplies for the islands from North America; with what they earned from supplying the West Indies, the Americans could buy more British manufactured goods. Nevertheless, although exports, especially to the Americas, may have contributed significantly to industrial growth, the domestic market was still more important in the late eighteenth century. It was not until the mid-nineteenth century that the British economy was fully geared to exporting.

Sezincote in the Cotswolds in Gloucestershire. Sir Charles Cockerell, who had been a banker in Calcutta, built this house in the early nineteenth century out of the fortune he had made in India. Unusually, Cockerell commissioned his house to be designed in an Indian style. His architect consulted Thomas Daniell (see page 305), an artist who had toured India and made many studies of Indian buildings.

The era of free trade

In an era of protection and closed markets, colonies to which access was guaranteed and from which competition was excluded, were very valuable for British exports. In the early nineteenth century Britain's industrial lead gave it access to markets in Europe and North America and as free trade began to spread in mid-century, in theory the whole world was opening up to Britain. But the empire still provided real economic advantages. Assumptions that empire could be 'exploited' to provide artificially cheap raw materials and captive markets are untenable: such things were not possible under a system of free trade extended to the colonies in the mid-nineteenth century. Nevertheless, in the later nineteenth century the proportion of British trade being carried on with its colonies and with other areas outside Europe and the United States increased markedly. The older industrial revolution industries, like cotton, did particularly well in these markets, while at the same time markets were declining in countries that had become fully industrialized. This was the period in which massive British investment also began to be placed overseas, predominantly in the countries where Britain was doing the greater part of its trade, such as its colonies of settlement and Latin America.

The short-term economic advantages of the empire to Britain in the later nineteenth century are clear: it was important in helping to provide export markets and an outlet for investment. But in the long term, did the British economy gain or lose during this period? One view is that possession of an empire exacerbated weaknesses becoming apparent in the British economy. Instead of modernizing its industry to cope with German and American competition in the difficult markets of Europe, Britain relied on easy markets within the empire or in countries where it could use its influence to obtain favourable terms. The funds so lavishly placed abroad should have been invested in new technology at home and the empire cost the taxpayer dear in bills for the army and the navy (according to a recent survey the British taxpayer paid two and a half times as much on defence as the French or German taxpayer). Others would disagree with this view, maintaining that it was natural for the British manufacturer to concentrate on markets in rapidly developing countries like Australia or Argentina, and that British investment, which could not be absorbed at home anyway, made this development possible and thus boosted British exports. Furthermore, the dividends earned on investment overseas enabled Britain to balance its deficits in commodity trade as imports began to exceed exports.

Was possession of an empire, on balance, an asset or a liability for the British economy in this period? Heavy commitment to a world outside Europe, of which the empire was a major part, probably did contribute to a decline in British competitiveness. It was no doubt natural for British manufacturers to shift their attention to new markets, especially to those with British connections, rather than to develop new products to compete in European markets. It was also no doubt natural for British people with money to invest to be willing to place it in such countries, even if, as many studies have confirmed, the return was not notably higher than on investments elsewhere. Such trends may, however, have discouraged changes within the British economy – including improvements in technology – which would have put Britain on a sounder competitive footing in the long term.

The new imperial economy

From the 1930s to the 1950s the proportion of Britain's trade going to the empire increased markedly: by the 1950s nearly half of all Britain's exports and imports were going to and from the empire. Empire trade helped to tide Britain through difficult times during and immediately after the Second World War, when other markets had collapsed and other sources of supply had been disrupted. When international trade revived in the late 1950s, however, both Britain and most of its imperial trading partners reverted to much wider patterns of trade, Britain being drawn into closer commercial links with Europe even before it sought entry into the European Economic Community. By the 1970s half of Britain's trade was with western Europe.

The economic balance sheet

The British as a whole did not get rich on the exploitation of their empire and become poor when this was no longer feasible. Nor, on the other hand, was empire the drug that corrupted the economic vigour of Britain, reducing it to an effete parasite. Britain's economic relations with its empire tended to reflect trends already established in the British economy and to strengthen certain of them. The creation of new colonial markets from which foreign competition was excluded encouraged

British manufacturers in the eighteenth century to increase the scale of their output. The quantity of goods going to these markets was probably not sufficient to 'cause' an industrial revolution but it facilitated one. The mature British industrial economy of the later nineteenth century was marked by dependence on markets outside Europe, a very high level of investment overseas, and reliance on 'invisible' earnings, from shipping and banking as well as from investments. Even without empire, Britain would no doubt have responded to the challenge of European and American industrialization by seeking new world-wide opportunities; for better or for worse, possession of an empire reinforced these trends. In the mid-twentieth century Britain could fall back on empire as a valuable economic prop, but it could not create an enduring imperial economy. In the late nineteenth century most British people had accepted that the benefits of empire justified a fairly high level of military and naval costs. By the 1960s there were too many other claims on Britain's financial resources and the declining benefits of empire did not seem to justify the costs. Changing economic relations with the empire both reflected and accentuated changes in Britain's economy as a whole – this is a pattern that was to repeat itself in other aspects of Britain's long engagement with empire.

AN IMPERIAL SOCIETY?

Throughout Britain's imperial history many British people have viewed the effect of empire on British society with misgivings. They have been fearful that empire was distorting and corrupting it. Concerns have traditionally focused on two main levels of society: the population as a whole (sometimes specifically 'the working class') and the elite.

Worries about the effect of empire on 'the people' are very old. One of the many adages transferred to Britain from Roman history was that the populace could be brutalized and corrupted by empire and the luxury that it diffused throughout society. These anxieties were particularly marked at the end of the nineteenth century, when they were aroused by what appeared to be strident popular enthusiasm for imperial wars, such as the South African War. Marxists argued that a section of the working class were profiting from imperialism and were therefore becoming a reactionary force in politics. George Orwell still deplored what he considered to be the British working class's commitment to empire during the Second World War. Working class acceptance of empire seemed to be beyond question but acceptance of empire or even enthusiasm for it were likely to have been no more than expressions of British nationalism. Although some industries, such as cotton manufacturing in the late nineteenth century, were very heavily dependent on imperial outlets, it seems improbable that calculations of their own economic interest had much to do with the views that working people might have about the empire.

Wealth made out of empire has long been regarded as suspect. Indian nabobs and West Indian planters were hated in the eighteenth century; randlords (South

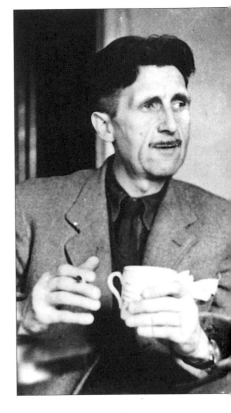

George Orwell spent the years 1922–27 in the Burma police. His experiences provided the material for a bitter indictment of British imperial rule in his *Burmese Days* of 1934. He believed that 'the wealth of England was drawn largely from Asia and Africa'.

African mine owners) were reviled at the end of the nineteenth century. The main fear was that great wealth suddenly acquired by unscrupulous upstarts would threaten established hierarchies and corrupt public life. Great fortunes made out of empire, like those of Clive or Rhodes, can be identified without any difficulty, but studies of the very rich in British history do not suggest that colonial wealth made a very major contribution.

The effect of empire on certain sections of the British middle classes was probably of greater social significance. In the nineteenth century India offered employment, which was both well paid and thought to be socially prestigious, in an army parallel to the British army and in a professional civil administration. Opportunities on such a scale became available much more slowly in other colonies. Government service in the colonies employed only some 1,500 people at the end of the nineteenth century, rising to about 20,000 in the 1950s. To official posts should be added comparable professional employment – law, medicine, or engineering – throughout the empire. Finally, the great wave of investment overseas, in which the empire had a part, attracted middle-class savings as well as the capital of the very rich.

The existence of a large 'professional middle class', 'service class', or even 'rentier class' is often seen as a distinctive feature of British society. To some social commentators this is also a characteristic British weakness. Such people, it is said, do not generate wealth and are peripheral to the British economy, yet they enjoy an undue prestige. They are an unfortunate legacy of empire. Whether Britain has been fortunate or unfortunate in its professional middle class, empire has nothing like sole responsibility for it. Those who sought employment in the empire were the kind of people who were attracted to the civil service, the professions, or the armed forces at home. There was no shortage of such people, even in the eighteenth century. Their numbers grew very rapidly in the nineteenth and twentieth centuries. For would-be public servants the empire provided a range of extra posts beyond those available at home, even though most people who had a choice seem to have preferred to stay in Britain.

Empire is often seen as a formative influence on the education of the British upper classes and of ambitious middle-class families. Most prestigious positions abroad were filled by people who had at least been to public schools and in some cases to universities. About one fifth of those matriculating at three Oxford colleges between 1874 and 1938 are known to have found employment in the empire. But the public schools and the universities seem to have captured imperial service, rather than the needs of empire bringing about changes in them. Certain public school masters talked a great deal about the mission of their schools to prepare the young for duty in the empire. Serious imperialists, however, were highly critical of the 'flannelled fools' and 'muddled oafs' of the public schools, so often assumed to have been moulded to the needs of empire. One critic conceded that obsession with 'character' and 'athletic sports' had produced the kind of man who did 'yeoman's service for the empire'. Yet, he added, 'it seems a thousand pities that he has not been trained ... to face the problems of race, creed and government in distant corners of the empire with a more instructed mind'. The competitive examination for the East India Company's service, later the Indian civil service, was based on existing academic subjects and was intended to favour candidates from Oxford. The assumption was that the empire needed the best products of schools and universities, trained in the most exacting subjects, the classics and mathematics. Branches of knowledge developed in nineteenth-century Britain with strong imperial applications, such as geography, geology, anthropology, and forestry. Their academic prestige, however, remained low almost until the end of empire.

COMMONWEALTH IMMIGRATION

Until as late as 1961 the outflow of British people to the empire was greater than any corresponding inflow. Such an inflow had, however, begun early. In the eighteenth century there was always an 'American' community living in London, even though the difference between 'American' and 'British' was hard to define. There were also a number of black people settled in Britain. How many is not known, but even in the eighteenth century they were said to be sufficiently numerous and sufficiently widespread for 'every man who has ever stepped beyond the place of his birth' to have seen one. In the 1950s, however, a long tradition of small-scale immigration gave way to a much more rapid acceleration.

The *Empire Windrush* brought 492 people from Jamaica to work in Britain in June 1948.

Most of the new immigrants came from Commonwealth countries in the Caribbean and South Asia. Out of 35,000 estimated to have arrived in 1955, the great majority were from the Caribbean. Of the 115,000 estimated for 1961, just over half were still from the West Indies. Thereafter, greater numbers came from South Asia. Since some inflow of new immigrants from outside Europe was a consequence of postwar economic growth in most of western Europe, Britain would presumably have shared in this inflow with or without an imperial past. Shortages of labour in certain sectors of the British economy were acute in the postwar period. But the imperial past seems very largely to have determined who actually came to Britain. Many West Indian people might well have gone to the United States, rather than to Britain, if tight restrictions had not been imposed in 1952; but in general, whether pushed by disaster, as with the Asians expelled from Uganda, or seeking opportunities for improvement, people from colonial and ex-colonial territories were drawn by language and common traditions to the United Kingdom.

The extent of this influx prompted the British government to impose the first restrictions on movement to Britain from within the empire in the Commonwealth Immigration Act of 1962. The ostensible purpose of the 1962 and subsequent acts was to limit immigration and thus to facilitate the absorption of those already in Britain as full members of British society. Many of the immigrant communities believe, however, that this purpose has not been fulfilled and that their acceptance has been far from complete. While their presence in Britain seems clearly to be a legacy of empire, whether the hostility that they have encountered also represents the influence of the imperial past is more debatable.

Other European countries have difficult race relations. In some cases, like that of France, there is also a long history of large-scale colonial involvement, and the minorities in the eye of the storm, immigrants from North Africa, are, like those in Britain, from ex-colonial territories. In Germany, on the other hand, the colonial

Commonwealth immigration and the 1962 act

Like free trade, the free movement of people throughout the empire became a strong principle of British imperial statecraft. In 1948, in response to assertions by ex-colonies of their right to regulate immigration, Britain proclaimed its continuing commitment to free entry in a British Nationality Act. All citizens of the colonial empire or the Commonwealth were recognized as also having British citizenship, which gave them a right to come to Britain.

In the 1950s the policy of free entry began to be reconsidered. Effectively excluded from the United States and attracted by labour shortages in Britain, West Indian people were beginning to come in some numbers; by the late 1950s so were people from India and Pakistan. From 1955 the British government began to consider a policy of restriction in response to reports of tensions in areas that had received large numbers of new immigrants. Ministers concerned with maintaining good relations with the colonial empire and the Commonwealth, however, were strongly opposed to restrictions. Riots in Notting Hill, an area of London with a concentration of West Indians, seemed to provide concrete evidence of potentially serious problems. In 1961 the government announced its intention of introducing a bill to restrict access to Britain; this became law the following year. Only those who had obtained vouchers for certain kinds of employment would be admitted. The Home Secretary, R.A. Butler, privately told his colleagues:

> The great merit of this scheme is that it can be presented as making no distinction on grounds of race and colour, although in practice all would-be immigrants from the old Commonwealth countries would almost certainly be enabled to obtain authority to enter ... We must recognise that, although the scheme purports to relate solely to employment and to be non-discriminatory, its aim is primarily social and its restrictive effect is intended to and would, in fact, operate on coloured people almost exclusively.

The Labour party had opposed the 1962 act, but it too had shifted towards a policy of restriction by the 1964 general election. This shift was reinforced by the failure of one of the party's leaders to hold an apparently safe seat, where his opponent campaigned on the issue of race. Both parties moved towards a policy of restrictions on immigration balanced by Race Relations Acts, which were intended to reduce discrimination against immigrants already settled in Britain. Labour passed a new Immigration Act in 1968 and Conservatives added fresh restrictions. Labour was responsible for the measures against discrimination, which Conservatives accepted. When Enoch Powell broke ranks in 1968 to warn that by allowing even restricted immigration, Britain was 'engaged in heaping up its funeral pyre', he was disowned by the Conservative leadership. Anti-immigration feeling therefore found an outlet less through the established political parties than through extra-parliamentary organizations, such as the National Front, founded in 1966, which urged that immigrants should be repatriated.

Enoch Powell. In his speech of 20 April 1968 Powell compared himself to the Roman senator who saw the Tiber 'foaming with much blood'.

commitment outside Europe was short and superficial and the minority attracting strongest hostility, the Turks, had no part in it. These examples suggest that the movement of non-European peoples to Europe in recent years is a development certainly not confined to Britain and that racial antagonism is not necessarily dependent on the experience of empire, still less on the specifically British experience of empire.

Moreover, the hostility experienced by immigrants from the Commonwealth may not be very different from the hostility experienced by other immigrants to Britain. Xenophobia seems to have been a part of the English view of the world from long before any large-scale imperial involvement. There is much to indicate that the British embarked on their imperial ventures with a disposition to dismiss non-European peoples, and other Europeans as well, as inferior. A golden age of innocence in early English dealings with non-European peoples, such as the native Americans in the early days of settlement, is hard to find. Chattel slavery may have been a status alien to English law and custom, but Africans were already feared and despised before the British became extensive slave owners. Foreign travellers in the eighteenth century recorded descriptions such as 'a chattering French baboon', 'an Italian ape', 'a beastly Dutchman', or 'a German hog'. Jewish immigration at the beginning of the twentieth century produced an Aliens Immigration Act of 1905, very similar in intention to the Commonwealth Immigration Act of 1962.

Some parts of the imperial experience may even have moderated antagonism to non-white peoples. Even if their assumptions were extremely paternalistic, anti-slavery and mission campaigns purported to be based on recognition of equality – 'Am I not a man and a brother?' But by the late nineteenth century views on a hierarchy of races were much more pronounced. Such views were common to most Europeans, but for the British they were reinforced by the extent of British imperial power. Almost by definition, non-European peoples were subject peoples and their destinies were controlled by Britain. To admit them as equal British citizens in Britain itself required a major break with the world view of many British people's past. Research into the reactions of British people to the first wave of immigrants from the 'new' Commonwealth found that hostility to them was especially marked among those who had served overseas.

With the passing of the years, however, fewer and fewer are left in Britain with any experience of empire. Those who most stridently advocate racist views in contemporary Britain do not seem to have any imperial nostalgia. Indeed, they have to deny the imperial past, at least implicitly, in insisting that people from minority communities have no historical connection with Britain.

It is unlikely that the new communities who started to move to Britain in the 1950s would have been absorbed easily, even if Britain had had no imperial past. As it was, the experience of empire probably sharpened deeply engrained xenophobia against an inflow of those not merely regarded as foreigners but also with all the connotations of subject peoples.

EMPIRE OR EUROPE?

In general, possession of an empire seems to have accentuated certain trends already recognizable in pre-imperial England. A people confident of their uniqueness became yet more confident that they were God's special people. For most of them, empire offered a mission to spread freedom, Christian truth, and improvement around the world. For some, empire enabled their race to demonstrate its superiority over other races. Empire helped to direct Britain's trade into a world-wide pattern which endured for a very long time. It also helped to scatter British people very widely around the world.

Cumulatively, therefore, the effect of empire was to turn Britain away from Europe. Yet Britain could never isolate itself entirely from Europe. What happened in Europe was always of the utmost consequence for Britain – the very worst possibility was that it would be invaded and conquered from Europe in time of war. Britain's rulers therefore had to play something of a balancing act between empire and Europe.

For much of the period covered by this book the choices hardly presented themselves. Empire and Europe seemed to be linked. Empire gave Britain the resources and the standing to play a major role in Europe and, since the main danger to empire was thought to come from the ambitions of other European powers, a successful European policy could neutralize such dangers.

Commonwealth to Europe

Did Britain jettison empire in order to embrace Europe? Britain's commitment to Europe certainly coincided with the loosening of its ties with the colonial empire and the Commonwealth. In 1961 the British government formally took the decision to apply for membership of the European Economic Community and, after two rejections by President de Gaulle, finally obtained entry in 1973. 1961, the year of the crucial decision to apply for membership, was also the year in which the British Cabinet decided to restrict Commonwealth immigration into Britain and in which two African colonies, Sierra Leone and Tanganyika, were granted independence. In the previous year the Prime Minister, Harold Macmillan, had warned the South African Parliament that 'a wind of change' was sweeping through Africa.

After 1961 there could be no doubt that a major realignment of British priorities from empire to Europe was taking place. However, there is little to suggest that Macmillan or his ministers either foresaw the need for such a shift or deliberately planned to bring it about. It seems rather that by 1961 long-term changes were forcing them reluctantly to make choices. On one hand, the success of the EEC had become unmistakable. More and more British trade was being done with the Community. On the other hand, Commonwealth and colonial trade links were weakening. Militarily, Britain had been committed to Europe since 1945, and the Commonwealth response to Britain's intervention at Suez in 1956 finally demonstrated that a serious Commonwealth diplomatic and military alliance was out of the question. Decolonization had begun in West Africa long before Britain decided to apply for membership of the EEC and a momentum was well under way by 1961.

On the surface at least, it seems that far from deliberately trying to clear the decks of Commonwealth or imperial encumbrances before going into Europe, ministers believed that a commitment to the Commonwealth and membership of the EEC were fully compatible. Commonwealth countries were publicly assured that Britain would only go into Europe on terms that guaranteed the continuation of their trading links with Britain. A Britain made stronger by membership of Europe would be a more effective member of the Commonwealth. Most Commonwealth leaders, however, viewed such assurances with scepticism. At a Commonwealth

The preferred solution to the claims of empire and Europe was usually for the British to apply what they liked to think of as their diplomatic finesse to Europe, while deploying the bulk of their armed forces outside Europe. For very long periods this arrangement seemed to be feasible. By the late nineteenth century, however, hard choices were having to be made. Were Germany, for instance, with its immense military capacity, to become wholly dominant in Europe, both Britain and its empire would be at Germany's mercy. To prevent this happening, Britain was drawn into ever closer arrangements with France and Russia and eventually felt bound to fight a vast continental war from 1914 to 1918 to ensure that France was not defeated. In a crisis the interests of Europe had been put first, but there had really been no question of choice: Britain's empire outside Europe had not been under any significant threat and the resources of that empire could be used for the European war.

Choices had again to be made in the 1930s, during the Second World War, and in the years after the war. The hostility of Germany, Italy, and Japan posed threats both in Europe and world-wide in the 1930s. Britain tried to maintain forces on all fronts, but the major concentration, as Australians were only too aware after the Singapore debacle of 1942, was inevitably on Europe. The ending of war and the creation of NATO meant a totally new permanent commitment to Europe. At least until 1989 this was always put first. Commitments to empire had to take second

prime ministers' conference in 1962, the terms on which Britain proposed to enter the EEC were bitterly attacked. An exasperated Macmillan commented that 'Poor Ted Heath [Edward Heath, Britain's chief negotiator with the Community], who is only accustomed to Europeans, who are courteous and well informed, even if hard bargainers, was astounded by the ignorance, ill manners and conceit of the Commonwealth.'

Whatever Macmillan may have thought, Commonwealth leaders had real grounds for scepticism. British negotiators sincerely wished to protect Commonwealth interests, but they were not prepared to let them wreck the negotiations. Britain did not want to have to choose between empire and Europe, but if choices had to be made there was no doubt what the choices would be. In 1951 Churchill had put the colonial empire and the Commonwealth before Europe. In 1952 even Macmillan had insisted that to 'join a Federation on the continent of Europe ... is something that we know in our bones we cannot do ... Britain's story and her interest lie beyond the continent of Europe'. By 1961 priorities had been changed irrevocably.

Commonwealth prime ministers' meeting, 1962. The cordiality of the group photograph contrasted with the acrimony about Britain's application to join the EEC.

place. Any question of major reinforcements from home in order to sustain British rule in India in 1946 or 1947, for example, was ruled out. Even so, Britain's ambitions to play a world role may have outrun the realism of the military planners. In November 1951 Churchill told his Cabinet: 'I never thought that Britain or the British Commonwealth should, either individually or collectively, become an integral part of a European federation ... Our first object is the unity and consolidation of the British Commonwealth and what is left of the former British empire.' British membership of the European Community was not to be effectively pursued for another ten years, when any imperial alternative was no longer being taken very seriously. Commitment to an imperial role was by no means the only reason for British caution about Europe in the 1950s. The 'special relationship' with the United States, for instance, still had a powerful hold. As so often, empire reinforced other considerations. By the time Britain was seriously approaching Europe many crucial decisions about the future of the Community had been taken without Britain. The British may well be deluding themselves if they suppose that different decisions would have been taken had Britain become a member much earlier, but by delaying they had deprived themselves at least of the opportunity of trying to influence those decisions.

If the British are now judged to be bad Europeans, empire cannot bear the whole blame. But empire has helped to engrain in the British a sense that they are different and superior to other Europeans.

NOT MUCH OF AN ALIBI

Millions of British people were able to lead more fulfilling lives through greater opportunities presented by emigration to Australia, Canada, or New Zealand. Some of those who went to areas with large indigenous populations engaged deeply, if on their own terms, with the societies in which they lived and reaped the benefits of contacts with cultures very different from their own. It would be condescending to suppose that the mercilessly caricatured pukka sahib or his memsahib or even the soldiers mainly confined to brutalizing barracks went untouched by strange lands and strange peoples. Nevertheless, for all the vast widening of horizons for so many people involved, it is still difficult to see empire as doing other than reinforcing the collective British insularity and self-sufficiency. Empire had to be on British terms. By and large British institutions and British society were not transformed by it. There were important exceptions, like the churches and the monarchy, but in most respects the empire was shaped as far as possible to British expectations, rather than the reverse. If the British are reluctant to merge their identity in Europe, so were they reluctant to merge their identity in the empire or the Commonwealth. Federal imperial institutions that would have involved genuine power sharing were never likely to win acceptance in Britain, let alone in the colonies. A world-wide British identity, embracing Canadians, Australians, and New Zealanders, was eventually found incompatible with new senses of national identity in those countries, but few

British people had shown any real interest in it, for all the networks of kinship built up by emigration. The terms of Britishness were always fixed in Britain itself, to which others had to conform or remain outside. Most British people have not shown conspicuous enthusiasm for widening concepts of Britishness in Britain to include being a Muslim, a Sikh, or a Hindu.

Britain's involvement with empire must be seen within the context of other and often older strands in the shaping of Britain. The kind of empire the British tried to create reflected the sort of people the British already were. To recognize that is not to belittle the importance of the imperial strand. Britain's imperial past has too often been identified with a relatively short period of the high imperial era of the end of Victoria's reign. Then it looks like an exotic growth whose 'impact' can easily be detected. That approach gives a distorting impression of the length and the depth of the British commitment to their empire. Empire was the work of the British people as a whole over centuries, not something imposed on them by a minority over a short space of time. Not surprisingly, an imperial enterprise in which so many people were involved for so long was not an exotic one, extraneous to the main currents of British history. It was central to them. In what they tried to do overseas, the British behaved much as they did at home. Empire revealed what was characteristic of them, although it exaggerated certain characteristics. If empire is responsible for the present discontents of Britain, it is the responsibility of whole generations of British people. It is not much of an alibi.

'The dreadful consequences of a general naturalization', 1751. This cartoon shows that dislike of foreign immigration into Britain has a long history. Britannia pours out her bounty to assorted foreigners while her own children have to emigrate to find work. The unwelcome immigrants include a 'blackamore' and a 'Musselman' – that is, a Muslim.

CHAPTER 13

K. S. Inglis

Australia

Invitation card to Australia's Centennial State Banquet, 26 January 1888. The imagery on this card celebrates the past that made Australia British – with medallions of the 'discoverer' Captain James Cook and of the first Governor of New South Wales, Arthur Phillip. It also celebrates Australia's continuing links with Britain: Queen Victoria is flanked by the flags of the still separate Australian colonies.

The centenary of British settlement in Australia happened to arrive just as Queen Victoria's Golden Jubilee ended. In Sydney, on 26 January 1888, orators still aglow from the imperial festivities of 1887 imagined mighty futures. The three million Britons inhabiting the southern continent would become by 1988 thirty, or fifty, or a hundred million, living in an empire not merely intact but enlarged. Sir Henry Parkes, Premier of the senior colony of New South Wales, proclaimed his hope that 'the red line of kinship' would 'unite us to England for generations to come' and foresaw a time when 'there is no spot on earth where British freedom does not reign'. Having lived in Australia for half the country's British history, Parkes was an archetype of the successful emigrant from Europe to a new world. In the centennial year the Queen – whom he had met on one of his visits to the old homeland – approved his appointment as Knight Grand Cross of the Order of St Michael and St George, an imperial fellowship created to honour Britons abroad.

This centennial optimism is in contrast to the mood of the mid-century. In 1849 Henry Parkes had spoken the language of rebellion. When the imperial authorities tried to revive the transportation of convicts to New South Wales, he was at the centre of a Great Protest Movement, speaking with admiration of the American revolutionaries as models for maltreated colonial subjects. No more convict ships were sent to Sydney, and the Colonial Secretary duly advised the Governor of Van Diemen's Land that he too could expect no further shipments of felons: England should not force the colonists 'into a furious opposition … extinguishing all loyalty and affection for the mother country'.

The agitators had known in their hearts that Britain would give in if only they shouted long and loudly enough. Colonists all over the empire benefited forever from the loss of the United States: thereafter, they could nearly always count on the Crown's advisers to remove sufficient discontents to cool any campaign for cutting ties with Britain. Not much bluster was necessary to gain self-government for each of the Australian colonies after 1850. At the festivities of 1888 everybody knew that when politicians around Australia could finally agree on the terms of a federal union, the Queen would be advised to give it her blessing. She did so in 1900, just in time for the Commonwealth of Australia to greet the new century, representing a modest victory for an idea first given a name early in her reign – nationalism.

That word was employed in the title of one centennial publication, Robert Thomson's *Australian Nationalism: An Earnest Appeal to the Sons of Australia in Favour of the Federation and Independence of the States of our Country*. Thomson was a republican, one of a few who had been provoked by the triumphal imperialism of the jubilee year to articulate a different vision for their land. He embraced 26 January 1788 – convicts and all – as a date not to be sneered at, one that in time to come would be 'classed in the world's history with the founding of Rome, the landing of the Pilgrim Fathers, or the storming of the Bastille'. But true Australian nationalism, he believed, required some other event to celebrate. 'There will be but one greater day in our own Australia's annals, and that will be the anniversary of the Declaration of her Independence.' Thomson and his allies envied the Americans for having in 1776 an external enemy against whom they could go to war and shed blood. How were Australians to achieve that necessary experience? Thomson looked around the world and let his eye fall on China. At the first threat of invasion from that quarter, he proclaimed, men would exchange pens and tools for rifles, women would embroider uniforms and prepare comforts for casualties, and no girl would look at her lover if he had not enlisted. The ensuing war would baptize the independent nation whose making it had precipitated. That was a tall order. If the making of Australian independence required an invasion by the armies of the ailing Manchu empire, the nationalists would be waiting forever.

When the bicentenary of British settlement was commemorated in Sydney on 26 January 1988 – Australia Day, as that anniversary was now called – the population

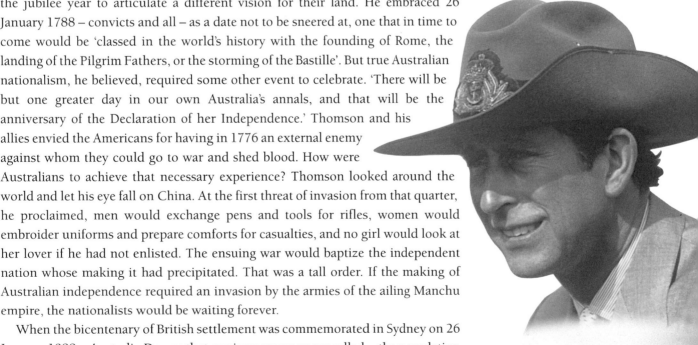

Prince Charles at the Bicentennial, 26 January 1988. The only voice from Britain belonged to the Prince, who made a short, mellow, post-imperial speech, and even he looked Australian: millions saw on television the balding royal head protected from the summer sun by a version of the slouch hat Australian men used to wear to imperial wars.

had reached not fifty but only sixteen million, of whom a proportion unimagined in 1988 had lines of kinship running not to England, Wales, Scotland, or Ireland, but to a host of countries from Italy to Vietnam. The empire was history, embodied in the pageantry of the day by old ships re-enacting the arrival of the first fleet and by the presence of Prince Charles. A second fleet, of tall ships assembled from all over the world, sailed into Sydney harbour representing the newly multicultural nation. The organizers held their breath to see how Aborigines – a people dispossessed in 1788, out of sight and mind at the festival of 1888, and now demanding the restoration of ancient land – would respond to the ships and to the whole show. A threat of boycott or resistance from any other group comprising less than 2 per cent of the population would not have been grave; but Aborigines, if enough of them chose, had the power to spoil the festival. Ominously anti-bicentennial slogans had appeared on walls, proclaiming 200 years of oppression and declaring that white Australia had a black history. In the event some thousands of Aborigines demonstrated noisily but genially.

AN INDEPENDENT AUSTRALIA?

When, if ever, between 1888 and 1988, had Australia become independent? P.J. Marshall observes in his introduction (page 10) that while the beginning of the British empire in general is difficult to date, its virtual end can be located in the 1960s. In the story of those colonies of settlement that became Dominions, however, the founding date is easily fixed and it is the terminal moment that is hard, perhaps impossible, to identify with precision. Dates may matter less than interpretation. In 1988 the historians W.J. Hudson and Martin Sharp published a book – the first on the subject, as they remark with justified surprise – entitled *Australian Independence*, devoted to a question that has always baffled those

'Bravo boys! Pull together!' Britain coaches the newly federated Australian colonies on their first outing together.

Australians who bothered to ask it. 'When, Precisely?' that last chapter is headed. Answer: 'Australia became an independent nation state, an independent kingdom on 11 December 1931.' That was when the Statute of Westminster was proclaimed, putting an end to all control by the British Parliament over the affairs of Australia, New Zealand, Canada, South Africa, and the Irish Free State. This date, they believed, was more significant than October 1942, when the measure was ratified in Canberra, for the Australians had held the power to do that at any time after 1931. And it was more significant than 1901, despite a popular and even academic assumption that the act of the British Parliament creating the federation contained some declaration, or concession, of independence.

Although the makers of federation were apt to use rhetoric signalling autonomy – Alfred Deakin, the Prime Minister, liked to describe himself and his compatriots as independent Australian Britons, until well into the twentieth century, Australian politicians were wary of talking about independence from Britain because they feared that a mother country whose children had chosen to leave home would no longer feel any obligation to protect or favour them. Unlike the Irish, South African, and Canadian governments, those of Australia and New Zealand had no substantial body of supporters pressing for a break from Britain. Stuck as they were to the south of Asia, where everybody else's Far East was their near north, they believed that a lingering measure of dependence on Britain might guarantee their shores the protection of the Royal Navy; more particularly, they wanted to be sure that the British government would build, pay for, and maintain the promised naval base at Singapore, to guarantee their security should Britain's ally Japan become the enemy. They imagined, moreover, that while the British government recognized a continuing constitutional link, it would be more inclined to supply Australia, in the phrase coined by S.M. Bruce, Prime Minister of Australia in the 1920s, with 'men, money, and markets'. Bruce and other Australians involved in drafting what became the Balfour formula on imperial relationships in 1926 wallowed happily in the calculated ambiguity of language that could mean independence or dependence, separateness or cohesion, according to Irish or Canadian or South African or Australian or New Zealand or British taste. This formula, which delayed for a few more years a formal independence Australian politicians did not want, was praised by the Solicitor-General, Sir Robert Garran. 'Contradictory? Yes. But it works. Mystical? Yes. But it works. The British have a genius for sliding into constitutional changes that derive not from statute law but from practice.' After 1931 Australian governments stalled for another decade, until John Curtin's Labor government ratified the statute, and did so then only because lawyers advised that it would be technically helpful in validating wartime laws. (The New Zealanders did not get around to it until 1947.) If 11 December 1931 is the true date of independence, it has not been celebrated as significant or even remembered. Nobody mentioned the statute on 26 January 1988, and after that it was invoked only by republicans to whom an 'independent kingdom' of Australia was a contradiction.

Anzacs and independence

The Digger hat worn by Prince Charles at the bicentennial celebration in 1988 felicitously connected vestigial monarchy with the Anzac tradition – 26 January with 25 April. That date, the anniversary of the day Australian soldiers landed at Gallipoli in 1915, had come to occupy the place Robert Thomson imagined in 1888 for a day greater in Australian annals than 26 January. By 1930 dawn services, marches in city and country, ceremonies at war memorials, and reunions of old comrades, together displayed Anzac Day as both a more popular and a more solemn expression of nationalism than Australia Day. Anzac Day commemorated the shedding of blood, the baptism of the nation. Big words waiting for more than a century were released by the Australians' (and, if they were remembered, the New Zealanders') achievement on the cliffs of Turkey. It could be described as something like a declaration of independence. In an editorial on the first anniversary of the landing entitled 'Anzac Day: the Birth of a Nation', the *Freeman's Journal* in Syndey declared: 'Before the Anzacs astonished the watching nations … we were constantly admonished by our daily journals to remember that we were nothing better than a joint in the tail of a great Empire … Anzac Day has changed all that … we are at last a nation, with one heart, one soul and one thrilling aspiration.' These words, celebrating the deeds of an army called the Australian Imperial Force, come out of Irish Catholic Australia. In Australia, as in Ireland, the degree of enlistment indicates that the British cause in the war of 1914–18 was more popular among Irish Catholics than was Sinn Féin. Turks on Gallipoli, assuming that the Anzacs were mercenaries, threw over pamphlets urging them to desert. German guards asked Australian prisoners why on earth they had volunteered to fight England's

Anzac day parade: part of the women's contingent on the 1919 parade at Melbourne to commemorate the landing in 1915 at Gallipoli, a place etched into Australian memories by the bravery shown by their troops and the heavy losses they incurred.

AWM H01894

war. But while Archbishop Daniel Mannix of Melbourne, friend of Sinn Féin, was prominent in the successful campaigns of 1916–17 to prevent the Australian Imperial Force from being reinforced by conscripts, the proportion of Irish Catholics who joined the AIF was close to the proportion of their ethnicity and faith in the population. That was about one in four: more than in any other country of emigration in or beyond the empire.

The eventual failure of the campaign, far from diminishing the use of Gallipoli in national mythology, actually enhanced it. Whatever the causes of the incompetence that the soldiers experienced all the way from Alexandria to Anzac Cove and the survivors endured all the way back, the potency of the legend enabled Australians to assure themselves that it was not the fault of the men from the Dominions. In France the English journalist C.E. Montague was to hear, as he recorded in his bitter war memoir, 'the old Australian sneer' about the capacity of the English: '… they wanted to have it quite clear that in England's war record they were not involved except as our saviours from our sorry selves'. As the basis for a legend in which Australians were still loyal to the empire but mature enough to be full partners in it, Gallipoli was perfect, failures and all. English politicians had thought of the campaign, English officers led it; the Anzacs simply fought, heroically. 25 April might never have gained its unique character in Australia and New Zealand if Britain had come out of the campaign with more glory. 'And what should they know of England who only England know?' No wonder Kipling, celebrating outriders of empire as the best of Britons, went down so well among Australians.

But the legend faded. By the 1990s the whole imperial enterprise had become alien to many Australian minds, and the men who had volunteered for the AIF were seen as having fought and died in somebody else's war. 'It is deeply ironic', one historian wrote in 1985, 'that many of the achievements recalled on Anzac Day were made in the service of another nation.' Other, usually older, historians reply that Australians were pursuing rational self-interest when they supported the imperial and allied cause. How one votes on that issue depends on judgements about German war aims. But for anybody who wants to understand the British empire it is not enough to wonder whether particular Australians calculated that they would be worse off if Germany won the war. What matters is how key words – 'empire', 'nation', 'country', 'British' – were interpreted at the time. That editorial writer in the *Freeman's Journal*, far from thinking that Australians at Gallipoli were serving another nation, believed that they were making his and their own. In the year of the Gallipoli landing, school teachers in South Australia administered to their pupils an oath beginning: 'I love my country, the British empire.' On 1914–18 war memorials I have found no inscription saying men fought and died for both country and empire: evidently the two words shared so much meaning in the inscribers' minds that it did not make sense to separate them. The people who made the memorials were still 'independent Australian Britons'.

War memorial. The 60,000 Australian dead of the First World War were commemorated by some 3,000 war memorials, the majority, as in this case, with the figure of an Australian soldier. These memorials are a constant reminder of the traumatic effects of the First World War on that generation of Australians.

The Pacific war and independence

Paul Keating, who became Prime Minister in 1991, encouraged the notion that Australians at Gallipoli were fighting other people's wars and that a truly Australian tradition of warfare dates back only to events of 1942 when Australian soldiers resisted a Japanese army that had invaded the neighbouring colony of New Guinea (Papua New Guinea) and held the enemy on the Kokoda trail. As one historian put it a few years earlier: 'Only in meeting the Japanese threat during the Second World War did Australian servicemen actually fight to defend Australia. In national terms the Kokoda trail has a better claim than Gallipoli to be the focus of a day of remembrance and thanksgiving.' It is true that in 1942, unlike 1915, bombs fell on Australia and an invasion of Australia seemed to be a real possibility. But we should also recognize that Australians had volunteered to serve the imperial cause no less enthusiastically in the Second World War than in the First, and that on the Kokoda track and elsewhere they were conscious of having inherited the Anzac tradition.

As expressed by Keating and others in the cause of a republic, the celebration of Australian valour in the Pacific war went with a tendency to 'bash the Poms' for abandoning Australia. The British, they claim, knew that the defences of Singapore were not strong enough to resist a Japanese attack, but they fooled Australians into believing it was invincible. Cooler heads blame Australian politicians for indulging the naive and parsimonious hope that in return for imperial solidarity Britain would underwrite the forward defence of the southern Dominions. Though there was no connection between the fall of Singapore in February 1942 and the ratification of the Statute of Westminster eight months later, the timing is symbolically appropriate. The Commonwealth of Australia was now independent of Great Britain whether its people liked that condition or not.

Australians in New Guinea. By August 1942 the Japanese had conquered most of New Guinea. 54,000 Australians with American support then drove them back in a long and bitterly contested campaign which was the first one that Australia had fought essentially on its own.

While the Japanese were sweeping south in 1942, Australian Prime Minister John Curtin issued his historic declaration of transferred dependence: 'Australia looks to America, free of any pangs as to our traditional links or kinship with the United Kingdom.' A plaque below an American eagle in Canberra bears monumental testimony to the response: 'In grateful remembrance of the vital help given by the United States of America during the war in the Pacific, 1941–1945.' The words were unveiled by Queen Elizabeth II in 1954 when she became the first reigning monarch to visit Australia. The British High Commissioner sat uncomfortably through the ceremony, having advised against the Queen's involvement on the grounds that the Australian–American memorial was part of a campaign 'to work up enthusiasm for the US'. He was not wrong, though its purpose might have been more precisely described as part of an attempt to ensnare the United States. Following the end of the war this new link was at the centre of Australian foreign policy, reaching its disastrous climax in Vietnam when Australia sent troops to support the United States.

TOWARDS A REPUBLIC

The royal tour of 1954 was an immensely popular enterprise, as Australians marvelled at having the face on the stamps and the money smiling live in their own streets. In retrospect, that visit looks like a monster beano to mark the end of empire. The Queen's later tours generated less and less excitement both because, to use the words of the nineteenth-century English writer Walter Bagehot, they let too much daylight in upon magic, and because a new pattern of immigration was creating a population decreasingly British in origin and sentiment. The decline of enthusiasm paralleled a decline in trade between the Queen's United Kingdom and Australian realms: during the twenty postwar years the proportion of Australian exports going to the United Kingdom fell by half from around 40 per cent to below 20. A series of symbolic changes also registered the erosion of the imperial connection. The British Prime Minister Clement Attlee dropped the word 'British' from 'British Commonwealth' in 1948, making the Australian Prime Minister R.G. Menzies 'feel very sick'. The word 'British' on Australian passports shrank, then vanished. From 1964, moreover, the holders of those passports could no longer enter Britain at will, but had to queue with people from India, Pakistan, and the West Indies. For many Australians this experience was a bruising revelation that the empire in which they had grown up was disappearing. Worse, they soon had to wait in that queue while European foreigners streamed through in the company of British citizens, partners in the European Economic Community now that the fickle old mother country had embarked on a policy of anti-imperial preference. Three decades on, that queue – defining Australians as aliens – could still rankle. 'I note that traditional allies of the UK, like the Germans and Italians, obtain preferential treatment by virtue of EC membership', wrote an Australian of British parentage to a newspaper in 1992, urging Paul Keating on to the republic.

Little by little Australia was heading in that direction. In 1993, for example, the oaths taken by new citizens and by federal ministers were both amended to remove pledges of allegiance to 'Her Majesty, Queen Elizabeth II, her heirs and successors'. No doubt the tribulations of those heirs and successors were helping sentiment for the monarchy to wane; but even without them, the British character of Australia, where two-thirds of the people now had mixed ethnic origins, were causes enough to achieve clear majorities in the polls for some kind of republic. Rational misgivings had to do with what kind of republic, and with a tendency among reformers to expect the republic to work magic, such as persuading Asians to take more Australian exports. As the centenary of federation approached, most people expected the 'independent kingdom' of 1931 to become a republic – still with a recognizably British political system, and no more and no less independent than other nation states in an era of multinational companies, supranational satellite television, and floating currencies.

How much of the country's British heritage will be recognized in the Australian republic of the twenty-first century is an open question. Retrospective Brit-bashing may well become less popular. Truths uncomfortable for nationalists may or may not be recognized, especially in the history of racial policies. The 'White Australia' policy (the exclusion of non-European immigrants) was firmly in place by 1900 despite serious British objections. In the years before colonial self-government, settlers were less tolerant than imperial officials towards the old inhabitants; indeed, they were given the name 'Aborigines' by men in London who believed that in these and other colonies of British settlement, the natives had to be protected from their usurpers.

By the 1990s one piece of recovered history had begun to have large consequences for post-imperial policies towards Aborigines. Until 1992 courts considering Aboriginal land claims had ruled that in British law Australia had become in 1788 *terra nullius* (nobody's land), thus requiring no treaty with the nomadic occupants before the intruders could acquire rights over it. Then in the late 1980s the historian Henry Reynolds showed that the doctrine of *terra nullius* had prevailed in British Australia only by the mid-nineteenth century after more than fifty years of uncertainty during which some authorities in Britain and in Australia considered that these hunters and gatherers did have rights to the land they occupied. In 1992 the highest court in Australia's British-derived legal system, influenced by Reynolds's finding, ruled that native title to land existed when British colonization began, and had not been extinguished by subsequent legislation. How to apply that decision seemed to present more difficulties than how to turn the independent kingdom into a republic. The musings of British governors and civil servants in the nineteenth century had become momentously relevant in what one might have thought was a post-British Australia.

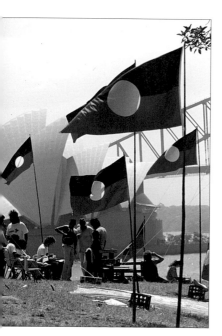

Aborigines claim land near Sydney, 1988. Such claims are a legacy of Australia's colonial past, since from the first British landing no recognition was accorded to any Aboriginal right to land. To draw attention to their grievances, Aborigines plant their flag on what they claim as their own.

Africa

CHAPTER 14

Toyin Falola

Africans who had first-hand acquaintance with British rule had to cope with rapid changes – some too fast for their comprehension, many others significant but too slow to be noticed. Before their very eyes, the old boundaries of indigenous states were re-drawn, sovereignty was lost, and the old elite received a blow from which it did not recover. How was the British empire assessed by those who experienced it? By the end of the nineteenth century the brilliant minds of the time saw what was going to happen. Chroniclers such as Akiga Sai of the Tiv and Samuel Johnson of the Yoruba were already talking of a dying past and the dawn of a new civilization. In the early twentieth century, with colonization an established fact, the majority of the new educated elite under colonial rule were impressed by the cultural contacts, accepted assimilation as a way of life, and dreamt about 'progress' – shorthand for the westernization of Africa and an eventual transfer of power to them. But after 1945 this optimism gave way to disillusionment: African nationalist movements were tired of an empire they regarded as oppressive and exploitative and anti-colonial struggles intensified. Subsequent generations, survivals of colonial rule and children of independence, regard the British empire and its legacy as part of the historical evolution of Africa and its development process.

THE ANATOMY OF CHANGE

British rule is nothing if not about change, in spite of Africa's continuity with its past. Today, English-speaking Africa cannot be defined without this legacy. The short duration of British rule and the survival of many aspects of indigenous culture led to a grand misconception and a misleading conclusion: that the impact of the empire was minimal and not enduring. This is one way to minimize the shock, stupefaction, and turmoil of an extraordinary conquest by underplaying it as a small episode in Africa's long history. The fact that in Africa today western values compete with the Islamic and the traditional, and the most modernizing sectors of African societies and the most influential political and economic ideas are western, is largely a product of imperialism. Certain changes made by the British were so decisive in their impact as to mark a major break with the past: these included the monetization of society, the commercialization of land, the integration of Africa into a world economy and international politics, the transfer of power from an old elite to an educated one, the emergence of permanent armies, the use of English, and the introduction of western medicine, education, sports, aesthetics, and architecture. Those who underplay the significance of the empire wrongly assume that pre-colonial traditions and institutions can be revived with ease to serve contemporary needs. The relevance of the past cannot be denied, but so far no one has come up with any model that does not bear the imprint of colonial changes. The patchwork of British rule is the foundation of many countries in modern Africa.

An early settler laager at Bulawayo. Bulawayo was the centre of the rulers of the Ndebele people, whose lands were included in the area claimed in 1889 by the British South Africa Company of Cecil Rhodes. In 1890 the first settlers moved into the area that came to be known as Southern Rhodesia. In 1893 Ndebele resistance to further incursions led to defeat in war and the loss of land to white settlement. By 1930 fifty million acres in Southern Rhodesia had been allocated to Europeans, by comparison with twenty-nine million acres for Africans.

Contact with the British widened the interaction with the outside world – well beyond the ties already established by the Atlantic slave trade, European exploration, and Christian missionary activities. To many areas, British rule brought for the first time a large number of aliens, notably Asians and Europeans. These settlers both benefited from and contributed to the economy but their presence generated tension where they settled in large numbers, as in southern and East Africa, or when they were too slow to depart after the end of British rule. Confrontations were most intense and violent in Kenya and Southern Rhodesia. In Kenya, for instance, there was bitter warfare from 1952 to 1956, leading to the death of about 10,000 people.

During the second half of the nineteenth century the map of Africa was virtually redrawn by European powers. By the end of the century the shape of Britain's stake in Africa was clear. The French controlled the largest territorial empire, but Britain had acquired colonies in some of the most heavily populated parts of West Africa, the most important of which were the Gold Coast and Nigeria. Occupation of Egypt gave Britain the richest asset in North Africa. In eastern, central, and southern Africa, Britain's territorial acquisitions were enormous: British rule ran continuously from the Cape to Lake Nyasa and from Zanzibar to Egypt. Since independence, colonial boundaries and even the names have largely been retained with only a few changes, such as the amalgamation of British and French Cameroon, the amalgamation of Tanganyika and Zanzibar to form Tanzania, and the renaming of the Gold Coast and Southern Rhodesia as Ghana and Zimbabwe.

There is a firm commitment to these boundaries by most of Africa and by international organizations like the Organization of African Unity and the United Nations. Yet colonial boundaries reduced the large number of pre-colonial states to a few new countries and the artificiality of the exercise – 'drawing lines on maps where no white man's foot ever trod', as Lord Salisbury described it in the nineteenth century – will continue to create problems. A typical African country is an agglomeration of hostile neighbours struggling to define common grounds for unity and stability. Disputes arising from the partition of one ethnic group between different countries and the inability of groups to live together have led to a series of political problems, including well-known cases of secession and civil war in Nigeria, frontier changes in Cameroon, aggression in Uganda, and prolonged warfare in Sudan.

When Britain carved out its African empire in the nineteenth century it imposed new forms of government and administration based on British models, gradually replacing age-old patterns of authority based on the power of the elders, chiefs, secret societies, and age grades. Many countries are now arguing over whether to sustain or jettison this secular form of government, especially where Islamic ideology presents an alternative, as in Sudan, Nigeria, and Egypt. English-speaking Africa, with its roots in an entirely different intellectual and cultural climate, does not provide a strong foundation for a secular state. The modern secular state is in trouble because of its failure to integrate the diverse people within its boundaries and to create a superior identity to that offered by religious and what remains of traditional identities. The civil service, police, army, and judicial system are all inherited from the British. Islands of privilege without responsibility, none of these institutions has developed any clear mission other than as an avenue for corruption. In some cases, these new institutions are inappropriate; in others, their responsibilities are not well defined. The army, as demonstrated in the case of Nigeria, is the most notorious of all: its leadership is accountable to no one but itself; it is the worst threat to the civilian society and the most formidable obstacle to building any viable democracy. Thus, the break with the British past has been limited and English-speaking Africa is characterized neither by any sustainable renewal nor by a retreat to ancient traditions but by its imperial legacy.

Capitalism as the economic ideology of the state has a similar beginning. During the colonial period Britain determined the direction and pace of the economy. The motivation was clear: colonies were markets in which to sell goods manufactured abroad and estates to produce raw materials. In addition, every colony was to be self-supporting so that there would be no need to use external funds. The basis of the British colonial economy included the exploitation of mineral and agricultural resources, the domination of external trade by foreign firms, and the use of the colonies as markets for British manufactures. In short, colonial Africa became a paying economic proposition for the British. For instance, in the 1956–57 financial year trade in British West Africa was worth a total of £503 million.

Gold Coast cocoa farmer. Cocoa was developed almost entirely on the initiative of African farmers. In the 1890s farmers in the Gold Coast (Ghana) started to grow cocoa on a large scale; by the end of the First World War farmers in parts of Nigeria were doing the same. It proved to be a successful export crop.

In order to achieve these changes, the British had to adapt the pre-colonial economy to the needs of the empire. This included the introduction of a new currency, new forms of financial organization, and new procedures: sterling replaced indigenous currencies such as cowries; banks were created for the first time; and the continent became more monetized than ever before. The greatest change came in the area of transportation, with new roads, artificial harbours, and railways. These facilities brought for the first time lorries, cars, and trains. Roads and railways created the modern transport revolution, making possible greater movements of goods and people. The cost of moving goods from the coast to the hinterland was reduced substantially – in the case of Accra to Kumasi in the Gold Coast, railways cut the cost to less than one sixth of what it had been. Peasants were persuaded to grow cash crops by offering them attractive prices. Taxation was used as an instrument not just to raise revenue but to ensure production: because peasants had to pay tax in money, they were forced to produce and sell. To create markets for British products, steps were taken to ensure that colonial subjects would either like or depend on foreign goods. The elite began to cultivate habits for imported items, further promoting the importation of goods from Britain. In the estimation of many of the elite and those who wanted to become like them, people's social standing could be measured by their use of the English language, the wearing of British-type clothes, and the adoption of British manners. In this way the behaviour and preferences of elite groups assured the spread of British material culture in Africa.

Some Africans gained from the new colonial economy. The larger political units created by the new countries increased the volume of trade. Where export crops succeeded, those who farmed or traded on a large scale prospered. Africa became less reliant on imported textiles as imported machinery enabled more to be produced locally. Africans benefited from the new transport systems, which enabled them to travel more easily. People moved from the countryside to new colonial towns or to growing older ones, where they enjoyed new amenities such as hospitals, schools, and improved roads.

There was, however a price to be paid for economic change. The British did not see rapid development of their colonies as a priority. Rather they pursued a policy of wealth transfer, keeping under their control the monetary reserves accumulated by the increased export of African commodities (see page 131). Reliance on a few export crops created a less diversified economy. Production of food crops declined in some areas where attention shifted permanently to export crops. Old land tenure systems were disrupted and land became an object for sale, with the result that many were dispossessed. There was a widening gap between the cities and the countryside. The provision of social facilities like dispensaries, hospitals, schools, and playing fields was never adequate.

As was to be expected, Africans complained about all aspects of exploitation and deprivation. One serviceman from the Gold Coast who lived through it all and had fought for the British during the Second World War published an interesting poem – a parody of Psalm 23 – in the *Accra Morning Post* in the 1940s, to lament the hardship of the age:

> The European merchant is my shepherd,
> And I am in want;
> He maketh me to lie down in cocoa farms;
> He leadeth me beside the waters of great need;
> The general managers and profiteers frighten me.
> Thou preparedst a reduction in my salary
> In the presence of my creditors.
> Thou anointest my income with taxes;
> My expense runs over my income
> And I will dwell in a rented house for ever!

There were extenuating circumstances. After the devastating wars of the nineteenth century and the resistance to conquest, a long period of peace and stability followed. This facilitated Britain's consolidation of its empire and the pursuit of its interests, but English-speaking Africa was also to make some gains out of it, largely by way of infrastructure (new roads, railways, telephone, and telegraphs), education, and social services. To be sure, the gains were small, and usually accidental, but they provided the basis for the post-colonial expansion and reforms.

English-speaking Africa inherited the post-1945 structure and problems, with limited opportunities for a rapid economic takeoff owing to inadequate trained manpower and capital, political immaturity, limited business experience, and a weak economy. Even today, technology is primitive – for instance, the majority of the peasants rely on such age-old tools as the hoe and cutlass, telephone facilities are lacking in most places, and food and good drinking water cannot be stored for many days. Existing communications continue to be expanded largely to promote external trade. Thus, rather than build a new railway system, the older colonial tracks from the coast to the hinterland are retained and priority is given to roads leading to the centres of export production. Internal transport systems are ignored primarily because governments do not think that they will generate revenues and foreign reserves and believe that urban centres are more important than the countryside.

As before, there is a dependence on external markets – a continuation of colonial patterns of trade – for the sale of raw materials and the purchase of finished products, technology, and even food. In the words of the Organization of African Unity, dependence makes the African economies 'susceptible to external developments and with detrimental effects on the interests of the continent'. The economic legacy of wealth transfer out of the continent includes the staggering amount of money needed to repay and service debts to western financial houses, the exchange of raw materials for manufactured goods, and the rather poor and fluctuating prices externally fixed on African exports. To these, African leaders have added a new one: huge sums of money stolen from the state are stored abroad, in the now proverbial Swiss banks. In post-independent Africa the economy is dominated by the state, which has interfered more and more in the attempt to stimulate economic growth, develop those sectors ignored by private investors, and distribute national resources to as many people and areas as possible. Interference has included price control of all products, rationing of key imports, establishment of industries by government intervention, fixing interest rates for banks, expulsion of aliens, and nationalization of foreign companies. Many countries have retained capitalism (for example, Nigeria and Kenya) while some (for example, Tanzania) have experimented with a different model, that of socialism. Neither has a success story to tell.

The legacy of social transformation is permanent in many aspects of life. Today, as in British Africa, education is seen as a way of imbibing western values, securing employment, and becoming part of the 'modern' generation. Since the end of empire the educational legacy has been improved upon by expanding facilities at all levels, adapting the curriculum to indigenous African culture, and training more women. But education is still not universal. Moreover, in the course of expansion quality has been sacrificed: even the early universities that made a good start, such as the University of Ibadan in Nigeria and the University of Makerere in Uganda, have failed to sustain their reputation. The discipline of students declines, along with the social status of their teachers.

Two other aspects of the social legacy are language and religion. Colonial rule, through its schools, made possible the rapid spread of the English language. English also became the language of commerce in the import sector and banking. In the new urban areas, it was the language that many people had to use to communicate with one another. Above all, it was the language of politics and administration. Since independence, English has been retained as the official language. Except in East Africa where Swahili and Somali enjoy pre-eminent status, proposals to use indigenous languages are unpopular because of the suspicion that one group wants to use its language to dominate others. While the use of the English language has facilitated interactions within and outside Africa, it remains essentially elitist, thus limiting its relevance for development and inter-group relations.

Islam and Christianity preceded the British conquest. Islam has been spreading since the eighth century; Christianity came to most areas after the fifteenth century, with European penetration, although it did not make many converts until after 1840. Christianity was able to spread with the empire, although the British encouraged religious plurality and showed no hostility to Islam. Both religions are now firmly established, and their competition is one cause of instability in some countries like Sudan and Nigeria.

There has been a population increase, notably after 1945, partly because of improved nutrition and access to medical facilities. Urbanization accompanied British rule everywhere, as new commercial, mining, and administrative centres were created and as migration to the cities became a means of seeking a better standard of living. In these centres, medical, sports, and entertainment facilities were provided as well – significant additions to social changes and the landscape. What most Africans now define as progress includes access to these benefits and living in these cities, while their leaders continue to face the problems of increasing population and urbanization. Thus, African beneficiaries of western education and religion have been transformed into a new elite, with values and visions of the future different in many ways from those of their pre-colonial predecessors. Monogamy, greater materialism, enhanced status for women, and the abandonment of local religions are some of these new values.

A mosque at Khartoum, 1960. Although the British overthrew a Muslim regime in conquering the Sudan in 1898, their policy was one of toleration. Islamic law was practised, and subsidies were paid towards the building of mosques. In the Sudan, as elsewhere in their African colonies, the British – without intending to do so – provided a framework within which Islam could spread.

THE INTERPRETATION OF CHANGE

Arguments about Britain's African empire revolve less around the fact of change than its interpretation. Critics on the far right judge most changes as having been beneficial to Africa: the continent, they claim, was saved from barbarism and drawn into an advanced civilization. On the far left, critics maintain that the changes were extremely destructive, laying the foundations for today's underdevelopment. Yet such perspectives are little more than reflections of ideological difference. Those on the right can be discredited as nostalgic apologists of empire, an easy thing to do since most of their leading lights are either former colonial administrators or British scholars more interested in the glory of the British expansion than its excesses in distant lands. Those on the left appeal to the victims of colonial exploitation, but are prone to exaggeration (such as their misleading conclusion that colonialism wiped out indigenous textiles). They underplay the survival of indigenous institutions (in such things as food habits, ceremonies, architecture, and language). They also underrate creative responses to British rule (such as the fusing of English with vernacular languages to form creole).

By its very nature, imperialism is perverse. It involves the domination of one group by another. To those who are dominated it is humiliating and degrading, to say the least. The sovereignty of the pre-colonial nations was terminated, denying them the ability to determine the pace and pattern of growth and to define their place in the international system. The majority of Europeans belittled the intelligence of Africans, dismissed many aspects of their culture as primitive, and treated them as an inferior race. Yet there were also things that English-speaking Africa can celebrate. The people resisted alien rule. In many places westernization was not adopted wholesale: many people retained substantial elements of their culture and institutions. Islam and 'traditional' religions, African music, art, dance, dress, and architecture survived the empire. Adaptations to change, the syntheses of old and new cultures (such as the combination of western and indigenous medicine in the treatment of specific diseases), and innovations in all aspects of life were a few of the monumental African responses to British rule. Nationalism and the renewal of old ethnic identities helped to restore the human dignity that British subjugation had taken away. Except for South Africa, racism did not last in Africa: any complaint of inferiority can no longer be attributed to the humiliation and racism of the empire but to the failure of the continent to acquire the respect of the international community. Independence was eventually achieved, a restoration of the sovereignty that Africans had lost.

ANGLO-AFRICAN RELATIONS TODAY

While the empire crumbled, its members continued to be loosely united in the Commonwealth, a major strategy for keeping the empire alive. Successive British governments worked to ensure co-operation with English-speaking Africa so as to maintain the international balance of power and safeguard Britain's economic assets

The Masai *moran*. The Masai of Kenya were able to retain an outwardly traditional way of life in spite of the pressures of colonialism. Although they lost access to much of the land that used to be available to them, they remained a cattle-keeping pastoral people, whose young men lived together as warriors.

in former colonies. No African state has formally become a member of a western alliance system, but military co-operation with Kenya, for instance, has been very close. In addition to providing technical and financial assistance on its own account and through the Commonwealth, Britain has signed many bilateral military, political, and economic treaties with its former colonies. There remain tensions in Anglo-African relations, however, caused by the desire of Britain to remain master. Britain's equivocal attitude to minority rule in South Africa and external military intervention in Africa, especially as part of cold war politics (for example, in Tanzania in 1964 when British troops intervened to protect the government of Julius Nyerere from a mutiny in its own army), and the limited financial and technical aid to Africa are three sore points. There is some resentment of Britain's leadership in the Commonwealth, and passionate and inflamed rhetoric about the uselessness of this voluntary association. While all English-speaking countries have received aid in one form or another from Britain, they have shown little gratitude because they see it as receiving back part of their 'stolen wealth', too small to be useful and never without a political price. Breaking loose from Britain has been difficult – it remains at once a best friend and a well-known enemy. Looking inward has not been easy either: African unity remains a myth while efforts at regional economic integration are unsuccessful.

Ghanaian high life band. From the 1920s a distinctive form of popular music evolved in what was the Gold Coast through a mixture of African and European instruments. High life uses western guitars with African percussion instruments. This group of the 1960s includes two famous musicians, Eric Ageyman and A.B. Crentsil.

DISAPPOINTED EXPECTATIONS

The more things change the more they stay the same. The African elites have now been in power long enough for their record to be assessed by African peoples and by scholars and it is difficult to reach any conclusion other than it has been a disappointment. The nationalists have failed to redeem their promises. The optimism of independence has given way to despair and frustration. 'Seek ye first the political kingdom and all else shall be added unto you' – Kwame Nkrumah's great slogan of the 1950s – is not wrong, but what followed was unexpected: poverty, drought, environmental degradation, political instability, military dictatorship, decadence, violence, inter-group conflicts, and warfare. The nationalism of the colonial era was short-lived. African nations who were full of confidence in their early years are now chronic debtors, with their citizens scattered around the world – making up the largest number of migrants and refugees.

There are now Africans to compare with the officers of the British empire. If a towering figure like Lord Lugard, the soldier and colonial administrator, is described as authoritarian, many of his African successors are no different; indeed they are worse if we include such an inglorious career as that of Idi Amin of Uganda. Nor can we fail to note that many African successors to the British district officers are arrogant, ignorant, and contemptuous of their own people. The colonial officer was focused on his mission, even if he was motivated by profit; but his African successor is not driven by any higher ideals. If colonial Africa was undemocratic, the military regimes that followed are much more brutal and dictatorial and less rational. In parts of colonial English-speaking Africa, where schools were well run and where there was a peaceful political order, people now talk of the period as the golden age of this century. Even in places where the performance of the British administration was poor and exploitation intense, contemporaries still talk about the hope they had, a belief that progress would come in their lifetime, in contrast to the hopelessness of the present and the future.

The cure to Africa's ills in the 1960s seemed simple: correct the mistakes of British rule. At the end of the century few would say the same thing, not because the mistakes have been corrected – far from it – but because many more have been added, not by the empire but by Africans themselves.

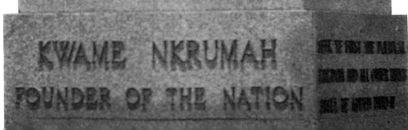

KWAME NKRUMAH
FOUNDER OF THE NATION

British Rule in India: An Assessment

CHAPTER 15

Tapan Raychaudhuri

Historical writing about India under the Raj has been hag-ridden by the strong emotions that often inform ostensibly rational debates. The preoccupation with giving good or bad marks to British rule has overshadowed exercises in serious analysis. Yet it would be futile to pretend that any historian can attempt to assess what actually happened without any trace of prejudice.

As P.J. Marshall says in his introduction (see pages 12–13), there is no unanimous British view of the imperial past. There are historians and social scientists in all parts of the world who consider imperialism in all its forms as morally unacceptable and a source of misery to the subject population – a historical phenomenon without any redeeming features. British historians with radical views do not disagree with this severely negative judgement.

Yet it would be true to say that in Britain the dominant academic and popular perception of the imperial past, and of the Raj in particular, is far from negative. The focus is now often on the factiousness of Indian society, the historical roots of the country's problems stretching way beyond the advent of the British, the peculiarly Indian character of Indian poverty for which it is wrong to blame the colonial rulers, and the very positive economic gains that flowed from imperial policies at least in parts of the country. In short, some academic perceptions of the Raj in Britain now see South Asia's problems of poverty, illiteracy, internecine conflicts, and the rest as being indigenous in origin and having little to do with the 190 years of British rule. Further, in this view, the empire did more good than the critics of imperialism are willing to recognize.

The approaches adopted by some of the other authors in this book, as summarized by P.J. Marshall in his conclusion (see pages 370–81), also tend to undermine any unequivocal condemnation of the Raj or of the British empire in general. In the first place, it is argued that any general judgement about imperialism and its consequences is likely to be invalid because of the diversity of conditions throughout the empire. Secondly, the subject populations are elevated into important players in the game, almost as important as the rulers themselves, if not in fact even more so. In such an analysis, the conquered are no longer passive victims but active co-operators in the relevant actions including the act of conquest. The benefits or otherwise of imperial rule are to a large extent traced to what they, and not the rulers, did or did not do.

In the course of a heated debate on Japan's war record, a Japanese historian pointed out that nations do not reassess their historical past radically unless they have gone through the experience of social revolution or crushing defeat in war. Since Britain has been spared such experiences, public perceptions of the imperial

District Officer. This drawing of a District Officer dispensing justice to village people appeared as an illustration to an account of the Indian civil service by one of its members, Philip Mason, in a book called *The Men who Ruled India; the Guardians.* Both the drawing and the title of Mason's book reflect the ethos of an idealistic service who saw themselves as guardians of 'their' people.

Mughal elephant armour. This armour of the early seventeenth century was one of many rich objects brought back from India by Robert Clive, the conqueror of Bengal, and his son Edward, Governor of Madras 1798–1803.

past appear to be in broad agreement that it would be unthinkable that a British monarch should apologize like the Japanese Emperor for ancestral misdeeds to an erstwhile subject people. In popular perception – and right-wing historiography – of course there were no misdeeds for which apologies are due.

If it is difficult for the average British citizen to take a negative view of the imperial past, it is almost equally difficult for the citizens of a former dependency that has gone through a prolonged struggle for independence to acknowledge any benefits of colonial rule. In post-independence India, serious thinkers and historians who see anything good in the imperial record can probably be counted on the fingers of one hand. Even the best known among these persis-tent admirers of the Raj, Nirad C. Chaudhuri, has described the British in India in the late nineteenth and early twentieth centuries as 'the Nazis of their time'.

THE EXPERIENCE OF RULE

British conquest began in Bengal in the 1760s. By the mid-nineteenth century it was virtually complete. The area that is now India, Pakistan, and Bangladesh was either under direct British rule or governed by princes who were subordinate allies of the British. The order created by conquest lasted until 1947.

Conquest and 'pacification'

When the English East India Company made a bid for political power in the mid-eighteenth century, first in the eastern and southern parts of India, the Mughal empire that once exercised control of the greater part of the subcontinent had been reduced to a shadow. Several regional powers, some of which still owed formal allegiance to the Emperor and even paid revenue to him, were fighting for supremacy and the company entered the fray to secure and enhance their commercial gains.

The Indian empire was acquired, not in a fit of absent-mindedness, as has sometimes been alleged, but, in the words of a British historian, in pursuit of the public and private greed of the company's servants. Hilaire Belloc advised a child that it should 'Always keep a hold of nurse for fear of finding something worse'. Similar claims have been made for British rule in India, probably correctly. But the initial experience of the conquest was horrendous both in Bengal and southern India. Ghulam Hussain, a contemporary historian, who was otherwise full of admiration for the British, especially for their courage and military skills, described how his countrymen were groaning under the company's yoke. The company's servants indulged in an orgy of loot and this systematic plunder was at least one major cause of the famine of 1770. Although there are reasons to question the accuracy of claims that the famine wiped out a third of Bengal's population, the ruinous effects on the region's economy are not in doubt. The wars in the south, where Haidar Ali, the ruler of Mysore, devastated territories under British control, produced similar consequences. And taxes collected from these provinces and from the company's subordinate Indian 'allies' funded the military machine for the conquest of more territories and the consolidation of empire.

That empire was nearly destroyed by the great rebellion of 1857, described inaccurately as the Mutiny. The result of complex and multiple causes, the rising expressed the accumulated anger of many sections of the population in north and central India – dispossessed princes, disgruntled soldiers, and a harassed peasantry from whom the company's army was largely recruited (see page 50). The rebels committed acts of great brutality and were suppressed in equally brutal ways. The British in India bayed for even more bloody revenge. The rebellion created a legacy of racial hatred which permeated all aspects of the relationship between the ruler and the ruled.

The leaders of the rebellion feature prominently in the demonology of British imperial history. It is significant that they were and are viewed very differently in India. Leaders like the Rani of Jhansi and Kunwar Singh are revered heroes in folk memory and nationalist myth has elevated the rising to the status of the First War of Independence. Such total disjuncture in perceptions is a significant comment on the relationship between the rulers and the subject population.

Pax Britannica

When India passed under the direct rule of the Crown in 1858 there was no one left to challenge British authority: the prolonged wars that had disturbed peace in many parts of the subcontinent during the decline of the Mughal empire and the era of conquest – some 160 years in all – were finally at an end. Banditry, a by-product of wars and anarchy, was soon crushed. For the first time in the history of the region, the entire subcontinent was ruled by one centralized government in a peace that the British regarded as one of their greatest gifts to India.

Peace, of course, is preferable to war and lawless anarchy, but the benefits of peace were not accessible to all concerned in the same way. If one remembers that the rebellion of 1857 occurred some thirty-five years after the main wars of

Santal Rebellion, 1855. The Santals were a 'tribal' people who lived in the wooded hills to the west of Bengal. Like other peoples who had lived apart from the main body of Indian society, they resisted the pressures of colonial rule and their resistance contributed to the sporadic violence of the Indian countryside. The Santals rebelled against tax demands and the incursions of settlers and traders from the plains. As this picture shows, Santals faced the fire of the British Indian soldiers armed only with bows and arrows.

conquest were over, it becomes obvious that many people in India were less than happy with the British peace. The peasants and the tribal people who constituted the majority of the population rose repeatedly in rebellion in many parts of the country throughout the eighteenth and nineteenth centuries. The immediate causes of these risings varied, but most were rooted in the massive dislocation caused by the process of conquest and consolidation. The people driven to rebellion in sheer desperation included peasants forced to give up cultivation during the period of plunder, tribes deprived of their hereditary rights to the free use of forest resources, tenants rack-rented or expropriated by landlords created under the new tenures, and cultivators hopelessly indebted to moneylenders (who benefited from the new laws of contract) or forced to cultivate indigo by white planters on totally unacceptable terms.

The forces of law and order were almost invariably deployed in favour of their oppressors. The new legal system was incomprehensible and too expensive to be of any use to the poor. Before the British, justice in matters of civil dispute usually took the form of arbitration by village councils. Such arbitration must have favoured the privileged, but the less fortunate were not ruined. The new equality before the law meant that a Brahmin could now be hanged, but such triumphs of justice were of little consolation to the peasant who lost his land to the moneylender or the landlord. The intricacies of the land tenure system and the incomprehensible laws enmeshed the agrarian population in ruinous law suits. There is also plenty of evidence that the people lived in mortal fear of the rapacious police. When a village was robbed, often the first concern of the villagers was to hide the fact from the police lest they should ransack their homes. Folk songs in every part of the subcontinent record memories of such varied misery. There are none rejoicing in the advent of the Pax Britannica.

There were others who shared the unhappiness of the underprivileged. Pious and learned Hindus or Muslims had in the past been rewarded by grants of rent-free land. Under the British their descendants were deprived of their livelihood if they failed to prove that the grants were authentic. The bulk of officials who had served the regimes conquered by the British, especially the Muslims, were reduced to penury. Indians had been appointed to high offices of state in the early days of the East India Company's rule, but this practice ceased totally from the late 1780s: a new stereotype – that Indians were dishonest and undependable – became an integral part of the official dogma. Nevertheless, the lower ranks of the colonial bureaucracy had to be opened to Indians, a fact that is now cited in support of the argument that the subject population were active players in the task of government and decision making. Memoirs of middle-ranking Indian bureaucrats leave one in little doubt that they had very little effective power and that they resented the severe restrictions on their career opportunities. The fact that the British bureaucrats in India were among the highest paid by international standards and at times affected a lordly style aggravated the resentment.

Of course, there were sections of the population who were delighted with their prospects under British rule, a fact that explains the enthusiasm for the Raj that persisted well into the twentieth century. The Indian princes and the big landlords, secure in their possessions and privileges, never lost that enthusiasm. The new professional classes and those who had the benefit of western-style education also long retained their faith in the beneficence of British rule, but they criticized many features of that rule from the 1820s onwards. And their criticisms were not directed only to matters that concerned their self-interest: the abject misery of the Indian peasant is a recurrent theme in the writings of Indian intellectuals in the nineteenth century.

LEGACIES OF THE RAJ

India, far more than any other part of the British empire, was the great testing ground for colonial rule and its capacity to leave enduring legacies: a huge population was ruled over a long period by a regime that was by most standards strong and well-equipped.

Development or underdevelopment?

When one reads the European accounts of India and other major Asian civilizations from the early modern age, one often has the impression of reading descriptions of a first world, to use a contemporary expression, written by people from less fortunate climes. Even in the mid-eighteenth century Clive compared Murshi-dabad, a provincial city in Bengal, in some ways favourably with London.

The information available concerning the record of India's economy under colonial rule is extremely imprecise. We know very little about the trends in population, output, or life expectancy until the last decades of the nineteenth century. Certain things are however clear. The population increased, if at all, at a very slow rate – never even 1 per cent per annum until 1921 when reduced mortality through control of epidemic diseases pushed the figure to 1.3 per cent. Agricultural data is undependable but it seems that although in Punjab and parts of southern India there was some growth in productivity, the record in the rest of the country was dismal. In some parts of the country agricultural output had stagnated or actually declined during the twentieth century so that the population as a whole had considerably less to eat per head in 1947 than in 1900. Insecurity of tenure, the heavy cost of borrowing, and minimal investment in irrigation all contributed to this poor record. The development of railways and the market for agricultural crops, both national and international, encouraged specialization in crop production and stimulated the production of cash crops, including the higher value food grains such as high-quality rice and wheat. The consequent gains were often at the cost of lower value food grains – coarse rice, barley, or millet – the main source of food for the majority of the population. India, never an importer of food grains in the past, became dependent on imports, and per capita availability declined until the trend was finally reversed in the 1970s.

Not surprisingly, the successor states of the Raj were among the poorest countries of the world. It is estimated that in India some 48–53 per cent of the rural population were below the poverty line in 1947: in other words, nearly half the population could not afford the minimum amount of food required to sustain the human body. Average life expectancy was twenty-nine years. Nearly 88 per cent of the population was illiterate and the rate of illiteracy was even higher among

'A loom with the process of winding off the thread'. This painting of *c.*1792 depicts the Bengal weavers who produced cotton goods for export throughout the world by the East India Company. In the first half of the nineteenth century Indian weavers such as these lost their export markets and part of their domestic markets as well to the competition of machine-made cloth from Britain.

women. A very high proportion of the predominantly rural population were either landless or had no secure rights in the land they cultivated. Although some of the agriculturalists who could afford to cultivate the higher value crops had prospered and were to prosper even more in the newly independent states, these constituted a very small proportion of the rural population, as did big landlords with vast estates who lived off their rental income without contributing to agricultural production in any way.

Of course, there was a great deal of poverty in pre-colonial times as well but it would be a mistake to see India's twentieth-century poverty as a continuation of pre-modern patterns. Modern underdevelopment is the product of a vicious circle, low income–low saving–low investment. In 1600 when agriculture had to support a relatively small and very slowly increasing population (the subcontinent had an estimated population of about 100 million as compared to some 1,000 million in the 1990s), poverty did not mean near starvation. Famines had certainly been a part of Indian life since very ancient times. But in the past these calamities had been caused by crop failure. In the nineteenth century, on the other hand, one would have expected food grains to move to areas of shortage, helped by a modern system of transport. Yet as late as 1899 famine mortality remained high because vast sections of the population now lacked the purchasing power to buy food even when it was available.

By 1947 India had not developed an industrial base to compensate for the poverty of the countryside. For much of the span of British rule India's population was probably more dependent on agriculture than it had been before the conquest. In the pre-industrial world, India's manufactures like textiles were among the staples of international commerce and a flourishing class of merchants plied their trade from East Africa to the Philippines and as far north as Moscow and St Petersburg. Early in the nineteenth century India lost its export trade in manufactures and became a net importer of manufactured goods and a supplier mainly of agricultural products to Britain for the first time in its history. The consequent limited growth in agriculture did not compensate for the decline in manufactures caused by the loss of export markets and of the demand from the courts and the armies of the rulers who had been deposed by British conquest, as well as by the competition of machine manufactures imported from Britain. Such modern industries as developed from the late nineteenth century remained relatively insignificant. All newly industrializing countries have been dependent on favourable state policies in almost every part of the world. In India the favourable terms granted to British exporters and the doctrine of *laissez faire* meant that Indian industries received no protection and hardly any encouragement by the state until the mid-1920s, and then only in response to persistent Indian pressure.

By the end of British rule India had a small industrial sector – consisting of mines, light consumer goods, and a major iron and steel industry – and it was served by an infrastructure, especially a railway network, that compared well with

Sampling raw cotton, 1872. This warehouse for raw cotton at Calcutta is an indication of how, from being an exporter of cotton cloth, nineteenth-century India became a major exporter of raw cotton with which other countries manufactured cloth.

that of other dependent countries. But the railway network was heavily oriented to the needs of exports and imports. The majority of India's villages lacked even mud roads serviceable round the year. Modern irrigation, impressive in scale – especially in the Punjab and Sind – benefited only 6 per cent of the cultivated land.

Perhaps the one point of strength in the Indian economy at the time of independence was the existence of a highly resilient entrepreneurial class, recruited to a large extent from castes and communities with long-standing commercial traditions, who had made the most of the limited opportunities available under colonial rule. Though facilities for technical education had been severely limited and there was hardly any demand for high skills, Indian universities and education abroad had produced large numbers of professionally trained personnel with technical skills that later proved to be of value in efforts to develop the country.

Thus, when power was transferred, South Asia was a typically underdeveloped region, with a vast and growing population, stagnant agricultural output, a small industrial sector, and inadequate infrastructure. In per capita terms India was nearly at the bottom of the international ladder both in commerce and in modern industry. Very low per capita income, low saving, and hence low investment completed the vicious circle. This was not the logical outcome of the buoyant pre-industrial economy of the sixteenth and seventeenth centuries, but a reflection of the workings of the colonial economic relationship. This is not to say that on the eve of the British conquest India was on the verge of an industrial revolution which was frustrated by colonialism. But the nature of economic change induced by the colonial nexus surely precluded the possibilities of industrialization. It also created bottlenecks which proved to be serious handicaps for later efforts at industrialization.

Politics, identities, and conflict

In 1947, when the British left India, they transferred power to two – and if one counts Burma, three – successor states. Of these, one, Pakistan, has since broken up into two states. India, Pakistan, and Bangladesh have all adopted Westminster-style parliamentary systems of government, with periods of lapse into military dictatorship in the case of the last two. The administrative system, including the judiciary, created by the British has survived decolonization though it has been extended and modified to cope with the tasks of economic and social development as well as the phenomenal increase in population. Parliamentary democracy and the rule of law, despite many challenges and violations, may be said to have become integral parts of the political culture in Britain's erstwhile dependencies in South Asia.

On the face of it, this fact reflects the triumph of an ideology that is western, especially British, in origin. It is not, however, the end result of smooth or continuous developments sponsored by the Raj. The British created representative institutions not as a conscious preparation for Indian independence, but to try to induce limited numbers of Indians to co-operate with the administration and thus to limit opposition to the government and reduce some of its costs. Except during the last ten years of their rule, when elected governments in the provinces had some real power, subject to the authority of the provincial governors and the Viceroy, the British bureaucracy who ruled the country was not accountable to any representative body in India. The right to vote for legislatures with strictly limited powers was granted to only 2 per cent of the population in 1919 and then to 10–13 per cent in 1937. It was the governments of India and Pakistan who introduced adult suffrage and accepted the principle of elected governments accountable to elected legislatures. This was a quantum leap, not the logical climax of gradual evolution. The transition was from oligarchic and autocratic government to representative democracy even though this was no doubt badly flawed in many ways.

The successor states also inherited the administrative organization of the Raj and the traditions that went with it. These were not best suited to the tasks of social and economic development attempted after independence. The inordinately expensive judicial system and a proverbially corrupt police which was often a law unto itself remain heavy burdens for the underprivileged in India.

New political identities leading to rivalries and conflicts developed within the British political and administrative framework. These are an enduring legacy of the Raj. Such developments were only partly the deliberate creations of British rule: they were essentially by-products of the workings of colonial government and its interactions with indigenous society.

The primary object of British rule was to protect and enhance the interests of Britain in India. This provided the one element of continuity in the otherwise ad hoc and shifting policies which are often cited in support of the theory that it is impossible to generalize about the motives and consequences of imperialism. So long as there was no conflict with the dominant purpose, the welfare of Indians was often an important consideration, especially at the level of idealistic decision makers. Besides, a contented subject population was essential for stable government. The record, however, suggests that conflicts between British interests and policies likely to benefit India in the long run were frequent enough.

As the British in India could be counted in thousands and the subject population were several hundred million in number, co-operation and acquiescence on the part of Indians were essential for the functioning of colonial rule. This political co-operation had to be bought at a price – providing some access to resources and devolving some power. Elite groups competed for these benefits and they did so partly on the basis of groups and alliances that already existed in indigenous society, and partly on the basis of 'constituencies' defined in

Sir P.T. Rajan. Rajan, who was educated at Oxford and became a barrister, served as a minister in the government of Madras from 1930 to 1937. In the last years of colonial rule British India was to a considerable degree governed by Indian ministers within a framework of overall British control.

their own terms by the rulers who saw Indian society as a mosaic of different interests, communities, and peoples.

As people began to see themselves in new ways through interaction with western thought and the British presence, social identities acquired a new political importance. We do not encounter in the pre-British past either the idea of an Indian nation or any consciousness of a Hindu community spread across the subcontinent. As the idea of nationhood and political rights seeped into elite consciousness, the facts of being an Indian, or a Hindu, or a Bengali, acquired meanings that were entirely new. When the new rulers distributed seats in local bodies and legislatures or allocated funds for education on the basis of communities and in some instances of castes, communities and castes became the focus for political competition. Social and doctrinal difference, which had very rarely been the cause of civil conflict, now informed competition and political antagonisms. The British perception that Hindus and Muslims were two mutually antagonistic monoliths, a notion not rooted in facts, became an important basis for allocating power and resources.

Rioting in Calcutta, August 1946. The episode known as 'the great Calcutta killing', in which about 4,000 people lost their lives, was one of many violent conflicts between Hindus and Muslims in the events leading up to the ending of British rule and the partition of India.

Hindu–Muslim rivalry and the eventual partition of India was the end result and the British policy makers, when they did not actually add fuel to the conflict, were quite happy to take advantage of it. For example, Muslim leaders who opposed the nationalist claim to speak for all Indians were certainly courted as potential allies, though at the last moment there was desperate anxiety to prevent the partition of India because it was considered a threat to Britain's world-wide strategic interests.

Indian nationalism – the idea that the very diverse population of the sub-continent constituted a nation – was also of course a product of British rule in India. The rulers did not encourage the idea and their publicists pooh-poohed the notion that a people so diverse could ever be a nation. Yet the emergence of a colonial elite, in many ways homogenous in terms of their expectations and frustrations and sharing a language and common assumptions, as well as unification under a single administration, laid a basis for pan-Indian nationalism.

The overt racism of the British in India, which affected the institutions of government, contributed powerfully to the growth of nationalist sentiment. All Indians, whatever their status, shared the experience of being treated as racial inferiors. Higher levels of appointment were virtually closed to non-whites. British people reacted violently against proposals that would make them subject to the authority of Indian judges. The Viceroy Lord Curzon commented that the British in India got away with murder because no white jury would find a white man guilty of killing a native. As late as 1930 British officers were advised in a secret army memorandum that they should not kick Indians. The life stories of Indian celebrities are full of episodes of racial insults. The perception of shared bondage gave credibility to the notion of shared nationhood.

The ideals of the Indian nation that emerged in 1947 grew out of the movement for independence. The new Indian nationalism was inspired by the ideals of representative democracy as practised in Britain and denied to India. It was also inspired by ideals of social equality, but the exigencies of the struggle for independence have limited the extent to which these ideals have been applied after 1947. Aware of the country's great poverty and pervasive social injustice – problems that the colonial government left untouched – the nationalists adopted programmes that would ameliorate some of the misery. But since they sought the support of all social classes, and the interests of the poor clashed with those of the privileged, the tendency was generally to avoid conflict and maintain the *status quo*. The landless and the sharecroppers have, for instance, remained where they were, but the rural classes, who had some rights to land and had come to constitute a strong base for nationalism, were rewarded at independence: their chief enemy, the big landlords, lost their land as did the Indian princes.

The effort to mobilize support and sustain an organization based on multiple ethnic elements and mutually conflicting interests created the basis for a unique nation state, more diverse than any other known to history. Unlike the Soviet Union, it was created with the active consent of the constituent elements and has survived with that consent largely intact for some fifty years. The absorption of the princely states, the two-fifths of Indian territory that was ruled by autocrats under British protection, into democratic systems with popular support also gives post-1947 India a further edge over the record of colonial rule.

The cultural legacy

The introduction of a western style of education brought an enthusiastic initial response from the new colonial elite who wanted a better knowledge of the English language as a key to careers under the new regime and who were, to a large extent, responsible for the new initiative. They also sought access to western science and humanities in the belief that these would generate progress. British policy makers like Thomas Macaulay, contemptuous of oriental cultures, wished to create a class of people who would be western in all but appearance. The need for functionaries who spoke the rulers' language was of course a consideration and the missionaries, who were among the chief propagators of western-style education, hoped to Christianize India.

The long-term effects of western education were very different from what the pioneers had expected. It acted as a catalyst – generating processes of change that went way beyond simple adoptions of western cultural artefacts. India was not Christianized: if anything, the new appeal to reason that shook the Hindus' faith in their own traditions also militated against the acceptance of Christian dogma. While the products of the new centres of higher learning remained enthusiastic for one feature or another of western civilization, liberal democratic and egalitarian ideals had much greater appeal than that of the constitutional monarchy enshrined in Britain's unwritten constitution. So much so that at one time educational administrators seriously considered the exclusion of British history, with its record of struggle for citizens' rights, from the curricula of Indian schools and colleges.

One major end-product of the cultural encounter was the articulation of a distinctively Indian nationalism. This emphasized the shared cultural traditions of India's diverse population and the belief that the Indian civilization had unique powers of assimilation which had created out of diverse and often warring elements a unified culture, the basis of a future Indian nation. While this message of co-existence and unity was carried, up to a point successfully, to the mass of population mobilized in support of the movement for independence, the new political culture was also potentially divisive. Basically, it was the culture of the urban classes exposed to western-style education. Its inspiration was liberal humanism and the democratic ideals of the west and these had little meaning for the Indian masses. Some of those ideals were communicated to the poor and the under-privileged through Gandhi's self-consciously Indian life-style and the charisma that the leadership and their followers acquired by courting persecution. But as a number of historians now point out, the masses interpreted the message of nationalism in their own terms, very different from the concerns of the middle class. There was an element of naivety in the modernizing leadership's expectation that deep-rooted attitudes and beliefs could be altered by waving the magic wands of reason, science, and technology. The leaders of Indian nationalism were generally committed to secularism, in the sense that it was right for the state to remain neutral or indifferent in matters of religion. The mass of Indian people have not always shared this belief. For them religion and politics have often been seen as inseparable.

Western education did create a class of people intellectually and in some ways psychologically in tune with developments of modern civilization in Europe and America. Since they provided the leadership of the nationalist movement, it would be obviously incorrect to describe them as denationalized. The encounter with western thought triggered off an outburst of creativity in literature and the arts that is remarkable by any standard. Much of this creative effort celebrated the new national consciousness. Access to a world language remains a great asset for the educated classes in India. The fact that the Indian Union has the second largest group of technically trained personnel in the world has certainly been facilitated by this linguistic inheritance of the Raj. Yet the fact remains that after some 180 years of exposure to English education less than 2 per cent of the population understand English. The percentage was even smaller in 1947 when there were 17 universities and 200 colleges in the subcontinent as against 140 and 2,000 respectively in the Indian Union alone today. And nothing has happened to bridge the chasm created by this cultural dichotomy. Macaulay believed that western culture would percolate down to the masses. This has not happened. The elite's way of thinking remains incomprehensible to the masses. Probably this fact, rather than the much discussed ethnic diversity of India, poses a real threat to its solidity as a nation state.

THE COLONIAL PAST AND THE SUBCONTINENT'S FUTURE

The vestiges of the Raj are very much present in the life of the subcontinent today. Despite attempts to shake it off, especially in Bangladesh, English remains the dominant language of intellectual discourse and, in India, effectively the language of administration as well. More important, the beliefs and attitudes that inform elite concerns as well as state policy can be traced back to the catalytic encounter with western thought under imperial auspices. The chasm that divides the masses from the privileged derives in part from this fact of western 'influence'. It is difficult to foresee an end to these legacies of the colonial past in the near future. One totally negative inheritance of that past, antagonism between Hindus and Muslims – converted at the state level into Indo-Pakistani conflict and Indophobia in Bangladesh, also seems destined to persist. On the positive side, the aspirations towards democracy, economic growth, and social equity that emerged in the colonial era – if not exactly with the blessings of the Raj – are now integral to the life of the subcontinent's population. It would be unwise to speculate about their chances of success.

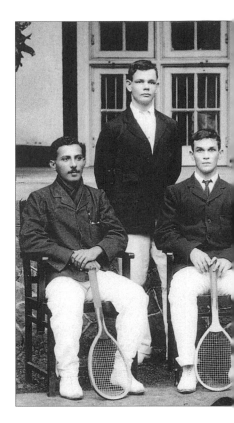

Doctors at a Bombay hospital, 1905. The Jamsetjee Jijibhoy Hospital was a well-equipped institution with Indian doctors trained to the same professional standards as their European colleagues. It had been founded to relieve the poor of Bombay, but its capacity of 296 beds could do little to meet the needs of the city's vast slum population. The gap between the worlds of the Indian doctor and of his potential patients was very wide indeed.

Empire in Retrospect

How should the British imperial record be judged? For some this is an easy question to answer. Empires or imperialism are by their very nature evils that cannot be condoned. 'Imperialism', Toyin Falola writes, 'is perverse. It involves the domination of one group by another.' Since empires rest on a denial of the right of people to rule themselves and to determine their own destinies, they are entirely inadmissable. That is the beginning and the end of the matter.

The destiny of the people of a colony is indeed in the hands of others. Moreover, the interests that imperial regimes pursue will always in the last resort be their own. That is certainly a perverse situation. Yet before the twentieth century few regimes anywhere in the world have been accountable to the wishes of those they ruled. Many large states in Asia, for instance, were ruled by people who were ethnically quite distinct from the mass of their subjects. In judging any past system of rule, questions about its origins or its intentions therefore seem ultimately to be less crucial than questions about how it affected those under its authority. Did British rule improve the lives of the people subject to it? Or did they suffer deprivations that went beyond the material and included social disintegration, cultural impoverishment, and loss of identity? Current debates about what happened to those under imperial rule almost inevitably merge into debates about the legacy of the empire for future generations living in independence after the end of empire. What did the British empire bequeath to those who succeeded it?

CRITERIA OF JUDGEMENT

Any assessment of how the British empire affected the lives of those ruled by it has to begin by defining criteria. What were the interests of the ruled? It has for long been assumed that the peoples of the world all have roughly similar ambitions. They wish to be citizens of nation states and members of 'modern' societies, marked by liberal secular values and democratic government and with economies based on industrialization and technological innovation. If British colonial rule laid the foundations of nation states with such attributes, then it might be commended; if it was judged to have retarded such developments, it was to be deplored. 'Modern' nation states in this sense were in fact precisely what most colonial nationalists, with the very obvious exception of Gandhi, actually wanted and what at least the first generation of leaders of new states tried to bring about.

The concept of modernity and its trappings now, however, look more questionable. It is often argued that the modern nation states of Africa are a disastrous importation of an alien foreign model. Many Asian and African people regard liberal or secular values as a western imposition, hostile to their own culture. The appropriateness of industrialization as a goal for many countries now seems to be highly questionable. In short, the criteria by which the interests of the ruled are to be judged are not entirely self-evident, nor are they immutable. Nevertheless, certain standards still command a degree of consensus. Few deny that wealth is better than poverty, that education is desirable, or that a government that is accountable to its subjects and rules by law is to be preferred to a dictatorship. It is not unreasonable to judge the British empire by its capacity to create such conditions.

Alternatives to empire

'What if?' questions about the past can only be answered in the most speculative and tentative way, but any assessment of the British imperial record is somewhat unreal without considering possible alternatives to it. Those who condemn the British empire need to give some thought to what the world would have been like without it. There is one conspicuous example of a people who avoided imperial domination and achieved most of the conventional goals of modernity by their own efforts. That example is the Japanese. Japan was left free of virtually all direct European contact from the 'closing' of the country in the 1630s to its forcible 'opening' in the 1850s. Then, building on social and economic developments during the period of seclusion, Japan's own rulers were able to borrow extensively from the west, without losing control over their own affairs, and to launch Japan into modernity by the end of the nineteenth century.

Impressive as this model of autonomously directed change may be, it is probably not one that is easily applicable to other parts of Asia or to Africa. The combination of a long spell of isolation and a highly developed capacity both to resist intrusion and to absorb and adapt the methods of the intruders was a very unusual one. There is very little evidence that before the twentieth century other countries were developing the kind of economic, social, and political foundations from which a modern state and an industrial economy could emerge. Nor was it easy for them to escape European domination. Apart from Japan, only the most remote and landlocked parts of the world, were able to do so. The fate of most non-European countries was either – like China, Iran, or Turkey – to have their autonomy seriously compromised by European pressure or to be incorporated into a colonial empire. Those who did not fall to the British were likely to yield to the Russians, the French, or the Germans, although the old colonial systems of Spain, Portugal, and the Netherlands were also expanding and Belgium, Italy, and the United States were becoming new colonial powers. By the later nineteenth century rule by another European power was a very real alternative to rule by the British.

THE BRITISH AND OTHER EMPIRES

Comparative colonial history is on the surface a beguiling subject. For the British in particular it is one in which a great deal of national self-esteem has been invested. For many British people it is axiomatic that their record in the establishment of colonies of settlement overseas and as rulers of non-European peoples was very

'In the Rubber Coils'. This *Punch* cartoon of 1906 reflects British revulsion at stories of atrocities inflicted on Africans in the Congo by the administration of Leopold II, King of the Belgians, who ruled the Congo as his personal domain. The Congo was the case where what seemed to be the abuses of foreign colonial rule acquired the greatest notoriety in Britain.

much superior to that of any other power. Other European countries oppressed their fellow citizens overseas and drove them to revolt; the British, after the American misadventure, learnt to nurture links of freedom, which evolved into that unique institution, the British Commonwealth of Nations. In the tropics, while the Spanish and Portuguese imperial regimes were sleazy and corrupt, the Dutch nakedly mercenary, the Germans and the Russians brutally militaristic, and the French overbearingly chauvinistic in imposing their own cultural values, the British ruled with a high-minded concern for the good of the ruled. Others tried to resist the pressures of nationalism, only to go down to defeat – for example, the Dutch in Indonesia and the French in Algeria; the British entered into partnership with their nationalists and extricated themselves from empire with grace and goodwill.

How well founded are these widely held beliefs? Any attempt to assess the British imperial record against that of other nations is complicated by the fact that there was nothing comparable to the most important British colonial enterprises in the empires of other powers. Like the British Americans of the Thirteen Colonies, Spanish and Portuguese communities overseas threw off metropolitan rule in the early nineteenth century. The British colonies of settlement in the nineteenth century and the Dominions of the twentieth century therefore have no counterparts in any other modern European empire. The British Indian empire was also unique in its vast scale. No other European colony had comparable resources or so huge a population.

Where direct comparison can be made, similarities between different varieties of European colonial rule are likely to be very much more marked than any differences. The eighteenth-century slave systems were very much the same: assertions that one European system might be more humane than others have no real substance. The late nineteenth or twentieth-century empires in Africa, on which many valuable comparative studies have been done, also have very strong underlying similarities. Administrative techniques and styles of course varied, as did systems of education or the layout of towns. The practical effects of such differences were, however, felt almost exclusively by the urbanized elites. The lives of the vast mass of African people varied very little, whether they happened to be ruled by British, French, Germans, Belgians, Portuguese, or Spanish. What mattered was whether they lived in colonies dominated by settlers or by large commercial enterprises, or where African chiefs were largely left to their own devices.

From the point of view of the ruled, European empires were in essentials very similar and it was not especially desirable to be a citizen of one rather than of another. There are obvious reasons for the similarities. Western European societies had much in common and had the same underlying interrerests in their imperial systems. Moreover, whoever the rulers may have been, the way in which a colony was ruled was much influenced by the ruled. The British Indian empire was an

Indian empire. African colonies were built on African people. The proposition that the ruled, as well as the rulers, make empires has been demonstrated at every stage in this book, even though the extent of indigenous participation, and thus of continuity between the colonial and the pre-colonial orders, is much less evident to Toyin Falola and to Tapan Raychaudhuri than it is to the authors of most of the other chapters.

THE DISTINCTIVENESS OF THE BRITISH

If the general similarities between the European empires mean that crude stereotypes about British benevolence and the exploitation practised by others have little substance, British colonial rule anywhere in the world still had distinctive features. The British brought common law traditions to whatever legal system they devised, with at least a theoretical respect for the accountability of government and the right of the individual, even if the rights of white individuals were usually more secure than those of non-whites. Until the rise of the great American missionary societies, Protestant missionaries overseas were almost exclusively British. Protestant organizations at home acted as a kind of conscience for British imperial rule – very potent in the age of anti-slavery, weakening later, but still active to the end of the empire. There was no European parallel to this. The unwillingness of the British government after 1945 to be dragged into major colonial wars is irrefutable, even if it is not easy to explain. It was not matched on the continent until the ascendancy in France of General de Gaulle.

Were the British more 'racist' than other Europeans? While all Europeans believed in a hierarchy of 'races' and practised discriminatory policies based on such beliefs, the British had an especially marked sense of racial hierarchy which was matched by very rigid policies. The extent of British racism emerges at many points in this book. British colonies of settlement were very hostile to non-white immigrants. Clearly demarcated boundaries were intended to exclude 'natives' from the British residential areas of colonial towns. As David Fieldhouse says, 'In a general sense ... the empire was racist' in the way that business opportunities were distributed. The roots of South African apartheid, the most inflexible of all systems of racial segregation, can clearly be found in the period when Britain still had ultimate responsibility. The British were never inclined to condone racially mixed marriages, which were common in some other empires, and they rarely treated people of mixed race as in any way the equal of whites.

THE DIVERSITY OF EMPIRE

By the rough criteria of material wellbeing, levels of education, and the political accountability of governments, there is now a huge range between countries that were once part of the British empire. One-time colonies of settlement, South Africa apart, would conventionally be assumed to score very heavily on all counts. The economic and educational achievements of the city-states in the Far East, Singapore and Hong Kong, are remarkable and put them ahead of Britain itself in both respects On the other hand, some parts of the former British empire are now among the poorest countries in the world and have suffered from civil war, military government, or other forms of dictatorship.

Although the colonial past cannot be held to be exclusively responsible for what has happened in the years since independence, the huge disparities in the present political and economic fortunes of former colonial countries accurately reflect the enormous degree of diversity that existed within that empire. It incorporated territories and peoples who differed very widely from one another and for whom British rule took very different forms and meant very different things. To judge the British imperial record as a whole is thus a largely fruitless exercise. Its successes or its failures have to be related to particular areas at particular times. They depended on the nature of the British presence in any territory and on how its people responded to that presence. The history of the British empire is a kaleidoscope of interactions between rulers and ruled. Any verdict on the empire must take account of the wide range of ways in which the British tried to rule and of the equally wide range of responses that they met.

Different patterns of rule

That British rule could take many different forms in different parts of the empire is a conclusion that comes out of every chapter. A.J. Stockwell shows how difficult it is to find uniformity of practice in imperial government and therefore to know what the British legacy in this field actually was, let alone to pass judgement on it. The British certainly took with them a commitment to British institutions and forms, but what actually happened in the colonies varied very widely indeed. Self-government was granted quite early in some territories, while it was withheld almost to the end in others. In some cases the British sought to preserve what they regarded as 'traditional' rulers and to administer indirectly through them; elsewhere they pushed such people aside and dealt directly with the mass of the population themselves. British policies even within the same territory could embody contradictory elements: aspirations to consolidate colonies into larger and what, it was hoped, would be more stable units clashed with persistent tendencies to see colonial populations as conglomerates of different ethnicities, tribes, and castes, and to treat such elements in different ways. It is not therefore very surprising that the political legacy handed down to those who rule ex-British colonies is so diverse. Within the territory of the new nation some populations had been integrated into an enduring sense of national identity over a long period; in others diverse communities had very little sense of national unity. In some colonies representative government and popular participation in politics were deeply rooted; in others the great majority of the population were voting for the first time when independence came. Some new countries inherited quite powerful state structures – already, as in South Asia, staffed to a high level by their own nationals;

in East or Central African colonies rudimentary government machines were being run by British officials almost to the end.

David Fieldhouse identifies certain underlying consistencies in the economic management of empire: at least until the mid-twentieth century colonies had to pay their way and balance their budgets from their own resources; stable currencies and exchange rates were very much encouraged; protective tariffs were actively discouraged. But he also shows a great variety of practice. In some tropical colonies agriculture was dominated by European-owned plantations, in others by relatively small-scale peasant production. Some newly independent states inherited quite elaborate infrastructures of harbour facilities, railways, or irrigation systems. Others inherited very little. In Kenya, a rich colony by African standards, a network of single-track railways was established in the colonial period, but as late as 1958 all but 2 per cent of the colony's roads were dirt tracks. Some colonies on the eve of independence had diverse economies which might include a manufacturing sector; others depended on a single crop for any export earnings. Smaller West Indian islands and poorer African territories lacked even that.

Reception of Governor.
An African artist records the arrival of a high British official at a port on the East African coast. As this picture implies, British power on the East African coast rested on a few naval ships and on African soldiers.

No systematic anglicizing

Andrew Porter describes how what he calls the 'incoherent', the 'spontaneous', and the 'unconscious' on the British side had at least as much of a role as 'purposeful diffusion' in the dissemination of British culture. The British were never systematic anglicizers, for all their confidence in their own values. Even if they had been, the limits on the diffusion of new cultural influences in societies where the mass of the population were poor and the colonial governments had few funds to spend on education were obvious. Mass literacy, let alone the mass learning of English, were only seriously attempted in most parts of Asia or Africa after independence.

Thomas R. Metcalf finds no single model for British colonial cities, even if British architectural forms were widely imitated and adapted. Different types of town grew from different impulses: trading towns, government towns, garrison towns, mining towns, and hill stations. The British were not assertive planners of towns: with rare exceptions, like New Delhi, local populations were left largely free to build as and where they pleased. For most of the nineteenth century, the functions of British urban government at home were generally somewhat limited; British colonial authorities did not try to regulate many aspects town of life either.

THE LIMITS OF POWER

Whatever the British might or might not try to do, what actually happened in any colonial situation depended to a large extent on those over whom the British ruled. To make that point is not to argue that force and coercion were not important in British imperial practice, but to recognize the constraints on the use of force that A.J. Stockwell has described. The British fixed boundaries and established the units of empire to which the inhabitants of these demarcations, however arbitrary they might appear in ethnic terms, had little alternative but to accommodate themselves. The enduring quality of ex-colonial boundary lines are a tribute to the efficacy of colonial power in that sense. Within their colonial boundaries, however, British power was often more negative than positive. It could stop people doing things, but it could not compel them to do something else. The British could destroy states that resisted them and crush rebellions. They could deprive elites of their privileges – sending the Asantahene of Ashanti in the Gold Coast (Ghana) into exile in 1896 or deposing Indian princes and incorporating their states into British India. The criminal law could be invoked to prohibit what were regarded as barbarous customs, such as widow burning or infanticide. Under conditions of free trade and reasonably cheap communications, British manufactured imports could eliminate some competing products, such as Indian handloom cloth. Improved communications and world-wide wars spread disease and high mortality. On the other hand, the British could not determine who would emerge to replace older elites that had lost ground under their rule. They had only a limited power to change people's beliefs or their social customs. Nor could they of themselves generate economic growth. Until very late in their rule they could not prevent

Caste, tribe, or class?
Social change in India and Africa under British rule

'England has to fulfil a double mission in India,' wrote Karl Marx in 1853, 'one destructive, the other regenerating – the annihilation of the old Asiatic society, and the laying the material foundations of western society in Asia.' Such expectations were very common in the age of empire. What were thought of as 'traditional' Asian and African societies would be fundamentally changed under the rule of Britain, the most 'modern' society in the world. Modern societies were based on social classes, which largely depended on a person's wealth: as people enriched themselves they would move upwards socially. Traditional societies were thought to be rigid and unchanging. Hindu India was believed to have created the most inflexible system of all: the caste into which they were born determined the position that Hindus would occupy for the rest of their lives. Pre-colonial African societies were assumed to be divided into tribes that also allowed virtually no social mobility.

It was confidently expected that colonial rule would break the stagnation of ages in India and Africa. New opportunities for acquiring wealth would enable people to enrich themselves and a new society based on class would emerge. Marx anticipated that: 'Modern industry, resulting from the railway system, will dissolve the hereditary divisions of labour, upon which rest the Indian castes, those decisive impediments to Indian progress and Indian power.'

At first sight, such expectations seem not to have been fulfilled. Castes are very much alive in modern India, as are tribes in much of modern Africa. But to assume from the survival of castes and tribes that Indian and African society did not change under colonial rule would be entirely

mistaken. Indeed, castes and tribes in their modern forms are not simply survivals of the past. They are actually the creations of the colonial period and reflect changes that took place then.

The British of course did not invent caste; but the ranking of Hindus into an apparently inflexible caste system may actually have been strengthened under colonial rule. What the British believed to be Hindu law was transmitted to them by Brahmins, members of the priestly or highest caste. The Brahmin interpretation of the law embodied their view of a caste hierarchy. In enforcing their interpretation the British probably gave it a sanction that it had not had before.

What is called tribalism in modern Africa also owes much to the colonial period. Colonial rule gave tribes a much sharper definition. Censuses classified people by tribe and in certain colonies land was allocated in 'reserves' on the basis of tribe. Far from the towns dissolving tribes, groups of urban migrants tended to emphasize their tribal identities as they competed with other groups for jobs, housing, and ultimately for power by organizing political parties that had a tribal basis.

What of classes in colonial India or Africa? It is certainly possible to identify Indian and African working and middle classes. The development of a middle class was particularly marked among business people and those who pursued professions in the towns, while the urban poor can be regarded as a working class. Similar changes took place in the countryside, where colonial policies generally encouraged the individual ownership of land, leading to the emergence of a middle class of substantial farmers who owned their land and of a landless class who worked on it.

By the end of colonial rule many individuals identified both with those of a similar caste or tribal background and with those who seemed to have the same position in society as they did. African and Indian society can therefore be described in terms of castes and tribes as well as in terms of class divisions. It would, however, be misleading to see one set of categories as traditional survivals and the other as a modern development. Both are in a sense modern. Colonial rule changed people, but it did not do so in any simple pattern derived from western or British models.

Jomo Kenyatta and a general. While officers of the Kenyan army continued to wear British uniform after independence, President Kenyatta appeared in public in what he regarded as appropriate African dress for a modern Kenyan.

disease or significantly reduce death rates in Africa or Asia. Whether these things happened and, if they did, the extent to which they happened, depended to a very large measure on the peoples whom the British ruled.

THE DIVERSITY OF RESPONSES TO EMPIRE

British imperial rule restricted choices but it also created opportunities to which the people whom they ruled responded in very different ways.

Political responses

A.J. Stockwell describes the opportunities that existed for obtaining a measure of power under the British. The British empire, like all empires, depended for its working on 'collaboration' (a word that should be used in this context in a neutral way without any of the overtones of disapproval usually attached to it). Put simply, the British could not run any colony without delegating much of the task to the ruled themselves. Opportunities existed for easing the British out of almost all effective power, as in the colonies of settlement that achieved responsible government, or to staff their bureaucracies and wield local influence on their behalf in Asia or Africa. British ground rules, usually based on racist assumptions as to who was fit or not fit to have access to power, determined the outlines of what was on offer. But there was still much room for local intiative to exploit this. How power was in practice divided between the British and their subjects therefore varied from colony to colony, but the regimes were never exclusively British.

Economic responses

The economic gifts that the British offered were investment, markets, technology, and financial services such as banking or insurance. As David Fieldhouse stresses, these gifts were not of course free. Nothing resembling modern aid programmes existed until the Colonial Development and Welfare Acts of the mid-twentieth century. Colonial communities that could afford to pay the interest on loans or purchase the technology and the services got the benefits. Within the empire certain commercial groups, not all of them necessarily white, were able to take advantage of what was on offer and to prosper. Parsis in Bombay, Chinese merchants along the Malay coast or in Hong Kong, and certain African trading families in West African ports all did well in the nineteenth century. Before the depression and the great fall of prices in the 1920s and 1930s many white farmers in the colonies of settlement and some peasant producers in India and West Africa made good livings. For the mass of its poor, the empire had very little to offer. It gave them mobility to search for work, mostly in labouring jobs, either in the mines or the cities or in the plantations, but, at least until the twentieth century, it could not even preserve its Indian subjects from huge famine mortalities. Indeed, in Tapan Raychaudhuri's view, the consequences of empire for the great mass of Indians were overwhelmingly adverse.

Rolls Royce and proud owner in Hong Kong. Successful Chinese business people have been able to reap the rewards of enterprise within a colonial framework since the mid-nineteenth century.

Cultural responses

According to Andrew Porter, 'The spread of education and ideas was determined by what the colonial peoples wished to take.' He shows that, contrary to British expectations, the empire provided a framework not only for the diffusion of Christianity and the English language, but within which religions other than Christianity and languages other than English could also spread. People could not be forced to convert to Christianity or to learn English. Whether they did so was largely determined by the nature of the society. As a very crude generalization, Muslims throughout the empire were at least initially inclined to be more self-sufficient and to show less interest in British culture than did some non-Muslims. Response also depended on economic circumstances. Poverty was no obstacle to conversion to Christianity, but learning English usually required a prior literacy in another language. The poor were not usually literate in any language and the British lacked the resources to make them so.

Given a largely free hand by the British to shape their environment and develop their own institutions, the inhabitants of colonial cities gradually imposed their own stamp on what had originated in imperial purposes. A major theme of Thomas R. Metcalf's chapter is the shift, even before the end of empire, from the colonial city to the national city – that is, that cities ceased to reflect the characteristics of a world-wide British empire and instead took on the characteristics of the emerging nation state in which they were situated.

John M. MacKenzie again brings out the theme of diversity: in this case diversity of artistic responses. The art of the white societies in Australasia, Canada, and South Africa was at first heavily influenced by British models, but by the end of the nineteenth century distinct national schools had evolved. Indigenous artistic traditions survived in non-European societies to act as an inspiration both for new generations of African and Indian artists, trained in western styles and techniques, and for some European artists seeking new ways of expressing themselves. Thus the art history of the empire is, like so many other aspects of its history, a story of the exchange of ideas and the merging of traditions.

JUDGEMENT ON EMPIRE

The extent to which British initiatives and responses by colonial peoples varied to produce very different results from colony to colony makes it almost impossible to offer any definitive judgement on the British imperial record as a whole. Given the highly polemical purposes that interpretations of that record have so often been made to serve in the past, caution in pronouncing judgement is no doubt salutary. The history of the British empire is, however, concerned with issues that were of great importance at the time, both to Britain and to the peoples ruled by Britain, and that are still very relevant to the contemporary world. The British record in dealing with such issues invites critical assessment, even if the assessments may differ for different phases of the empire.

The Victorian empire

Throughout the nineteenth century Britain waged repeated wars outside Europe. In the 1850s, for instance, the British were fighting in New Zealand and at the Cape. British forces invaded Iran and China, where they helped to burn the Summer Palace at Peking. The Burmese were attacked and huge forces had to be deployed in desperate battles to suppress the revolt of the Bengal sepoys and to reconquer much of northern India. Yet for all for all its violence and an undoubted brashness and over-confidence, especially in mid-century, the Victorian empire had a creativity that its later successors lacked.

Britain's lead over the rest of Europe meant that, for much of the nineteenth century, a connection with Britain was likely to bring real compensations, even if the connection was imposed by force and bloodshed. Britain was an unrivalled source of emigrants, capital, technology and expertise of all sorts. It was the cheapest supplier of most manufactured goods and the biggest market for all sorts of food and raw materials. The British were the proud custodians of a culture and a set of values that many other people found very attractive indeed.

At a high price to its indigenous peoples, a flood of British immigrants transformed Australia, New Zealand, and Canada during the nineteenth century. India was certainly not transformed in the same period, but among small groups in cities like Calcutta and Bombay there was a remarkable merging of British and Indian culture. Outside the port cities in the second half of the nineteenth century the railways brought economic opportunities to some sections of the rural population and new schools and colleges extended education. Modern historians do not depict the anti-slavery movement as a simple crusade of good against evil. They recognize both the ambiguities of motives and the failure of the abolitionists to create new opportunities for black people in the Caribbean, let alone in West Africa. Even so, the movement represents a massive involvement by the British public as a whole and by part of its political leadership in a concern for non-European people. It is doubtful whether involvement on this scale has ever been repeated in British history.

The British empire in the twentieth century

Given the likely alternatives, to have drawn the British ticket in the nineteenth-century lottery of empires may not, on balance, have been an altogether unhappy accident. By the end of the century, however, brash creativity was giving way to wary caution. During the twentieth century the attractions of the British ticket began to diminish. Other options beckoned, including the prospect of independence.

The British committed their empire to two World Wars. Many of those who fought were clearly proud to have done so and identified themselves closely with Britain's cause. The wars stimulated political and economic changes which weakened Britain's hold on the empire, yet they inflicted much suffering, not just

Opposite: End of empire in Kenya, Nairobi, 12 November 1963. This ceremony was one that was repeated over and over again in different colonies: the Union Jack was hauled down and the national flag run up in the presence of British dignitaries and the new national leaders.

on the largely volunteer fighting men but on huge numbers of non-combatants as well. Having taken a full role in the partition of Africa in the last quarter of the nineteenth century, the British did little to encourage political or economic development there until the era of the Second World War. In South Africa in 1910, by granting virtually complete power to run their internal affairs to the new Union government chosen by an almost entirely white electorate, the British eased themselves out of any further attempts to play a significant role in relations between white and black. The new imperial adventure in the Middle East left the British embroiled in Palestine and achieved little elsewhere. Facing an economic recession and nationalist challenges, the British were generally forced on the defensive in the interwar period. Yet, as K.S. Inglis demonstrates for the Australian case, through such tactics as 'calculated ambiguity of language', Britain was generally successful in conciliating different varieties of Dominion nationalism and even showed some dexterity in playing for time against Indian nationalism.

The Second World War and its immediate aftermath may have stimulated a revival in Britain's imperial creativity, but it was much too late. For all the idealism invested in the Commonwealth, it could not make the British option competitive over all the other options that were now on offer. While extricating themselves from empire with real skill, even if their former subjects, as in the Punjab where some 250,000 people were killed, were not always so fortunate, the British began to turn towards another option themselves as they sought entry into Europe.

It is sometimes argued that the difficulties of the contemporary third world indicate that the British should have prolonged their rule. There is, however a good case for suggesting that a full transfer of power in India should actually have been attempted in the 1930s rather than being delayed into the 1950s or later. By 1947 the British had no capacity left to govern India in any form. Although British colonial rule in Africa was more purposeful in promoting economic development and in the provision of health and education in its last phases than it had ever been in the past, there is nothing to suggest that the British government or the British electorate were prepared to commit the resources that would have made any very significant impact on African problems. Nor could British colonial officials long retain the authority to impose their solutions on these problems in the political climate that was emerging after the Second World War. In short, it is hard to see the end of empire as premature. A world that had been shaped by empires had outgrown even the largest of those empires.

Reference guide to The Cambridge Illustrated History of the British Empire

British Imperial Territories from 1783

Further Reading

British Imperial Territories from 1783

This is a list of territories either ruled by Britain or over which, during the period of this book, Britain exercised a dominant influence. The name given to each is that by which it was known under British rule. Terms like 'protectorate' or 'responsible government' are explained on pages 152–53. Dates at which independence was attained are given for all territories, with two kinds of exceptions: territories marked * were still British dependencies in 1995; the old Dominions, marked †, are of course independent countries in the fullest possible sense, but the date at which they attained their independence is very difficult to determine. The letter and number after each entry are references to one of the maps of the empire on the endpapers.

Aden [P9] The port was seized by the East India Company from the Arabs in 1839 and ruled by the company until 1858, when it was transferred to the Crown as part of British India. Aden became a separate colony in 1936. Inland territory was brought under British protection by treaties with Arab chiefs from 1873 and formed the Aden Protectorate. In 1963 Aden joined the South Arabian Federation, which became independent as South Yemen in 1967.

*****Anguilla** [M9] The island was settled from St Christopher in 1650 and brought under Crown rule in 1663. Its government was united with St Christopher from 1882 until 1967, when it declared its separation. It was brought back under direct British administration in 1969.

Antigua [M9] The island was settled from St Christopher in 1632 and brought under Crown rule in 1663. It became independent as Antigua and Barbuda in 1981.

*****Ascension** [N10] The island was first occupied in 1815 by the Royal Navy as a precaution while Napoleon was held on St Helena. It was placed under civil administration from St Helena in 1922.

†**Australia** [R, S11] The Commonwealth of Australia was created in 1901 by the union of New South Wales, Queensland, South Australia, Tasmania, Victoria, and Western Australia.

Bahamas [L9] The islands were settled from 1629 and brought under Crown rule in 1717. Bahamas became independent in 1973.

Bahrain [P9] The emirs of Bahrain entered into treaties of protection with Britain from 1882. Full independence was proclaimed in 1971.

Barbados [M9] The uninhabited island was settled in 1625 and brought under direct Crown rule in 1663. It became independent in 1966.

Basutoland [P11] The territory of its African ruler was annexed by Britain in 1868. Basutoland was transferred to the Cape Colony in 1871 but returned to British protection in 1884. It became independent as Lesotho in 1966.

Bechuanaland [O, P11] After the dispatch of a British military expedition in 1884, a protectorate was proclaimed in 1885. Part of Bechuanaland was transferred to the Cape Colony in 1895, but the rest remained under British protection until it became independent as Botswana in 1966.

*****Bermuda** [M9] The islands were claimed in 1609 and settled by a London company from 1612. Bermuda was brought under Crown rule in 1684.

Bhutan [Q9] Border territory was taken from Bhutan after a war with the British in 1864. In 1911 the ruler of Bhutan signed a treaty with Britain, guaranteeing his internal autonomy in return for British control of his foreign policy. The connection ended with Indian independence in 1947.

*****British Antarctic Territory** Islands were claimed from 1819 and claims to part of the continent defined in 1908 and 1917. The 1959 Antarctic Treaty laid down regulations for activities in Antarctica.

British Columbia [B2] Following a treaty in 1846 with the United States, colonies were established on Vancouver Island in 1849 and on the mainland in 1858. The two colonies were united in 1866, and British Columbia became part of the Dominion of Canada in 1871.

British Guiana [M10] In 1831 a single colony was created out of three Dutch possessions – Berbice, Demerara, and Essequibo, which had been conquered in 1796 and 1803 and were annexed to Britain in 1814. The colony became independent as Guyana in 1966.

British Honduras [L9] From about 1636 British logwood cutters settled on coastal sites. Spain contested Britain's right until 1786. The settlement was administered from Jamaica from 1862 until 1884, when it became a separate colony. In 1981 it became independent as Belize.

*****British Indian Ocean Territory** [Q10] In 1965 islands that had been dependencies of Mauritius and Seychelles were placed under direct British administration. In 1976 all the islands except the Chagos group were returned to Seychelles on independence. Britain retained the Chagos islands, largely for defence purposes.

British Kaffraria [F5] A colony was established in 1847 after war on the frontier of the Cape Colony with the Xhosa ('Kaffirs'). In 1866 it was incorporated into the Cape Colony.

British New Guinea [S10] A protectorate was established in 1884 to pre-empt German claims. It was transferred to Australia and renamed Papua in 1906.

British Somaliland [P10] The coast was brought under protection from Aden in 1884. Boundaries were fixed in 1897 and a separate colony set up in 1905. The Italians occupied it from 1940 to 1941. It became independent as part of Somalia in 1960.

*****British Virgin Islands** [M9] The islands were settled from 1666 and brought under Crown rule in 1713.

Brunei [R10] The Sultan of Brunei was brought under British protection in 1888. His territory was occupied by the Japanese from 1942 to 1945. He became ruler of an independent state in 1983.

Burma [R9] In three wars, beginning in 1824, 1852, and 1885, the British conquered the territory of the Burmese kings. British Burma was administered as part of India until 1937, when a separate government was created. The Japanese occupied Burma from 1942 to 1945. It became independent in 1948.

†**Canada** [L, M8] The Dominion of Canada was created by the coming together in a Confederation in 1867 of Canada East and Canada West together with New Brunswick and Nova Scotia. British Columbia was added in 1871, Prince Edward Island in 1873, and North West Territory in 1870. Newfoundland joined the Confederation in 1949.

Canada East [C2] In 1760 the British conquered French Canada, which became the British colony of Quebec in 1763. In 1791 Quebec was divided into two separate colonies – Upper and Lower Canada. Lower Canada was renamed Canada East in 1840. It was the nucleus of the province of Quebec in the 1867 Confederation.

Canada West [C2] The colony originated in the creation of Upper Canada by the 1791 division of Quebec (see previous entry). In 1840 Upper Canada was renamed Canada West. It was the nucleus of the province of Ontario in the 1867 Confederation.

Cape Breton Island [C2] Conquered from the French in 1758, the island became part of Nova Scotia from 1763 until 1784, when it was made a separate colony. In 1820 it was again incorporated into Nova Scotia.

Cape Colony (Cape of Good Hope) [E5] The Dutch settlements at the Cape were seized by the British in 1795 and 1806. They were annexed by Britain in 1814. The Cape Colony was granted responsible government in 1872 and became part of the Union of South Africa in 1910.

*****Cayman Islands** [L9] The islands were ceded by Spain in 1670. They were administered from Jamaica until they became a separate colony in 1959.

Ceylon [Q10] Coastal areas were conquered from the Dutch by the East India Company in 1796 and transferred to Crown rule in 1802. The King of Kandy was deposed and the whole island brought under British rule in 1815. Ceylon became independent in 1948 and adopted the name Sri Lanka in 1972.

Cook Islands [K11] The islands were annexed in 1888 and transferred to New Zealand in 1901.

Cyprus [P9] The island was placed under British administration by treaty with Turkey in 1878. It became a colony in 1914 and gained its independence in 1960.

*****Dependency of South Georgia and the South Sandwich Islands** [N12] British claims date from James Cook in 1775. British control was established in 1908 and 1917 over what were called the Falkland Island Dependencies until 1962.

Dominica [M9] The island was captured from the French in 1761 and annexed by Britain in 1763. The French occupied it again from 1778 to 1783. Dominica became independent in 1978.

Egypt [P9] Nominally a Turkish province but effectively independent, Egypt was conquered and occupied by Britain in 1882. It was a British protectorate from 1914 until 1922, when it became independent, but with strong treaty obligations to Britain. British occupation of the Canal Zone lasted until 1954.

Eire [O8] The whole of Ireland was an integral part of the United Kingdom until 1922. Then the twenty-six southern counties became the Irish Free State with Dominion status. In 1937 the name Eire was adopted. In 1948 Eire left the Commonwealth to become the Republic of Ireland.

Ellice Islands [T10] Placed under British protection with the Gilbert Islands in 1892, the islands became part of the colony of the Gilbert and Ellice Islands from 1916 until gaining independence as the separate state of Tuvalu in 1978.

*****Falkland Islands** [M12] The first British occupation in 1765 was contested by Spain. The British withdrew in 1774 but returned in 1833. Colonial rule was established in 1841. The islands were briefly occupied by Argentina in 1982.

Fiji [T11] Missionaries and settlers took up residence on the islands from 1835. In 1874 they were annexed to the British Crown at the invitation of the Fiji chiefs. Fiji became independent in 1970.

Gambia, The [N9] Forts were settled by traders from 1661. They were placed under Crown rule to be administered from Sierra Leone in 1821. The Gambia became a separate colony in 1888, to which inland territory was added as a protectorate in 1894. It became independent in 1965.

*****Gibraltar** [O9] The fortress was conquered from Spain in 1704 and British possession was confirmed by treaty in 1713.

Gilbert Islands [T10] A protectorate was established together with the Ellice Islands in 1892 and it became part of the colony of the Gilbert and Ellice Islands from 1916, until gaining independence as Kiribati in 1979.

Gold Coast [O10] Forts were settled by traders from 1631. They were placed under Crown rule administered from Sierra Leone from 1821 to 1874 with an interval under merchant control from 1828 to 1843. A protectorate was extended inland from 1830. In 1874 the colony of the Gold Coast was created. Further territory was added until its final boundaries were fixed in 1904. Part of German Togoland was included in 1919. The Gold Coast became independent as Ghana in 1957.

Grenada [M10] The island was conquered from France in 1762 and was annexed to Britain the following year. The French reoccupied it from 1779 to 1783. It became independent in 1974.

Heligoland [E2] The island was seized from Denmark in 1807. In 1890 it was ceded to Germany.

*****Hong Kong** [R9] China ceded the island in 1842. Additional territory was acquired in 1860 together with the New Territories on the mainland on a ninety-nine-year lease from 1898.

India [Q9] The East India Company established its first coastal settlements from 1609. A process of territorial expansion accelerated from 1757, leading to great extensions of direct British rule after the conquest of Indian states, together with the reduction of other states to the status of subordinate allies of the British, subject to what was later called paramountcy. Company rule was replaced by Crown rule in 1858. From

1876 British monarchs were given the title of Empress or Emperor of India. In 1947 a partitioned British India attained independence as India and Pakistan. Bangladesh seceded from Pakistan in 1972.

Ionian Islands [E3] In 1809 the British drove the French out of what before 1797 had been Venetian territory and annexed the islands in 1814. The islands were ceded to Greece in 1864.

Iraq [P9] The former Turkish province of Mesopotamia was conquered by the British in the First World War. In 1920 Britain was granted a mandate. In 1922 an autonomous Iraq was bound by treaty obligations to Britain. Iraq became formally independent in 1932. Britain reoccupied Iraq from 1941 to 1945.

Jamaica [L9] The island was conquered from Spain in 1655. It became independent in 1962.

Kenya [P10] A British share of East Africa was demarcated with Germany in 1886. In 1888 the British share was annexed by the Imperial East Africa Company. The British East Africa Protectorate under the Crown replaced the rule of the company in 1895. In 1920 it became the colony of Kenya, which attained independence in 1963.

Kuwait [P9] The Arab emirate signed treaties of protection with Britain from 1899. Kuwait became fully independent in 1961.

Labuan [H4] The island, ceded by the Sultan of Brunei, was annexed in 1846 and became a colony in 1848. It was incorporated into North Borneo in 1890.

Malacca [H4] The settlement was seized from the Dutch in 1795 and occupied until 1816. In 1824 the Dutch ceded it to the East India Company. It became part of the Straits Settlements in 1826.

Malaya [R10] The British signed treaties of protection with Malay rulers from 1874 to 1930. In 1896 some of these states were grouped together as the Federated Malay States. Malaya was occupied by the Japanese from 1942 to 1945. All the Malay states, together with the Straits Settlements except for Singapore, were incorporated into a new federation in 1948. This was the basis on which Malaya achieved independence in 1957. In 1963 Malaya joined with Singapore (which seceded in 1965), North Borneo, and Sarawak to form Malaysia.

Maldive Islands [Q10] A British protectorate was proclaimed over the islands in 1887. The islands were declared to be independent in 1965.

Malta [O9] In 1798 the French occupied the island belonging to the Knights of St John. The British drove out the French in 1800 and annexed Malta in 1814. It became independent in 1964.

Mauritius [P11] The island was conquered from France in 1810 and annexed by Britain in 1814. Mauritius became independent in 1968.

*****Montserrat** [M9] The island was settled in 1632 and brought under Crown rule in 1663. It was occupied by the French in 1664–68 and 1782–84.

Natal [F5] Territory was annexed in 1843 and British settlement followed. Natal was granted responsible government in 1893. Zululand, under British authority since the end of the Zulu War in 1879, was transferred to Natal in 1897. Natal became part of the Union of South Africa in 1910.

Nepal [Q9] The Himalayan kingdom fought a war with Britain from 1814 to 1816. During the war the first of large numbers of Nepalese Gurkha soldiers were recruited into the British Indian army. A British Resident was appointed to the Nepalese court from 1816. Nepal has exercised full independence since the ending of British rule in India in 1947.

Nevis [M9] The island was settled from St Christopher in 1628 and came under Crown rule in 1663. It was united with St Christopher in 1882 into a single government.

New Brunswick [C2] A separate colony was created out of Nova Scotia in 1784. New Brunswick was granted responsible government in 1854 and became part of the Canadian Confederation in 1867.

Newfoundland [M8] English ships were probably fishing off the Grand Banks from the late fifteenth century. The island was annexed by Sir Humphrey Gilbert in 1583 and brought under Crown rule in 1713. Newfoundland was granted responsible government in 1855, but returned to colonial rule in 1934. It joined the Canadian Confederation in 1949.

New Hebrides [T11] The islands were settled by French and British planters and missionaries during the nineteenth century. In 1906 a joint Franco-British administration was set up. New Hebrides became independent as Vanuatu in 1980.

New South Wales [I5] The eastern coast of Australia was claimed by James Cook in 1770 and the first settlement by convicts took place in 1788. New South Wales was granted responsible government in 1855 and became part of the Commonwealth of Australia in 1901.

†**New Zealand** [S12] James Cook claimed the coast of North Island in 1769 and of South Island in 1770. In 1840 British rule was established by treaty with the Maoris. New Zealand was granted responsible government in 1856.

Nigeria [O10] A consulate was established in 1851 at Lagos, which was annexed in 1861. The Niger Districts Protectorate was created around the Niger delta in 1885, followed in 1886 by a sphere allocated to the Royal Niger Company up the river. Further annexations were made from 1892 to 1898. Crown rule replaced that of the company in 1900. Northern and Southern Nigeria were united in 1914. Part of German Cameroon was added in 1919. Nigeria became independent in 1960.

North Borneo [R10] Territory was ceded by the Sultan of Brunei to a group which became the North Borneo Company in 1881. North Borneo was brought under Crown rule in 1906. It was occupied by the Japanese from 1942 to 1945. As Sabah, it became part of Malaysia in 1963.

Northern Rhodesia [O, P10] Territory known as Northern Zambesia was allocated to the British South Africa Company in 1891. Crown rule replaced company rule in 1924. Northern Rhodesia became part of the Central African Federation with Nyasaland and Southern Rhodesia in 1953. In 1964 it gained independence as Zambia.

Nova Scotia [C2] France ceded Nova Scotia to England in 1621 but recovered it in 1632. By the Treaty of Utrecht it again passed to Britain in 1713. Further territory was added in 1763. Nova Scotia gained responsible government in 1846 and became part of the Canadian Confederation in 1867.

Nyasaland [P10] Mission settlements were established from 1875. In 1891 the Central African Protectorate was proclaimed over the area, which was known as Nyasaland from 1907. Nyasaland became part of the Central African Federation with Northern and Southern Rhodesia in 1953 and gained independence as Malawi in 1964.

Orange Free State [O11] Afrikaner trekkers from the Cape in the 1830s set up a state which was annexed by Britain from 1848 to 1854. Thereafter the Orange Free State enjoyed virtual independence until it was conquered in 1900 during the South African War. Responsible government was granted to it in 1907 and it became part of the Union of South Africa in 1910.

Palestine [P9] Turkish rule over Palestine was brought to an end by British conquest in 1918. Britain was granted a mandate over it in 1920. The mandate was abandoned in 1948. A Jewish–Arab war followed, out of which emerged the state of Israel.

Penang [H4] In 1786 the East India Company established a settlement, which became one of the Straits Settlements in 1826.

*Pitcairn Islands** [K11] The first settlement was made in 1790 by the *Bounty* mutineers. Crown rule was established in 1838.

Prince Edward Island [C2] The island (then known as the Island of St John) was captured from the French in 1760 and annexed by Britain in 1763 as part of Quebec. In 1769 it became a separate colony. It joined the Canadian Confederation in 1873.

Qatar [P9] The rulers of Qatar entered into treaties of protection with Britain from 1916. It became independent in 1971.

Queensland [I5] The first settlement was made at Moreton Bay in 1824. Queensland became a colony with responsible government separate from New South Wales in 1859. It became part of the Commonwealth of Australia in 1901.

Rhodesia [P10] The area of Southern Rhodesia was conquered from African peoples from 1890 to 1893 and settled by the British South Africa Company. With the demise of the company, the colony of Southern Rhodesia passed under Crown rule with responsible government in 1923. With Northern Rhodesia and Nyasaland, it formed part of the Central African Federation from 1953 to 1964. In 1965 its government unilaterally declared its independence as Rhodesia. Rhodesia turned into Zimbabwe in an internationally recognized independence in 1980.

Rupert's Land and North West Territory [B, C2] Much of the north of Canada was claimed by the Hudson's Bay Company, which traded from coastal posts from 1670. Inland posts were developed by both the Hudson's Bay Company and the North West Company from 1774. In 1869 the company surrendered its rights to the Crown and the territories were transferred to the Dominion of Canada in 1870. In the same year a separate province of Manitoba was created out of an area previously called the Red River Settlement.

St Christopher (St Kitts) [M9] In 1623 St Christopher became the first island in the Caribbean settled by the English. It came under Crown rule in 1663. The French occupied it from 1782 to 1783. In 1882 the government of Nevis was combined with St Christopher. St Christopher and Nevis became independent in 1983.

*St Helena** [O10] The island was annexed in 1651 and settled by the East India Company in 1661. It came under Crown rule in 1834.

St Lucia [M9] The island was captured from the French in 1778, but returned to them in 1783. In 1796 and in 1803 it was captured again, to be permanently annexed by Britain in 1814. St Lucia became independent in 1979.

St Vincent [M9] The island was captured in 1762 and annexed the following year. The French occupied it from 1779 to 1783. St Vincent and the Grenadines became independent in 1979.

Sarawak [R10] The Sultan of Brunei appointed James Brooke Rajah of Sarawak in 1841. Further territory was added in 1861 and 1905. The Japanese occupied Sarawak from 1942 to 1945. The rule of the Brooke family was replaced by Crown rule in 1946. Sarawak became part of Malaysia in 1963.

Seychelles [P10] The islands were conquered from France in 1794 and administered from Mauritius from 1811 until they became a separate colony in 1888. Seychelles gained independence in 1976.

Sierra Leone [N10] A company founded settlements, largely for freed slaves, in 1787. The settlement was taken over by the Crown in 1807. Inland territory was incorporated as a protectorate in 1896. Sierra Leone became independent in 1961.

Sikkim [Q9] A British Political Officer was appointed to supervise the government of the kingdom in 1890. The ruler's autonomy was restored in 1918 under continuing British protection. This protection was withdrawn with Indian independence in 1947.

Singapore [R10] The island was settled in 1819 and became part of the Straits Settlements in 1826. It joined Malaysia in 1963, leaving it to become an independent state in 1965.

Solomon Islands [T10] A British protectorate was established from 1893 to 1900. The Japanese occupied the islands from 1942 to 1945. They became independent in 1978.

†**South Africa** [O, P11] The Union of South Africa was created in 1910 out of the Cape Colony, Natal, the Orange Free State, and the Transvaal.

South Australia [I5] An act of Parliament was passed in 1834 to create a new colony and the first colonists from Britain arrived in 1836. South Australia was granted responsible government in 1855, becoming part of the Commonwealth of Australia in 1901.

South West Africa [O11] The port of Walvis Bay was declared to be British territory in 1878 and annexed to the Cape Colony in 1884 when the Germans began to set up a colony in the surrounding area. The German colony was captured in 1915 and became a South African mandate in 1919. It attained independence as Namibia in 1990.

Straits Settlements [R10] Malacca, Penang, and Singapore were placed under a joint government in 1826 under the East India Company. It was administered under the government of India from 1858 and as a separate colony from 1867. Malacca and Penang became part of the Malayan Federation in 1948. Singapore remained a separate colony.

Sudan [P9, 10] Egyptian rule over the Sudan was overthrown in the 1880s by the Mahdist revolt. Acting nominally for Egypt, Britain reconquered the Sudan in 1898 and established a joint Anglo-Egyptian condominium over it. It became independent in 1956.

Swaziland [P11] Britain established a joint protectorate over Swaziland's rulers with the Transvaal in 1890. In 1906 Britain assumed the protectorate on its own. Swaziland became independent in 1968.

Tanganyika [P10] Britain conquered what had been German East Africa during the First World War. In 1919 Tanganyika became a British mandate. It attained independence in 1961 and united with Zanzibar to form Tanzania in 1964.

Tasmania [I6] European settlement on the island then known as Van Diemen's Land began in 1803 and a colony separate from New South Wales was established in 1825. It attained responsible government in 1856 and became part of the Commonwealth of Australia in 1901.

Tobago [M10] The island was captured in 1762 and annexed the following year. The French captured it in 1781 and retained it at the peace of 1783. It was again conquered by the British in 1793 and annexed to the British empire in 1814. Its government was united with Trinidad in 1888.

Tonga [T11] The ruler of Tonga signed a treaty of friendship with Britain in 1879. He placed himself under British protection in 1900. Tonga attained independence in 1970.

Transjordan [P9] The British conquered what had been part of a Turkish province in 1918 and received a mandate for it in 1920. Transjordan was separated from Palestine in 1921 and an Arab kingdom was created in alliance with Britain by a treaty of 1923. It became independent as Jordan in 1946.

Transvaal (South African Republic) [P11] Afrikaners trekking out of the Cape in the 1830s established their own state. Britain annexed it from 1877 to 1881 and conquered it in 1900. It was granted responsible government in 1906 and became part of the Union of South Africa in 1910.

Trinidad [M10] The island was conquered from Spain in 1797 and annexed in 1814. Its government was joined with Tobago in 1888. Trinidad and Tobago became independent in 1962.

*Tristan da Cunha** [N11] The island was first occupied in 1816 by the Royal Navy as part of precautions while Napoleon was on St Helena. It was administered as a colony under St Helena from 1938.

Trucial States (Trucial Oman) [P9] Britain signed treaties of protection with Arab rulers from 1887. The United Arab Emirates became independent in 1971.

*Turks and Caicos Islands** [M9] The islands were settled in 1678 and annexed to the Crown in 1766. They were administered from Jamaica and Bahamas until they became a separate colony in 1973.

Uganda [P10] The Imperial British East Africa Company annexed the share of East Africa allocated to Britain in 1888. The company signed a treaty with the kingdom of Buganda in 1890. With the demise of the company, Buganda became a Crown protectorate in 1894. Other protectorates were established in 1896 and the colony of Uganda was created in 1905. Uganda became independent in 1962.

Victoria [I5] Port Phillip was settled from Tasmania in 1834. A separate colony of Victoria was set up in 1851 and granted responsible government in 1855. It became part of the Commonwealth of Australia in 1901.

Weihaiwei [R9] The port was leased from China in 1898. It was returned to China in 1930.

Western Australia [H5] The coast was first settled in 1826. The Swan River Colony was established in 1829. Western Australia was granted responsible government in 1890 and became part of the Commonwealth of Australia in 1901.

Zanzibar [P10] The first British Consul was established on the island in 1841. A British protectorate was declared over its Sultan in 1890. Zanzibar became independent in 1963 and part of Tanzania the following year.

Further Reading

INTRODUCTION *The World Shaped by Empire*

a) General histories of the British empire, covering the whole or a substantial part of the period of this book:

C.C. Eldridge, *Victorian Imperialism*. London: Hodder, 1978.

R. Hyam, *Britain's Imperial Century, 1815–1914: A Study of Empire and Expansion*, 2nd edn. London: Macmillan, 1993.

L. James, *The Rise and Fall of the British Empire*. London: Little Brown, 1994.

T.O. Lloyd, *The British Empire 1558–1983*. Oxford: Oxford University Press, 1984.

B. Porter, *The Lion's Share: A Short History of British Imperialism 1850–1983*, 2nd edn. London: Longman, 1984.

b) J. Morris, *Pax Britannica*. This trilogy (London: Faber) is a vivid evocation of the last hundred years of the empire. The individual volumes are: *Heaven's Command: An Imperial Progress*, 1973; *Pax Britannica: The Climax of an Empire*, 1968; *Farewell the Trumpets: An Imperial Retreat*, 1978.

c) A.N. Porter (ed.), *Atlas of British Overseas Expansion*. London: Routledge, 1991. This provides maps which supplement those in this book.

Chapter 1 *The British Empire at the End of the Eighteenth Century*

R. Anstey, *The Atlantic Slave Trade and British Abolition, 1760–1810*. London: Macmillan, 1975.

A. Calder, *Revolutionary Empire: The Rise of the English-Speaking Empires from the Fifteenth Century to the 1780s*. London: Jonathan Cape, 1981.

P.D. Curtin, *The Rise and Fall of the Plantation Complex: Essays in Atlantic History*. Cambridge: Cambridge University Press, 1990.

P. Lawson, *The East India Company: A History*. London: Longman, 1993.

Chapter 2 *1783–1870: An Expanding Empire*

C.A. Bayly, *Imperial Meridian: The British Empire and the World 1780–1830*. London: Longman, 1989.

_____, *Indian Society and the Making of the British Empire*. Cambridge: Cambridge University Press, 1988.

G. Blainey, *The Tyranny of Distance: How Distance Shaped Australia's History*. Melbourne: Macmillan, 1966.

J.M. Bumsted, *The Peoples of Canada*: vol. I, *A Pre-Confederation History*. Toronto: Oxford University Press, 1992.

J. Walvin, *England, Slaves and Freedom, 1776–1838*. Basingstoke: Macmillan, 1986.

J.M. Ward, *Colonial Self-Government: The British Experience 1759–1856*. London: Macmillan, 1976.

Chapter 3 *1870–1918: The Empire under Threat*

M. Beloff, *Imperial Sunset*: vol. I, *Britain's Liberal Empire 1897–1921*, 2nd edn. London: Macmillan, 1987.

J. Eddy and D. Schreuder (eds), *The Rise of Colonial Nationalism*. Sydney: Allen & Unwin, 1988.

R.J. Moore, *Liberalism and Indian Politics, 1872–1922*. London: Edward Arnold, 1966.

A. Offer, *The First World War: An Agrarian Interpretation*. Oxford: Clarendon Press, 1989.

R. Robinson and J. Gallagher with A. Denny, *Africa and the Victorians: The Official Mind of Imperialism*, 2nd edn. London: Macmillan, 1981.

P. Warwick (ed.), *The South African War: The Anglo-Boer War 1899–1902*. London: Longman, 1980.

Chapter 4 *1918 to the 1960s: Keeping Afloat*

M. Beloff, *Imperial Sunset*: vol. II, *Dream of Commonwealth 1921–42*. London: Macmillan, 1989.

J.M. Brown, *Modern India: The Origins of an Asian Democracy*, 2nd edn. Oxford: Oxford University Press, 1994.

J. Darwin, *Britain and Decolonisation: The Retreat from Empire in the Post-War World*. Basingstoke: Macmillan, 1988.

J.A. Gallagher, *The Decline, Revival and Fall of the British Empire*. Cambridge: Cambridge University Press, 1982.

W.R. Louis, *Imperialism at Bay, 1941–1945: The United States and the Decolonization of the British Empire*. Oxford: Clarendon Press, 1977.

N. Mansergh, *The Commonwealth Experience*: vol. II, *From British to Multiracial Commonwealth*, 2nd edn. London: Macmillan, 1982.

Chapter 5 *For Richer, for Poorer?*

G.N. Blainey, *The Rush That Never Ended: A History of Australian Mining*. Melbourne: Melbourne University Press, 1963.

D. Denoon, *Settler Capitalism: The Dynamics of Dependent Development in the Southern Hemisphere*. Oxford: Clarendon Press, 1983.

D.K. Fieldhouse, *Colonialism 1870–1945: An Introduction*. London: Weidenfeld & Nicolson, 1981.

D.R. Headrick, *The Tentacles of Progress: Technology Transfer in the Age of Imperialism, 1850–1940*. New York and Oxford: Oxford University Press, 1988.

J. Iliffe, *The African Poor: A History*. Cambridge: Cambridge University Press, 1987.

M.B. McAlpin, *Subject to Famine: Food Crises and Economic Change in Western India, 1860–1920*. Princeton, NJ: Princeton University Press, 1983.

Chapter 6 *Power, Authority, and Freedom*

B. Anderson, *Imagined Communities: Reflections on the Origin and Spread of Nationalism*, 2nd edn. London and New York: Verso, 1991.

J.A. Gallagher and R.E. Robinson, 'The Imperialism of Free Trade', in J.A. Gallagher, *The Decline, Revival and Fall of the British Empire*. Cambridge: Cambridge University Press, 1982.

R. Heussler, *British Rule in Malaya: The Malayan Civil Service and Its Predecessors, 1867–1942*. Westport, CT: Greenwood Press, 1981.

E. Hobsbawm and T. Ranger (eds), *The Invention of Tradition*. Cambridge: Cambridge University Press, 1983.

P. Kennedy, *The Rise and Fall of the Great Powers: Economic Change and Military Conflict from 1500 to 2000*. London: Unwin Hyman, 1988.

A. Seal, *The Emergence of Indian Nationalism: Competition and Collaboration in the Later Nineteenth Century*. Cambridge: Cambridge University Press, 1968.

J.M. Ward, *Colonial Self-Government: The British Experience 1759–1856*. London: Macmillan, 1976.

Chapter 7 *Empires in the Mind*

R.W. Bailey, *Images of English: A Cultural History of the Language*. Cambridge: Cambridge University Press, 1992.

P.D. Curtin, *The Image of Africa: British Ideas and Action, 1780–1850*. London: Macmillan, 1964.

A. Nandy, *The Intimate Enemy: Loss and Recovery of Self under Colonialism*. Delhi: Oxford University Press, 1983.

E. Said, *Orientalism*. London: Routledge, 1978.

R.A. Stafford, *Scientist of Empire: Sir Roderick Murchison, Scientific Exploration and Victorian Imperialism*. Cambridge: Cambridge University Press, 1989.

B. Stanley, *The Bible and the Flag: Protestant Missions and British Imperialism in the Nineteenth and Twentieth Centuries*. Leicester: Inter-Varsity Press, 1990.

Chapter 8 *Imperial Towns and Cities*

A.J. Christopher, *The British Empire at Its Zenith*. London: Croom Helm, 1988.

G. Davison, *The Rise and Fall of Marvellous Melbourne*. Melbourne: Melbourne University Press, 1978.

R.G. Irving, *Indian Summer: Lutyens, Baker and Imperial Delhi*. New Haven: Yale University Press, 1981.

P. Kanwar, *Imperial Simla: The Political Culture of the Raj*. Delhi: Oxford University Press, 1990.

A.D. King, *Colonial Urban Development: Culture, Social Power and Environment*. London: Routledge & Kegan Paul, 1976.

T.R. Metcalf, *An Imperial Vision: Indian Architecture and Britain's Raj*. Berkeley: University of California Press, 1989.

R.J. Ross and G.J. Telkamp (eds), *Colonial Cities*. The Hague: Nijhoff, 1985.

Chapter 9 *British Emigration and New Identities*

G.C. Bolton, *Britain's Legacy Overseas*. Oxford: Oxford University Press, 1973

J.M. Bumsted, *The Peoples of Canada*, 2 vols. Toronto: Oxford University Press, 1992.

S. Constantine (ed.), *Emigrants and Empire: British Settlement in the Dominions between the Wars*. Manchester: Manchester University Press, 1990.

B. Guest and J.M. Sellers (eds), *Enterprise and Exploitation in a Victorian Colony: Aspects of the Economic and Social History of*

Colonial Natal. Pietermaritzburg: University of Natal Press, 1985.

K.S. Inglis, *The Australian Colonists: An Exploration of Social History*. Carlton, Vic.: Melbourne University Press, 1974.

G.W. Rice (ed.), *The Oxford History of New Zealand*, 2nd edn. Auckland: Oxford University Press, 1992.

Chapter 10 *The Diaspora of the Africans and the Asians*

B. Brereton, *Race Relations in Colonial Trinidad 1870–1900*. Cambridge: Cambridge University Press, 1979.

K.L. Gillion, *Fiji's Indian Migrants: A History to the End of Indenture in 1920*. Melbourne: Oxford University Press, 1970.

D. Lowenthal, *West Indian Societies*. London: Oxford University Press, 1972.

V. Purcell, *The Chinese in Malaya*. London: Oxford University Press, 1948.

K. Saunders (ed.), *Indentured Labour in the British Empire, 1834–1920*. London: Croom Helm, 1984.

H. Tinker, *A New System of Slavery: The Export of Indian Labour Overseas 1830–1920*, 2nd edn. London: Hansib, 1974

Chapter 11 *Art and the Empire*

M. Archer, *India and British Portraiture, 1770–1825*. London: Sotheby Parke Bennet, 1979.

C.A. Bayly (ed.), *The Raj: India and the British, 1600–1947*. London: National Portrait Gallery, 1990.

E. Berman, *The Story of South African Painting*. Cape Town: Balkema, 1974.

G. Docking, *Two Hundred Years of New Zealand Painting*. Melbourne: Lansdowne, 1971.

J. R. Harper, *Painting in Canada: A History*, 2nd edn. Toronto: University of Toronto Press, 1977.

P. Mitter, *Much Maligned Monsters: The History of European Reactions to Indian Art*. Oxford: Clarendon Press, 1977.

B. Smith, *Imagining the Pacific: In the Wake of the Cook Voyages*. New Haven: Yale University Press, 1992.

_____, *Place, Taste and Tradition: A Study of Australian Art Since 1788*, 2nd edn. Melbourne: Oxford University Press, 1979.

Chapter 12 *Imperial Britain*

P.J. Cain and A.G. Hopkins, *British Imperialism: Innovation and Expansion 1688–1914*. London: Longman, 1993.

_____, *British Imperialism: Crisis and Deconstruction 1914–1990*. London: Longman, 1993.

R. Holland, *The Pursuit of Greatness: Britain and the World Role 1900–1970*. London: Fontana, 1991.

J.M. MacKenzie (ed.), *Imperialism and Popular Culture*. Manchester: Manchester University Press, 1986.

P. B. Rich, *Race and Empire in British Politics*, 2nd edn. Cambridge: Cambridge University Press, 1990.

V. Robinson, *Transients, Settlers and Refugees: Asians in Britain*. Oxford: Clarendon Press, 1986.

A. P. Thornton, *The Imperial Idea and its Enemies*. London: Macmillan, 1959.

Chapter 13 Australia

G. Davison, J.W. McCarty, and A. McLeary (eds), *Australians 1888*. Broadway, NSW: Fairfax Syme & Weldon, 1987.

B.L. Gammage, *The Broken Years: Australian Soldiers in the Great War*. Ringwood, Vic.: Penguin, 1990.

W.K. Hancock, *Australia*. Brisbane: Jacaranda Press, 1986.

W.J. Hudson and M.P. Sharp, *Australian Independence: Colony to Reluctant Kingdom*. Carlton, Vic.: Melbourne University Press, 1988.

J. Jupp (ed.), *The Australian People: An Encyclopedia of the Nation, Its People and Their Origins*. North Ryde, NSW: Angus & Robertson, 1988.

H. Reynolds, *The Law of the Land*. Ringwood, Vic.: Penguin, 1987.

Chapter 14 Africa

C. Achebe, *Things Fall Apart*. London: Heinemann, 1958.

C. Achebe et al (eds), *Beyond Hunger in Africa: Conventional Wisdom and an African Vision in 2057*. London: James Currey, 1990.

G.B.N. Ayittey, *Africa Betrayed*. New York: St Martin's Press, 1992.

A.A. Boahen, *Africa under Colonial Domination 1880–1935*, abridged edn., Vol. VII of *A General History of Africa*. London and Berkeley: James Currey, University of California Press, and Unesco, 1990.

B. Davidson, *Modern Africa: A Social and Political History*, 3rd edn. London: Longman, 1994.

Chapter 15 British Rule in India: An Assessment

C.A. Bayly, *Indian Society and the Making of the British Empire*. Cambridge: Cambridge University Press, 1988.

_____ (ed.), *The Raj: India and the British, 1600–1947*. London: National Portrait Gallery, 1990.

J.M. Brown, *Modern India: The Origins of an Asian Democracy*, 2nd edn. Oxford: Oxford University Press, 1994.

N. Charlesworth, *British Rule and the Indian Economy, 1800 to 1914*. London: Macmillan, 1982.

S. Sarkar, *Modern India 1885 to 1947*, 2nd edn. Basingstoke: Macmillan, 1989.

B.R. Tomlinson, *The Political Economy of the Raj, 1914–47: The Economics of Decolonization in India*. London: Macmillan, 1979.

Contributors

EDITOR **P.J. Marshall**, former Rhodes Professor of Imperial History, King's College, University of London.

Toyin Falola, Professor of African History, University of Texas at Austin.

David Fieldhouse, former Vere Harmsworth Professor of Imperial and Naval History, University of Cambridge.

K.S. Inglis, William Keith Hancock Professor of History, Social Science Research School, Australian National University.

Benjamin E. Kline, teacher in the California university system.

John M. MacKenzie, Professor of Imperial History, University of Lancaster.

Ged Martin, Reader in History and Director of the Centre of Canadian Studies, University of Edinburgh.

Thomas R. Metcalf, Professor of History, University of California at Berkeley.

Andrew Porter, Rhodes Professor of Imperial History, King's College, University of London.

Tapan Raychauduri, former Professor of Indian History and Civilization, University of Oxford.

A.J. Stockwell, Reader in History, Royal Holloway, University of London.

Acknowledgements

Every effort has been made to obtain permission to use any copyright material listed below; the publishers apologize for any errors or omissions and would welcome these being brought to their attention.

PICTURES

Cover (*The Ganges Canal, Roorkee (Saharanpur District)* 1863 by William Simpson 1823–1899), British Library (OIOC WD 1012); *Title page*, 31 (*A Patrol under the Command of Captain Fisher Charged by Macoma's Kafirs in Van Beulen's Hoek, Kat River* by Thomas Baines 1822–75), Bonhams, London/Bridgeman Art Library; *Half title*, 331, Imperial War Museum/Camera Press, London; 7, 53, 63, 69, 93, 96, 100, 135, 147, 154, 173, 180, 183, 192, 208, 237*l*, 247, 258, 284, 324*c*, 366, Hulton Deutsch Collection; 9, 77, 372, Punch Publications; 13, S.K. Dutt/Camera Press, London; 14–15, 46 (*Raja Dhian Singh on Horseback, Punjab Plains c.*1840), 251, 312*t*, 363 (*Sulkeah (Calcutta)*) by J.L. Kipling), courtesy of the Trustees of the Victoria & Albert Museum; 17 (*West India Docks* by T. Rowlandson 1756–1827 and A. Pugin 1762–1832), British Library, London/Bridgeman Art Library; 19 (*The Surrender of Yorktown, 1781* by Louis Nicolael van Blarenberghe 1716–94), Lauros-Giraudon/Bridgeman Art Library; British Library, London: 21 (OIOC WD 959), 23 (*Warren Hastings in European Court Dress* by unknown Mughal artist, OIOC OR 6633, F.67a), 48 (OIOC W 2868), 71 (OIOC B 9854), 106–7, 123*t* (OIOC 448/4), 133 (OIOC B 2033), 139 (OIOC B 12639), 142 (OIOC B 10757), 169 (OIOC), 178 (OIOC PIB 27/lE), 220 (OIOC V 6600), 224 (*South East View of Fort St George, Madras* from *Oriental Scenery* Part II plate 7 acquaint 1797 by Thomas and William Daniell, OIOC X 432, B 327), 226 (*Native Shop in Jaun Bazar Street, Calcutta* from *India Ancient and Modern* by William Simpson, 1784.d.2), 232*t* (OIOC B 2012), 239 (*New Government House* by James Moffat *c.*1802, OIOC WD 476), 245 (OIOC Album 42 4350), 297 (Add MS 15513-4), 299 (OIOC P 430), 302 (OIOC F 597), 303*t* (OIOC F 106), 303*b* (OIOC WD 2089), 312*b* (OIOC P 2126), 327 (*Sezincote* drawn and etched by J. Martin, OIOC P 1601), 337 (BMC 3124), 362 (*A Loom, with the Process of Winding off the Thread* by Arthur William Devis 1763–1822, OIOC P 805), 365 (OIOC Photo 134/2), 369 (OIOC B 10496); 26, 51 (*Defence of Arrah House against Three Mutinous Regiments and a Large Body of Insurgents under Koer Singh*, lithograph after William Taylor 1808–92), 98, courtesy of the Director, National Army Museum, London; 27, 234, 360, Illustrated London News Picture Library; 30, 159, 264, Mary Evans Picture Library; 32, Library of Congress; 38 (*The Entrance of Port Jackson and Part of the Town of Sydney, New South Wales*), 39, 298, 338, Mitchell Library, State Library of New South Wales; 40, 236, Mansell Collection; 42, National Library of Australia/ photographer J.W. Beattie, Album 229; 43, courtesy of the Trustees of the Wedgwood Museum, Barlaston, Staffordshire; 44 (*William Wilberforce* by George Richmond 1809–96), 58 (*William E. Gladstone* by Carlo Pellegrini 1839–89), 59 (*Alfred Milner, Viscount Milner* by Hugh de Twenebrokes Glazebrook), 61 (*Joseph Chamberlain* 1896 by John S. Sargent 1856–1925), 168 (*Thomas Babbington, First Baron Macaulay* 1849 by John Partridge 1790–1872), 218 (*Rudyard Kipling* 1899 by Sir Philip Burne Jones), 286 (*Sir Thomas Stamford Bingley Raffles* by George Francis Joseph 1764–1846), 324*t* (*Garnet Joseph Wolseley, lst Viscount Wolseley* by Paul Albert Besnard, *b* (*Horatio Herbert Kitchener, lst Earl Kitchener of Khartoum* by Charles Mendelssohn Horsfall), *c*, courtesy of the National Portrait Gallery, London; 45, 167, Foreign & Commonwealth Office Library Photograph Collection, London; 57, 111, 113, 116, 118, 121, 126, 136, 141, 143, 148, 152–3, 156, 160, 162, 185, 187, 198, 199, 206, 222, 232*b*, 246, 249, 282 (*Trinity Estate* from A

Picturesque Tour of the Island of Jamaica by James Hakewill 1825), 289, 305, 350, Royal Commonwealth Society Collection; 62, Bodleian Library, Oxford, 2523.c.24; 64, 204, Museum Africa; 67, 84, 86, 270, 344, Imperial War Museum, London; 79, 80, Crown Copyright/ Imperial War Museum, London; 90, 378, Burt Glinn/Magnum; 95, 119, 172, 348, 381, Topham Picture Source; 101, Associated Press; 103 (*Hong Kong Harbour c.*1848 by unknown Chinese artist), by permission of Urban Council Hong Kong from the collection of Hong Kong Museum of Art; 104, 215, 279, Popperfoto; 110, 256, Coo-ee Historical Picture Library; 115, E.T. Archive; 122, 123*b*, courtesy of Dr Elizabeth Whitcombe; 127 (*Shearing the Rams* 1890 by Tom Roberts, Australia, 1856–1931, oil on canvas on board, 180.3 x 119.4 cm), Felton Bequest, 1932, National Gallery of Victoria, Melbourne; 144, 233 courtesy of Sally Carpenter; 145, courtesy of John Swire & Sons Ltd; 158, JIS Photo, courtesy of the National Library of Jamaica; 164, courtesy of the Library of Parliament, Parliament of the Republic of South Africa; 170, courtesy of Sally Carpenter/ photo by La Belle Aurore; 175, National Archives of Canada/C 396; 177, Alexander Turnbull Library, Wellington, New Zealand, ref. no. F96972 1/2; 190, grateful appreciation is expressed to the Baptist Missionary Society of Didcot, UK, who provided the photograph of the portrait which hangs in the Baptist Missionary Society offices; 195, Royal Geographical Society, London; 207 (*Baptism of the Maori Chief, Te Puni, Otaki Church, New Zealand* 1853 by Charles Decimus Barraud 1822–97), National Library of Australia, NK 1103; 211 (*Rammohan Roy* by Henry Perronet Briggs 1791(?)–1844), City of Bristol Museum & Art Gallery; 213, reproduced from James Wells *Stewart of Lovedale* 1919, opp. p. 214/by permission of the Syndics of Cambridge University Library; 219 (*The Village Club* by Henry Edward Detmold from *The Jungle Book* by Rudyard Kipling), Bridgeman Art Library; 228–9, courtesy of John Rennie, from negative courtesy of Mrs Margaret Cairns/photo: Herbert Beard, *c.*1900; 231 (*Adelaide, Hindley Street from the Corner of King William Street* by James William Giles 1801–70), National Library of Australia, U1378/NK54; 237*r*, 267, 343, Coo-ee Picture Library; 240, National Archives of Canada/C 2837; 242, 243, Bridgeman Art Library; 244, by courtesy of the Royal Architectural Library, RIBA, London; 254 (*A Primrose from England* lithograph by John Robert Dicksee 1817–1905 after Edward Hopley 1816–69), National Library of Australia, NK 833; 259 (*Natives of New South Wales As Seen in the Streets of Sydney* from *Views in New South Wales and Van Diemen's Land* by Augustus Earle 1793–1838), National Library of Australia, NK 1239/3; 262, Government Printing Office Collection, State Library of New South Wales; 263, courtesy of the Mitchell Library, Glasgow; 268, Saskatchewan Archives Board, photo no. R-A1071; 274, Popperfoto/ photo: Joyner; 276, National Library of Australia; 281*t*, 293, Range/ Bettmann; 281*b*, Wilberforce House, Hull City Museums, Art Galleries and Archives; 291, courtesy of The West India Committee; 296, Natural History Museum, London; 300, Tate Gallery, London; 301, 324*br*, E.T. Archive; 306 (*Under a Southern Sun* 1890 by Charles Conder, Australia/Great Britain, 1868–1909, oil on canvas 71.5 x 35.5 cm), Bequest of Mary Meyer in memory of her husband Dr Felix Meyer, 1975, Collection: National Gallery of Australia, Canberra; 307, Royal Geographical Society, London/Bridge-man Art Library; 308*t* (*Aboriginal Head/Charlie Turner* 1892 by Tom Roberts, Australia, 1856–1931, oil on canvas on paperboard 39.4 x 29.8 cm), Art Gallery of New South Wales; 308*b*, National Library of Australia, NK 2181; 309, 314, 315, courtesy of South African National Gallery; 310, National Gallery of Canada, Ottawa/photo: copyright NGC/MBAC; 313, 316–17, Pitt Rivers Museum, University of Oxford; 318, Joanne O'Brien/Format; 329, George Orwell Archive, University College

London/photo by Vernon Richards; **332**, photo by Michael Charity/ Camera Press, London; **335**, Press Association; **339**, **353**, Camera Press, London; **342**, Australian War Memorial, negative number HO 1894; **346**, Penny Tweedie/ Panos Pictures; **354**, Sybil Sassoon/Robert Harding Picture Library; **355**, Juliet Highet/Life File; **356**, Popperfoto; **357**, Norah Vivian's drawing from *The Men who Ruled India*; *the Guardians* by Philip Woodruff, Jonathan Cape, 1954; **358**, The Board of Trustees of the Royal Armouries; **375**, National Museums of Tanzania; **377**, photo by David Channer/Camera Press, London.

OIOC = Oriental & India Office Collections

TEXT

page 161 R. Kipling, superscription to 'In the House of Suddhoo', *Plain Tales from the Hills*, 3rd edn. London: Macmillan, 1890.

page 193 L. Bennett, *Anacey Stories and Dialect Verse*. Kingston: Pioneer Press, 1950.

page 193 V.S. Naipaul, *A House for Mr Biswas*. London: Deutch, 1961, 398.

pages 218–19 R. Kipling, 'The Ladies', 'Chant-Pagan', and 'Recessional', in T.S. Eliot (ed.), *A Choice of Kipling's Verse*. London: Faber, 1963.

page 218 R. Kipling, 'The Supplication of Kerr Cross', in A. Rutherford (ed.), *Early Verse by Rudyard Kipling 1879–1889*. Oxford: Oxford University Press, 1986.

page 256 L. Esson, 'The Shearer's Wife', cited K. Alford, *Production and Reproduction: An Economic History of Women in Australia 1785–1850*. Melbourne: Oxford University Press, 1984, 189.

page 291 E.R. Braithwaite, *To Sir, with Love*. London: Bodley Head, 1969, 39.

Index

Italic numbers indicate
illustrations, maps, and captions.

Aborigines, Australian see
    Australia
Accra 102, 183, 214, 228–9
Achebe, Chinua 192–3, 192
Acholi 191
Adelaide 231, 233
Aden 34, 384
Afghanistan 28–9, 29, 300
African Association 194
African National Congress 69,
    172
Afrikaners see South Africa
Aga Khan 248
Ageyman, Eric 355
agriculture 16, 16–17, 19–20,
    25, 37–8, 43–4, 57, 60, 68,
    70, 102, 110, 117, 118, 121,
    122–3, 122, 123, 125–34, 126,
    127, 130, 133, 196, 198, 227,
    228, 259, 267, 277, 278,
    280–91, 282, 326, 327, 350,
    350, 362–4, 362, 363
Aitken, Max (Lord Beaverbrook)
    322
Alexander (the Great) 224, 240
Alexander, William 21
Algeria 324, 372
American colonies 10, 16–19,
    27, 159, 320, 327, 372
American Revolution 18–20, 19,
    322, 339
Amery, L.S. 267
Ames, Mary Frances 62
Amin, Idi 294, 356
Amritsar 98, 99
Anand, Mulk Raj 192
Anguilla 384
Antigua, 16, 160, 291, 384
Arabs 82, 84, 157, 182
architecture
    hill stations 232, 232, 234–5
    imperial London 166–7,
        238
    mining towns 234–5, 234
    styles 167, 224, 228, 236–7,
        236, 237, 238–44, 239,
        240, 242, 243, 244, 327
    town planning 225–31,
        226, 231, 233–4, 233,
        243, 252
Arden-Clarke, Sir Charles 177
Argentina 12, 157, 265, 328
Arrah House 51
art
    crafts 303, 311
    history painting 299–301,
        299, 300, 301

indigenous traditions
    311–15, 313, 314
'township art' 315, 315
in colonies of settlement
    306–15, 306, 307, 308,
    309, 310
in exploration and science
    296–8, 296, 297, 298
in India 302–5, 302, 303,
    305, 312, 312, 314
Ascension 384
Ashanti 181, 376
Asiatic Society of Bengal 194,
    213
Aswan dam 121
Attlee, Clement 85, 96, 100,
    172, 182, 345
Auckland 177, 277
Aurangzeb 303
Australia 384
    Aborigines 37, 42, 42, 176,
        187, 220, 231, 259, 274,
        297, 308, 308, 313, 315,
        340, 346
    agriculture 37–8, 110,
        127–9, 127, 132, 256–7,
        256–7
    art 38, 127, 296, 297, 306,
        306, 307, 308–9, 308, 315
    British origins 254, 254,
        255, 263–9, 267
    communications 116, 117,
        119, 261–2, 262
    constitution 41, 68–9, 165,
        325, 340–3, 342, 345–6
    convicts 36–9, 38, 39, 258,
        263
    defence of 87, 94, 344–5
    economy 38, 90, 98, 138,
        146, 328
    education 209, 250
    first settlement 36–40, 37,
        38, 176, 263
    identity 13, 97, 252, 258–9,
        263–5, 268, 269, 272–8,
        276, 320, 338–46, 338
    military contribution 57,
        77, 78–9, 79, 87, 87, 89,
        262, 270–1, 270, 342–3,
        342, 343
    mining 37, 136–7, 136, 234,
        254
    population 8, 42, 68, 187,
        220, 254, 258–9, 265,
        267, 339–40
    religion 209
    towns 38, 68, 230–1, 231,
        233–4, 237, 237, 238–9,
        238, 241, 248, 249, 250,
        253, 257, 259, 264, 272

'white Australia' policy 68,
    276, 277, 346
    women 256–7, 256–7, 258
Awadh (Oudh) 50, 303

Baden-Powell, Robert 53, 63,
    63
Bagehot, Walter 345
Bahamas 384
Bahrain 384
Baikie, William 194
Baines, Thomas 31, 299, 307
Baird, Sir David 299
Baker, Sir Herbert 167, 240, 243,
    243, 244
Balfour, A. J. 82, 341
Balfour Declaration (1917)
    82–3; (1926) 92, 97, 273, 325
Ballarat 234
Banda, Hastings 101, 101
Bangladesh 358, 364, 369, 386
Banks, Sir Joseph 194, 196, 296,
    297
Barbados 19, 123, 282, 384
Barberton 258
Baring, Evelyn (Lord Cromer)
    74, 150, 158, 196
Barnato, Barney 135
Barnett, Correlli 80
Barrack-room Ballads 218
Barrow, John 188
Basutoland (Lesotho) 147, 384
Bathurst (Australia) 136
Bathurst (the Gambia) 230
Battiss, Walter 314
Bechuanaland (Botswana) 119,
    384
Beerbohm, Max 321
Beit, Wernher 135
Belgium 371
Bell, Sir Henry Hesketh 185
Bell, Sydney Smith 169
Belloc, Hilaire 148, 359
Benares 303
Bendigo 136, 136, 234
Bengal 16, 20–21, 22–3, 26, 46,
    50, 71, 181, 189, 189, 194,
    211, 213, 249, 250–2, 312,
    326, 358–9, 360, 362, 380
Bennett, Louise 193
Berlin conference (1885) 73
Bermuda 384
Bevin, Ernest 82
Bhownaggree, Mancherjee 171
Bhutan 384
Birch, James 163
Bird, Isabella 168
Birney, Earle 273
Blantyre 101
Bleak House 324

Boers see South Africa:
    Afrikaners
Bogle, Paul 158
Bombay 16, 20, 26, 137, 142–3,
    227, 238, 241, 245, 245, 250,
    312, 369
Botha, Louis 69
Botswana see Bechuanaland
Boys Brigade 62, 63
Boy Scouts 62, 63
Brahmo Samaj (Society for the
    Transcendent Deity) 211
Braide, Garrick 210
Braithwaite, E.R. 291
Braque, Georges 314
Brassey, Thomas 116
Brazil 43
Brisbane 231, 276
Bristol 16
British Antarctic Territory 384
British Broadcasting Corporation
    216, 262
British Columbia 260, 261, 275,
    384
British Commonwealth of
    Nations see Commonwealth
British Empire Exhibition,
    Wembley 308, 311, 312
British Guiana (Guyana) 7, 32,
    43, 281–2, 285, 287, 289, 291,
    295, 384
British Honduras 384
British Indian Ocean Territory
    384
British Kaffraria 384
'Britishness' 13, 223, 273–4, 279,
    290–1, 319–22, 336–7
British New Guinea (New
    Guinea) 55, 153, 344, 344,
    384
British North America 34–6, 35,
    109 see also Canada
British Somaliland 384
British South Africa Company
    65, 73–4, 348
British Virgin Islands 384
Broken Hill Proprietory
    Company Ltd (BHP) 137
Brooke, James 154, 158
Brown, George 214, 266
Bruce, S.M. 341
Brunei 154, 384
Brunel, Isambard 114
Brydon, Dr 300
Buchan, John 60
Buddhism 179
Buenos Aires 12
Bulawayo 348
bungalow 236–7, 236–7, 239
Burke, Edmund 31, 156, 319

Burma 72, 74, *74*, *86*, 179, 312, 329, 364, 380, 384–5
Burmese Days 329
Butler, Lady *300*
Butler, R.A. 332
Buxton, Thomas Fowell 31, 85, *204*, 220

Cabot, John 10
Cairo 163
Calcutta *13*, 20, 137, 145, 195, 197, 211, 213, 225–7, *226*, 238–41, *239*, 248–53, *249*, *251*, *302*, 312, *363*, *366*
Calwell, Arthur 277
Cambridge University 201
Cameron Highlands (Malaya) 235
Cameroon 55, 349
Campbell-Bannerman, Sir Henry 66, 174
Canada 385
   agriculture 126, *126*
   art 306, 307–8, 310, *310*, 315
   British origins 10, 254, 263, *263*, 265–9, *268*
   communications 68, 113, 116, 117, 120, 126, 214, 260–2
   constitution 35–6, *35*, 152, 155, 164–5, 325
   economy 90, 98, *109*, 110, 117, 120, 126, 137, 138
   education *199*, 201, 209
   French in 19, 34, 35, 36, 40, 42, 53, 93, 161, 175–6, *175*, 241, 255, 260, 264
   French language 34, 36, 187, 260
   identity *268*, 269–78, 320
   military contribution 32, 77, 78–9, *78*, 80, 87, *87*, 270–1, *270*
   population 8, 34, 68–9, 258–60, 274
   racial prejudice 275–7
   relations with US 27, 28, 35
   towns 68, 230, 233, *240*, 241, 253
Canadian Pacific railway 117, 126, 261, 266, 307
canals 70, 72, 114–15, *115*, 120–1, *122*, 124
Canberra 272, 341
Canton 20, *21*, *111*
Cape Breton Island 385
Cape Colony (Cape of Good Hope) 31, *31*, 40–2, *40*, 65, *65*, 69, 155, 176, 187, 213–14, 259, 274, *307*, 385, 388
Cape Coloured *see* South Africa

Cape Town 40, *164*, 201, 225–6, 228–9, *228–9*
Carey, William *190*, 191, 203, 213
Caribbean *see* West Indies
Carpenter, Mary 247
Cartier, George 264
Cawnpore (Kanpur) 50, 227
Cayman Islands 385
Cecil, Lord William 201
Central Africa 101, 104–5, 114, 116, 119, 175, 196, 208, 375
   see also Northern Rhodesia, Nyasaland, Southern Rhodesia
Central African Federation 101, *101*, 104, 165
Central Asia 28–9, *28–9*, 54
Ceylon (Sri Lanka) 31, *116*, 152, *160*, 226, 246–7, 280, 285, 287, 288, 293–5, 312, 385
Chagos Islands 384
Chamberlain, Joseph 57, 60–2, *61*, 64–7, 85, 89, 92, 150
Chandigarh 244
Charles, Prince of Wales *339*, 340, 342
Charters Towers 272
Chaudhuri, Nirad C. 358
Chiang Kai-Shek 276
Ch'ien-lung *21*
Chile 12
Chilembwe, John 212
China 7, *11*, 12, 20, *21*, 23, 33, 55, *55*, 103, *111*, *145*, 148, 150, 201,157, 158, 286, 287, 339, 371, 380
Chinese 103, 145, 163, 181, 275–7, *276*, 286–8, *286*, *287*, 292–3, 378, *378*
   Chinese language *187*
Chisholm, Caroline 257
Christchurch 209, 233
Christianity 23, 24, 30, 44, *44*, 45, *45*, 49, 190–91, *192*, 196, 197–8, 200, 203–14, *206*, *207*, *213*, *217*, *247*, 250, 290–1, *291*, *325*, 352, 368, 379
Churchill, Winston *69*, 85, *86*, 89, 94, 167, 171, 177, 181, 260, 276, 319, 335, 336
City of London 16, 151
Clarkson, Thomas 44
Clive, Edward 358
Clive, Robert 20, 171, 313, 326, 330, *358*, 361
Cobden, Richard 31, 85, 323
Cockerell, Sir Charles *32*
cocoa 102, 129, 131, *350*
Colley, Sir George *159*
Collins, Michael 176
Colombo 226
Colonial Development (and Welfare) Acts 91, 124, 146, 378

Colonial and Indian Exhibition 311
Colonial Office (British) 24, 101, 131, 247, 265, 323
Commonwealth
   British influence 94, *96*, 151, 173, 184, *215*, 319, 354–5, 381
   definition 92–3, 97–8, 217, 273, 345, 372
   and Europe 334–6, *335*
   immigration from 318, *318*, 331–3, *331*
   India and Pakistan 92, 100
   Ireland 176
   literature 191–2, *191*, *192*
   monarchy 91, 171, 325
   Second World War 87
   South Africa 278
   troops 90
communications 16–7, *16*, 26, 33, 47, 49, 57, 68, 70, 72, 108–9, *109*, 113–25, *113*, *116*, 118, *119*, *123*, 126, 127–8, 141, 212–17, *215*, 233–4, 260–3, *262*, 350, 351, 363–4, 375
Conder, Charles *306*
Congo 115, *372*
Congress (Party) *see* Indian National Congress
Connaught, Duke of *164*
Conservative party 58, *61*, 64, 67, 84–5, *97*, 173–4, 332
convicts *see* Australia
Cook Islands *217*, 277, 385
Cook, James 23, 36, 259, 296–9, *296*, *297*, *298*, 313, *338*
Coomaraswamy, A.K. 312
Cornish 255
Cornwallis, Lord *19*
cotton *16*, 17, 20, 25, 43, 70, 117, 118, 131, 139–41, 227, 288, 327, 329, *362*, *363*
Coward, Noel 321
Crentsil, A.B. *355*
cricket *11*, *160*, 250, 271
Cripps, Sir Stafford 94, 100, 172, 181
Cromer, Lord *see* Baring, Evelyn
Crown Colony government 152, 154–5
Crowther, Bishop Samuel Adjai 190, 206, *206*, 210
Cuba 43
currencies 91, 98, 111, *111*, 112, 184, 350
Currie, General Sir Arthur 266
Curtin, John 341, 345
Curzon, Lord *13*, 70, 77, 84, *170*, 173, *173*, 181, 189, 203, 244, 367
Cyprus 28–9, 181, 182–3, *182–3*, 385

Dalhousie, Lord 47
Daniell, Thomas 305, *305*, *327*
Daniell, William 305
Dar es Salaam *167*
Darjeeling 235
Darwin, Charles 220
Dawson City 137
Deakin, Alfred 341
Deb family 211
Declaration of Independence (1776) 13, 339
decolonization 84–5, 94–7, *97*, 102–5, 146, 152, 166, 181–4, 217, 292–5, 340–1, *380–1*, 381
De Gaulle, Charles 334, 373
De Lesseps, Ferdinand 115
Delhi (New Delhi) 50, 167, 169–70, *169–70*, 211, 242–3, 243, 253
Dependency of South Georgia and the South Sandwich Islands 385
diamond mining 65, *65*, 129, 134–6, *144*
Dickens, Charles 324
direct rule 162–3
Disraeli, Benjamin 58, 115, 171, 322
'divide and rule' 45, 165
Dominica 385
Dominions, the 76, 78, 81–3, 85, 88, 90–3, 96–8, 112, 152, 168, 171, 176, 216, 270–4, *270*, 305–11, 315, 325, 340, 372, 381 *see also* Australia, Canada, Ireland, New Zealand, South Africa
Dube, J.W. 172
Duff, Alexander 220
Durban 229
durbar 169–70, 171
Durham, Lord 164
Dyaks 158, 294, 295
Dyer, General *98*, 99

East Africa 56, 73, 78–9, *79*, 87, 102, 104, 119–20, 165, 175, 191, 196, 252, 375, *375 see also* Kenya, Tanganyika, Uganda, Zanzibar
Easter Rising (Dublin) 266
East India Company 16, 21, 22, 24, *26*, 30, 47, 118, 120, 133, 153, 154, 185, 195, 197, 211, 224, 225, 227, 302, 313, 319, 331, 358–9, 361, *362*, 384
Eaton, Timothy 266
Eden, Anthony *90*
education 45, *45*, 70, *71*, *156*, 173–4, *187*, 189, 194–203, *198*, *199*, 211, 216, *244*, 250, 267, 268, 290–1, 330–31, 352, 364, 368–9

Edward VII, King *170, 301*
Egypt *28–9, 58,* 72, 74–5, 90, *90,* 95, 114, 115, *121,* 150, *150,* 155, 157–8, 163, 196, 227, 273, 334, 385
Eire 385 *see also* Ireland
Elizabeth II, Queen 269, 273, 325, 345, 346
Ellice Islands 385
Emerson, William 244
emigration *see* migration
Empire Day 62, *63,* 171, 216
Empire Marketing Board *130,* 216
English language 8, 71, 161, 185–91, *187,* 192–3, 200, 260, 269, 275, 279, 349, 351, 352, 354, 369, 376, 379
Enigma of Arrival 193
enosis 181, *182*
environment 122–3, *122, 123*
EOKA 182, *182*
European Economic Community 98, 113, 128, 328, 334–7, *335,* 345
Eyre, Governor 158

Falkland Islands 10, 105, 166, 385
famine
 East Africa 134
 India 132–4, *133,* 359, 363
 Sudan 134
Far East, 54–5, *55,* 88, 89, 91, 94, *148,* 155 *see also* China, Japan, Malaysia, Singapore
Farouk, King 158
Farquhar, J.N. 205
Fashoda 76
Federated Malay States *see* Malaysia
federation 150, 164–6, *340,* 341
Federation of the West Indies *see* West Indies
Fiji 7, *143,* 252, 288–9, *289,* 294–5, 385
film *see* media
First World War 69, 72, 76–9, *77, 78–9,* 80–3, *80, 83, 84,* 270, 270–1, 342–4, *342, 343*
Foreign Office (British) 86, 88, 155
Forster, E.M. 321
Fort William College 197, 213
Foveaux, Major Joseph 39
France 54–6, *55,* 72–3, 75–6, 78, 84, *90,* 155, 157, 158, 335, 371, 372, 373
Frazer, J.G. 195
Freetown 45, 46, 201
free trade 25, 26, 32–3, 59, 60, 66, 90–1, 110–11, *110,* 138–41, 227, 327

Fulani 162
Furneaux, J.H. 227

Gallipoli 13, 77, 97, 271, 342–4, *342*
Galton, Francis 196
Gambia, The 113, 230, 385
Ganda 191
Gandhi, Mahatma *98,* 99, 174, 177, *178–9,* 180, *180,* 181, 190, 248, 252, 277, 284, 368, 370
Garran, Sir Robert 341
Garvey, Marcus *293*
Geddes, Patrick 253
General Agreement on Trade and Tariffs 113
George III, King 16, 325
George V, King 78, *170,* 215, *215,* 273
George VI, King 269, 273, 325
Germany 54–6, *55,* 65, 72–3, 78, 84, *153,* 155, *167,* 335, 371, 372
Ghana *see* Gold Coast
Gibraltar 166, 385
Gilbert, Sir Humphrey 296
Gilbert Islands 385
Girl Guides 63
Gladstone, William Ewart 58–9, *58,* 74, 267, 322
Glasgow 17
Godlonton, Robert 214
Gold Coast (Ghana) 96, 102, 104, 112, *113,* 131, *162,* 177, 181, 183, 188, 201–2, 214, 228–9, *215,* 350–1, *350, 355,* 356, 376, 385
Goldie, Sir George 116, 155
gold mining 37, 39, 65–6, *65,* 129, 134–7, *135, 136,* 234–5, *234, 254, 258,* 275–7, *276,* 286, 308
Gordon, General 75, 76, 160, 322, *301*
Gorton, John 269
Graham, Maria 225
Grand Trunk railway (Canada) 116
Grand Trunk road (India) 161
'Greater Britain' 12, 59–60
Great Exhibition (1851) *14–15,* 250, 311
'Great Game', the 29
Great Trek *see* South Africa
Greaves, Constance *309*
Greece 181, *182*
Greenwood, Arthur 267
Gregory, Augustus 307
Grenada 385
Grey, Earl 29–30, 42
Grey, Sir George 264
Griqua *see* South Africa
Guggisberg, Gordon 202

Gujaratis 245, 248
Gurkhas *80,* 90, 386
Guyana *see* British Guiana

Haggard, Rider 320
Haidar Ali 359
Haileybury College 197
Halhed, Nathaniel 213
Halifax (Nova Scotia) 16, 266
Hancock, W.K. 269
Harare *see* Salisbury
Hardinge, Lord 243
Harrison, George 135
Hastings, Marquess of 47
Hastings, Warren 22, *23,* 156, 173, 304, 313
Hausa 163, 220
Haussmann, Baron 167
Havell, E.B. 312
Havelock, General 322
health and disease 142–3, *142–3,* 228, 229, 230, 236, 252 *see also* medicine
Heath, Edward 335
Heligoland 385
Henry VII, King 10
Henty, G.A. 63, 320
Hinduism 177, 200, 205, 210–12, *211*
Hitler, Adolf 177, 267, 270, 273
Hobson, J.A. 67
Hodges, William 224, 297, *298*
Hola Camp 171
Home, Robert *190*
Hong Kong 10, 34, *55,* 103, *103,* 105, 166, *187,* 201, 253, *286,* 374, *378,* 385
Hong Kong and Shanghai Bank 103
Hoo Ah Kay 292
Horton, James Africanus 45
House for Mr Biswas, A 193
Hudson's Bay Company 16
Hudson, W.J. 340
Hughes, Richard 38
Hughes, William 173
Hussain, Ghulam 359
Hyde, Robin 270, 278

Ijebu 204
immigration *see* migration
Imperial Airways 116, 119, *119*
Imperial British East African Company 73, 198
Imperial Institute 196
Imperial Jamboree (1924) *63*
indentured labour 276–7, 284–6, *284,* 288
independence *see* decolonization
India 385–6
 agriculture 70, 132–4, 362–3

army 12, 23, 26, *26,* 50, 56, 78–9, 79, *81,* 87, 89–90, 94, 156, *243, 360*
art *299, 300,* 302–5, *302, 303, 305,* 311–12, *312,* 313, 315
British conquest 16, 20–3, 22, *23,* 46–8, 47, 154, 199, 319, 326, 358–9, *358*
British depictions of 161, 189–90, *189,* 218–19, 220, *220,* 221, 299, 321, 323, 357–8
British monarchy and 24, 30, 153, 169–70, 171, 325–6, 301
British women in 236, 247
civil service 49, 160, 162, 195, 197, 218, 331, 357, 361
communal conflict 163, 182, 366–7, *366,* 377
communications 113–14, 115, 116, 117–19, 120, *123,* 124, 213–14
constitutional change 71–2, 85, 94, 99, 364–5
defence of *28–9,* 29, 86, *86,* 89
education 49, 70–1, *71, 198,* 200, 211, *244,* 368–9
famine 132–4, *133,* 359, 363, 378
health 142–3, *142–3, 369*
independence 13, 93, 96, 100, 102, 165, 175, 182, 381
Indians outside India 7, 7, 102, *118,* 122, 245, 248, 266–7, 276–7, 284–7, *284, 287,* 288–9, 292, 294–5
industry 70, 90, 111, 117, 137, 139–40, *139,* 145, 331–2, 363–4, *363*
irrigation 120–1, *122*
languages 185–6, 188–91, *190,* 194, 195, 213, 214
law 23, 48, *48,* 168, *168,* 360
nationalism 71–2, 98–9, *98,* 171, *173,* 174, 177, *178–9,* 179–81, 367–9
religion 44, 205, 207, 210–12, *211,* 220
states (princely) 16, 21–2, 22, 46–8, *47,* 153, 155, *169,* 361, 368
textiles 20, *139,* 326, *362, 363*
towns 13, 16, 20, 24, 50, 137, 143, 169, 197, 224, *224,* 225–6, 226, 227,

230, 232, 232, 235,
    236–7, *236–7*, 238–44,
    239, 242–3, 245, 245,
    248–53, *249*, 303, 327,
    363, 366, 369
Indian Mutiny *see* Indian
    Rebellion
Indian National Congress 71,
    98–100, *100*, 165, 171, 172,
    174, *178–9*, 179–82, 216
Indian Rebellion 50, *51*, 70, 118,
    149, 160, 161, 176–7, 230,
    241, 247, 301, 322, 359,
    380
Indians, North American 18,
    220, 259, 274, 315
indirect rule 93, *93*, 162–3, *162*
Indochina 54, *55*
industry 70, 109–10, 118, 137,
    138–41, *139*, 144, 327, 352,
    363–4, 370
informal empire 11–12, *11*,
    156–8, *156*
infrastructure 113–125, *113*,
    115, *116*, *118*, *119*, *121*,
    122–3, 351, 375
Inkata Freedom Party 279
International Monetary Fund
    146
investment 53, 57, 91, 117,
    124–5, 128, 131, 326–30, 363,
    364
Ionian Islands 386
Iran 12, 20, *28–9*, 29, 371, 380
Iraq 77, 78, 84, 88, 153, 386
Ireland 9, *9*, 88, 176, 249, 320,
    342–3, 385
    Irish 9, 17, 151, 176, 248,
    255, 320
irrigation 120–24, *121*, *122*, 364
Isandlhwana 158
Islam 177, 199–200, 210–12,
    244, 347, 352, *353*, 354
Israel 90 *see also* Palestine
Italy 54, 335, 340, 371

Jabavu, J.T. 214
Jacob, Swinton 241
Jalalabad *300*
Jamaica 16, 154, 158, 193, 228,
    282–3, *282*, 290, *331*, 386
Jamaican Rebellion (1831) 44;
    (1865, Morant Bay) 46, 158,
    158, 220, 221
Jameson, Dr 65
Jameson Raid 65, *65*
Japan 32, *81*, *86*, 87, 94, 103,
    112, 335, 344–5, *344*, 357–8,
    371
Jardine Matheson 103
Jews 82–3, 182
Jhansi, Rani of 359
Jinnah, Muhammad Ali 100,
    100, 223

Johannesburg 135, *135*, 214,
    233, *234*, 235, 248, 315
Johnson, James 210
Johnson, Samuel 347
Johnston, Harry 221
Jones, Alfred 198
Jones, The Revd Michael Daniel
    265
Jones, Sir William 195
Joy, G.W. *301*
Jungle Book, The 218, *219*

Kabul *300*
Kaffir Wars *see* South Africa:
    British wars with Africans
Kalgoorlie 137
Kano, Sultan of *93*
Kanpur *see* Cawnpore
Karachi 249
Kaunda, Kenneth 101
Keating, Paul 269, 344
Kelly, Ned 309
Kenya 102, 104, *104*, 105, *118*,
    119, 130, 171, 177, 182–3,
    202–3, 229, 241, 244, 294,
    348, *354*, 355, 375, *377*,
    380–1, 386
Kenyatta, Jomo 177, 182, *377*
Kettle, Tilly *303*
Kew Gardens 197
Khan, Sher Bahadur *220*
Khan, Wazir 211
Khartoum 160, *301*, *353*
Khoikhoi *see* South Africa
Kikuyu *104*, 162, 203
Kim 218
Kimberley *64–5*, 65, 135, *144*,
    235
Kingi, Wiremu 177
Kingsley, Mary 205, 222–3, *222*
Kingston, Jamaica 228
Kipling, Rudyard 59, 62, 63,
    161, 189, 218–19, *218*, *219*,
    320, 343
Kitchener, Lord 75, 158, 324,
    324–5
Koelle, S.W. 190
Krio 45, *45*
Kruger, President 65–6, 214
Kuala Lumpur 244
Kumasi *162*
Kuwait 386

Labour party 68, 84–5, *96*, *97*,
    174, 332
Labuan 386
Lagos 229
Lahore 218, 230
Laird, Macgregor 116
Lampson, Sir Miles (Lord
    Killearn) 158
Lancashire 139–40
Lang, John Dunmore 261
Laski, Harold 172

Latin America 33, 57, 150, 157,
    327, 372 *see also* Argentina,
    Brazil, Chile
law
    English 38, 322, 341, 373
    law and order 161, 360
    property rights 122, 281,
    346, *346*, 350, 360–1,
    377
    rule of law 168, 171, 373
    varieties of law 168, 170
    in Australia 341, 346, *346*
    in British Africa 168, 350,
    352
    in Canada 161
    in India 22, 48, *48*, *72*, 168,
    168, 221, 360–61, 377
    in Malaysia 168
    in South Africa 161, 168,
    278
    in the West Indies 22, *158*,
    281
Law, Bonar 322
Lawrence, T.E. 83, *84*
League of Nations 84, 93, 153,
    155, 223
Le Corbusier 244
Leeward Islands 20, 165
Lenin, V.I. 67
Leopold II, King 372
Lesotho *see* Basutoland
Lessing, Doris 192
Liberal party 58, *58*, *61*, 66–7,
    68, 173–4
Light, Colonel William 233
Lismer, Arthur *310*
Liston, Bishop 266
literature 191–4
Liverpool 17
Livingstone, David 194, 208,
    208, 298–9, 307
Lloyd George, David 77, 83, 84,
    85
London 16, *16*, 166–7, 238 *see
    also* City of London, Colonial
    Office, Foreign Office,
    Parliament
London University 201
Lovedale *213*, 214
Low, David 321, *321*
Low, Hugh 163
Low, Robert 322
Lucknow 50, 211, 230
Lugard, Sir Frederick (Lord
    Lugard) 93, *93*, 162, 189, 201,
    356
Lutyens, Sir Edwin 167, 243, *243*
Lyttelton, Oliver 217
Lytton, Lord 235

Macarthur, John 127
Macartney, Lord *21*
Macaulay, Thomas 168, *168*,
    173, 188, 368–9

Macdonald, John A. 266, 269
Mackenzie, Alexander 173, 266
Mackinnon, William 155, 198
Macmillan, Harold 101, 104–5,
    147, *147*, 334–5
Macmillan, W.M. 216
Macquarie, Lachlan 308
Madras 20, *26*, 179, 224, *224*,
    225, 227, 240, 241, *358*,
    365
Mafeking *52–3*, *53*
Magna Carta 320
Maher, Charles *39*
Maine, Sir Henry 195
Majuba Hill 159, *159*
Makarios, Archbishop 182, *182*
Malacca 386
Malawi *see* Nyasaland
Malaya (Malaysia) 7, 74, *86*, *95*,
    150, 155, 161, 163, 165, 166,
    181–3, 198, 244, 252, 285–8,
    292–4, 386, 388
Malaysia *see* Malaya
Maldive Islands 386
Malta 56, 386
Manawapou 177
Manchester 44, 227
Manchuria 55
Mandalay 74, 179
mandates (League of Nations)
    83, 153
    Iraq 83, 84, 88, 153
    the Pacific 84
    Palestine 82–5, 94, 153
    South West Africa 84, 153,
    388
    Transjordan 83, 84, 153
Mannix, Archbishop Daniel 266,
    343
Maori *see* New Zealand
Maori Wars *see* New Zealand
Maples, Chauncy 205
Maqhubela, Louis *315*
Marchand, Colonel 158
Marconi, G. 262
Marshman, Joshua 203
Marx, Karl 377
Mary, Queen *170*
Maryland 18
Masai 130, *354*
Mason, Philip *357*
Massachusetts 18
Massachusetts Bay Company
    152
Massey, Prime Minister 266
Mau Mau 104, *104*, 182
Mauritius 7, 31, *185*, 280, 282,
    284–5, *284*, 289–91, 295, 386
Meath, Lord 64
media 212–17, *213*, *215*, 262
    broadcasting 215–17, *215*,
    262
    film 215–16
    newspapers 213–14, 215

printing and publishing 212–14, *213*

medicine 45, 142–3, *143*, 197, *247*, 354, *369 see also* health and disease

Melbourne 68, 230–1, 233–4, 238–9, 241, 248, 249, 250, *342*

Menzies, Sir Robert 269, 345

Merrett, Joseph *309*

Mesopotamia *see* Iraq

Middle East 29, 83–4, *83*, 88, *90*, 94 *see also* Arabs, Egypt, Iran, Iraq, Palestine, Suez canal, Suez crisis, Transjordan

migration 7, *7*, 29, 34, 68, 254–79, 280–95, 318–20, *318*, 324, 331–3, *331*, *337*

  Africa 7, *234*, 280–85, 287–8, 293–5

  Asia 68–9, 276–7, *276*, 284–7, *284*, *286*, 292–5

  Australia 98, 136, 186–7, 254–60, *254*, *257*, 272, 276–9, *276*, 345

  Canada 98, 187, 254–5, 258–60, 262–8, *263*, 272–3, 276–9

  China 276–8, 286–7, *287*, 292–5

  Commonwealth *318*, 331–4, *331*

  England 17, 265, 267–8

  India 7, 102, 276–7, 284–5, 287–9, *287*, 292–5

  Ireland 17, 265–6

  New Zealand 40, 186–7, 254–9, *257*, 262–5, 267, 276, 278–9

  North America 17–19, 34

  Palestine 83

  Scotland 17, 263, *263*, 265–7, *267*

  South Africa 40, 187, *234*, 254–5, 258–9, 263, *264*, 265, 267, 277–9

  Wales 265

Mill, James 311

Mill, John Stuart 158

Milner, Sir Alfred (Lord Milner) 59, *59*, 84, 196, 214

mining 37, 39, 65–6, 129, 134–7, *135*, *136*, *144*, 234–5, 275–7, *276*, 286, 308

Mirzapur 227

missionaries, mission societies 23, 24, 45, *45*, 190–1, 196, 197–8, 203–9, *204*, *206*, *207*, *208*, 210, 211, 213–14, *213*, *247*, *291*, *325*

Mombasa *118*, 241

Montague, C.E. 343

Montreal 68, 241

Montserrat 386

Monypenny, W.F. 214

Mornington, Lord *see* Wellesley, Marquess

Morris, Jan (James) 52, 80

Morris, William 311

Morrison, Robert 190

Mountbatten, Lord Louis 100, 165, 182

Movement for Colonial Feedom 172

Mritunjaya *190*

Mughal empire 20–1, 153, 188, 241, 244, 326, 358–9, *358*

Muller, Professor Max 195

Murchison, Sir Roderick 194

Murshidabad 361

museums 167, 169, 313, *313*

Muslim League 100, 165, 182

Mussoorie 235

Mysore Wars 299, 359

Naipaul, V.S. 192–3, *193*

Nairobi 229, 244, *380–1*

Namibia *see* South West Africa

Nanaimo 265

Nana Sahib 50

Naoroji, Dadabhai 171

Napoleon Bonaparte 26, 56, *109*, 115

Narayan, Jayaprakash 174

Narayan, R.K. 192

Nasser, Gamal Abdul *90*

Natal 41, 65, 69, 229, 238, 274, 276–9, 386

National Congress of West Africa 181

National Front (Britain) 332

NATO 89, 335

Navy League *54*

Ndebele *41*, 204, *348*

Nehru, Jawaharlal 100, *178–9*, 181, 244

Nelson, Admiral 301

Nelson (New Zealand) 199

Nepal *80*, 386

Netherlands 56, 371, 372

Nevis 386

New Brunswick 164, 265, 386

New Delhi *see* Delhi

Newfoundland 10, 386

New Guinea 55, *152–3*, 344, *344*

New Hebrides 155, 386

New South Wales 36–40, 128, 138, 268, 271–2, 338–9, *338*, 386

New Zealand 386

  agriculture 122, *123*, 128–9, 256–7, 262

  art 306, *308–9*, 309, 310, 315

  British origins 254, 263, 265–8

  communications 117, *262*

constitution 41, 152, 155, 177

economy 98, 138

education 199–200, 201, 267

identity 264, 269–71, 274, 277–8, 320

Maori 40, 42, 176–7, *177*, 187, 199–200, *207*, 220, 259–60, 274, *274*, *308–9*, 309, 311, 315

Maori Wars 40, 149, 176–7, *177*

military contribution 78–9, *79*, 80, 87, 270, *270*, 342–3

mining 40, *123*, 137

religion 206, *207*, 208–9, 267, 268

towns 233, 257, 277

white population 40, 42, 68–9, *177*, 255, 258, 259–60, 274

women 256–7, *257*

Nigeria 93, *93*, 112, 116, 131, *141*, *143*, 162, 163, 166, *170*, 192, 201, 204, 210, 220, 228–9, 347, 349, *350*, 352, 386

Nkrumah, Kwame 95, 104, 177, 183, 356, *356*

Nolan, Sir Sidney 308–9

Norfolk Island *39*

North American colonies (later United States) 10, 16–19, 27, 159, 320, 372

North Borneo 294, 386

Northern Rhodesia (Zambia) 101, 102, 104–5, 386

Nova Scotia 16, 19, 34, 164, 387

Nyasaland (Malawi) 101, *101*, 102, 104–5, 201 212, 387

Nyerere, Julius 355

Oman 157

Omdurman 75, 158, *325*

Ontario (Upper Canada) 34, 36, 164, 187, *199*, 233, 259, 308, 385

Ootacamund 235

Opium Wars 33, 103, 158

Orange Free State (Orange River Colony) 41, 65, 69, 165, 387

Orange Order 249

Organization of African Unity 349, 351

Orientalism 196

Orwell, George 329, *329*

Otago 199, 201, 209

Otaki 315

Ottawa *240*, 241

Ottawa conference (1894) 126, (1932) 112, 126

Ottoman empire *see* Turkey

Oudh *see* Awadh

Oxford University 197, 201, 330–31

Pacific islands 84, *217*, 280, 297–8, *297*, 314

Pakistan 93, 100, *100*, 120–1, 223, 358, 364, 365, 369, 386

Palestine 77, 82–5, 94, 153, 182, 387

Palmer, Major William *302*

Palmerston, Lord 32–3, 267

Parkes, Sir Henry 338–9

Parkinson, Sydney *296*, 297

Parliament (British) 11, 16, 24–5, 43–4, 97, 149, 151, 168, 170–3, 322

Parsis 245, *245*, 378

partition 72–6, 83–4, 102, 165, 174, 179, 180, 182, 349, 367

  Africa 72–6, *73*, 102, 349

  Bengal 181

  India/Pakistan *100*, 165, 175, 180, 182, *366*, 367

  Middle East 83–4

  South East Asia 72, 74, 75

Passage to India, A 321

Pathans *198*, 220

Paton, Alan 192

'Pax Britannica' 33, 359–61

peasant farming *121*, 129–31, *130*, 360

Peking *21*, 380

Penang 225, 227, 248–9, 387

Peninsular and Oriental (P and O) 118

Pennethorne, Sir James 166–7

Pennsylvania 18

Perak War 161, 163

Perham, Margery 247

Persia *see* Iran

Persian Gulf *29*, 34

Perth 231

Peshawar *198*, 211

Pfander, Carl 211

Philip, Dr John *204*

Phillip, Arthur *338*

Picasso, Pablo 314

Pietermaritzburg 229, 238

Pitcairn Islands 387

Pitt Rivers, Arthur 313

plantation farming 43–4, *116*, 131–2, 278, 280–90, *282*, *284*

Plassey 20

Pope, Alexander 155

Port Arthur 39, *148*

Port Elizabeth 229

Port Said *90*

Portugal 18, 25, 56, 371

Potatau I, King 177

Powell, Enoch 173, 332, *332*

Pretoria 241, 244

Prince Edward Island 387

printing *see* media
Privy Council 168, 170, 281
protectionism 59, 109–13, 125, 138–41, 144, 363
protectorates 83, 152–3
publishing *see* media
Puck of Pook's Hill 219
Puni, Te *207*

Qatar 387
Quebec (Lower Canada) 19, 34, 36, 53, 161, 164, 187, 209, 241, 260, 277, 385
Queensland 128, 237, *237*, 387
Quit India Movement 180

Rabuka, Colonel 294
race 59–60, 69, 172, 196, 217, 220–3, *220*, 222, 225–6, *226*, 227, 228–31, 233, 234, 236, 247, 248–50, *249*, 274, 275–9, 287–8, 331–4, 337, *337*, 348, *348*, 355, 367, 373
radio *see* media
Raffles, Thomas Stamford *286*
Rahman, Tunku Abdul 182
railways 33, 49, 57, 68, 113, 115–20, *116*, *118*, 123, *123*, 126, 137, 233–4, 261, 278, 363–4
Raj, the (definition) 48
Rajan, Sir P.T. *365*
Raleigh, Sir Walter 152, 296
Rathbone, Eleanor 247
Reeves, William Pember 267
religion 23, 24, 30, 44, 45, *45*, 49, 168, 177, 179, 190–1, 192, 196, 197–8, 199–200, 203–12, *204*, 205, *206*, 207, *207*, *208*, 210–12, *211*, 213–14, *213*, 217, 223, 244, 247, 250, 290–1, *291*, 324, 347, 352, *353*, 354, 369, 379
Renaldi, Francesco *302*
Renison, Sir Patrick 177
representative government 152, 153, 154, 374
responsible government 35–6, 41, 97, 138, 152, 155, 165, 378
Reynolds, Henry 346
Rhodes, Cecil *64–5*, 65–6, 73, 101, 119, 135, 155, 201, 330
Rhodesia *see* Southern Rhodesia
Risley, Henry *220*
rivers 113, 114, 116, 120, *141*
Roberts, Lord 65, *65*, 324, *324–5*
Roberts, Tom *127, 308*
Robinson, The Revd Charles 196
Robinson, J.B. 135
Roosevelt, President 95, 260
Roy, Raja Rammohun 211, *211*
Royal Academy 300
Royal Colonial Institute 64

Royal Geographical Society 194, *195*
Royal Niger Company 73
Royal Society 194, 297
rubber 132, 140, 198, 227
Rupert's Land and North West Territory 387
Ruskin, John 311
Russell, Earl (Lord John Russell) 24
Russia 28–9, *28–9*, 54–6, *55*, 96, *109*, 148, 371, 372

Sai, Akiga 347
Said, Edward 196
Said, Muhammad 115
Said, Seyyid 157
Saklatvala, Shapurji 172
Salisbury (Harare) 229
Salisbury, Lord 58, 75, 156, 349
Samoa 277
San ('bushmen') *see* South Africa
San, Saya 179
Santal Rebellion 360
Sarawak *154*, 158, 294, 295, 387
Savage, Prime Minister 270
Schon, Heinrich 190
schools 45, *45*, 71, *156*, *187*, 198–203, *198*, *199*, 211, *244*, 267, 268 *see also* education
Schreiner, Olive 192
Schreiner, W.P. *172*, 229
Scotland 263, 265–7, 319–20
   Scots 17, 151, 249, 260, 319–20
Scouting for Boys 63
Second World War 81, 82, 85, *86*, 87–9, *87*, 91–2, 97, 99, 344–5, *344*
self-government 59, 69, 85, 91, 95, 96, 98, 99, 101, 146, 155, 165, 170, 173, 277, 339
Senegal 73
Serampore 213
Seven Years War 18–19, 159
Seychelles 387
Seyyid Ali, Sultan 156
Sezincote *327*
Shah Jahan 243
Shanghai *11*, 12, *145*
Sharp, Martin 340
Shaw, Flora (Lady Lugard) 247
Shepherd, Lord 289
Sherwood, Dr Marcia *98*
shipping *17*, 33, 108–9, *109*, 113–16, *113*, 118, 127–8, 260–2, *281*
Shuja-ud-daula, Wazir *303*
Siam (Thailand) 55, *55*, 157
Sierra Leone 45, *45*, 46, 188, 201, 206, 283, 334, 387
Sikhs 220
Sikh Wars 48
Sikkim 387

Simla 232, *232*, 235
Singapore 7, 13, 34, *55*, 166, 226, 227, 248, 253, 286, *286*, 292, 294, 341, 344, 373, 387
Singh, Dhian *46*
Singh, Kunwar 359
Singh, Ranjit *46*, 48
Slachters Nek 187
slavery 7, *7*, 8, 18, 20, 25, 30, 33, 43–6, *43*, *44*, *45*, 131, 171, *206*, 207, 220, 228, *228*, 280–4, *281*, *282*, *283*, 287–8, 289–91, *291*, 321, 327, 333, 380
Sloane, Sir Hans 313
Smith, Adam 109
Smith, Donald A. 266
Smith, Ian 101
Smith, Robert *303*
Smuts, Jan Christiaan 69, *69*, 92, 260, 264
Sokoto, Sultan of 93
Solomon Islands 387
Sotho *41*, 309
South Africa 387
   agriculture 129, 130, 131, 132
   Afrikaans language 260
   Afrikaners 40, *40*, 59, 65–7, *65*, *67*, *69*, 101, 159, *159*, 161, 165, 176, 187, 241, 244, 260, *264*, 274, 279
   art *31*, 306, *307*, 309–10, *309*, *314*, 315, *315*
   British wars with Africans *31*, 41, 42–3, 69, 149, 158, 307
   Cape Coloured *172*, 228, 274
   communications 116, 117, *119*, 213–14
   constitution 152, 155
   early British rule *31*, 40–1, *41*
   education 201, 267
   Great Trek, the 40, *40*, *41*, *264*
   Griqua *41*, 204
   industry 140
   Khoikhoi 40, *41*, 42, 176, *204*, 228
   languages 137–8, 161, 187, 192, 213–14, 260, 273, 275, 279
   law 161, 168
   military contribution 78–9, *79*, *87*, *270*, 271
   mining 42, 65–7, 135, *135*, 136, 137, *144*, 172, 235
   racial discrimination 69, 172, 229–30, 274, 277, 278–9, 355, 373
   railways 119, 261
   San ('bushmen') *314*, 315

towns 225–6, 228–9, *228–9*, *233*, 234, 235, 238, 241, 244, 248, *258*, 272
Union 69, *164*, 165, *172*, 261, 271–2, 274, 381
white identity 98, 264, 275–9
white population *228*, 254–5, 258, 259, 264, 265, 267
Xhosa 31,*40–1*, *41*, 42–3, 149, *204*, 213–14, *213*, 229, 384
Zulu *41*, 158, 220, 229, 278–9, 309–10
see also South West Africa
South African Republic *see* Transvaal
South African War (1881) 159, *159*, 176; (1899–1902) 41, 52–3, *53*, 57, *57*, *59*, 64–7, *64–5*, *67*, *69*, 76, 135, 149, 165, 176
South Australia 39, 128, 343, 387
South Carolina 18
Southern Rhodesia (Rhodesia, Zimbabwe) 65, 73, 101, 102, 104–5, 140, 201, 204, 229, 348, *348*, 387
South West Africa (Namibia) 55, 84, 153, 388
Soyinka, Wole 192
Spain 18, 25, 56, 371
Spofforth, F.R. 271, 272
sport *11*, *160*, 161, 185, 271, 272, 273, *274*
Sri Lanka *see* Ceylon
St Christopher (St Kitts) 387
St Helena 387
St Lucia 387
St Vincent 387
Stalin, Joseph 38
Stalky and Co 63
Stanley, H.M. 208
Statute of Westminster 97, 168, 341, 344
Steel, Flora Annie 236
Stephen, George 266
sterling *see* currencies
Stoffels, Andries *204*
Straits Settlements *see* Malaya
Strijdom, Prime Minister 273
Sudan 72, 75, 155, 158, 160, 301, *301*, *325*, 349, *353*, 388
Sudbury, Ontario 275–6
Suez canal 72, 74, *90*, 114, 115, *115*, 227
Suez crisis 90, *90*, 95–6, 115, 273, 334
sugar 7, *16*, 19–20, 25, 43–4, 70, 128–9, 131, 132, 228, 277, 278, 280–5, *282*, *283*, 288, 326, 327

Swahili *213*
Swazi *41*
Swaziland 388
Sydney *38*, 68, 230–1, 238, 248, 250, 253, *259*, 264, 338–40
Syria 77

Tagore, Abanindranath 312
Tagore family 211
Tagore, Rabindranath 194, 312, *312*
Tamihana, Wiremu *177*
Tamils 285, 294
Tanganyika (Tanzania) 55, 78, 102, 167, *167*, 293, 294, 334, 348, 355, 388
tariffs 59, 60–1, 66, 90, 109, 112, 138–41
Tasmania (Van Diemen's Land) 37, 39, *42*, 297, 388
Tata family 141, 171
Taubman, George Goldie 116, 154
taxation 22, 26, 48–50, 125, 152, 155, 159, 200, 201, 322, 328, 350, 359
telegraph 47, 114, 215, 261, *262*
Tennyson, Alfred 221
Thailand *see* Siam
Thatcher, Margaret 13
Thibaw, King *74*, 179
Things Fall Apart 192
Thiong'o, Ngugi wa 192
Thomson, Robert 339, 342
Tilak, B.G. 179
Tipu Sultan ('Tipoo') 299, *299*, 305
Tiv 347
tobacco 17, *19*, 326
Tobago 388
Togo 55
Tonga 388
Toronto 68, 233, 253
town planning *see* architecture
trade
   with Africa 45–6, 72–3, 91, 113, *113*, 130–1, *130*, *141*, 349–51
   with China 20, 21, 23, 26, 33, 103, *111*, *145*, *378*
   with India 20, 25, 26, 70, 90, 226–7, *362*, 363–4, *363*
   with Japan 26, *32*

   with West Indies *16*, 25, 44, 228, 289, 326–7
   in eighteenth century 16–17, 108–9, 326–7
   empire trade 25–6, 57, 60, 68, 77, 90–1, 109–13, *109*, *126*, *130*, 138–41, 327–9, 334
     slaves 7, 17, 23, 43–4, 280
     trading ports 226–31, 245
Transjordan 84, 153, 388
Transvaal (South African Republic) 41, 65–6, *65*, 69, *69*, 135, *159*, 165, *258*, 274, 388
Trinidad 32, 43, 152, 155, 166, 192–3, 281, 282, 289, 388
Tristan da Cunha 388
Trollope, Anthony 264
Trucial States (Trucial Oman) 388
trusteeship 93–4, *93*, 156, 223
Tshatshu, Dyani ('John') *204*
Tswana *41*
Turkey 77, 83, *84*, *182–3*, 371
   Ottoman empire 20, *28–9*, *29*, 153, 155
Turks and Caicos Islands 388
Turner, J.M.W. 305

Uganda 102, *118*, 150, 191, 201, 294, 349, 352, 356, 388
Unilateral Declaration of Independence (Rhodesia) 101
United African Company 116
United Nations 82, 182, 349
United States of America 7, 16, 28, 87, 89, 91–2, 94–6, 327, 345, 371
Universal Negro Improvement Association *293*
universities 45, 201, 250 *see also* education

Vancouver 277, 384
Van Diemen's Land *see* Tasmania
Van Horne, Sir William 307
Varma, Ravi 312, *312*
Victoria 39, 128, *136*, 138, 271–2, 275, 388
Victoria, Queen *30*, 49, 52, 63, 76, 80, *153*; 171, 325, 337, 338–9, *338*
Vietnam 340, 345

Vimy Ridge 270
Virginia 10, 17, 18, *19*, 326
Voortrekker Memorial *264*

Waitangi, Treaty of 177
Wakefield, Edward Gibbon 268
Wales 265
Welsh 151, 255
Wales, Prince of (1875) 301
Wandiwash 20
Ward, William 203
Wavell, Lord 182
Webber, John 297–8, *297*
Wedgwood, Josiah 43
Weihaiwei 78, *148*, 388
Wellden, J.E. 63
Wellesley, Marquess 47, 197, *239*
Wentworth, William Charles 268
West, Benjamin 300
West Africa 43, 45, 46, 73, 78–9, *79*, 87, 102, 104, 114, 116, 120, 130–1, 162, 181, 190, 214, *222*, 228–9, 378 *see also* Cameroon, Gambia, Gold Coast, Nigeria, Sierra Leone
Western Australia 39, 137, 261, 388
West Indies
   cricket *160*
   federation 165–6, 295
   government 152, 154–5, 293, 295
   indentured labour 132, 284–5
   literature 192–3, *193*
   migration to Britain 318, 331–3, *331*
   military contribution 87
   nineteenth century society 287–91
   revolts 158, 221
   slavery 7, 20, 43–4, 46, 131, 207, 220, 228, 280–4, *281*, *282*, *283*, 287, 289–91, *291*, 327, 333, 380
   sugar 19–20, 282–4
   value of 12, 16–17, *16*, 32, 326–7
   see also Antigua, Barbados, British Guiana, Jamaica, Leeward Islands, Trinidad

'Westminster model, the' 173, 364
wheat 25, 57, 60, 68, 70, 117, 126, *126*, 128
'white Australia' policy *see* Australia
White Highlands (Kenya) 119, 130
Whitlam, Gough 273
Wilberforce, William 44, *44*, 85
Wilkins, Charles 213
Williams, Eric 43
'wind of change' *147*
Windward Islands 20, 165
Witwatersrand *see* Johannesburg
Wolfe, General 300
Wolseley, Lord 324, *324–5*
women
   education 45, 70–1, *71*
   fertility 283
   gender imbalance 256, 258–9, *258*
   role and social position 248, 251–2, *251*, 320, 353
   in colonies of settlement 256–7, *256–7*, 309
   in tropical colonies 246–7, *246–7*
wool 25, 37–8, *110*, 117, *123*, 127–9, *127*, *259*, 267
World Bank 146
World Council of Churches 210
Wren, Sir Christopher 239, 243
Wyatt, Matthew 167

Xhosa *see* South Africa

Yorktown *19*
Yoruba 347

Zaghlul Pasha 172
Zambia *see* Northern Rhodesia
Zanzibar 150, *156*, 157, 241, 388
Zimbabwe *see* Southern Rhodesia
Zulu *see* South Africa

British Imperial Territories in 1939

K   L   M   N   O

7

8

Canada

Newfoundland

UNITED
KINGDOM

Eire

9

Bermuda

Gibraltar

Malta

West Indies - (see Inset)

British
Honduras

The Gambia

Nigeria

Sierra
Leone

Gold
Coast

10

British
Guiana

Ascension

Northern
Rhodesia

St Helena

South West
Africa

Cook Is.

Pitcairn Is.

11

South
Africa

WEST INDIES

Bahamas

Tristan
da Cunha

Turks &
Caicos Is.

Falkland Is.

South
Georgia

British
Virgin
Is.   Anguilla

St Christopher   Antigua
Nevis   Montserrat

South
Sandwich Is.

Dominica

12

St Lucia   Barbados

St Vincent

Grenada

Trinidad &
Tobago